Senator Fulbright

Senator Fulbright

PORTRAIT OF A PUBLIC PHILOSOPHER

by Tristram Coffin

E. P. Dutton & Co., Inc.: New York: 1966

FIRST EDITION

Grateful acknowledgment is made to Dr. Jan van Loewen and the International Copyright Agency, London, England, for permission to quote from *Becket,* by Jean Anouilh, translated by Lucienne Hill, and published in the United States by Coward-McCann, New York, N.Y., 1960.

ILLUSTRATIONS

Senator Fulbright

I

IN THE UNEASY days of February, 1966, a new face came into the American consciousness.

From the small and glowing screen in the living room, above the bar, in the shop window, it stared with a quizzical and questioning air. Man, what is your fate?

This was not the face of the usual television idol, but of a prophet of these new and strange times of atoms and revolutions and wars in far places. The face was essentially thoughtful—a long forehead with the lines of an intense frown of concentration, a firm chin, the clear blue eyes of a thinking man peering over his Ben Franklin glasses. His manner was a blend of ironic good humor, sharp inquiry and gentle Southern courtliness. He was the junior Senator from Arkansas, J. William Fulbright, chairman of the Foreign Relations Committee.

He sat leaning forward slightly in his leather chair, his shoulders hunched, as he addressed the Secretary of State sitting before him like an expressionless Buddha.

"All I am pleading with you and have been very awkwardly I think—is that this isn't the kind of conflict that warrants a vast escalation, a vast escalation of money and many thousands of deaths. I think it is not that kind of vital interest, as I can cite many other instances. I also think that the great countries, especially this country, is quite strong enough to engage in a compromise without losing its standing in the world and without losing its prestige as a great nation."

The camera lingered on the face, the light shining on his spectacles, catching in a very moving way the earnestness of the appeal. The world, or much of it, has been haunted by that moment. For what Fulbright was conveying was that man, for his own survival, must find a substitute for war. It is too costly, too dangerous, too inhumane. The atom has made war an instrument of universal death.

There is a curious inevitability about the role in which Senator Fulbright finds himself. All his life has pointed him toward this contest on the main stage with the warmakers. He has felt its tug, and resisted it only to be drawn by the tide of events. He is not a man who would choose to fight on street corners. He prefers to sit back and read history, not make it. He is a scholar in the gentlemanly tradition of Thomas Jefferson. Yet, again and again, his outrage against what Emerson referred to as, "Things are in the saddle and ride mankind," has driven him, usually alone, to do battle with such fearsome bullies as Joe McCarthy, such public idols as General Douglas MacArthur, and such popular dogmas as the Cold War militant. Finally, now, in a face-to-face contest with his old friend, Lyndon B. Johnson. In each crisis, Fulbright has risen painfully, reluctantly, from his deep chair, put down his book, adjusted his glasses to see over them, and come out fighting.

This last battle began in the muggy summer of 1965, after American intervention in the Dominican Republic and a sharp escalation of the war in Vietnam. The Senator from Arkansas sees his country as having two faces, one reasonable and humane, the other passionate and self-righteous. The Cold War, he believes, has emphasized the wrong profile by its gut appeal to mass hatred, its huge arms buildup, its Messianic drive. After the Cuban missile crisis, America seemed to pause and show the face of reason. Then John Kennedy was assassinated. His place was taken by a man who came from the emotional, highly patriotic, Populist tradition of Southern poor white politics. (Fulbright belongs to the other tradition, conservative, aristocratic, intellectual.)

The Senator watched in horror—that is the only word for it—as Johnson adopted his own foreign policy with a whoop and a holler, which seemed in Fulbright's eyes, to be a blend of Texas Populism, Teddy Roosevelt and John Foster Dulles. Guns and prayers and exhortations to defeat the Devil.

Senator Fulbright's outrage came to a head after American forces were landed in the Dominican Republic. He saw this as reckless use of force, and spoke out. There is much of the Cassandra in this man.

In the Vietnam hearings, in his appeal to Secretary Rusk, Fulbright saw the war in Asia as a small war inflamed into a large one. Two huge powers, the United States and China, were drifting toward a collision. Women, children, peasants, hospital patients were being destroyed by terrorism, napalm and bombs in the great impersonality of modern war. More civilians than soldiers were casualties. The longer the conflict endured without victory, the more terrible the temptation to use the atom bomb. Was it worth it?

To those who find an epic heroism in war and a near religious fervor in battling Communism, this quiet dissenter is an archfiend. President Johnson's private comments about him are, by report, unprintable. But to the hundreds of thousands who have written or wired the Senator, one phrase recurs again and again, to his embarrassment. It is "Thank God." Fulbright does not pretend to have a private line to the deity.

There is a mood of desperation in these letters, as if behind the neatly curtained windows of Main Street and Suburbia, U.S.A., lies grave doubt about the war. Handwritten, they say for example: "You seem to be a lone voice calling in the wilderness of misunderstanding . . . I hope someday you will be President and all wars ended . . . Please do not become discouraged by the criticism and abuse you are getting . . . Your statements seem like a breath of fresh air after all the hot air and hostile winds that blow from Washington . . . Thank you for your efforts to achieve a more rational and humane foreign policy."

Or a practical suggestion from Arkansas: "I respectfully suggest that the warmongers and grafters who favor war go to the Arkansas or Mississippi river bottoms during a three-day rain, and crawl around on their bellies in the mud, slime and snakes. I don't suggest that they be shot at. I don't even suggest throwing rocks at them every time they stick their heads up. I do suggest green persimmons be thrown at them and all the time they are dodging the green persimmons, they are being yelled at, 'Go home, Americans. We don't want you.' And after three days and nights of such pretended warfare, that the war wanters vote for or against war."

And a Washington society columnist, Scottie Lanahan, led her list of the ten best-looking men in the capital with Senator Fulbright, explaining that in a man personality and features are both important.

This making of Fulbright, a man who shuns crowds and emotional scenes, into a public idol was explained by an objective observer, *The*

Manchester Guardian. "If President Johnson, Mr. McNamara and Mr. Rusk are always being shown by events to have got things wrong," *The Guardian* said, "it is inevitable that more attention will be paid to the analysis of their critics. And alongside the education provided by the news headlines of the day, the critics themselves have become more effective. A turning point came with the hearings of the Senate Foreign Relations Committee, and it is fitting that Senator Fulbright, the hero of these encounters, should have paid tribute to those who pioneered the struggle when nobody else was interested. 'It is only when the Congress fails to challenge the Executive,' he said, 'when politicians join in a spurious consensus behind controversial issues, that the campus and streets and public squares of America are likely to become the forums of a direct and disorderly democracy.' "

The Senator was honestly surprised by the furor, pro and con, and remarked, "In a democracy dissent is an act of faith. Like medicine, the test of its value is not its taste but its effects, not how it makes people feel at the moment, but how it inspires them to act thereafter. Criticism is more than a right; it is an act of patriotism, a higher form of patriotism, I believe, than the familiar ritual of national adulation."

Further, the Constitution bids the Senate to give the Executive "advice and consent" on foreign policy. Also, there was a widespread feeling on Capitol Hill that the President had been too clever in using a generous and general resolution passed in 1964 as his authority to make war, that this use was both a violation of the confidence of those voting for it and of the Constitution.

Fulbright thinks of himself as a teacher. His Senate critics acidly call him "the schoolmarm." His faith is to seek the truth and bring it to his classroom: the Foreign Relations Committee, through which the Senate gives its advice and consent on foreign policy. Until recently, for more than a quarter century the Committee was little more than an amiable, if sometimes pompous "consenter." Such past chairmen as Walter George, Tom Connally and Arthur Vandenberg served as Administration ringmasters.

The Senator from Arkansas has gradually transformed the Committee into a forum for great inquiries and debates. The result—the hearings have a depth and range unknown in the days when Senators and Secretaries of State were curtsying to one another.

At the outset of the Vietnam hearings, he announced in his pleasant drawl, "All we seek is some information and enlightenment, so that our country's judgment, the judgment of our people, of this committee may be as wise as possible."

At the hearings, he questioned the ancient and honorable institution of war. He criticized the unthinking, hip-hip-hooray brand of American politics. He declared that Communist states are not the evil demons our folklore has pictured. He took a hard look at the wisdom and veracity of the Administration. Most of all, Fulbright tried to draw the American people into a debate on foreign policy.

Although dissent is a way of life with him, his reasoning is never frivolous. He thought "unconditional surrender" as a war aim was an error, because it unduly prolonged the horror of war. In 1946, he had proposed that President Harry Truman resign, because he believed at that crucial turning point in world affairs, one party should be wholly responsible for the conduct of American policy, and the Republicans had then won control of Congress. Later he was the only Senator to vote against funds for Joe McCarthy's investigations, because he saw them as witch-hunts intimidating honest officials and eroding the integrity of government. He tried to block a resolution giving President Eisenhower a free hand in the Middle East, because he considered it a dangerous encouragement to meddle in deep waters. As a minority of one, he argued with superb logic against the unhappy Bay of Pigs adventure in Cuba. Events proved him correct. He took on the full might of the Pentagon in his "military memorandum," criticizing generals and admirals for engaging in extremist propaganda.

Nor is he daunted by his lonely storming of the citadels of power. After all, as a freshman Representative in 1943 he led the United States out of its isolationism into a system of world organization. The Fulbright resolution: "Resolved, That the House of Representatives hereby expresses itself as favoring the creation of appropriate international machinery with power adequate to maintain a just and lasting peace, among the nations of the world, and as favoring participation of the United States therein through its constitutional processes," passed 360 to 29. It officially ended American isolationism and led directly to the founding of the United Nations.

This modest and neatly waistcoated gentleman from Arkansas is regarded in Washington with high emotion. President Truman called him "an overeducated Oxford SOB," a reference to his Rhodes scholarship. Walter Lippmann has written, "The role he plays in Washington is an indispensable role. There is no one else so powerful and also so wise. Not only has he been the bravest and wisest of advisors. He is also the most farseeing and constructive." President Johnson's very close personal friend, columnist William S. White, wrote, "What the Fulbright people really represent is a new and embittered crypto pacifism-isolationism." *The New York Times* said editorially, "Senator Fulbright often speaks out as the conscience of American foreign policy." The ultrarightists have distributed hundreds of thousands of tracts entitled, *Fulbright, Freedom's Judas-Goat.*

He is so popular among the young, receiving astounding ovations at college campuses in his speaking appearances, that some commentators believe he has fallen heir to the Kennedy idolism. At a recent White House dinner for 121 Presidential scholars, Fulbright "found himself very much the man of the hour with the young students," according to *The Washington Post.* They left their tables to gather around the Senator. The young American non-Communist radicals see him as a sort of modern saint, and at a recent peace march in front of the White House, a huge sign carried by a bearded youth said: "We are succumbing to the arrogance of power, SENATOR FULBRIGHT."

No one pretends to understand him completely. He is a complex human being—at times witty, erudite, earthy, sardonic, melancholy, a sparkling furnace of ideas, both shrewd, and innocent to the point of naïveté, candid, and nearly always quietly and magnificently courageous. His critics argue that he is querulous, irritating and impractical, and has never properly understood the menace of global Communism.

A line in Jean Anouilh's play, *Becket,* whose title character he greatly resembles, gives the spirit of the man. Becket tells King Henry II, "One has to gamble with one's life to feel alive."

He is full of paradox. Fulbright seems, at one moment, to abhor conflict. When others beg him to enter the fight, he grumbles, complains and vacillates. But once there, he plays to win, and gets a very real exhilaration out of it. He was a University of Arkansas star halfback and at Oxford won his half-blue at lacrosse, the world's roughest sport.

He is equally at ease at a white tie diplomatic function and a church supper at Yell County, Arkansas. He likes country-cooked spareribs, and often goes to the Farm Women's Market on Saturday mornings in search of them. He feels suffocated without long moments of solitude, and detests noise, confusion, bores and demagogues. When he first heard Joe McCarthy speak, he said, "My God, that man is a boor!" This old-fashioned word meant to him that McCarthy was a primitive man with no concern for his fellows or truth. He is a believer in such nineteenth-century virtues as thrift (he drives a ten-year-old Mercedes and rides tourist class on airplanes, although he is well to do). He lives quietly on the rim of Rock Creek Park in Washington, and the house, inside and out, has an air of rather conservative good taste. He reads history in bed, and his favorite TV fare is "Bonanza."

The Senator values physical exercise, and his Burning Tree golf dates are sacred. He and Mrs. Fulbright used to ride bicycles through the park. Early in the morning while the mist is still rising from the stream, he walks alone in the park, a modest figure in a cap along the path.

He has a very few old and treasured friends, such as Walter Lippmann and Eugene Black, former president of the World Bank, but no close associates on Capitol Hill. His aloofness sometimes has hurt the feelings of Senators who have tried to be friendly, and yet this would surprise him. He is not consciously distant. Fulbright simply exists within himself much of the time, and assumes others want to also. Some Senators say he is lazy, because they cannot understand a fellow who may sit for some time without speaking or moving. The usual politician is kinetic.

Every evening after the hubbub of the day has passed, Fulbright sits alone in his office, the lights low, putting events and thoughts into perspective. This is a creative and selective process. He decides which of his thoughts are ready to leave his private world and enter the public arena. He has an uncanny sense of timing, and once when an assistant objected to an advanced idea in a speech, Fulbright said, "I agree it may startle people some today. But six months from now they will come to accept it." He was right.

The Senator reviews his own convictions constantly. He reversed himself 360 degrees in two years on foreign aid and the Gulf of Tonkin resolution, and frankly said so. He said, "What the hell, knowledge is not static. What good does it do to argue that the sun revolves around the earth when science can prove the opposite?"

The Senator from Arkansas is like a cable, several strands wrapped in one. He is a successful politician, and has been elected five times. In 1962, his strength with the voters was such that he frightened the racist demagogue, Governor Orval Faubus, out of the race against him. According to Arkansas political gossip, the White House has been encouraging Faubus to take on Fulbright in 1968.

He is, as Karl Meyer wrote, "a public philosopher." He is an investigator to rank with Pecora and Walsh. His orderly inquiry into the Reconstruction Finance Corporation revealed a trail of corruption flowing from private industry to the Government and the White House during the Truman days and led to the abolition of the RFC and other reforms. He is a social critic of the American scene to compare with De Tocqueville and Mark Twain, whom he often quotes in his speeches.

In the latter role, he has candidly, for a politician, described those factors within the American society that send us blundering and awkward into war and foreign involvement. These are: a basic fundamentalism with its good-evil seesaw (the good can do no wrong and evil must be destroyed), an arrogance that inevitably rises with power, McCarthyism that tries to silence opposition, a Messiah complex or belief in Manifest Destiny ("there is a bit of missionary in all our souls"), and a conformist Diplomatic Establishment with its high priests, such as Dean Acheson, John Foster Dulles and Dean Rusk. He ponders in that vein of irony so typical of him: "The idea of being responsible for the whole world seems to be flattering to Americans, and I am afraid it is turning our heads, just as the sense of global responsibility turned the heads of ancient Romans and nineteenth-century British. A prominent American is credited with having said recently that the United States was the 'engine of mankind' and the rest of the world was 'the train.' . . . What romantic nonsense this is. And what dangerous nonsense in this age of nuclear weapons."

His words reveal what is not at first apparent in this rather aloof and imperturbable individual. It is that a strong and swift stream runs beneath the surface. He cries out for reason in a world of passion and violence. He is outraged that the great promise of man and the progress of science and culture are forever being strangled by wild men with guns and armies at their call. He told Arkansas voters in 1944, "I hate war, not only because it destroys our young men, our families, our property, but because it will sooner or later destroy our system of free enterprise. War will inevitably make us slaves of an organized bureaucracy, and this would happen whether we won or lost. The democratic system of free enterprise is not designed for war."

Today he sees the world drifting to the final holocaust. This is not simply rhetoric. His feeling at times that man has lost control of his fate, as in the Greek tragedies, accounts for his moodiness.

In mid-April, 1966, as the Vietnam war screwed up another notch and the President turned his anger on the Senator, Fulbright sat in his office with a reporter. He was tired and distraught. He rubbed a finger across his forehead as if to wipe out pain.

He said wearily, "I feel so isolated and discouraged. Good God, I'm discouraged. The war fever is increasing. We Americans are so powerful, and so self-righteous."

Yet he has the strength to pull himself over his despair. A few nights later he was having dinner with several young Senators at the home of Senator Frank Church of Idaho. They were dejected and frustrated. He told them, "Events don't stand still. The world moves. We may plunge into disaster overnight, that I'll admit. But we may elude this fate, because there is so much change going on in the world. The British election, now, has made Harold Wilson more independent. It is this kind of glimmer of hope that means we have to keep on doing what we are doing."

What Fulbright has been doing, particularly since his Dominican Republic investigation, vastly disturbs the Foreign Policy Establishment. He has been trying to prove, to an ever-widening audience, that the basis for our huge military program, foreign aid, and network of treaties—that is, fear of a Communist monster—is false, and needs to be changed. The Establishment encompasses the State Department, the Pentagon, defense contractors, the CIA, the AFL-CIO hierarchy (thanks to its foreign policy adviser, Jay Lovestone, former head of the American Communist Party and now a hard-line cold warrior), AID, journalists, professors and what Kenneth Galbraith calls "the New York foreign policy syndicate—the Dulles, McCloy, Lovett communion with which, I am sure, Secretary Rusk would wish to be associated and of which Dean Acheson is a latter-day associate." (Robert A. Lovett, former Secretary of Defense, is a partner of the Wall Street banking firm of Brown Bros., Harriman & Co. John J. McCloy, former High Commissioner for Germany, and board chair-

man of the Chase Manhattan Bank, is in private law practice now.)
Galbraith said, "The syndicate . . . has provided the grace notes of
American foreign policy for twenty years."

The holy writ of The Establishment is the Truman Doctrine of
1947. "I believe it must be the policy of the United States to support
free peoples who are resisting attempted subjugation by armed minorities or by outside pressure."

To this Fulbright says we must give up old myths and face new
realities: a Communist system continually fracturing and altering its
new faces; megaton weapons and transoceanic missiles; revolutions in
Asia, Africa and Latin America against colonialism and feudalism; a
vast imbalance of wealth and food in the world; the population
explosion and extreme nationalism. Clinging to the old myths, he
said, "can reduce foreign policy to a fraudulent game of imagery and
appearances." The Senator pointed out on the Dominican Republic
episode, "We failed to perceive that if we are automatically to oppose
any reform movement that Communists adhere to, we are likely to
wind up opposing *every* reform movement, making ourselves the
prisoners of reactionaries who wish to preserve the *status quo.*"

The Senator believes the United States has overextended and
overcommitted itself, and we have neither the wisdom nor resources
to play guardian angel to the world. He would channel foreign aid
through an international agency, such as the World Bank, because the
United States tends to become too intimately involved in a nation we
assist. "The Vietnam war began as a foreign aid program," he says
wryly.

He admits the constant danger of aggression. He would treat this
disease by two means. First, he would try to temper the bloated
nationalism of a nation, say as China, by cutting away its isolation
with trade, scientific and cultural exchanges and cooperative ventures.
In a broad sense, he is one with modern sociologists who say the way
to cut down crime in the slums is not to hire more police and arm
shopkeepers with Colts, but to discover the basic causes—poverty,
boredom, idleness and self-pity—and cure them. He held unique
hearings on May 25, 1966, during which two leading psychiatrists
testified, concerning the cause and cure of the "sickness" of nations.

Second, if actual aggression occurs, or is about to occur, it should
be met by united action, either through the United Nations or
regional groups as the Organization of American States. He blamed

the Johnson Administration for moving in, in his view, recklessly and alone, into the Dominican Republic without waiting for the O.A.S.

Senator Fulbright's biting critique of the Dominican adventure was in a very personal way a cruel ordeal for him. It cost him the old friendship of Lyndon Johnson. The Senator does not give his friendship lightly, and Johnson had been his one intimate associate on Capitol Hill. Reporters overhead in the press gallery had often seen the two sitting together in the front row, Johnson's arm around the chair of the other, telling one of his fabulous stories. (They are like a chapter out of a Robert Penn Warren novel, but more earthy.) Fulbright would be grinning in enjoyment. The erudite Arkansan was fascinated by the dynamic up-and-go and brilliantly shrewd personality of the Texan. Johnson was equally drawn by the culture of the other, and a mutual friend has said, "There is no one Lyndon Johnson admired or needed more than Bill Fulbright." There is a parallel in the friendship of King Henry II, the rough and shrewd Norman monarch, and Thomas à Becket, the highly educated Saxon. They became bitter enemies when Becket became the Archbishop and took the side of the Church against the Crown. It was then that Henry cried, as Johnson well might today, "Will no one rid me of him?" (This is from the Anouilh play *Becket.*)

As late as August 7, 1964, Fulbright was the champion advocate of Johnson's policy in Asia. He overcame many doubts in the Senate to drive through the resolution to give Johnson unlimited authority to act. His sense of guilt over this role has been a powerful goad since.

The landings in the Dominican Republic in late April, 1965, and the widening of the Vietnam war brought troubling doubts. He tried to talk to Johnson, but there was no communication. "Understand each other? It wasn't possible. We were like two deaf men talking."

In these private talks during that summer, President Johnson ignored or brushed off Fulbright's advice. The President gravely misjudged the Senator as one who has "no stomach for a fight," according to Washington columnist Mary McGrory. He accepted the popular cliché that Fulbright was "lackadaisical" and too quixotically independent ever to get a following. He would fuss and fume in private, but go along publicly.

The Senator groaned and puzzled over his dilemma for weeks. Then on September 15 he spoke.

Fulbright carefully exonerated Johnson, "The principal reason for the failure of American policy in Santo Domingo was faulty advice given to the President by his representatives in the Dominican Republic at the time of acute crisis." Johnson, though, tends to personalize criticism, and he reacted as Henry II: "Becket is attacking me and he has betrayed me. I am forced to fight and crush him."

Johnson's problem was, he could not reach Fulbright. He has no ambitions, thus no price tag. He has no secret vices, and so cannot be elbowed into silence. He is in the grip of a conviction and so untouchable.

In a frustrated fury, the President has attacked his old friend with all the apparatus available to a Chief Executive. Commentators have been startled by the verbal violence—through Administration spokesmen, in-House columnists and Capitol Hill loyalists—thrown at the Senator. The aim has been to stun the heretic into silence and discredit him with the public. This was the way Johnson, the broncobuster of the Senate, handled recalcitrant members.

In a sense, the President's anger was justified. If Fulbright had not spoken out so clearly, if he had not scheduled the Vietnam hearings, the dissent would have been confused, and Johnson could have had his way. This, many believe, would have been to step up the war and possibly broaden it to Cambodia and defy the Chinese with the threat of nuclear bombardment.

Yet, and this will fascinate the historians, the Johnson Administration may come around to accepting many of Fulbright's views, while not forgiving him for their advocacy. This reaction is a familiar pattern in his career. Ideas of his that were denounced as heresy are within a year or two quietly adopted by those in power.

Some even believe that, one day, Johnson will call Fulbright and say, "You're so damn smart, get me out of this mess."

The breakup of the friendship affected both men personally. The President moved to the right, shunning even such a handpicked successor as Democratic leader of the Senate, Mike Mansfield, who also held moderate views on Vietnam. Johnson consorted closely with Everett Dirksen, the Republican leader, a charming relic of the Taft bloc, and even praised the right-wing Texas Senator, John Tower, a Republican, for his superpatriotic stand on Vietnam.

For a while the Senator from Arkansas tried to preserve the private friendship with the President. He never criticized him publicly or carried the quarrel on his shoulder. He sent the President a modest letter proclaiming his personal loyalty and admiration, but defending his right to criticize for the good of the Administration. Johnson did not answer it. Fulbright defended his old friend to others. He ended a conversation that obviously troubled him by saying, "I think you are making a great fault in imputing these faults to the President. It just is not creditable to me."

Lyndon Johnson has been unable to be this dispassionate toward an antagonist. He has seemed driven by a need to hurt Fulbright. One incident took place at a large Democratic fund-raising dinner in Washington in May, 1966, before an audience of Administration officials, Congressmen and lobbyists. The Senator sat at the head table, some seats down from the President.

Johnson rose to speak. He looked out on the audience, and then turned his head to stare harshly at his old friend. In a voice hoarser than usual, the President said, "I am glad to be here with my old friends—and members of the Foreign Relations Committee."

Senator Fulbright made an ironic bow, but nothing in his political life has been so personally wounding.

He listened as Johnson demanded that the Democratic Party back him on Vietnam and punish the dissenters. This reminded Fulbright unhappily of Joe McCarthy's threats to "purge" Senators who failed to support him. A week later, the Senator read the transcript of a Johnson speech at a political dinner in Chicago. He insisted that voters "read carefully the statements of every public official and every candidate for every office . . ." and note those "ready to turn on their own leaders, their own country, and their own fighting men," and denounced his critics as "nervous Nellies."

Senator Fulbright remarked with a note of finality, "How could we have been so wrong about this man!"

Nonetheless, the Senator resisted invitations to denounce the President or cripple his legislative program. He hoped as the months rolled on the man in the White House would want to hear his ideas on an Asian peace. He was willing to gamble that the President's aching need for public approval would bring him to his critics, and ask their help.

But this hope, too, turned to ashes. In mid-June, 1966, an incident took place. Senator Fulbright was at the White House for a ceremonial occasion, and the President took him by the arm and led him into his private office. The two were alone for an hour. Lyndon Johnson spoke in a rapid-fire manner, almost without interruption.

He pulled memoranda from his pocket and read them, mentioning the deity frequently, in his attempt to justify his policies in Vietnam. He seemed to Fulbright frantic in his desire to convert his old friend. The Senator was only able to get in a few troubled words, but these, he thought, were lost. He mentioned later, "The President is all wrapped up in a religious war."

On June 29, after the bombing of oil depots at Hanoi and Haiphong, Fulbright was asked whether he had lost all hope of persuading the President to a more moderate course. Yes, he said, he no longer had any such illusions.

The only path left open to him was one he had traveled many times before—against General MacArthur's "total victory," Joe McCarthy, John Foster Dulles' brinkmanship, and intervention in the Dominican Republic—the open forum of public debate and discussion. It was a lonely path and the wind would be heavy.

II

SENATOR FULBRIGHT is a modern Prometheus. He defies the gods and myths of modern society to save man from the horror of atomic doom. Like Prometheus he is not moved by arrogance or rebellion, but rather by a concern for man, in the plural and abstract. More often than not, the Senator confesses his own inadequacy and his intense desire to give up the lonely struggle. He cannot. He keeps hoping the good and the reasonable in man will overcome the evil and the passionate.

The beginning of his fear of atomic disaster, of man destroying himself in a final, foolish rage, can be fairly well pinpointed. It did not arise from the shock of Hiroshima and Nagasaki, but rather from a series of hearings in which he acquired understanding of the atom bomb from the scientists, and in the process, accepted their apocalyptic view.

The hearings took place in September, 1945. Senator Brien McMahon of Connecticut, another freshman, had introduced a bill for the peaceful use of atomic energy. Its aim was to shift control from the military to civilian authorities. (The bill was passed, but the military got their way after all when President Truman overruled the Atomic Energy Commission on the production of a hydrogen bomb.) Fulbright sat through most of the sessions which wandered from one borrowed committee room to another.

The witnesses were scientists, generals and admirals. Most of the pertinent questions were asked by the Arkansan. He asked Rear Admiral William R. Purnell, the Navy's expert on atomic warfare, "Do you feel that there is a defense against this weapon?"

"I do not know of any defense," the admiral replied. "The people who made the bomb have thought about any possible countermeasures, and of ways to evade them."

The Senator, his forehead creased into a frown of concentration, asked, "Do you suppose there will be any warning of the attack starting the next war?"

"No, and we will have no time to develop countermeasures. The war might last only thirty minutes."

The Senator from Arkansas nodded his head. He quickly grasps the far-reaching revolutionary nature of the new realities of this time—the bomb, overpopulation, African and Asian nationalism, the revolts against feudalism in Latin America, while most American politicians think the world goes on just as before.

"Is it possible we might attack first?"

"No, sir, that is impossible under our Constitution."

"Then, in an event of a paralyzing attack," Fulbright said, thinking ahead, "we are at a disadvantage. We are the most vulnerable. If we have any defense it must be in the political field. We must have a strong world organization." He was trying to fit this radical weapon into a rational world.

"That is not in my field, sir."

The Senator then expressed a view he has repeated many times, in many different ways: "This seems so much more powerful than ordinary weapons, our conventional ideas do not apply. We've always thought defenses could be developed for anything, so we wouldn't have to worry."

Here was the genesis of his famous 1964 speech, "Old Myths and New Realities."

Admiral Purnell said dryly, "There must be an exception to every rule."

The witness the following morning was Dr. J. Robert Oppenheimer, the fragile-looking research director of the Los Alamos bomb project. He explained, "All we did was to take a tree ripe with fruit and shake it hard. Secrecy is not possible. The nature of the world is not secret. Our policy is not secret. You cannot keep the atom secret."

Fulbright asked, "Can we keep the techniques of the atom bomb a secret?"

"That is like asking why don't you stop beating your wife," Dr. Oppenheimer answered with a slight smile. "The immediate problem, it seems to me, is to get confidence among the nations, not force them apart by trying to build up a great secret. Other countries will say—keep your secrets. We'll do it another way. The intolerable state is very close. It is only necessary for other nations to decide to pursue an independent course in atomic research."

Senator Fulbright inquired if there was any defense.

"There are no specific countermeasures. There never will be. Our bomb cannot be exploded before it hits the target. I will offer to wager half my savings, small as they are, to anyone who can explode a bomb made at our place before it reaches its destination. The atomic bomb is the two-billion-dollar straw that may break the camel's back."

"Could our one hundred and forty million people be wiped out in one attack?"

"I am afraid that is true. The atomic bomb has weakened the military power of the United States. Ten or twenty years from now atomic bombs will be very cheap."

Fulbright commented, "We in government have a real job, to make sure the people understand the importance of this new power."

The scientists would try to help, Dr. Oppenheimer told him.

Almost twenty years later, the Senator was saying, "The acquisition of nuclear weapons by smaller nations, if it occurs, will act as a great equalizer, giving them power out of all proportion to their size and resources, and further undermining the advantage of size and wealth enjoyed by nations like the United States and the Soviet Union. . . . What is urgent for both the Communists and the free world is the prevention of nuclear war. This single objective, the survival of the civilized societies of the earth, is the one elemental interest which all nations have in common. . . ."

The reaction of the United States and its protagonist, Soviet Russia, to the nuclear challenge shocked Senator Fulbright, and greatly influenced his thinking. Nations were no more rational than individuals.

A bitter struggle took place within the United States. The military, encouraged by Dr. Edward Teller, the Hungarian émigré scientist, pressed for greater weapons, and was upheld by President Truman. When Dr. Oppenheimer resisted making the hydrogen bomb, saying it would bring on a nuclear arms race, he was driven out of the Government in a trial which the conservative Alsop brothers compared to the Dreyfus case. Senator Fulbright said of this, "One of the most dramatic and most recent examples of the sickness which afflicts us—a bitterness, a suspicion, a kind of primitive ruthlessness—is the case of Dr. Oppenheimer. The decision is a tragedy of the first magnitude, appropriate to the genius of the ancient Greek poets. . . . This is but the latest chapter in the development of anti-intellectualism which is spreading throughout the country."

Unhappily, Dr. Oppenheimer's prophecy was correct, and a monstrous arms race between the United States and Russia took place, each polluting the atmosphere until the Nuclear Test Ban Treaty which Fulbright steered through the Senate. Of this race, Fulbright said, "There is a kind of madness in the dialogue of the nuclear age, an incredulous response to terrors beyond our experience and imagination. There are few examples in history of nations acting rationally to prevent evils which they can foresee but have not actually experienced."

The question is often asked why a man so concerned with the human fate could be indifferent to the plight of the Negro in the South. It is difficult to place him exactly on this issue. He is neither a hard-line segregationist, nor a champion of integration.

When he first entered politics in Arkansas in 1942, he favored an all-white Democratic primary. Six years later, he encouraged the president of the University of Arkansas in a private exchange of letters to admit Negroes, and this was done. He has taken part in a gentlemanly manner in the Southern filibusters, never engaging in such Confederate demagoguery as the sedate Senator Richard Russell of Georgia, or, for that matter, Lyndon Johnson. He signed the Southern manifestos, and prepared a scholarly brief asking the Supreme Court to delay desegregation in Little Rock. He would not take sides in the Little Rock school desegregation crisis. He was one of the first Southern Senators to have a Negro, a young graduate student, on his office staff.

He has urged the Administration to go slow in enforcing equal rights in the South, but at the same time has asked his voters to abide by the new laws. On a "Meet the Press" program May 15, 1965, Senator Fulbright said he favored Federal legislation to assure the Negro's voting right. He termed the white violence at Selma, Alabama, "deplorable, regrettable and tragic—the last gap in opposition to Negro equality." He pronounced what is the essence of his present belief: "The country has spoken. From here on it is the law of the land."

The reasons for his attitude toward civil rights are threefold. He was, first, born at the wrong time and place. At no time, in the early formative years, from his childhood in Fayetteville, Arkansas, to his return from Europe as a young man, did this issue ever come clearly before him.

Fayetteville, the university town in the northwest corner of the state, where he lived until he went to Oxford, never straying more than one hundred miles from it, is a neutral enclave in the Confederate South. It was settled by Missourians and was sympathetic to the North in the Civil War. During the Senator's boyhood, not more than fifty Negroes lived in Fayetteville. The town claims to have been the first in the South to integrate its schools.

At Oxford and later traveling about Europe as an apprentice foreign correspondent, Fulbright had no contact with Negroes; he did not see the issue as an intellectual and social challenge. The chances are that had he been born twenty years later, Fulbright might have been a leader of moderate forces in the South.

Second, he has a sort of tacit agreement with his voters. He once told an interviewer, "My people have rather strong feelings on this subject, and since they permit me a great deal of freedom in foreign policy, I think I should respect their wishes."

Third, a man as scholarly as Fulbright tries to focus his attention on a few great issues. Even so he complains very much he cannot follow up all the leads and clues in foreign policy, and recently wrote a friend, "It is a struggle for me to find the time for things I should be reading these days."

Senator Fulbright was probably not deeply aware of the impact of the civil-rights issue until Little Rock. Since then, he has been embarrassed and confused by the immensity of the issue and the emotions aroused by it. When questions on civil rights are asked by reporters during interviews, he becomes a little irritated. Look, he says, "Will the country, Arkansas or I be better off, if I am defeated taking a stand on civil rights too far in advance of my voters?" Or, he may say, "You can't pass a law, and tell a man he must love his neighbor. A characteristic of man since his centuries of fighting for survival under the most primitive conditions is fear of the stranger. The stranger invaded his hunting ground, stole his grain and took away his woman. There exists today this residual fear of anyone who looks differently, who believes differently, who talks a strange tongue. It's man's greatest problem in his groping for survival in the nuclear-missile age. We simply have to work at it by exercising self-discipline, and trying very hard to understand the stranger. I don't see how you can solve it by passing laws."

His mind has been trained in the scientific discipline, and he does not think a man should talk about a subject unless he knows a great deal about it. The careless phrases of politics bore and irritate him. When he wanted to find out what kind of a policy the United States should have, realistically, toward Communist China, he called in thirteen scholars and bombarded them with questions. The scholars may not be any more correct, in the long run, than the impulsive hunches of Lyndon Johnson, but their theories do have a scientific validity. They have been tested and checked. They are based on history and accepted scientific theory, rather than one individual's irascibility and seat-of-the-pants feeling.

Any new clues to world behavior Senator Fulbright snatches up mentally and examines. Thus, scanning through the *Atlantic Monthly,* he was attracted by an article by Dr. Jerome D. Frank, the Johns Hopkins psychiatrist, and corresponded with him. They have had several talks, and Dr. Frank appeared before the Foreign Relations Committee on May 25, 1966.

Dr. Frank wrote, "I have been struck by the parallels between the behavior of nations today and that of mental patients," and suggested the Cold War may be a "sickness."

A nation will develop, through fear, a hostility toward one or more nations, and the enemy is transformed into a "non human" who may be destroyed with no moral compunction. Dr. Frank said, "The image of the enemy is remarkably similar no matter what nation is in the role. He is always a kind of subhuman monster: cunning, crafty and cruel. . . . Enemies act toward each other in ways that confirm their reciprocal image." As hate grows, so does one's own self-righteousness. "Our side is seen as intellectually superior but guileless and therefore easily victimized, peace-loving, honorable and fighting only in self-defense."

The Senator expanded this thought in a number of speeches, particularly those on "The Arrogance of Power." He said at one point, "There is a kind of voodoo about American foreign policy. Certain drums have to be beaten regularly to ward off evil spirits— for example the maledictions which are regularly uttered against North Vietnamese aggression, the 'wild men' in Peking, Communism in general, and President de Gaulle."

Dr. Frank also suggested the "self-fulfilling prophecy." We act toward an enemy in such a way that he is moved to react toward us in a way we predicted and dreaded. The threats and insults and bomb waving swapped by the United States and Russia from 1946 to 1963 forced both into an extravagant arms race, which may not have been either prudent or necessary. Senator Fulbright sees this happening today in the relations between the United States and China.

The Senator thinks the social sciences should be drawn into intelligence at a high level, so we may have more precise knowledge of friend and foe alike. The anthropologist and historian and psychiatrist may be much more understanding in charting a course for American policy with China than Secretary McNamara's computers or Secretary Rusk's rigid ideology. Thus, Fulbright was quite interested as Dr. Frank told the Committee that an enemy, if he believed deeply in his cause, could not be bombed into negotiations.

The psychiatrist said, "People who are fighting for their ideals seldom, if ever, can be forced into surrendering by punishment. The notion that one can cause people to abandon their ideologies by inflicting pain should have died with the Christian martyrs."

The Washington diplomatic establishment is as hidebound as Great-Aunt Lucinda, and regards the Senator's tours into the groves of academia for new knowledge as terribly avant garde. The foreign policy bureaucracy which, according to Joseph Kraft, is filled with "sluggish foreign service officers," goes out of its way to denigrate Senator Fulbright. One ambassador of a major Western ally says that the Secretary and his assistants repeatedly have told him, on their initiative, that the gentleman from Arkansas has no credibility and standing in the United States. In cozy cocktail briefings for key foreign correspondents, the Secretary and his staff make a point of running down the Senator.

Every time Senator Fulbright makes a speech, the research divisions of the State Department, the Pentagon and the CIA comb through it, searching for points to be refuted. When the Senator urged that the Vietcong be brought into negotiations, word went to our mission in Saigon to come up with a rebuttal. The result was a memorandum from the deputy ambassador, William J. Porter, which claimed the Vietcong had no popular support. This memorandum was then "leaked" to one of the newspaper columns that act as a private stiletto for the President and Secretary Rusk.

The Senator has been denounced by so many so often these little conspiracies amuse him. In 1962, just before he began his campaign for reelection, his administrative assistant, Lee Williams, a young Arkansas lawyer of American Indian ancestry, sent him a note: "As a result of your Senate speeches, press conferences, television appearances and other public utterances in the past two weeks, you have succeeded in arousing the ire of practically every organized segment of world opinion. This is reflected in the mail you have received during the period. The following is a list of groups from which you have had messages indicating their displeasure with your expressed opinion: John Birchers, McCarthyites, Goldwaterites, Thurmondites, Dixiecrats, militarists, isolationists. Zionists, Germans, Catholics, Chinese Nationalists, Koreans, NAACPers, Communists, private powerists, veterans, farmers' cooperatives."

The Senator laughed.

He is able to show such detached amusement for a simple reason. He has no ambition to be other than what he is. He has no need for a consensus. He does not want to be President, leader of a popular revolt or Cabinet member. He declined a bid to be president of Columbia University to fill Nicholas Murray Butler's post. He fled almost in panic when John Kennedy hinted he wanted him for Secretary of State.

This incident took place in November, 1960, after the elections. Word leaked out to the Senator from the back door. A newsmagazine was preparing a cover story on the future Secretary of State and was gathering background material. A fellow Senator told him he had heard "the word."

"What does he want me for?" Fulbright said unhappily. "I wouldn't be worth a damn. People are always complaining I don't know how to run the Committee. Imagine me in that great factory downtown?" The prospect was appalling.

John Kennedy had picked him with considerable political shrewdness. The Secretary should have international prestige, and only one other man, Adlai Stevenson, rated in the same league with Fulbright. Kennedy, though, was considerably annoyed at Stevenson for not withdrawing in his favor at the Democratic convention, and considered him a man unable to make up his mind.

The Secretary should have the respect of the Senate and the Foreign Relations Committee.

The Secretary should have public acceptance. While the public knew him only as a vague and respectable figure, the foreign policy commentators and scholars who would be writing of the State Department rated him very highly. Walter Lippmann, whose advice Kennedy sought, valued Fulbright as one of the rare wise men.

The Secretary should be a prudent counselor, but not engage in public wrestling matches with the President over policy, and he should not harm the Administration politically. Would naming a Southerner toss away the Negro vote? A few delicate inquiries showed it would not. Would the Jews be upset by Fulbright, since he had chided the Zionists for influencing American foreign policy in the Middle East? Some would, and some wouldn't.

Senator Fulbright's view of Kennedy, at this point in time, was hopeful but not enthusiastic. Kennedy had been a member of the Foreign Relations Committee, mostly *in absentia*. Much of the time he had been away campaigning, and Fulbright thought of him as a dilettante in foreign policy. The Senator from Arkansas had been a zealous backer of Lyndon Johnson for the Presidency, because, as he said, "We need an older man with experience to get things done." And, during the campaign of 1960, Fulbright was disturbed to hear Kennedy speak quite emotionally about Cuba, and remarked at the time, "He's out-Nixoned Nixon."

As the rumors piled up and colleagues called him, Fulbright was embarrassed. He did not want to be Secretary of State, yet he did not feel he could turn down the office if Kennedy asked him to take it. With a characteristic directness, he decided the best strategy was to head off the bid. He saw his chance when the newspapers reported the President-elect would pay a visit to Senator Dick Russell, chairman of the Armed Services Committee, and the leading sachem of the Senate.

Fulbright went to see Russell. The two dukes of Congressional feudalism sat in Russell's second-floor office in the old Senate Office Building, and Fulbright said he had a damned delicate matter to talk over. These reports that Jack was going to tap him for Secretary of State. Probably nonsense. But suppose it is true! My God, imagine me trying to run that bureaucracy, highballing out to the airport to meet the Prime Minister of Pogo Pogo, complimenting the French Ambassador's wife on her latest hairdo, the days cluttered up with smoke-filled conferences, playing nicey-nice to Congressional committees, fighting the bureaucratic wars with Defense and CIA and the White House staff, jetting overseas to apply new glue to the patchwork of alliances.

You know, Dick, he appealed to the other, I'd be a hell of a poor Secretary.

The Georgian listened with a grave and appreciative humor. He knew Bill Fulbright had to have elbow room and solitude, that he was impatient with others and couldn't tolerate boobs or boredom. Senator Russell said he would speak to Kennedy.

Fulbright thought the project had been dropped after the Kennedy-Russell meeting. However early in December, *The New York Times,* in a front page story by its White House correspondent, William H. Lawrence, a personal friend of the President-elect, flatly stated Fulbright was going to be Secretary of State. The announcement would be made in a few days.

The story appeared on a Wednesday morning. The next day, Senator Kennedy personally called Fulbright's office in the Capitol only to find the Senator was in Arkansas. Kennedy talked to an aide; it was most urgent that he speak to the Senator. "Give me his schedule, and I'll call him in Arkansas. If he calls in, tell him to please get in touch with me. I must speak to him."

The assistant gave President-elect Kennedy the schedule, where he would be at this and that hour. Senator Kennedy called later in the day, and seemed quite agitated. He had not been able to reach the Senator. Did the office have *any* idea where to contact him?

Fulbright simply laid low in the piney woods of Arkansas. This was about as clear a turndown as Kennedy could get. He gave up. Dick Russell had been right. Bill Fulbright didn't want the job.

This opens up conjectures. Would President Kennedy have gone ahead with the Bay of Pigs against the strong advice of his Secretary of State? Would President Johnson have ordered Marines into the Dominican Republic? Would he have escalated the war in Vietnam? Would he have been so adamant against dealing with the National Liberation Front?

The life Senator Fulbright has chosen and would not trade for all the tea in China is a delicately poised combination—the Committee chairman, the lawmaker with all the drudgery and routine hard work this involves, the politician doing chores for the folks back home (he is known as the "oleo king" for his repeal of discriminatory measures against "the lower-price spread"), the teacher, and, in carefully treasured odd moments, the scholar.

In the usual fraternal chitchat of the cloakroom, a colleague congratulated Fulbright on looking so fit in the winter of 1965–1966.

"I don't know why," the gentleman from Arkansas replied. "I was up until two o'clock this morning."

The other had visions of high-level crisis talks or, what the hell, a gay diplomatic party. He asked, "What were you doing?"

The Senator responded most enthusiastically, "Reading Chinese history."

He complains that he does not have enough time to think. The Senator comes to his office before most of his colleagues, reads the papers, goes over the mail, has a brief word with his staff, and then is off to a committee meeting. One day recently, he had three such meetings, one from ten until a little after noon, another beginning at two-thirty and a third starting at four. If he does not have to be on the Senate floor or go to a committee, Fulbright sees visitors in the afternoons. About ten times as many people want to see him as he has the time and interest for, and his tactful personal secretary, Kitty Johnson, has this problem to deal with daily. He will always squeeze out a half hour or hour for a man from whom he can learn something, as Jean Lacouture, the noted French authority on Vietnam, when he was in Washington. And he hardly ever turns away people from Arkansas.

The Senator rarely writes more than a few paragraphs of his speeches anymore. He makes notes and stuffs them into his pockets, and talks over the ideas with his staff. Lee Williams, his administrative assistant, is the devil's advocate. He tried, without success, to persuade Fulbright to give up or tame down his Dominican Republic speech. When the ideas are clear, the Senator has a long lunch or afternoon with Seth Tillman, a young political scientist from M.I.T. who has learned the Fulbright syntax. After Tillman turns in a draft, Fulbright worries over it, changing words here and there and sometimes writing a new paragraph.

In all that the Senator from Arkansas says in public there is a simple thesis, one that he spelled out for the American Newspaper Publishers Association on April 28, 1966: "I believe that the citizen who criticizes his country is paying it an implied tribute. At the very least it means that he has not given up on his country, that he still has hope for it. More often, the critic is motivated by high regard for the society he lives in and for its promise; in this case the vigor of his criticism is the measure of the gap he perceives between promise and performance. I do not think it is 'selling America short' when we ask a great deal of her; on the contrary, it is those who ask nothing, those who see no fault, who are really selling America short. . . .

"We are falling short because, in a curious way, we do not seem to believe in our power and greatness. The evidence of this lack of faith in ourselves is our apparent need for constant proof and reassurance, our nagging desire for popularity, our bitterness and confusion when foreigners fail to appreciate our generosity and good intentions. Lacking an understanding of the dimensions of our own power, we fail to understand our enormous and disruptive impact upon the world; we fail to understand that, no matter how good our intentions—and they are, in most cases, decent enough—other nations are alarmed by the very existence of such great power, which, whatever its benevolence, cannot help but remind them of their own helplessness before it. . . .

"When a nation is very powerful but lacking in self-confidence, it is likely to behave in a manner that is dangerous both to itself and to others. Feeling the need to prove what is obvious to everyone else, it begins to confuse great power with unlimited power and great responsibility with total responsibility; it can admit no error; it must win every argument no matter how trivial. . . ."

This is Fulbright talking to his own people. This is what history will record of him—if there is a history.

III

J. WILLIAM FULBRIGHT, despite his French cuffs, waistcoat, and Oxford degree, is as full of the Arkansas Ozarks as a razorback hog. His toughness, his earthiness which comes out in private male conversation, his dislike of great power, his independence all reek of a small town of the Southwest a generation ago.

Fayetteville, Arkansas, wasn't the jasmine-haunted South of William Faulkner, but a progressive university town founded by Missourians, flavored by Populism and looked more west than south. "It was," the Senator says reflectively, "a very serene place."

He was born on a muddy corn-hog farm in southern Missouri on April 9, 1905. A year later, his father brought the family to Fayetteville to get away from the mud and try his hand in business. The boy spent his life within the confines of Washington County and its ripe hills until, as a young man, he left for Oxford on a Rhodes scholarship.

It is difficult to imagine today how isolated a small town could be from the so-called mainstream of American life. There were no electronic media to flash the latest cry of the wounded child in Asia or the statesman's roarings from Washington. The main source of events was the little newspaper, *The Democrat,* and its chronicle of birth, marriage and death and local politics and church socials.

So the Senator's childhood was untouched by the clamor of the new American nationalism. Teddy Roosevelt was the President then. He seized Colombian territory, set up the puppet state of Panama and built the canal. He swung the big stick, and sent the American Navy into Santo Domingo to collect custom duties. He regarded foreigners, particularly those who disagree with him, with a picturesque contempt. He referred to Colombian officials as "bandits," "black-mailers" and "jackrabbits," and called the president of Venezuela an "unspeakably villainous little monkey." At one time, he thought of intervening militarily in that country and wrote his Secretary of State, "It will show those Dagos that they will have to behave decently." When the Senate blocked his "treaty" with Santo Domingo, he cried, "The Senate is wholly incompetent."

Teddy preached the gospel of "strenuous endeavor." He said in his piercing high voice, "Nothing in this world is worth having or doing unless it means effort, pain, difficulty. Let us therefore boldly face the life of strife."

And in the Senate, Albert J. Beveridge was crying, "God has not been preparing the English-speaking and Teutonic peoples for a thousand years for nothing but vain and idle self-contemplation and self-admiration. No! He has made us the master-organizers of the world to establish system where chaos reigns. . . . He has made us adepts in government that we may administer government among savage and senile peoples. . . . He has marked the American people as His chosen nation to finally lead in the regeneration of the world. This is the divine mission of America. . . . We will not renounce our part in the mission of our race, trustee, under God, of the civilization of the world."

Not having been suckled on this juice, Fulbright regarded it as "arrant nonsense" when he heard it espoused by such true believers as John Foster Dulles and Lyndon Johnson. The absence of this kind of nationalism from his bringing up is important to his philosophy.

Another key to his personality is the serenity and security of his childhood. This has been transformed into his great strength, his ability to move ahead alone, away from the crowd. He does not need a gang of well-wishers surrounding him, nor does he retreat when attacked.

His father was Jay Fulbright, a farmer and businessman of German ancestry. The name originally was Vulbrecht. He was not a learned man, although he spent two years at the University of Missouri. He was a quiet, self-contained, hardworking individual. The Senator describes him as "a man of calm, even temperament. He believed life would go on no matter what the crisis or calamity at hand." His mother wrote of him, "He knew self-reliance. He had little time for the man or woman who eternally leaned on someone else—the government, his employers or his parents. He was a stalwart, not afraid to take a chance and never whining when he lost. His mind worked as straight a line as anyone I've ever known. Fairness was his creed, simplicity his code."

There is much of his father in the Senator, in his complete lack of hysteria, his deliberate self-control, his willingness to walk alone. An incident of 1965 tells a story. Before his Dominican Republic speech, an assistant proposed, "I don't think you should say this all by yourself. You should get some other Senators to stand up with you. That fellow downtown only understands one thing, and that is power, and your voice alone isn't going to change him. It'll just make him mad. I'm sure I can get fifteen or so Senators to come to the floor, and say they agree with you."

Fulbright shook his head. "No," he said, "I don't want to involve anyone else. These are my ideas, and they may not agree with me. I don't want to embarrass them by inviting them to support me. I'm willing to stand by myself."

In 1906, Jay Fulbright came to Fayetteville, and began building a small-town business empire with German industriousness. He would buy into a little business, develop it by hard work and scrupulous attention to details, and put money into another venture. He died at fifty-six, the wealthiest man in town. He owned a major share in a bank, newspaper, bottling works with a Coca-Cola franchise, creamery and produce house, lumber company, a wagon works, and a small timber railroad. From old photographs, the Senator bears a marked resemblance to his father.

Jay Fulbright had a high sense of responsibility, and his son tells of one episode. His father made good personally on a bad loan he had recommended, although he had no legal responsibility to do so.

His son feels the same sense of responsibility to find out the truth behind American foreign policy, and make known his findings to the people. As many will attest, he pursues this with a rare diligence and stubbornness.

The family affluence, while it was no fortune, protected Fulbright from the damaging shock of economic insecurity that afflicted the lower class and much of the middle class of America in the 1920's and 1930's. This generation has been obsessed with the need to acquire material wealth, and has spent its greatest energies in this pursuit. Not so the Senator. He is less well-to-do than Lyndon Johnson, who was a poor boy almost five hundred miles south in the worn-out cotton lands of east Texas.

But, Fulbright has had the opportunity to indulge himself in knowledge, a rare privilege in his time.

His mother was the best-known person in northwest Arkansas. The Fayetteville library and a dormitory at the University of Arkansas are named for her. In her photographs, she is a small woman, sensibly dressed, with a strong chin and wonderfully alive eyes. An old friend of the family remarks, "There was always excitement around her, like sparks."

"Miss Roberta," as she was known, raised six children, took over the family enterprises when her husband died, wrote a column in the local newspaper, had the prettiest gardens in the county, and was a persistent reformer in local politics. She also found time to take classes at the university. She loved ideas and good talk. "God, how she loved to talk!" the Senator reminisces.

Her family name was Waugh. They were of English origin from Virginia and "literarily inclined, but not very good at making money," the Senator remarks. "Instead, the Waughs produced teachers and doctors. My Uncle Tom Waugh was a man of learning."

Miss Roberta attended the University of Missouri, at a time when few women were going to college, and taught school before she married. In her later years, she spoke what was her epitaph: "I've lived long. I've loved working. I've loved fighting in the argumentative sense. I abhor war. I believe it must be abolished. I wish I could have done more for humanity." She completed her college work and took a teacher's degree after her children were grown.

In her newspaper column, "As I See It," in what is now *The Northwest Arkansas Times,* she showed herself as a humanist and reformer. "Life is a dull thing when centered only in self," she wrote. "A glowing, burning thing when centered in others and in the world. . . . Could I wish for one faculty for the human race, it would be appreciation in its deepest sense. It is those who have this attribute who bring value to life, to human relations, to human endeavor. . . . Prejudice completely short of reason fires my flammable nature until a conflagration is all that can appease it. The rule of reason is a good one." She thought Franklin D. Roosevelt was "the greatest living exponent of the Democratic idea that everyone is entitled to opportunity, that government is for the people and by the people, and that Freedom is a human right."

She was an active force in the community. She cleaned out a corrupt courthouse. Once she heard the church board was going to oust the preacher whom she admired as an honest and courageous man. She stormed the board meeting, and said she believed in justice and the reverend was not receiving it. The board overruled her objections and fired him. She found the pastor another post.

When a provincial professor at the University of Arkansas tried to stir up feelings against instructors from the North, she wrote, "A university is no field for such tripe. This is concentrated prejudice and the essence of sectionalism. The Mason and Dixon line should be as dead as last year's calendar."

The Senator inherited her capacity for outrage, not entirely to the comfort of his staff. At the office Christmas party in 1961, his staff presented him with an unusual gift of wire all prettied up in tinsel paper and bright red ribbon.

"What is it?" he asked amiably.

"It's a muzzle, Senator."

He accepted the muzzle in great good humor, for he recognizes that his penchant for criticism brings in a torrent of letters and telephone calls, but he can no more strangle his hankering for reform than change his accent.

Miss Roberta was proud of her son's intellectual bent, and encouraged it. His father thought the boy should be trained to take over the businesses, and he worked summers. The summer after his first year at the university he worked in the college dairy, washing bottles and slopping hogs. Miss Roberta came to his rescue, and from then on he went to summer school. When her husband died, Bill was eighteen. He stayed out of the university for a semester to help with the family business, becoming an officer and director of several concerns. He was, as a newspaper noted, the youngest vice president of a railroad in the United States, the short line in northwest Arkansas, owned partially by the family.

Miss Roberta saw that running a lumber company and a Coca-Cola bottling works was not what her son was cut out for. She took control of the enterprises quite competently, and he went back to school.

This was a large family. The Senator had four sisters and a brother. Anna and Lucille and Jack were older, and the twins, Helen and Roberta, were younger. An old Arkansas friend remarked, "Bill's been very fortunate. He's always had very devoted and intelligent women to look after him and take care of him, all the way from Miss Roberta and the sisters to Betty, his wife."

Of this close-knit family, only the Senator, Anna (Mrs. Kenneth Teasdale, the wife of a St. Louis lawyer), and Jack, who lives in Memphis, are alive. Helen's husband, Hal Douglas, runs the family enterprises in Fayetteville, and is one of the few close friends of Fulbright.

In this highly literate atmosphere, both of his family and of a university town, Fulbright was mercifully spared the hellfire and damnation religion that souped up the backwoods camp meetings, burned into the spirits of millions of Americans of that generation and created the fierce good-evil dichotomy and evangelism that permeates so much of foreign policy today.

His own philosophy allows there is no all-beneficent man or all-evil one, and that most of us wander in between, with capacities for great good and impulses of sheer savagery. He has enormous faith in man as a logical being, and once said, "If I didn't believe that, I couldn't go on."

If the Senator were to put this in theological terms, he would probably say that God's special gift to man is his capacity for reason.

Fulbright's lack of contact with Fundamentalist religion in his childhood creates a certain blindness. He does not understand emotionally what motivates a Lyndon Johnson or John Foster Dulles in their absolute conviction they are angels of the Lord taming the forces of Satan.

In college, Fulbright was a sort of spirited all-American kid. In his second year he had a stripped-down Ford, and was fined $62 in a night court for speeding. He was the star halfback of the football team, and was the hero of the 1922 homecoming game against mighty Southern Methodist. A sports columnist of the day reported: "It was not Southern Methodist but Arkansas which dished out the fireworks. After an exchange of punts, early in the contest, the Razorbacks powered on down to the Mustangs' goal line. Bill Fulbright, the hero of the game, faked an end run, then passed to Homer Berry for a touchdown, 12 yards out. The homecoming crowd went wild!

"Later in the spirited melee, Fulbright hauled in an S.M.U. punt and galloped 40 yards into Mustang territory. When a Razorback drive finally ran out of steam, Fulbright dropped back to the 35 yard ribbon and booted a perfect field goal, giving Arkansas a highly surprising 9–0 lead."

The *Little Rock Gazette* said, "On the football field he [Fulbright] distinguished himself as a real triple threat man, making his first letter at the age of 17. Few men in the Southwestern Conference could surpass him in hurling passes as the S.M.U. and T.C.U. players can testify this year. His punting usually bordered on the sensational, more because of his uncanny accuracy than because of height or distance."

This driving desire to win the game remains, as several Presidents and Secretaries of State know. He hesitates, standing outside an argument before he is drawn in; then he plays to win.

At the university, Fulbright was also captain of the tennis team, a member of the glee club, and, by a one-vote majority, president of the student body. One classmate remarked: "He was a pleasant guy, but always a little apart and younger than most. He had acquaintances all over the campus but no close friends."

A professor remembers him: "He was quiet, rarely volunteering an answer. He was definitely an intellectual, a fairly rare breed at Fayetteville, and somewhere between a cynic and a philosopher. Even then, he was asking questions. Very pleasant and nice, but if you made an error, there would be his hand and he would ask you if you didn't mean such and such. It wasn't very smart to argue with him, because you knew he had studied the lesson."

The atmosphere of the community in which he lived all of his young life was, as the Senator has said, serene. It is an Arcadia. The family lived in a big rambling house on Mount Nord with a view of the pine green Ozarks from the front porch and surrounded by Miss Roberta's gardens. The boy hunted and fished and hiked all over the county, and has today the outdoorsman's love of natural beauty and exercise. He becomes tired and irritated if too long without it.

A friend who has watched Fulbright closely for years made an observation about his background: "You'll never understand Bill until you realize what a secure basis he had. The most important family in town. Never had to worry about money. Tremendous support from the family. Sparked and kept in high gear intellectually by Miss Roberta. At the university, the boy wonder. I'm sure this is why he could stand up to Joe McCarthy without flinching or challenge the President of the United States."

The history of Arkansas must have had an effect upon him, too. This is the only Southern state which does not have a single statue of a Confederate general in the statehouse.

Arkansas was dragged into the Civil War by a plantation-owning

Governor from the eastern section and hysterical newspaper accounts. The Governor in a message to the legislature said, "Without slavery her [Arkansas'] fertile fields will be deserts, and her people penniless and impoverished."

The Confederate Congress exempted from military service all who owned twenty slaves or more. This was odious to the small farmers of Arkansas who made up the majority. The war became known there as "the rich man's war and the poor man's fight." When the Confederacy insisted on shifting Arkansas troops across the Mississippi River, many refused to go. Others deserted later. While Arkansans were fighting in Tennessee, Federal troops moved in from the north. Areas of heavy fighting in Arkansas were devastated. The Arkansas College was left a roofless ruin. Hospitals were filled with the sick and wounded. Few young men were left to plant and reap. The state was burdened by a huge debt. Arkansas' best historian, John Gould Fletcher, wrote in his *Arkansas,* "It was the people of the state who had to make this war, abandoned and betrayed and alone."

To anyone who has read through all of Senator Fulbright's speeches, this has a familiar sound. Wars, according to him, are not made by the men who have to fight them but by zealots and fanatics. He said recently, "Who are the self-appointed emissaries of God who have wrought so much violence on the world? They are men with doctrines, men of faith and fiery idealism, men who believe in some cause without doubt and practice their belief without scruple, men who cease to be human beings with normal preferences for work and fun and family and become instead living, breathing embodiments of some faith or ideology. From Robespierre to Stalin and Mao Tsetung they have been capable as Djilas wrote of Stalin 'of destroying nine tenths of the human race to make happy one tenth.' "

A spirit of independence and iconoclasm rides high in Arkansas. The folk heroes are Andrew Jackson, a Populist Governor named Jeff Davis, and Jesse James. The Senator who mildly says he does not believe in "quiet acquiescence" is both part of this tradition and appeals to it. Philip Carter in the *Texas Observer* says the way Fulbright stands up to Presidents pleases the "stiff-necked rebellious independence" of the state. Nor do they mind when he criticizes the American psyche and calls the foreign policy adolescent. ("We have clung too long to our youth as a nation, during which our foreign policy consisted of a series of exhilarating and successful adventures. But we live now in a far more difficult and dangerous world in which we must come of age. Neither God nor nature has preordained the triumph of our free society.")

Carter quotes a Little Rock constituent, "I don't always agree with him, and Bill sometimes makes me mad as hell. But you've sure got to admire the courage he has to say exactly what he thinks." The *Blytheville Courier* pretty well expressed the spirit and outrage of Arkansas after the President removed Fulbright from his social list. The editor wrote, "Since war is intolerable, we would rather see our Senator in the doghouse while searching for a solution than in the White House dining room endorsing tired platitudes over glasses of Moselle."

Arkansans generally, according to Carter, believe he is "a brilliant statesman ('whether you agree with him or not') whose Olympian style and international prestige enhance the whole state—and, they add, he is a resourceful and willing champion of every vested interest from Lake Village to Siloam Springs. . . . Fulbright has always been an enigma—but they have listened to him and voted for him. To them he is neither prisoner nor paradox, but a hometown prophet to be honored by his own."

The Senator sometimes alludes to another factor in his life. This is the way fate comes along and picks him up and puts him down in a totally new situation—from small-town football hero to Oxford scholar, from Government lawyer to university president, from university president to Congressman. In each case, chance entered his life.

While he was still a student at Arkansas, an English professor saw the announcement of examinations for Rhodes scholarships at Oxford. The professor persuaded Bill Fulbright to make a try, and he went to Little Rock for the tests. He says now with a slight smile, "It was a damn good thing for me they were given out on a regional basis, rather than for the top scholar-athletes in the United States. I suppose the committee was intrigued at the idea of an Ozark hillbilly at Oxford."

He set off across the continent as excited as he had been when he began a football game, but with something more besides—the sense that here was a whole big world he had never seen and was about to explore—and he was eager as a jackrabbit to get across the road.

The Senator remembers to this day the exhilaration and wonder with which he wandered about New York City looking at the big buildings and shops, and trying to fit these wholly unfamiliar and exciting sights into his own small world. He had achieved by some miracle of chance that heart's desire, the liberty to test himself. A line from James Joyce suggests the mood of the boy from Arkansas as he began a great adventure alone: "There was a lust of wandering in his feet that burned to set out for the ends of the earth."

IV

SENATOR FULBRIGHT is both modest and charmingly deceptive when he talks about his years in England.

He told a writer for *Life* magazine, "All I did at Oxford is to have a hell of a good time—played games and studied the minimum."

The Senator enjoys at times presenting himself as a rather highly enameled lightweight and fussily respectable. Like many fighters, he prefers to go into the ring underrated.

The photographs of Fulbright at Oxford bear out his description and show a happy-go-lucky young man—exceptionally good-looking, elegantly dressed in tweeds, puffing a pipe, or as the youngest member of the lacrosse team.

He impressed fellow students at Pembroke College, Oxford, as a well-to-do young dilettante from the States. One recalls, "He was a mixture of the sporting and social type. Bill was very good at tennis and won his half-blue at lacrosse and took ardently to rugby. He was quite a socialite, too. We had these little clubs named after famous men, as the Johnson Club for Dr. Johnson, but they were really an excuse to get together and drink and talk not very seriously. Bill belonged to all of these, and was a most congenial fellow. He showed up, sometimes, too, at the philosophical society, which was usually limited to students of philosophy. One of my strongest impressions of him was one of indolence, from his slow speech and easy manner. It was quite a surprise to most of us when he became a world figure."

One man at Oxford who was not surprised was Ronald B. Mc-Callum, now the master of Pembroke College, a distinguished British scholar, historian and critic. He was Fulbright's tutor, had studied at Princeton, and was interested in the vigorous mind and competitive spirit of this drawling American. As the scholar read for honors in modern history, McCallum lead him into the high adventure of the study of the past.

The historian employs a discipline to which McCallum introduced Fulbright; he removes himself from immediate events, and looks upon the scene coolly and reflectively.

McCallum taught the young man from Arkansas, too, to question the cliché, the dogma, the hard sell. This saved Fulbright from the scars which many educated men of his generation suffered. As youths, they became fascinated with Marxism or other isms. Fulbright has never been trapped by doctrines, right, left or center. Instead, the tutor introduced him to scholarly social criticism.

The relation between tutor and pupil remains today. They correspond regularly. The Senator addresses him formally as "Master," and McCallum replies simply to "Fulbright." This correspondence, and it is dearly private, offers the Senator an opportunity to try out ideas, exchange thoughts and seek information in the objective pupil-tutor relationship.

Oxford was the base from which he took off for jaunts into Europe. He visited every country on the Continent but Spain and Russia. He traveled Europe third class, sprinkling lice powder on the train seat before settling down. He spent one summer with an archeological expedition in the south of France, another holiday in Poland with a cut-down car. He learned to ski and skate at St. Moritz. He was bored by the plethora of old people on the Riviera.

As president of the Johnson Society and Teasel Club at Oxford and a member of the joint Oxford-Cambridge lacrosse team, Fulbright was something of a minor celebrity, and was invited to a dinner party at Lady Astor's town house, where he met the Prince of Wales. When he came with the lacrosse team to the United States, and was received at the White House by President and Mrs. Coolidge, there is no evidence that he was awed by the Presidential presence.

After finishing his studies at Oxford—he received a bachelor's degree in 1928 and a master's in 1931—Fulbright went to the University of Vienna to study German. There at the celebrated Café Louvre on Wipplinger Strasse, he met M. W. Fodor, correspondent for *The Manchester Guardian* and the *New York Post*. Mike Fodor was probably the most highly respected foreign correspondent in Europe. He was a Hungarian émigré, stocky, balding, and had been a metallurgist of some distinction. During World War I, he was interned in England because of his nationality, and turned to journalism after the war as more interesting.

One of Fodor's former colleagues, who had been with the United Press in Vienna, recalls, "Mike taught more foreign correspondents their business than any man alive. He was a godfather and teacher and managing editor to us all. He helped Dorothy Thompson, for one, to get her start. Mike was quiet and intellectual and exuded integrity. He knew every ruler of Europe personally, and could recount in detail history and treaties and battles.

"About eight or nine o'clock every evening, we would come to the Café Louvre before we filed our dispatches, and look for Mike. We would try out our stories on him, and ask him questions. He knew everything from where to buy a good pair of shoes to the name of the Foreign Minister's mistress."

Fulbright, then twenty-six, fell in with the journalists, and Fodor took him on as an apprentice. The Senator recalls, "Every year Fodor went on a grand tour around Europe. I went with him, and sat in on the interviews as his assistant. It was most educational."

In this time with Fodor, Fulbright acquired a faith, that sticks with him to this day, in the integrity of the good foreign correspondent. In a number of crises, a careful reading of press dispatches has aroused in him a question about the veracity of Administration reports. He spends a good deal of his private time talking to correspondents from all parts of the world. At least one investigation of the Foreign Relations Committee was based on a personal memorandum from a *New York Times* correspondent.

Fulbright might have stayed on with Fodor and become a correspondent, but family affairs brought him back home to Fayetteville. The time had come for him to take over his share of running the businesses.

As a member of the civilized aristocracy of the Western world, he was an anachronism running the back country sawmill. It was a new aristocracy, not based on birth but on intellect. Many of its peers came from the middle class, as he did. They were crammed with knowledge of the history and culture of Western civilization. They contrasted oddly with such contemporaries as Al Capone, Billy Sunday, "Daddy" Browning and his sixteen-year-old bride, "Peaches," and Herbert Hoover.

Fulbright was restless but uncomplaining in Fayetteville, and when a chance came for him to leave, Miss Roberta did not try to stop him.

It seemed unlikely that he would ever settle down happily to running the bottling works and sawmill. A friend of his, a wealthy playboy, called him to Washington to help put his estate in order. Fulbright was installed in a great mansion, had a few business errands to run and a full social life. Those who knew him then remember a handsome, charming young man who wore casual sports jackets and pronounced a few words with a recognizable British accent, as "fragyle," in a soft Southern voice.

Fulbright traveled in a limited social set, among people of his own kind, and saw little of the politicians or the reformers. One evening he was invited to dinner at the home of a young married couple. The husband had known Fulbright at Oxford. The other guest was Miss Elizabeth Williams. She came from an old, aristocratic and moneyed Philadelphia family. Her father had been a cotton merchant. She attended a private school in Philadelphia, and came out very correctly at an old-fashioned tea.

The two guests had an argument at dinner. It was probably over politics and the New Deal, since she came from a conservative Republican background. Betty Fulbright remembers: "Bill said he would have to meet me again, so he could persuade me he was right."

It is entirely characteristic of the Senator that he should meet his wife at a small dinner party, and become quite interested because of a discussion. His arguments must have been effective, for Betty Fulbright is one of his better campaigners, the transplanted Philadelphia Main Liner greeting country women at a fried chicken dinner and enjoying it.

The Fulbrights were married in 1932 and have two daughters, Betsy, the wife of a Washington physician, Dr. John Winnaker, and Roberta, Mrs. Thaddeus Foote III. The latter's husband is related to Adlai Stevenson and is a lawyer. There are three grandchildren, two girls and a boy. Fulbright went to the George Washington University law school and graduated with honors, and thence into the antitrust division of the Department of Justice. He was one of the Government lawyers representing the NRA in the famous sick chicken case, in which the Supreme Court struck down the New Deal's attempt to set a minimum wage, abolish child labor and create consumer standards. (Of the decision, President Roosevelt said, "We have been relegated to the horse-and-buggy definition of interstate commerce.")

The young lawyer was never a vital, committed part of the reform and social revolution of the New Deal. He is essentially a teacher and critic and historian and not, as Roosevelt or Johnson, a conscious mover of mountains. So he left the Government to teach law at George Washington.

Then chance intervened in his life again. Dean Julius S. Waterman of the University of Arkansas heard he was teaching at George Washington, and wrote, "So long as you are teaching, why don't you come back home? We need you here." So, at thirty-one, he returned to Fayetteville to take up a career he had finally chanced upon, teaching. He has a good deal of sympathy for the young people of today who have such a hard time finding what they want to do, for he was well past his youth when he decided teaching was it. He became a lecturer at the law school.

The seven intervening years in Arkansas, 1936–1943, have a special place in his life. "Some of the happiest and best years of my life were then," he muses. "Betty and I lived in a modernized log house in a rustic area with our own spring. I loved the place."

The house was an old hunting lodge known as "Dancing Rabbit's Foot Lodge" with chinked logs, a Chinese-type roof and balconies as on a Swiss chalet, about ten miles out of town and surrounded by 110 acres. He dammed up a stream and made a pool for swimming. He raised cattle, chicken, hogs, vegetables and feed on the acres. He and Betty cured their meat, churned cream and rendered lard. She even learned to make soap in an outdoor kettle.

There is yet a part of Thoreau in Fulbright—a joy in solitude, a sense of wonder at the infinite variety and order of nature, pleasure in hard, physical work. He went out into the mornings hunting quail and watching the early sun dapple the wooded hills. One of Mrs. Fulbright's favorite pictures is the Senator stripped to his waist, in trunks, working in the garden.

Chance intervened again. In 1939, the president of the university was killed in an automobile accident. Next in line was Dean Waterman, about whom Fulbright has said, "I believe people instinctively sensed that here was a man who embodied the wisdom and understanding of centuries of suffering and struggle by the human race. To know him was to have hope that eventually the good in man's nature will prevail over evil." Dean Waterman declined the presidency and recommended Fulbright. This choice of a thirty-four-year-old law lecturer was not the most popular among the older faculty members, but it pleased the board of trustees and the Governor.

An old family friend recalled, "He looked more like a student than most of his students did, being addicted to a pipe, a station wagon and a tweed jacket." The first time he went to a football game as president in the battered station wagon, a freshman directing traffic yelled at him, "Back that wreck out of here. That's for the faculty. Can't you read?" One Arkansas historian has described his reign as "dignified, vigorous and determined."

Even in these busy, happy times, he thought of the world outside. Mrs. Fulbright remembers: "In those days when we needed a hospital for Fayetteville, Bill said, 'Think how much we could do in building hospitals and schools and roads, if all the money didn't have to go to wars.' He talked about the waste and destruction of war, and the need for peace to develop a nation intellectually, economically and morally."

In 1940, he was anguished by the war in Europe, and felt the United States must help Britain and her allies to survive. He was invited to address the University of Missouri and included in the draft he sent, "The weasling, timid and fearful policy of our isolationist Senators is one of the greatest dangers to our true interests." The university asked him to delete that sentence, since Senator Champ Clark of Missouri would be in the audience. He refused, and received a wire canceling his invitation to speak.

His tenure as president was brief, two years. The new Governor, Homer Adkins, was riled by remarks Miss Roberta made in her column. She wrote after his election that the voters had traded a statesman, Governor Carl Bailey, for a glad-hander and backslapper.

Adkins asked the legislature for authority to appoint a majority of the board of trustees, six of the ten, and obtained it. The board met in May to oust Fulbright, but students staged a mass meeting of protest. This was probably, the Senator says with a smile, one of the first politically inspired student protests in modern America.

The Senator was spared until June, 1941, Commencement Day. There had been omens. Mrs. Fulbright had invited the trustees to a luncheon, and five of the six Adkins appointees said they could not make it. The board met before noon in a tumultuous two-and-a-half-hour session. They asked Fulbright to resign. He said, "Why should I resign? If I am to be fired, why leave the people in doubt?" He went out and waited in the hall while the board decided to oust him. At the president's reception, he cheerfully congratulated the man he expected to succeed him.

That night in the rain he passed out diplomas while the students cheered him. He was their guy against the others.

This unexpected turn of events was the trigger that brought him to Congress. Congressman Carl Ellis, who had studied constitutional law under Fulbright, came to him and said, "I'm going to run for the Senate, and I think you should try for my seat."

Fulbright protested he didn't know anything about politics, and didn't have the temperament for it.

Ellis answered with the kind of logic Fulbright is unable to resist. He asked, "What about the lectures you gave us on the need for educated men in politics?"

He was the most unlikely candidate ever to run in the Ozarks. Mrs. Irene Carlisle of the Fayetteville newspaper wrote a year later, "The farmers and shopkeepers who decide the district's political destinies were not quite prepared for the somewhat slouchy young man who looked and acted like a bashful small town boy and admitted with a grin he had never run for any sort of office, didn't know the names of the ten counties in the district, and had never before set foot in six of them."

American politics is vulgar, and Fulbright, while he can be earthy, is not earthy in the sense of the TV commercial or the usual political pitch. He is unable to appeal to the low fears and prejudices and phony hopes of the multitude. Conservatives cry out that crooked politicians and fellow travelers are ruining the fiscal integrity. The liberal accuses the fat cats of cheating the little fellow. Real issues are ignored or so timorously discussed they are unintelligible. When Adlai Stevenson, with urging from Fulbright, proposed a nuclear test ban in 1956, Democratic politicians tried to get him to lay off. The idea was too new, too hot.

A candidate thinks, at least, he must convince the voters he shares their oddities. Hubert Humphrey had to prove to his Minnesota dairy farmers he hated oleomargarine, and would fight it to the death. Lyndon Johnson labored mightily for the oil depletion allowance for wealthy Texans. Paul Douglas with hordes of Polish-American voters in Chicago regularly offered to "liberate" Poland from Russian authority. New York Senators continually attack the Arabs, and defend Israel to the last cliché. Southerners for years had to walk with the "nigger-hating" poor whites.

Fulbright has said, "The process of being elected to the Congress in a predominantly rural community in the South is an experience that is not easy to describe. Until the summer of 1941, when I left the presidency of the university, I had never taken part, directly or indirectly, other than to vote, in any political campaign. But the process of introducing oneself, and talking to the people informally, in their business places and their homes, was the most interesting and satisfying experience of the campaign. With only a few exceptions, they were interested and friendly, although rarely did they indicate how they would vote. Generally speaking, they were more interested in me as a person than in my views about the broad principles of government.

"After three months of personal visits, with particular attention to those influential in political matters, the speaking campaign began. This phase of the campaign is very strenuous and downright hard work. Never having made a political speech before, the first few efforts were excruciatingly painful. I have seldom experienced a feeling of more abject despair and humiliation than the first time I spoke on the street corner of a small village with about a dozen curious listeners who apparently were not listening. However, it is amazing how soon one becomes accustomed to the sound of one's voice when forced to repeat a speech five or six times a day.

"As election day approaches, the size of the crowds grows; they are more responsive and more interested, and one derives a certain exhilaration from that which only a few weeks before was intensely painful."

Mrs. Fulbright remembers that campaign distinctly. "Bill thought he would have a most difficult time talking to a group without a prepared text," she reminisces. " 'What will I say to them?' he asked before the first meeting. He spoke from the back of a wagon at Garfield, and I know it was difficult for him to speak for fifteen minutes. But six weeks later, at the end of the campaign, he talked for an hour and enjoyed it. We roamed the district in a Ford with a loudspeaker, and made five stops a day. The first would be at eleven A.M., on a street corner with perhaps eighteen to twenty people there, and invariably a little boy with his mouth open and staring. The longer he was campaigning, the more Bill liked it. He liked talking to people and answering their questions."

Even in this arena, he remained essentially the teacher—a lecture, usually brief, and then the exchange of thinking through the question and answer. One observer of that first campaign remarked: "The people appreciated a politician who was willing to stand before them, and not simply entertain them with wild and woolly charges, but to answer their questions. I think he gave them a feeling of being closer to them and their interests than the usual candidate."

He went into the campaign as the underdog, a long shot. A young professor against a tough old professional. But he had a good deal going for him. He was a local hero, the college football star, Rhodes scholar, and popular college president. And he had been martyred by a clumsy Governor. He was immensely attractive personally, and he grew to get the feel of the audience and respond.

The young professor won, of course, and again chance put him on a new path.

V

THE NEW CONGRESSMAN from Arkansas drove across Memorial Bridge into a war-darkened city. The spotlights which dazzled the great dome of the Capitol were turned off. The Mall was dark.

When Fulbright had been here before, Washington was a small town whose business was politics. It lived in the excitement a reform administration brings. The dust was being stirred up, new ideas mixed into the soil, and overall there was a kind of gaiety.

Today the place was swollen, desks in the hall and shabby temporary buildings hastily put up. The New Dealer, the social worker, the politician were eclipsed by another breed, generals and dollar-a-year men. The latter were specialists from industry called in to allocate the steel and get the tools of war made. The social life was subdued and conversation hurried.

The somber business of war stimulated Fulbright, but in an unusual way. He wanted to banish it, its waste and terror and savagery. This was a conviction that came out of the conversation and lonely thoughts in the old house in Fayetteville, his history books, conversations with McCallum at Oxford, and the year with Fodor in Europe.

If, he argued, there had been a world peace-keeping body when Hitler came to assemble his legions, Germany could have been held down, and dehorned, the pistol taken away. The League of Nations might have done the job. But the United States, and specifically Congress, junked it. Today, the American Congress must lead the way, redeem itself. Fulbright had no very clear idea in the beginning how this might be done. He was a freshman and one among several hundred members of the lower House.

Chance, again, helped him. He came to the attention of Speaker

Sam Rayburn, who kept a lookout for bright young freshmen and was attracted by the university president from the neighboring state. "Mr. Sam" asked Fulbright what committee he would like.

"I'd like Foreign Affairs, Mr. Speaker," Fulbright said. "I think in a few years foreign poilcy, that is, how we organize the peace, is going to be the most important business before Congress."

The Speaker looked at him closely. "You may be right," he said. "I'll see that you get on the committee."

It was not considered a major committee, and it was ruled in a comic opera style by the Honorable Sol Bloom, a pompous little fellow who wore built-up shoes and spectacles on a black cord. He had been an impresario before he entered politics. He was not one to enjoy full discussion in his committee and wielded his gavel vigorously.

Soon after Congress opened, on January 29, 1943, Congressman Fulbright saw the chance to talk about peace. His old friend, Brooks Hays, used to say, "When Bill was a halfback at Arkansas, he would see a hole and put his head down and run for a long gain. That's the way he operated in Congress."

The hole, in this case, was "lend-lease." This was a device to give huge quantities of war materiel to countries fighting the Axis. The Administrator was Edward R. Stettinius, Jr., who had been borrowed from big steel to impress the Congressmen, and he appeared before the Committee on this day.

A handsome, white-haired and urbane individual, Stettinius read from his prepared statement: "A principle has been hammered out in the time of crisis. The principle of the total cooperation among nations in the waging of war, a cooperation in the interest of peace, and for the benefit of all, the only principle on which a war of alliance can be successfully waged."

At the end of the Committeee table, Fulbright made notes in a careful hand on the pad before him—"a cooperation in the interest of peace." Did they really mean it? This might be the hook for peace.

When his chance came to ask a question, Fulbright said, "Would you care to express yourself as to whether the lend-lease program might not be a proper vehicle, not only for winning the war, but of dealing with the peace to come?"

Stettinius obviously had not thought about it at all. No one in 1943 was thinking much about peace. But, he said tactfully, indeed lend-lease might be such an instrument.

The young Congressman spelled out his idea: lend-lease controlled the guns and butter; its agreements might include a provision for postwar cooperation in peace-keeping. Promises could be extracted during times of battle when ammunition was as dear as life. At this hour, the Battle of Stalingrad was raging, Americans had just landed in North Africa, and the fight for Guadalcanal was coming to a close. When the guns were silent, Fulbright argued, the Allies might be less willing to cooperate in a peace-keeping system, and then in another twenty years there might be another war.

Stettinius was accompanied by a bright young bureaucrat, Oscar Cox. This was a standard practice, to keep the dollar-a-year men from violating the sacred canons of protocol. Cox saw immediately what Fulbright had in mind. He showed his concern by a negative shake of his head and a frown. This was very out of channels.

Even at that time, Fulbright was not easily dissuaded from pursuing an idea. He said doggedly, "But you in Lend-Lease hold the thing of value which might be persuasive of postwar agreements. Don't you agree? Wouldn't it be more effective if you had something to say about the commitments to foreign nations?"

Chairman Bloom thought the time had come to squelch the brash young freshman. He said, "Perhaps, Mr. Stettinius, you do not care to answer."

But he did. The idea intrigued him personally. He thought a way might be worked out to get a closer meshing between the State Department and Lend-Lease on postwar aims.

Fulbright went on: "As a practical matter, you are the man who controls lend-lease. Now these agreements are sometimes a result of bargaining, aren't they? And in the drawing up of agreements after the war, aren't you in an excellent position?"

Bloom moved to stop this nonsense. He observed lend-lease was for a limited time only. And Cox said primly the agency could not interfere with the State Department.

The little flurry was noted with quiet appreciation and amusement around the table. The young man from Arkansas was going to be hard for Sol to manage. After the meeting broke up, Fulbright had several members come to him and suggest his was an interesting thought.

Three important members, in particular, encouraged him and steered Fulbright through the battle to put Congress on record. They were Luther A. Johnson of Texas, the ranking Democrat; Republican.

James W. Wadsworth, an aristocratic New Yorker who had served two terms in the Senate, and Republican Charles A. Eaton, who had been pastor of John D. Rockefeller's Baptist Church in Cleveland and later editor of *Leslie's Weekly*.

Representative Fulbright tried to interest the State Department in his idea. Unfortunately, the Department then was quite rigid and unimaginative, so much so that Roosevelt made foreign policy from the White House. The Department had been a haven for wealthy young men with good manners and a hankering for pleasant society, but with no enthusiasm for Dad's business. Foreign service officers were more used to handling matters of social protocol than peace-keeping.

Fulbright's first try was with Dean Acheson, then Assistant Secretary of State. Acheson was the epitome of the State Department man, a magnificently imposing social presence, a Yale Deke, Episcopalian, an awesome moustache and eyes that could activate a headwaiter by their hauteur. Fulbright's experience with him has not been particularly fortunate, largely because of the other's lack of enthusiasm for new ideas.

At the hearing before the Committee, Congressman Fulbright told Acheson, "I hoped lend-lease could be made a vehicle for something more important than the return of worn-out tractors. Doesn't the master agreement refer to the Atlantic Charter?"

Acheson stared icily at him. He told the freshman member he was "building up a false relationship" for lend-lease, that it would be "unfortunate" and "premature" to use lend-lease to discuss postwar relationships at this time. The monumental brush-off.

Fulbright was not subdued. He said, "There is one thing of special interest to me. That is the settlement of world problems through collective security." He asked Acheson if he didn't think lend-lease could be used effectively in the interests of peace? Why not put the word "peace" in the title of the act, along with "defense"?

Acheson had enough of this young man. He said if he were changing the language, he would use the word "war."

Fulbright said, "I am sorry you restrict lend-lease to so narrow an aim, purely for the prosecution of the war."

Acheson said coldly he could not envisage settlements reached through lend-lease.

The young Congressman wanted to continue the debate, but Bloom shut him off.

The historian may wonder, if Fulbright's plan had been adopted, could Russia's expansion into eastern Europe have been curtailed and the Cold War avoided? Fulbright is not one to brood over past omissions, but thinks in not using lend-lease, we gave away our best leverage.

"When I came to Washington in 1943," he recalls, "almost no thought had been given to the peace. Obviously Russia was going to be a problem. She had shut herself away from the world. She had been invaded twice in a generation by German armies. She was going to demand extraordinary precautions against new attacks from the West. We could have used lend-lease to bargain for a plan that would not have raped eastern Europe."

He tried his idea next on another Assistant Secretary of State, Adolf Berle, Jr., who eighteen years later was one of the leading protagonists of the Bay of Pigs invasion which Fulbright opposed.

Fulbright asked Berle if commitments on the control of force might not be written into the lend-lease agreements.

Berle replied, "I am not sure this would be proper. I will leave that to the chairman."

The chairman was only too glad to silence the heretic.

The only sympathetic attention came from the Secretary of War, Henry L. Stimson. He was a Republican, a scholar of world affairs, had been Secretary of War under President Taft and brought back by FDR for his bipartisan war cabinet.

Fulbright dug into his knowledge of history in his discussion with Stimson in the curious little committee room on the gallery floor of the Capitol. He pointed out that during the Napoleonic Wars the British gave loans without any thought of recovering the funds, but for the goodwill this would bring on the Continent.

He added with feeling, "The real benefit to the country will not be the return of material things, but the commitments we may get, and which may be founded on goodwill through the reorganization of the world. This seems to me inherent in the whole program, and is really the only benefit this nation can get out of the war."

Stimson said Fulbright's view had been stated "succinctly" and "accurately."

Fulbright's plan was lost in the machine. He then changed his tactics. He saw the Administration needed a push from Congress. Or perhaps some assurance from Capitol Hill that the legislative branch was concerned about the peace, and did want—this time—a world peace-keeping body. A simple resolution by Congress might be the ticket.

At a party Fulbright ran into Oscar Cox, the Stettinius aide, and tried the idea out on him. He was enthusiastic. He explained the Administration was leery of getting too deep into peace-keeping because of fear of Congress. Franklin Roosevelt had been in Woodrow Wilson's Administration, and was very sensitive to the Senate's action on November 19, 1919, in rejecting the Treaty of the League of Nations.

Fulbright received good advice from his friends on the Committee. They proposed that he bypass the chairman, and take his idea directly to the Secretary of State. He was almost certain to approve the resolution, and with this in hand Fulbright would have no trouble with Bloom.

Fulbright wrote Cordell Hull and was invited by the Under Secretary, Sumner Welles, to the Department.

By this time the freshman from Arkansas had delighted the White House and State Department by his maiden speech. It was a satirical reply to Congresswoman Clare Boothe Luce's "globaloney" attack on Administration foreign policy. She called it "the bigger and redder and more royal" international New Deal. The Atlantic Charter was "monumental generality and noble catchall" and "the four freedoms a virtuous platitude."

Ordinarily, through an old-fashioned gallantry in Congress, the words of a lady member are received with a blind amiability, and forgotten. Also, it is quite unwise to try to answer anyone with so biting a tongue as Mrs. Luce, or one connected with such a powerful publishing empire. One of the Arkansan's more cautious colleagues remarked, "Bill was just a plain damn fool, but it was great fun."

Reports of the day describe Fulbright's manner as he rose in the House as "courtly." He made a little bow to Mrs. Luce and said, "Although I am not unconscious of the sparkling beauty and suavity of manner of the honorable lady from Connecticut, yet I find I am not as susceptible to her logic and persuasion—at least on the floor of the House—as some of my colleagues appear to have been. . . . Her witty and scintillating remarks about Mr. [Henry] Wallace were quite equal to the sophisticated style of Walter Winchell and *Time* magazine. Not only is Mr. Wallace 'spasmodically sane' but he is full of 'globaloney,' a wonderful word which convulsed the gallery and will certainly live for many seasons in the folklore of Broadway."

She had, he thought, advocated "a narrow, imperialistic policy of grab" in asking that war be used to gain commercial advantages for the United States, specifically for American airlines. "Instead, our representatives should begin negotiations at once with our Allies to formulate a specific and concrete system for collective security of the nations of the world. . . . The time is getting short for the development and consideration of a program for peace. It must be done now while the minds and hearts of the people of this world are concerned with universal and fundamental issues . . . while danger and sacrifice give us humility and understanding."

So when Fulbright went to Under Secretary Welles he was received cordially. The Congressman said, "The only way people will take medicine is when they are sick or in a state of shock. The world is sickened and shocked by war. Now is the time for the Allies to agree on a plan for peace."

Welles asked what he had in mind.

Fulbright told him of his proposed resolution. Welles said the idea was admirable, and he would write the Congressman to that effect.

The timing was perfect. A year earlier Fulbright might have received an indifferent audience. A year later would have been too late. As Hull's memoirs revealed, at this exact time the wartime Allies were afraid the United States would back out after the war, as in 1919. There was a great deal of skirmishing, chiefly between England and Russia, over the future map of Europe. A Congressional resolution putting the United States into the postwar world would have a stabilizing effect; it would make wartime cooperation easier, too.

The next move by the Congressman was, in sports parlance, an end run. This was to keep Bloom from interfering with the resolution. Johnson, Wadsworth and Eaton quietly lined up committee members. Fulbright offered his resolution: "Resolved that the House of Representatives hereby expresses itself as favoring the creation of appropriate international machinery with power adequate to prevent further aggression and to maintain lasting peace and as favoring participation by the United States therein."

Bloom said the committee would have to consult with the State Department before it could consider the resolution.

Fulbright replied, "Mr. Chairman, I have a letter from Secretary Welles giving the Department's views."

Representative Wadsworth moved to report the resolution. It passed the Committee unanimously.

From here on the resolution moved through the labyrinth of Washington backstage dealings with a miraculous ease. This was due, in large part, to Fulbright's counselors. Representative Johnson talked to Sam Rayburn. He was for it, but recommended that Fulbright have a talk with Harry Hopkins and get the machinery of White House persuasion ready to move. Wadsworth and Eaton worked skillfully among the Republicans.

The meeting between Fulbright and Hopkins was dramatic, but not in the usual sense. They got along very well together. They understood each other. The drama was in the two personalities. Fulbright was the young professor, a rank amateur in politics, idealistic, hopeful, and yet aware of the terrible lessons of history. Hopkins, the "deputy President," was the old social worker turned politician, tired, more than a little cynical. He had schemed and connived and pushed through much of Roosevelt's program and now was helping him prosecute the war.

Hopkins suggested that Fulbright write the President a letter, so he would have something in writing. On June 26, 1943, the Congressman wrote the Chief Executive that he thought the Democrats had been remiss; they had not worked out a policy for postwar cooperation in peace-keeping. This could be done, Fulbright said, by Congressional action.

"I have always thought," he concluded, "that your own success has been largely due to your courage in boldly taking the lead in the development of progressive solutions for our troubles. I cannot believe that a timid and cautious policy at this time in regard to our foreign policy will contribute to the welfare of the world or of the Democratic Party."

Congressman Wadsworth was feeling out Republican sentiment. He made an offer to Speaker Rayburn. If the resolution could be put aside until September, he and Eaton and John Vorys of Ohio, another committee member, would work for its adoption at the Mackinac Island meeting of Republicans. At present, Wadsworth said, about fifty Republicans would vote against it. If it were explained to them properly, the antis could be held to ten or twelve.

This strategy was agreed to.

President Roosevelt wrote to Fulbright: "As you know I am fully in accord with the principles contained in your Resolution and with those contained in other resolutions of the same character that have been offered in the Senate. I believe that the adoption by the Congress of a resolution containing these principles would be in the highest degree desirable.

"I have been informed that the Speaker some days ago discussed the question of taking up this resolution with the Majority and Minority leaders and with Congressman Wadsworth and yourself, and it was agreed at that time that your Resolution would be taken up when the House reconvenes in September. I am, of course, in favor of having your Resolution acted upon as soon as there is reasonable assurance that no prejudicial amendments would be adopted and that the largest possible measure of support can be obtained for its passage."

Fulbright in his personal campaigning among members and on the lecture platform very carefully pointed out this was more than a scrap of paper. He told the American Bar Association in August, "It [the resolution] tells the world that the United States recognizes that any organization for peace must be based upon power adequate to enforce peace, and that the United States will share both in supplying that power and in the responsibility for the exercise of that power."

The "power" would not only be "the use of some kind of force, but may also include the power, if necessary, to control the productive capacity of instruments of aggressive warfare. The traditional police force which disturbs so many people may not be nearly so important as control of strategic materials and productive capacity."

This was repeated in his speech to the House, so that what Congress passed actually was an approval of the idea of a world body with teeth and guts to it. The Administration of Roosevelt, later of Truman, was hesitant and never went that far. Later, the Senate, in effect, went back on its approval by taking the heart out of the World Court, removing its compulsory jurisdiction.

The Senator still believes the nations must come to accept a delegation of limited power to an agency designed to prevent war. If it is either "sovereignty" or war, we should give up the former. He has said sardonically, "The professional patriots beat their breasts and wave the flag and shout 'sovereignty,' hoping to frighten us, like sheep, back into the corral of isolationism. In the minds of many the word 'sovereignty' has some mystical connotation in some way associated with divinity."

The debate began in late September. Hopkins, Rayburn, Eaton, Wadsworth and Vorys had done their work so well that passage without crippling amendments was certain.

Fulbright spoke briefly. The resolution was "simply the first small step in the building of a policy which I hope may have better results than that which we have followed in the past. We have now, throughout the world, ample evidence of the inevitable consequences of that policy. . . . This resolution is not a grant of power to the Executive; it is simply an expression by our people, through their representatives, that we intend to participate sincerely in an effort to bring order into the world. If this resolution is adopted, the Executive can negotiate as to the details with assurance that the people are willing to support any reasonable system of collective security. . . .

"We members of the House have an obligation to do everything in our power to see that the children of today's heroes do not have to do it all over again in twenty years."

This was for Fulbright an emotional speech. He would not say the same words today. He has learned too much about the blind streak of violence in men and nations to dare hope the world will be spared these recurring wars. His hope now is that the ferocity of the wars can be limited.

On the floor and afterward in the cloakroom, members crowded around to congratulate Fulbright. A senior Representative from Georgia came to his office to say it was the best speech he had heard in the House.

The isolationists, a small and gaudy band, cried out against the resolution. Their leader was Representative Hamilton Fish of New York. He called it "a very pious legislative resolution, more or less a beautiful mirage with very little substance . . . How can we solve postwar peace until we know the aims of Stalin and Churchill?"

Representative Clare Hoffman of Michigan, a spry little man whose tailored suits had no pockets, shouted (he never spoke in a normal voice in an argument), "The resolution means we are repealing the Declaration of Independence, that we are adopting a foreign policy which commits us to an allegiance with Great Britain and Russia. It is an insult." He accused Fulbright of being a British agent because he had been a Rhodes scholar.

Everett Dirksen of Illinois raised a series of carping parliamentary questions. Again, the ironic note of fate. Twenty-two years later, Dirksen, the Senate Minority Leader, supporting President Johnson, complained of the Senate Foreign Relations Committee hearings over Vietnam.

In the House in September, 1943, another opponent quoted radio commentator Fulton Lewis, Jr., as saying the resolution would "transform the world into a glorified WPA." Fulbright has kept him, too, as a persistent personal critic.

The high emotional point of the debate came when Congressman Eaton spoke. He was a handsome older man with flowing white hair and an impressive manner and voice. Standing in the well of the House, he said, "I have a personal interest for wanting to see this passed. I had seven of the finest boys in the world in my family, fine boys just as you have in yours.

"One of them died of his wounds over Holland on the thirtieth of July, another was killed near Nuremberg on the tenth of August. Five are left. I hate war. And, before God, I am going to vote for anything that I think will avert the necessity for sacrificing the young manhood of the nation.

"Let us stand up and face our responsibility and make this one gesture to show that we are in favor of abolishing forever wholesale murders in the cause of civilization."

On September 21, the bells rang throughout the House side of the Capitol and members came pouring in through the swinging doors as the clerk called their names in a loud, flat voice. When the vote was counted, the Fulbright resolution passed 360 to 29.

These were brave days. These were triumphant days. These were days of much hope.

VI

THE FULBRIGHT RESOLUTION and a companion measure in the Senate—it passed 85 to 5—cleared the international air. At least for the time being.

Cordell Hull wrote in his diary that his discouragement over the way the Russians turned away from postwar settlements was counterbalanced by the Fulbright resolution.

Soon after Congress acted, the foreign ministers of the Allied Powers met in Moscow, and there seemed less mistrust than before. Official reminiscences report both Britain and Russia seemed reassured that America would not run out after the guns were still.

Winston Churchill feared that the Soviet Union would try to take over the European continent by force of arms and subversion, and replace British influence there and in the Mediterranean. The Soviet leaders—Stalin and Molotov were two of the world's most suspicious individuals—thought the British were determined to destroy Communism. (When Molotov visited Washington and was an official guest at the Blair House, his aides regularly looked under the bed.) Roosevelt had been acting as a mediator, and both London and Moscow had more trust in him than in each other. So the news that the United States was going to take a major role in the postwar world had at least one effect: it brought the Allies together first at the Moscow conference, then Cairo and Teheran and San Francisco on the need for a peace-keeping organization.

President Roosevelt was so pleased by the Fulbright resolution he invited its author to one of the rare social evenings at the White House, and congratulated him, and asked him about himself and his plans. Secretary Hull sent him to London to represent the United

States at a forty-four-nation conference on postwar education, and he was elected chairman.

This is heady wine. So many triumphs in such a shallow reach of time tends to turn men into pompous bores, and they think about running for President. Not so Fulbright. He has always thought of himself as a messenger of time and chance.

Besides, there was so much to do. The people must be turned away from the old isolationism. He went back to Arkansas, and he spoke before Rotary Clubs and in church basements and school gymnasiums. What he said in Fort Smith was echoed at Eudora, all with his appealing earnestness: "The decision for peace is up to the people. If they falter and postpone the decision, there will be more war. We are paying in blood for our failure after World War I. The failure of the American people to think squarely on international relations stands in the way of world peace. We must develop a feeling of confidence that there will never be another war.

"I think events have conspired to force this nation to make its choice—either we must decide to become a regimented state, prepared to wage war at all times after the fashion of Germany, or we must take steps through collective security with the other nations of the world to see to it that world wars do not occur."

This was a voice of prophecy. Twenty-three years later, the United States had a defense budget of $61.4 billion, a spreading war in Southeast Asia, with several hundred thousand Americans troops involved, Marines in the Dominican Republic, peace-keeping forces in Germany, the Pentagon as the great source of power in Washington, dissent in the Senate attacked as traitorous, the Government's chief policeman, J. Edgar Hoover, able to kill a consular treaty with Communist nations.

Fulbright does not regard his talks to the people of Arkansas in the summer and early fall of 1943 as showing much prescience. "The choice was clear," he comments. "When there is no law and order, you have vigilantes taking over, general bloodshed, or the strongest powers carving up the world. We have become the vigilantes writing the rules and enforcing them in many parts of the world. It's a pretty big and expensive job for one nation."

The Congressman told the Lions Club in Fayetteville: "The postwar peace problem even now is to select the real aim of the war. Why are we fighting? Merely to put out a fire, or make sure the fire never consumes us again?" He spoke to a war bond rally in Little Rock:

"There is reason to hope this time we shall not withdraw into an illusory shell of isolation and permit violent forces to shape the world."

He believed this. His thinking was that the wartime Allies had suffered so much they would accept a joint responsibility for peace. Russia, at this point, was keeping its promises. The Red Army had started a massive offensive from the east, thus pinning down Nazi legions, while the British and Americans prepared the second front across the British Channel. He went on to Little Rock and told the United Commercial Travelers, "There is no hope for happiness and prosperity if we can't stop wars. Foreign policy is not remote. It is the most important business we have. War uses up resources, as we have seen from the depletion of bauxite reserves in Arkansas. War destroys men and creative talents. It causes inflation which may lead to later depressions." He suggested that the wild inflation following World War I in Europe and America brought on the great Depression of the 1930's.

This was spoken at a time when other orators were proclaiming the heroism of war and the splendor of its fighting men. Glorified violence was the daily diet of the American people. Hate of the enemy was deliberately created.

But here was the Civilized Man outraged by the very violence in the news. Here was the conservative who saw war as a radical and revolutionary force sweeping away order and culture. Here was the historian who recalled how war ended and leveled the most promising age of human thought, the golden age of Greece.

Few realize how deeply moved Fulbright has been by the tragedy of Greece. If he is a throwback to any period in history, it is to the years surrounding 431 B.C. in Athens. In his outlook upon life, his style of writing, he is of that period.

His philosophy might be a paraphrase of Aristotle's: "Since then reason is divine in comparison with man's whole nature, the life according to reason must be divine in comparison with [usual] human life. Nor ought we to pay regard to those who exhort us that as men we ought to think human things and keep our eyes upon mortality: nay, as far as may be, we should endeavor to rise to that which is immortal, and live in conformity with that which is best in us." His belief in the importance of the mind over passion echoes Anaxagoras, "All things were in chaos when Mind arose and made order." He answers his critics as Euripides: "A slave is he who cannot speak his thoughts." His comments on both the Dominican Republic and Vietnam adventures rival the irony of Aristophanes who depicted Greece as a blustering bully and its generals as fools.

He writes with the simplicity of the Greeks, rather than in the romantic style of most English and American literature.

Fulbright as a student read and never forgot the lesson of Thucydides' *History of the Peloponnesian War*. In conversation the Senator often refers with scorn to Alcibiades, the military hero and demagogue who led his nation into the fateful attack upon Syracuse. This attack brought on the terrible wars that destroyed the glory of Greece and deprived mankind for centuries of the clarity and reason of Greek culture.

Thucydides believed the war was brought on by the corrupting disease of power. Power, he wrote, created a desire for more power, and this inevitably brought on despotism and war. This is a theme that Senator Fulbright developed powerfully in his three controversial Johns Hopkins lectures in 1966. Like Thucydides, he believed that a nation, no matter how good its intentions, how democratic its system, must discipline itself against this abuse. He saw America falling into the same error as Greece. He agreed with Edith Hamilton who wrote that in the fall of Greece, through the corrupting influence of power, then war, "the cause of humanity was defeated."

This explains in part, for he is too complex ever to be explained by one thread, his lonely campaign against war in the cities and villages of Arkansas at the height of World War II.

On February 14, 1944, Fulbright announced he was a candidate for the Senate. His announcement was modest and pointed to the theme that dominated his life. He said, "Soon after I was established in Washington it became evident to me that there was no unity of purpose and no basic policy for the future upon which we and our friends could rely. It seemed to me that some understanding as to the future relations among the Allies was the outstanding need of this nation and of the world—for the efficient prosecution of the war, and as an essential basis for a peaceful world thereafter." If elected, he would pursue this in the Senate.

Some of his campaign managers argued this was too highbrow. This was a state where the usual brand of oratory was Populism whose targets were "Eastern bankers" or white supremacy, and whose style was a mixture of Fourth of July patriotism and Old Testament evangelism.

Fulbright said no, he would win or lose on this issue. He felt if he could win the election on building peace it would encourage faint hearts in Washington.

His chief rivals were Senator Hattie Caraway, the widow of Senator Thaddeus H. Caraway, running for reelection, and Governor Homer Adkins, the man who fired Fulbright as university president. No one in the state had the luster of Fulbright. President Roosevelt and Cordell Hull had praised him. He was written about in magazines and in the Memphis and St. Louis newspapers. He was young and attractive. (As a matter of political dynamics, Fulbright has always had a great attraction for women voters.)

He made his obeisance to the local gods, saying, "I am not for Negro participation in our primary elections."

The campaign, that is the Democratic primary, took place in the hot Arkansas summer. Men sweating in their shirt-sleeves crisscrossed the state. They told stories in a broad accent, lambasting their opponents gleefully, and entertaining the "folks" with music or variety. One wealthy candidate for Senator hired the "Grand Ole Opry" troupe of radio fame. The story is told of Betty Fulbright, the Philadelphia socialite, going through crowds, shaking hands and saying, "You go listen to 'Grand Ole Opry,' but be sure to vote for Bill Fulbright." This highly amused the Arkansans, enjoying the rich man's circus but voting for the young fellow.

The other candidates ganged up on Fulbright, and accused him of every crime in the books. He was denounced as being the pet of the C.I.O., a "nigger lover," friend of Communists, giving away U.S. gold to the world, and a British swell. One candidate always referred to him as "Lord Flushbottom." Thousands of scurrilous pamphlets printed out of state accused him of being a draft dodger. He was in his late thirties, had two children and was either a university president, manager of the Fulbright enterprises, or Congressman during the draft, and was never called.

This was his first real exposure to the bare fists of the Primitive. No one knew for sure how he would react. The sudden, thudding fierceness of the Primitive's attack often crumbles good and gentle men, as, for example, Senator Elbert Thomas, scholar and Mormon missionary, in his last campaign, and Senator Frank P. Graham, former president of the University of North Carolina. They are unable to cope with brutality and appear ineffective to the voters.

Fulbright, however, showed a quality that is one essential ingredient of his political successes. An Arkansas politician explained: "You'd never think it to see him—a nice fellow who never raises his voice—but the Senator is a real gutsy fighter. When they hit him low, he doesn't panic. He keeps on going and wins the knockout on points."

The *St. Louis Post-Dispatch,* in a story on the campaign, said of Fulbright that he "never raised his voice and never lost his balance."

He was also attacked in an ancient political ploy, the last-minute smear. Governor Adkins accused him of voting for a Negro and a Communist in Congress. This was an omen of the later McCarthy era. Fulbright had voted against a rider tacked on an appropriation bill in the House. The rider barred five men from Government employment, allegedly because they were Communists. One was a Negro, William Pickens. Fulbright said this was trial without a jury. The accused was given no chance to present his own case; it was a perversion of the Bill of Rights.

This shows another side of the gentleman from Arkansas: the conservative legal purist, the true, never-say-die believer in Constitutional government. As the McCarthy era was to show later, it was Senators such as these, and not the professional liberals, who stood up against the Brutes.

The Primitives, for their part, seem to be filled with a helpless choler against the Civilized Men, like Fulbright. They are, crudely put, their betters. The Primitives are the mob ransacking the palace after the revolution, not for anything of value but for the sheer physical pleasure of destroying treasures they could never possess. In every proletarian revolution, those in France, Nazi Germany, Soviet Russia, the intellectual is made captive or destroyed with a ferocity hard to understand. The American revolution was, by contrast, an intellectual one. It was not engineered by farmers and blacksmiths and clerks, but by the mental aristocracy of the colonies.

This last-minute attack did not bother the Senatorial candidate. He thought the electorate wanted to hear the issues. He told the Rotary Club, "The real issue is the ability to do something positive and constructive toward making a lasting peace."

At Pine Bluff he asked, "If we must be eternally using our best brains and energies and sacrificing our finest young men for war, how are we to make real progress in building our state?"

At Hot Springs, the famous spa in western Arkansas, he exhorted a crowd standing in the listless July heat under the waxy leafed magnolias and big oaks: "Total war can be prevented if we discard our prejudices and recognize our power and influence as a Christian nation to help organize the forces of peace-loving people to control the forces of aggression."

His campaign style was simple. A car with a loudspeaker went ahead of him, proclaiming that Congressman Fulbright would speak on the courthouse lawn or in the park. He arrived without any beating of drums or whanging guitar. He stood on the bandstand, a chair, or from the back end of a truck, speaking quietly and earnestly, "We have a choice. Either we must become overwhelming in power, at tremendous expense, or we must join in the formation of collective power to resist aggression in the future."

Some political correspondents will argue that neither then nor since have the Arkansas voters really understood what Fulbright was telling them.

In a sense, this is unimportant. If they grasp the bare bones, that is enough. If there is a rapport, if they think the candidate is on *their* side, if they think he is up to fighting *their* battles against all the misty forces that oppress modern man, he is their man. There was an unmistakable earnestness and sincerity about Fulbright that his opponents, hoarsely shouting their wares, did not have.

His final appeal was a full-page ad headlined, "That This Horror Shall Not Happen Every 20 Years," and a statement of his views on a world organization.

To the surprise of the forecasters, Fulbright ran well ahead in the first primary. Arkansas has two primaries. The first pits all candidates against one another; the second, the top two. He defeated Governor Adkins in the runoff primary, another irony in his career. In a smiling election-night statement, he said, "I'd like to stay in the Senate a hundred years, because it's going to take that long to bring the world around to nonskid peace."

Out of the hot, breathless summer came a man rewarded but not changed. As soon as the Senate met and he was sworn in and received his assignments—he was not given a place on Foreign Relations—he set to work. He and Senator Alexander Smith, a New Jersey Republican, and onetime lecturer at Princeton, organized the sixteen freshmen members. He drafted a letter which the sixteen sent to President Roosevelt. They believed the United States should take an active role in a world peace organization.

By then he had begun to understand a fact of life. It was not the old isolationists of 1919, Borah and Lodge, he had to contend with. It was, instead, a new and ruthless form of nationalism, Manifest Destiny, backed for the first time by something more than rhetoric because of the great war machine America was developing. Men's eyes were misting at the thought of exporting the whole American legend—the supermarket, chewing gum, Sunday school, the Fourth of July picnic, free elections—to all the less fortunate. The curse of power was showing itself.

In a radio talk, Senator Fulbright said, "Consultation and agreement is the only alternative to superfortresses and robot bombs. The chief thing about Dumbarton Oaks is the machinery by which these consultations can take place in an orderly manner. The making of a peace doesn't constitute merely a beautifully drafted constitution or a magic formula. It is a continuing process that must go on from day to day, year to year, as long as our civilization shall last. Our participation is not just signing a charter with a large red seal. It's a positive participation in all the little details and decisions which together shape the growing, living structure, making decisions by reason rather than the sword."

He had a prophetic sense of uneasiness. Nothing very sharp and clear. He expressed his doubts in an interview early in 1945. A writer called him off the Senate floor, and he came through the swinging doors from the cloakroom to the frilly little lobby where interviews take place.

The journalist made a complimentary remark.

Fulbright smiled and said, "I'm just a boy from the Ozarks where the hillbillies come from."

As the exchange of conversation moved away from opening banter, he said with a frown gathered together between his eyes, "Our foreign policy, I am afraid, is improvised from crisis to crisis." It didn't seem to have any overall purpose or continuity.

What ominous omens did he see?

"Hate," he said. He repeated the word, "Hate."

The other expressed a little surprise.

"If the powerful influences in the press have so poisoned the minds of our people that they do not desire to cooperate positively and concretely with our Allies . . ." He shrugged his shoulders in a gesture of futility. "Then an entirely different course than now proposed should be pursued. We have been unable in the past to disentangle our prejudices from our thinking on the big issues."

He was discouraged by the flavor of talk in the Senate, particularly among those with most power on the Foreign Relations Committee, Vandenberg and Connally, George and Austin. They did not want to give up any sovereignty to an international body. They demanded a veto power, so that the national decision was supreme. Damned if they wanted the Russian Reds or the British or the French telling us what to do.

The interviewer asked Senator Fulbright what the answer was.

In a mixture of gloom and irritability, he replied, "The Senate should be more creative. Instead of just negatively saying what we won't do, it should offer alternate courses."

He heard the distant thunder. He saw the little puffs of hot, fetid wind springing up and rustling the treetops. He sensed, but without any real knowledge, that the storm would be rough.

VII

As a boy, Senator Fulbright rode and hiked through the mountains south of Fayetteville. They are scarcely more than high hills, about two to three thousand feet high. The roads were full of sudden turns. A wagon would move easily along the dirt and gravel overhung with trees and, with no warning, find itself on the edge of a cliff and forced to turn sharply, the driver pulling hard on the reins and shouting to the horses or mules.

The Senator's life has been full of these sudden turns, and one took place on April 12, 1945. Franklin D. Roosevelt died unexpectedly at Warm Springs, Georgia. This and the events that followed changed the young Senator's world and hopes. He was forced to deep and skeptical thinking.

He had been emotionally and intellectually in tune with Roosevelt's last written statement: "Today we are faced with the preeminent fact that, if civilization is to survive, we must cultivate the science of human relationships—the ability of all peoples, of all kinds, to live together and work together in the same world, at peace."

The Senator from Arkansas assumed, with probably more optimism than Roosevelt had at the time, that the great powers, bled by the horrors of the war, would accept the challenge. He had, actually, been impatient with the President for not laying before the world a blueprint.

Fulbright had a few clues to what was on Roosevelt's mind from his conversations with him and Hopkins and younger men on the fringes. FDR saw that Russia would be a thorn in the postwar garden unless its deep suspicions of the West could be calmed. He had committed himself to that uneasy task.

The suspicions were part traditional; they grew out of the long isolation of Russia under the Czars. They were nurtured by British and American intervention against the 1917 revolution, and the obvious Western dislike and fear of Communism. This was complicated by the clash between Stalin, the epitome of Russian distrust, and Churchill, the bold stalwart of empire. Churchill had been one of the instigators of the 1917 intervention; a generation later he wanted to prevent that revolution from spilling over into Western Europe in the stream of war.

The undertows of doubts showed in the conferences over military strategy, and continued. Stalin demanded a second front at the earliest moment to relieve the pressure of 121 Nazi divisions and 3,000 planes smashing at Russia. Churchill wanted to clear the Mediterranean first. Roosevelt had talked of a second front in 1942 or 1943. The 1943 proposal even reached the stage of extensive planning and a name, Operation Roundup. Churchill, instead, plugged for the North African landings and then to Sicily. The Soviets interpreted the delay in the second front to mean the West would prefer to see Russia exhausted by its fight with the Germans, and became more bitter. The second front came, at last, on June 6, 1944, and the Russians in keeping with their 1943 promise launched an offensive from the east a few days later.

Roosevelt thought some of the Russian bitterness might be drawn out by his ambitious plans for postwar rehabilitation. The nations of the world would pool their resources: services, ports, transportation, knowledge and communication. Science would transform wastelands into fertile areas. Birth control would defuse population explosions. Excess populations could be moved en masse to new areas. The wealthier nations would contribute the most, but, as a reward, they would be spared the hell of war and revolution under some sort of world organization dominated by the big powers.

For a while after Roosevelt's death, a momentum kept the war and peace moving. The first United Nations conference that spring in San Francisco gave a slight glimpse of the problems ahead, in the controversy over the big power veto. The end of the war in Europe was in May. At the Potsdam Conference July 17–August 2, 1945, the Big Three rearranged the borders of Europe, Russia obtaining parts of Poland and Czechoslovakia and a presence in Germany (the drawing of Poland and the Baltic states into the Soviet system was already a *fait accompli*). Stalin agreed, in return, to allow "free and unfettered elections" in Finland, Bulgaria, Rumania and Hungary. The first atom bombs were dropped on Hiroshima and Nagasaki on August 6 and 9, changing the future of mankind irrevocably and, of more moment at the time, ending the war in Asia.

During the rest of the year, the Roosevelt policy began to come apart, perhaps because it expected too much of men and nations. Harry Truman was hardly the man to preside over the peace. He had no experience in foreign affairs. He was a small-town politician active in veterans' affairs, picked up by the Pendergast machine of Missouri, who had headed a popular Senate investigation of war contracts, and was pushed on the 1944 ticket by the Democratic national chairman, a Missourian. After Roosevelt's death he told Jim Farley unhappily, "I didn't want to be President. I wouldn't have accepted the nomination if I thought Mr. Roosevelt was going to die. I want to go back to the Senate. That's where I belong."

A few weeks after Truman moved into the White House, Senator Fulbright went to see him. He was disturbed by fresh signs of cracks among the Allies. What he wanted was reassurance, some word that the Administration was still thinking along the lines of the Fulbright resolution, that the new President was determined not to let the old animosities color and destroy the peace.

Truman greeted him in a most friendly manner. He was glad to see a Senator. He hankered for news of the cloakrooms and committees. For fifteen or so minutes, Senator Fulbright talked to him. Truman listened with an air of bright and untroubled innocence, and told him to come back again. It was good visiting with him.

Later, back on Capitol Hill, Fulbright said in dismay, "I didn't make a bit of impression on him. He didn't know what I was talking about."

The Senator was stunned. The President of the United States was walking blindfold off a cliff. Roosevelt had told him next to nothing, and Truman had made no effort to find out for himself what was going on. He looked at the papers certainly, but the items he read were not about international affairs, but mostly local politics and how the war was going and Congressional hearings.

This was unforgivable, but not unusual. Abraham Lincoln was as remiss with Andrew Johnson, and so the peace did not carry out the promise of the Gettysburg Address. And Vice Presidents had become accustomed to regarding their office as a useless appendage of the Constitution; they lacked any real duties or responsibilities or close association with the President or affairs of state.

At first vaguely, like shadows behind a window with the shade pulled, Fulbright could see the shattered pieces of foreign policy begin to form new patterns.

The President was still the main figure, of course. The greatest event in Truman's life before he came to the Senate was as the captain of Battery D in World War I. His heroes were the military, and at a White House ceremony awarding the Congressional Medal of Honor he said earnestly, "I would rather have this medal than be President." In his social contacts with Congressmen, he lobbied actively for military legislation, such as the continuation of the draft.

Truman also was an ardent advocate of Manifest Destiny, that peculiar combination of the missionary spirit, strong nationalism and belief in military power. When a delegation of five Senators, led by Charles Tobey of New Hampshire, came to see him and urged international control of the atom bomb, they were rebuffed from the outset. Tobey remarked later, "I could tell after five minutes, Harry was against us. So I didn't even take the resolution from my pocket."

The President's advisers on foreign policy were Admiral William Leahy, his new Secretary of State James F. Byrnes, and Senator Arthur Vandenberg. Leahy was one of the old Roosevelt team. He believed in military power as the great pacifier. It was the one language all nations understood. If the Russians acted up in the Middle East, send the fleet into the Mediterranean on "maneuvers." Leahy was a dominant influence, because he was in the White House and saw Truman several times a day.

Byrnes was a former Senator and Supreme Court Justice. In the Senate he had acted as a behind-the-scenes manipulator for Roosevelt. For this he was rewarded by apointment to the Court, but FDR made him his "Assistant President" when war came. He was the chief lobbyist and Congressional handyman for the President. Since Byrnes had been a court reporter in his youth and still knew shorthand, Roosevelt took him to the Crimean conference and dictated secret memoranda to him. Byrnes came to the office of Secretary committed to the Roosevelt policy, that is, trying to mollify the Russians and mediate between them and the British. He did not have the prestige and authority, and was undercut at home by Admiral Leahy and Senator Vandenberg and later Churchill himself. Byrnes was not helped, either, by the rapacious behavior of the Russians.

Vandenberg seemed less than heroic to Fulbright. The Michigan Republican, the ranking minority member on the Foreign Relations

Committee, was a handsome man, somewhat on the order of President Harding. He had white hair, a sonorous voice and a grand manner. He had been an isolationist prior to World War II, but was converted by Roosevelt's personal diplomacy and the influence of John Foster Dulles, then New York Governor Dewey's foreign policy consultant. Vandenberg had the gift of the pleasing generality, and Truman was mightily impressed by him. He gave Vandenberg what amounted to veto power over Administration foreign policy.

This the Senator exercised in two ways: he opposed giving up sovereignty to an international body, and advocated a tougher line with Russia. In this he followed general public opinion.

There was a paradoxical nature to American public opinion. It favored a world organization to keep peace, but thought it should be dominated by American ideals and policies, since we were the good guys. Senator Fulbright has given the most candid profile of the American psyche of any politician in modern times. This was a part of his analysis of all the elements of American foreign policy. He cannot endure the mists of ignorance through which most of us walk our entire life.

"We are not God's chosen people, any more than anyone else is, but simply a very rich, industrious and very lucky nation," he says. "We came to a rich, unused continent that had been spared the greed and ravages of wars and civilization. It was like stumbling on a gold mine. Because we are rich and powerful, we have a responsibility to behave intelligently and generously. But we have nothing like a mission to regenerate mankind.

"Nor are we revolutionary as we pretend. It isn't surprising that Americans are not drawn toward the uncouth revolutionaries of the non-Communist left in Latin America. We are not, as we like to claim in Fourth of July speeches, the most truly revolutionary nation on earth. We are, on the contrary, much closer to being the most unrevolutionary. We are sober and satisfied and comfortable and rich. Our institutions are stable and old and even venerable. Our revolution of 1776 was not much of an upheaval compared to the French and Russian revolutions and the current and impending revolutions in Latin America and Asia and Africa.

"Our heritage of stability and conservatism is a blessing, but it also limits our understanding of the character of social revolution, and sometimes the injustices which spawn them."

Our judgments on the world, then, in this view, are often provincial and isolated. "We are predisposed," Fulbright says, "to regard any conflict as a clash between good and evil rather than simply as a clash between conflicting interests. We are inclined to confuse democracy and freedom, which we regard as moral principles, with the way in which they are practiced in America. There is much cant in American moralism and not a little inconsistency. It resembles in some ways the religious faith of many respectable people who, in Samuel Butler's words, 'would be equally horrified to hear the Christian religion doubted or to see it practiced.' " Part of this ethic, too, he points out, is an unreasoning faith in the military.

What took place after Roosevelt's death, then, was the evaporation of the Roosevelt policies—vague though they were—and a moving in of the untutored-man-on-the-street view, through Truman and Vandenberg.

As Fulbright watched with dismay, the quarrelings of the Allies grew louder in the summer of 1945. Secretary Byrnes ran into trouble with Soviet Foreign Minister Molotov. He tried to reason with Molotov about his demands for military bases in Eastern Europe. Molotov replied stiffly that the United States was insisting on exclusive control of strategic bases in the Pacific.

Senator Fulbright entered the dispute, not as a major voice, but as a critic on the aisle with an idea on how to improve the play by cutting the second scene of the third act. He proposed we drop our demand for exclusive control of Pacific bases, and put them under a world trusteeship.

No one in authority paid any attention to his idea. It violated the American ethic. We had bought and paid for the bases with our sweat and blood, and damned if we would share them with others.

In the autumn of 1945, President Truman announced we were still manufacturing atomic weapons. He said, "We are the only people who can make atom bombs, and we'll keep it that way."

This wiped out any possibility of international control, which Fulbright thought was one key to the door of peace. It also led to the nuclear arms race which came to a pause in 1963.

The sudden turn was almost unbelievable. Two years before, Congress had passed the Fulbright resolution with enthusiasm. Now the whole spirit of international cooperation seemed to have withered away. Melancholy and doubt invaded his thinking.

On the surface, he was the promising young Senator on the up ramp. Bascom Timmons, the eminent journalist, called him "Presidential timber." Others recommended him as Harry Truman's running mate in 1948. Truman in presenting the United Nations Charter to Congress in the fall of 1945 said it carried out the Fulbright resolution, and a columnist reported the Senator stirred "with embarrassed pleasure." It was at this time he was approached to become president of Columbia University. He spoke at the "Town Meeting" and wrote articles for *The New York Times* and the *New Republic*. He was saluted at the National Press Club as "Three-hat Bill" for his remark that a politician should have one hat to toss in the ring, one to wear, and a third to talk through. He was interviewed by a noted sportswriter and proposed that athletics be used "to break down existing suspicions and misunderstanding and foster peace."

Fulbright was a minor public idol, the good peace guy.

But in the private chamber of his mind, he kept asking himself with a growing sense of futility, "What can I do?"

In the Senate, foreign policy was dominated by Vandenberg, "Ole Tawm" Connally of Texas, chairman of the Foreign Relations Committee, and Walter George of Georgia. Connally, in particular, regarded Fulbright as a damn upstart and would not make a place for him on his committee. He had been considerably miffed that the Fulbright resolution had originated in the House, and only the prodding of the White House led him to put a companion resolution through the Senate.

Fulbright decided to take his doubts and fears to the public. He appeared on an N.B.C. broadcast November 23, 1945, and said, "I have a very serious purpose in speaking to you. It is simply to ask of you, with all the conviction of which I am capable, to give serious and solemn thought, as citizens of this republic, to the policies which your government is currently following in its relation with other nations . . . I am asking you to give your best attention to our foreign affairs, because I know you want a decent world for your children. I am asking it because I have come to the conclusion that our government has lost its bearings, and is drifting about in a fog of indecision . . ."

Here the gentleman from Arkansas emerged as the rebel and critic. He was driven by a sense of helpless outrage.

Fulbright told the radio audience: "The basic principle upon which all civilized society has been founded since the beginning of history is simple and clear to anyone who will bother to think of it for a mo-

ment. Civilization began with the family unit. It progresses from that
through the tribe, the city state, the principality of the national state.
The fundamental principle upon which all successful communities
was based was law. Without these rules of conduct there was chaos,
every man against every other man. We can see that it is perfectly
natural and logical that this familiar principle should be extended
throughout the world. The threat of the atomic bomb forces us to a
decision earlier than we had anticipated."

There were two ways rules of conduct could be established, by the
sword or by agreement. "To do so by force," he said, "means
persistent and successful warfare until one nation imposes its will on
all others. For us to follow this policy is unwise and unlikely . . . It
has little chance of success, as the Germans have shown us twice. It
was by agreement that we established law among the original thirteen
independent sovereign states in 1789, a radical experiment at that
time. If we had not done so, it is practically certain that today there
would be several proud and belligerent little countries on this continent eager to defend their sovereignty with their lives and with a
standard of living and happiness comparable to that of Europe and
the Balkans of today. Washington, Madison, Jefferson, Hamilton and
Franklin were wise. They demanded and obtained the rule of law."

In exasperation, the Senator said, "In view of our own experience
and of all human history, I cannot understand why our present
government does not exert all its influence toward the creation of
rules of conduct applicable to all peoples."

The place to begin was by limiting armaments and the atomic
bomb. This could be done within the United Nations by amending the
charter. He wanted to abolish the veto and delegate "certain rule-
making powers" to the United Nations. But, he said, "our government, unfortunately, does not seem to appreciate the function of law
in the maintenance of peace." Instead, it was paying lip service to the
United Nations but insisting on absolute national sovereignty.

There followed a critique of American policy every bit as biting as
anything he has said since.

"The President professes a faith in the United Nations, but his
actions and statements are not designed to give any life or vitality to
that organization. We as much as any nation insisted upon the veto
provision in the charter. We propose large armed forces by conscrip-
tion; we demand exclusive bases in the Pacific; we insist upon our

right to participate in the affairs of Eastern Europe, and we keep the atomic bomb to ourselves under the guise of a self-appointed sacred trusteeship.

"We object to Russia's demand for bases in the Mediterranean and Dardanelles, we refuse her request to participate on an equal basis in the affairs of Japan. We complain of her actions in the Balkans, and would oppose any mention of the Panama Canal.

"We play by ear without the slightest regard for the harmony of the composition. Such a method of dealing with serious questions can only lead to disaster. We have a choice between two policies, armed might and imperialism or rules of law enforceable by the United Nations.

"If we are to rely solely on our own might for our security, we must arm to the teeth and increase our strength by the domination of strategic bases in the Atlantic as well as the Pacific. If we intend to find security under law and justice, every effort must be made to induce all the United Nations to accept enforceable rules of conduct superior to national sovereignty."

He ended with an appeal for public action. "It is your wealth," he said, "your homes, your loved ones that are the hostages of war. It is your responsibility to think, to discuss and to use every means at your command to give your government wisdom and courage in its quest for the right decisions."

This heresy by a soft-spoken, quietly well-dressed man in a broadcast studio put an end to all the boomlets of Fulbright for President or Vice President. He defied the rules of political loyalty. He wanted us to give the bomb to the world. The break with The Establishment was clean and neat.

When Truman saw in the newspapers what Fulbright said, he was outraged. One of his poker-playing cronies, Senator Carl A. Hatch of New Mexico, told reporters, "I deplore the fact that Senator Fulbright saw fit to condemn the Administration foreign policy in a radio address where it could not be challenged. I strongly believe critical speeches on such all-important subjects should be made on the floor of the Senate, where the speaker's denunciation might be subjected to the same critical analysis, debate and perhaps the same condemnation in which the Senator indulges."

There was a bewildered amazement in the inbred Washington political society, the Congressmen and bureaucrats and Cabinet members and journalists. What the hell was he trying to prove?

Throwing away bright chances, calling for something that just couldn't be. All right, suppose he felt that way; couldn't he keep quiet? This is the logic that infests Washington, and it makes criticism a monumental task of not only intelligence but guts and nerve.

Fulbright replied wryly to Hatch, "I am highly flattered that he considers the statement I made on Friday night worthy of the attention and time of the Senate. It never occurred to me that the Senator might even notice my remarks. Having heretofore made several remarks on kindred subjects on the floor of the Senate, I did not recall that he ever noticed them. It never occurred to me that a requisite of either a member of the Democratic Party or the Senate was agreement with the Administration policies."

This time, the Senator from Arkansas was alone. There was no chorus in the Senate behind him. This did not deflect him. He had his last say in the argument with Senator Hatch: "The only principle that has ever controlled the violent tendencies of mankind has been law. The only way to establish law is to delegate the power to create law to an institution which also has power of enforcement."

Senator Fulbright had negotiated the sudden turn of the road. The moment of hesitation was over. His goal was the same, but he no longer had the brimming hope of two years earlier. And his tactics had changed.

VIII

THE CHANGE IN Senator Fulbright's mood, to that of the scornful rebel, was quite clear during the Senate debate on the United Nations Charter. He said, "The double-dealing, the hypocrisy, the utter futility of the efforts of the world's leaders to secure peace during the past twenty-five years demonstrates conclusively that the old pattern of diplomacy is bankrupt and hopeless."

Yet there remains in this man an ability to create even while he is criticizing. Fulbright, as a good many observers have noted, is much like the young intellectual revolutionaries who ran the American Republic in its early days. They were not only capable of criticizing the old order, but they also made a new one and operated it with rare honor.

What the Senator sees as his greatest success came during this period of disillusionment—the Fulbright scholarship exchanges.

The idea grew out of his own experience as a scholar abroad, a chance conversation and a little-known incident of history. A Senator remarked to him what a hell of a mess we were in over surplus American war equipment overseas. Trucks, tractors, monkey wrenches, railroad lines, boats, telephones, hospitals, wire—everything a modern industrial army carries with it.

The United States was not going to gather up all the four million pieces of gear, ship them back home and dump them on the postwar economy. The country was not about to give the equipment away. This offended the merchant mind. The nations which badly needed the gear had no money. At best, they could promise to pay in the sweet by and by.

Senator Fulbright thought the dealings and arguments over surplus equipment might be another wedge to drive the Allies apart. He happily remembered an odd footnote to history in connection with the Boxer Rebellion and the indemnity.

At the turn of the century the Chinese Empire was carved up and taken over by Western nations, England, France, Russia; its mainland was overrun by Western troops, gunboats, missionaries and traders. Special concessions were granted the nations within China. Chinese were "shanghaied" as virtual slave laborers. Thousands were shipped to the United States to help build the Western railroads. The Boxers were a secret nationalist society whose motto was, "Uphold the dynasty, drive out the foreigners."

The Boxers seized Peking, among other places, with some government connivance, terrorized the Westerners and destroyed Western property. European and American ships and troops put down the rebellion, and the West demanded an indemnity of $333 million for the indignities they had suffered.

The American share was $26 million, and in an act of unexpected good sense, we placed $16 million in a trust fund for the education of young Chinese in the United States.

Senator Fulbright did some more research. He found that after World War I, part of Belgium's debt to the United States was converted to a student exchange program. This was under the aegis of Herbert Hoover. The Senator wrote Hoover, the great patriarch of the Republican Party, and asked his opinion of a plan he was dreaming about. This would be to convert the surplus war property abroad into a giant student exchange program. The equipment would be sold to X country, which would pay in its own currency. The funds would remain in X, and be used to pay the tuition, books and living expenses of American students, chiefly GI's to begin with, who would wish to study there.

Hoover replied enthusiastically. He had always wanted to expand the student exchange, and was prepared to propose an ambitious program with Latin America when the Depression intervened. He agreed it was a cheap and sure way to make friends for America abroad.

Fulbright then introduced his bill "authorizing the use of credits abroad through the sale of surplus properties abroad for the promotion of international good will through the exchange of students in the fields of education, culture and science."

The bill was referred to a subcommittee on surplus property of the main Military Affairs Committee. He came before the panel of Senators and explained in his most reasonable way, "The meat of the matter is simply that we have this large amount of property, no one knows how much it will bring, but whatever it brings will be difficult to convert into dollars. It will take the form of a credit established in these countries with their own currency, and I believe that unless we devote it to a purpose such as this, in the course of time, it will suffer the same failure as the old war debt.

"In other words, it will be canceled to some extent. There may be payments, but out of that method there will probably develop great friction and animosity. On the other hand, if a small part is used for education, it offers the chance of doing more over a longer period for better understanding between these countries than anything I can think of."

Here was a formula, a way out of a dilemma. Educators and veterans groups came sprinting to its support. The State Department beamed its approval. The Pentagon grumbled a bit, preferring to turn over the equipment lock, stock, and barrel to local generals. One Senator wanted to tack on a civil-rights clause, saying that no applicant should be discriminated against because of race or color, but Fulbright talked him out of it. He explained this would mean automatic hostility from the Southerners and kill the exchanges.

Fulbright told the Senate optimistically: "My belief in the program is based on the assumption that when foreigners come to our shores what they see will be good. In spite of our occasional strange aberrations, I believe that America is a great country, that its virtues outweigh its faults. If the people of the world can understand us, they will throw in their lot with us."

In a later and more philosophical mood, he told an interviewer, "It's never possible to prove what word or ideas may have changed the course of events, but we do know from history the narrow margins by which some great decisions are made. I remember reading once about the decisions of the Athenians to attack Syracuse, a decision which brought about the downfall of everything that Athens had attained. Maybe they would have done differently if they'd known a little more about Syracuse. That's what these exchanges give us, the chance for us to know more about each other."

The bill passed the Senate without dissent, and through the House in a breeze.

The Fulbright exchanges, though, have been too clear a target to escape the Primitives. The Primitive is suspicious of scholarship, he equates it with strange, new and radical ideas. The Nazis had the same hate-fear of intellectuals as of Jews. Stalin all but destroyed an entire generation of Russian intellectuals, imprisoning them or turning them into eunuchs. Joe McCarthy complained loudly and often that the Fulbright exchange harbored Communists and subversives. Senator Everett Dirksen called it suspiciously "global Federal aid to education." During the McCarthy era, a Senator confided to Fulbright he would have opposed the bill, because, "I don't want our impressionable American youth to be infected with foreign isms." Congressman John Rooney of Brooklyn, who controls State Department funds from his niche in the Appropriations Committee, refused to allow $309,000 for the travel of Fulbright dependents. He said stoutly, "This is a luxury the American taxpayer cannot afford." Rooney never expressed the same alarms about staggering military appropriations.

The main body of opinion, though, is that the Fulbright exchange program has been immensely worthwhile. President Kennedy called it "the classic modern example of beating swords into plowshares." The State Department says it is "the most fabulously profitable investment ever authorized by Congress."

An Oxford don told the Senator at a ceremony, "You are responsible for the largest and most significant movement of scholars across the face of the earth since the fall of Constantinople in 1453." Some 81,811 scholars have benefited from 1949 through June 20, 1966. Of these, 28,610 were Americans, and 53,201 foreigners. The first beneficiary was a young Burmese. Interestingly, the "Fulbrights" have been the greatest stimulus to training in the arts in American history. American singers, instrumentalists, conductors, painters, architects, designers, dramatists, dancers and those studying the cinema—2,350 of them all told—have studied abroad. America's reward, according to Howard Taubman, "is that it receives back from Europe men and women whose talents have been sharpened and whose horizons have been broadened. In their own work and in their influence on others they contribute to the nation's cultural flowering."

This is a bonus the selection committee never dreamed of when it chose the young football player from the Ozarks for a Rhodes scholarship. This man has put back in the pot much more than he took out.

A milestone was reached in 1964 when Yugoslavia became the

first Communist country, and the forty-ninth nation, to sign an agreement for exchanging students. Fulbright flew to Yugoslavia for the ceremonies.

It was a rewarding experience for him, proof of an idea he has held stubbornly and against great odds for more than two decades, which is that Communism, instead of being a huge boulder threatening Western civilization, is a careless group of stones in varied states of decay. Individual Communist states, as they mature, can not only coexist with, but become a part of, Western society.

The exchange program has a simple mechanism. Students are chosen by panels here and abroad. The American going overseas gets round-trip travel, economy class, tuition, books and a monthly living allowance. The American Fulbrighters are graduate students, elementary and secondary schoolteachers and professors. The foreign scholar gets round-trip fare and in some cases allowances. Usually the university to which he applies will have scholarships for foreign students. The foreigners have been widely placed throughout the country.

A good many Fulbrighters go into the Foreign Service. A few years ago 152 were counted in posts around the world. This is true, too, of the foreign Fulbrighters, many of whom serve in Washington embassies, the United Nations Secretariat, or have gone home to become ranking government officers.

The scholarships have made the Senator famous around the world and placed his name in the international language, accepted in standard dictionaries. To "fulbright" is to study abroad.

Senator Fulbright is prouder of this exchange program than of any other work. A sign of the bitterness of the White House at the Senator in early 1966 was a sneering comment on the exchange scholars. A columnist close to the White House wrote that the leader of peace pickets in Australia during Vice-President Humphrey's visit was a Fulbright scholar from New York.

At the same time the Fulbright student exchange bill was moving through Congress, the world was boiling with confusion and trouble, and another sharp turn lay ahead for the Senator.

In early November, 1945, the Senator told the Foreign Policy Association, "We are troubled by a feeling of helplessness. In spite of our professed intention to build an organization with adequate power, we have done little to achieve that end. Instead, we have fallen to quarreling with Russia like two dogs chewing on a bone. To be tough or soft toward a nation is not a policy. Our policy should not be merely to love or to hate Russia or any other people; it should be to obtain their assistance in the creation of a bona fide organization based upon law and with force and vitality in its system. To admit that war is inevitable is to forfeit the game before the contest has begun."

A few months later, the spirit of the Fulbright resolution of 1943 was junked. Senator Vandenberg was irritated by what he considered was Secretary Byrnes's too moderate attitude toward Russia. In the spring of 1946, he talked at length with John Foster Dulles on a new Republican position. Dulles was already on record as saying the United Nations was "relatively impotent and negotiations at Paris failed because the Soviet leaders consider American ideas of freedom to be obsolete."

Vandenberg then initiated, more or less formally, the hard line which has become a regular part of American foreign policy. He told the Senate, with Fulbright listening, "I assert my own belief that we can live together in harmony if the United States speaks as plainly on all issues as Russia does; if the United States just as vigorously maintains its own purposes and ideals as Russia does. If we abandon the miserable fiction that we somehow jeopardize the peace if our candor is as firm as Russia's always is, and if we assume a moral leadership we have too frequently allowed to elapse. We must have positive foreign policies." Manifest Destiny had been reborn as "moral leadership" against the Soviet Union.

This was not unexpected. The American public, and the large Polish communities in such cities as Detroit and Chicago, in particular, was outraged by an apparent double cross on Poland. In May, 1945, Harry Hopkins won a promise from Stalin that free elections would be permitted in Poland, and it would operate on a parliamentary system "as in Belgium and Holland." In return, Washington and London recognized the Soviet-sponsored Provisional Government of National Unity. Instead, Poland was converted into a Soviet puppet state, with the usual policy of police control and terror against oppositionists. In Czechoslovakia, the same process was beginning in 1946, a year after it was liberated by Soviet and United States armies.

While stiffening its policy toward Russia, the United States—at least in the regency of the White House, Senate Foreign Relations Committee, Pentagon and State Department—moved rapidly away from any international controls. The impulse was to go it alone.

The three barons of the Committee, Vandenberg, Connally and George, mutilated a resolution on the World Court. The resolution would have permitted the United States to accept the authority of the Court.

George said scornfully, "A large number of Americans think that by adopting resolutions and hastily entering into international agreement we can make certain and steadfast the peace of the earth. We are not going to put an end to war with laws or resolutions, or by adhering to every kind of international agreement which anyone can think of."

This was a poke at Senator Fulbright, who was backing the World Court resolution.

Vandenberg criticized the resolution and Connally offered an amendment which, in effect, killed the Court. His amendment gave the United States veto power over jurisdiction. In other words, we would decide when we wanted to let the court rule on a dispute involving us.

Senator Elbert Thomas claimed the Connally amendment was contrary to the United Nations Charter. But the amendment passed 51 to 12. Backing it were all of the old lords of the Senate and all of the isolationists.

In the spring of 1946, Harry Truman and Winston Churchill agreed informally to "contain" Russia, that is prevent it from moving deeper into the West, or, most specifically into Greece and the Mediterranean. This "containment" was not taken through the United Nations for probably two reasons, the Soviet veto and Churchill's lack of enthusiasm for international government. He was a quite sincere believer in power politics, and felt power was all that would restrain the U.S.S.R. The containment would depend largely on American power, since the United States was relatively undamaged by the fury of the war.

The Cold War was officially announced in Churchill's Iron Curtain speech at little Westminster College in Missouri, where he came as Truman's guest. There, in his great robes, Churchill said in his dramatic voice, "I do not see or feel the same confidence or even the same hopes at this time . . . A shadow has fallen over the scenes so lately lighted by the Allies' victory. Nobody knows what Soviet Russia and its Communist international organization intends to do in the immediate future, or what are the limits, if any, to their expansive tendencies."

The American military was moving so rapidly into foreign policy that the Foreign Policy Association said in October, "The United States now relies on military and naval strength in achieving its aims of foreign policy to a greater degree than ever before in its peacetime history, and the War and Navy Departments have an important part in shaping America's foreign relations . . . The President bears the responsibility of making sure that military agencies do not gain domination over foreign policy." *The Washington Post* editorialized, "Some of our military men seem to think their department is the State Department."

The same month, the War Department announced a strategy of "massive retaliation" aimed at Soviet Russia. A mass flight of B-29 bombers was set off on an around-the-world cruise designed to follow the borders of Russia.

These events were followed by the expansion of absolute Soviet control over Eastern Europe in violation of the Potsdam agreements. Which came first, the chicken or the egg, will be debated until kingdom come, but certainly events contrived one on the other.

During this storm of mutual suspicion and recriminations, Senator Fulbright began to waver in his beliefs. His faith in the United Nations, in the reasonableness of the Allies was smashed by torturing doubts as during March, April and May, 1946 a strident Cold War psychology, moves and countermoves, sprang from the earth.

He stood with a small band of Senators protesting the atomic bomb tests at Bikini. The plan was to drop bombs on an armada of old warships. A number of prominent scientists said the tests had no military value, but were rather a part of the game of atomic muscle flexing. Fulbright pleaded, "It would seem to me that at this particular moment, instead of making a contribution toward peace, it would contribute to the suspicion of other countries, particularly other members of the Security Council with whom we are now having some misunderstanding."

The tests were held.

On March 5, 1946, the Senator from Arkansas spoke bitterly, "When a great struggle ends, there is always some measure of disillusionment, a letdown, a taste of ashes in the mouth. Peace, it seems to some, is a pale, undramatic disappointing thing when the ghastly exhilaration of war fades into the past. It is then that unity falls away like a husk and division deepens. It is then that with unseemly haste we seek to forget the war; to forget the sacrifices of these young men for whom we all subconsciously feel a responsibility. It was in such an atmosphere that twenty-five years ago we made the decisions which resulted in the recent catastrophe.

"It is difficult for me to see the pattern of a healthy future in the atomic bomb, jet propelled airplanes, Mr. Stalin's latest five-year plan and Mr. Truman's Navy Day address. It is true that we survived the first meeting of the United Nations without drawing pistols and knives, although at times it looked like the thing to do."

This was a different Fulbright from the man who stood in the House two years before, speaking with such hope about his resolution. Something had left him, been pressed and twisted out—his faith in the reasonableness of man. The lesson he learned was mentioned later in a private conversation. He said, "Mankind is poisoned by fear of the stranger. It's a primitive and animal instinct, and I suppose a hundred thousand years ago it was a necessary part of the struggle for survival. This fear has been enlarged and turned into terrifying myths by man's imagination. There aren't any other creatures that kill and destroy for such illusory reasons as men. We have wars and massacres and injustices against the weaker. It's a pretty bad record, and a universal one. The only way to get over this is to know more about the stranger. No one is ever as bad as you picture him in your imagination and fear."

In April, 1946, he thought there was a last chance for the giants, America and Russia, to sit down together amicably on international control of atomic energy. The United States, then, was the sole possessor of the bomb. If Russia rejected a reasonable plan, he reasoned, it would "indicate Russia's intentions are not peaceful."

This was not to be, and for reasons unknown to the Senator. There was great conflict within the Administration, and in Russia, too, over international control. In June, 1945, seven leading atomic scientists presented to the Secretary of War a plan which called for our renouncing the use of nuclear weapons, and international control by rationing uranium. Secretary of War Henry L. Stimson proposed privately to Truman that we offer the secret of the atom to the Soviets, since they were certain to get it themselves.

The Administration position was shown in November, 1945, although the United Nations was then setting up a commission to develop an international control plan. Secretary of State James F. Byrnes said no international body could compel the United States to release A-bomb secrets. This was because the military, specifically

General Leslie R. Groves, the head of the wartime atomic project, did not believe the Soviets would have a bomb at the earliest in ten years, and possibly sixty years. As it turned out, the Russian physicist, Pyotr Kapitza, had theorized in 1941 on the possibility of a bomb, and the Soviets began working on it in 1943. Kapitza, incidentally, was placed under house arrest for urging Russian scientists to press for international controls.

An American plan for international control, the Baruch Plan, which satisfied few of its drafters, according to David E. Lilienthal, then chairman of the Atomic Energy Commission, was put together. It was a system for a stage-by-stage climb to true international control with a stiff inspection system. Lilienthal quotes one expert as saying, "A really efficient system of inspection would be so contrary to the traditions of the Russians and their philosophy of government that they would consider such a proposal as an attack upon their whole system and way of life." Bernard Baruch later confided to Lilienthal the inspection plan was the core of the Soviet objection. The Russians also complained it would allow the United States to keep its bombs and plants almost indefinitely, but would place Russia's uranium under immediate control.

At any rate, the Soviets turned down both the Baruch Plan and a private plea by American scientists for an international control conference of world scientists. The reason seems plain; they were in striking distance of their own bomb, which was exploded in August, 1949.

During this period of international tension, the American people generally were busily trying to keep up with the Joneses, and Senator Fulbright said, "Most of us are so busy these days building a better mouse trap that we have forgotten to build a civilization. Why do we all refuse to face the truth when we know that in a world torn by disagreement, refrigerators and electric dishwashers are of no ultimate use?"

In his dismay and concern, Senator Fulbright turned the corner into the Cold War. He recalls now this came when the Russians were so deaf to our plans for international control of the atom. On May 17, 1946, he made a speech which is one of the most tortured of his career. Like most Americans, he became frightened of this brutal, authoritarian force, and thought some way must be devised to keep it within its cage, or, like the Vandals, it would destroy civilization.

He said, "I confess that I am troubled and find it exceedingly difficult to arrive at any convictions about the future of our international relations . . . Six months ago I thought the major problem was to overcome the traditional isolationism of this country and persuade our people to devote our power and influence to the establishment of law based on justice. I believe that the great powers had endured so much suffering and destruction they would be determined to work together for the prevention of war. It seemed unbelievable that any of them would run the risk of war either by aggressive action or by neglecting their international responsibilities. But during the last few months Russia has traveled far along the path to aggression, and the United States has neglected its responsibilities at home and abroad.

"A year ago in Washington there was considerable enthusiasm for the United Nations now being created. Today there is a profound sense of frustration and futility about the future."

He devoted a part of this address to his own change of mood about Russia: "There are doubts in the minds of many of us that Russia will ever submit to rules of conduct in any field." Since then, he has revised this dogmatic concept; he now believes that nations evolve constantly, under pressures of the world and internal longings of their peoples. A "sick" nation, one which refuses to be bound by laws, may be cured by a greater participation in the world community. A nation during this period of sickness should be both treated and quarantined.

"It is with profound reluctance," he said, "that I have concluded that the recent actions of Russia are not consistent with a desire to bring peace to the world under the aegis of the United Nations. During the past several months the question which haunts us most persistently is, is it the purpose of Russia to dominate the world through a subtle combination of infiltration and force, or is she only seeking security?" He did not answer finally.

He listed as Russia's criminal acts—"her ruthless stripping of Manchuria, her extravagant demands of reparations from Italy, and for bases in Tripoli and the Dardanelles, the annexation of the Baltic States and Polish territory, the violation of her pledges to reestablish free governments in the Balkans, and her refusal to permit official representatives or citizens of her former Allies to enter any of these territories under her control, except under the most stringent restrictions."

It was still possible, he thought, "to restrain Russia's ambitions within reasonable bounds and to reassure her as to the friendly and pacific purposes of the Western world."

His way of doing this was to unify Western Europe politically and militarily as a balance against the U.S.S.R. Walter Lippmann has written, "He was, I think, the first American public man who realized that if Western Europe was to coexist with the Soviet Union it would have to unite. And he is the first responsible American statesman to be saying that the necessary counterweight to the development of the Communist power is a much closer political and economic integration of the Western world."

This period, one of such turmoil and doubt for the Senator and the world, ended for him on a note of comedy.

A few days before the 1945 Congressional elections, he was eating alone in the Senate cafeteria and a girl reporter for a press association sat down to talk with him.

He asked her what she thought would be the outcome of the elections, and she replied the Democrats would lose control of Congress.

"That would be one hell of a fix," Fulbright said in surprise. "Imagine that—a President of one party and Congress of another. There would be a stalemate, and at a time when we need to be united."

"What would you suggest?" she asked.

"Truman should resign. First, he would appoint a Republican Secretary of State to succeed him."

There was no Vice President. Truman had succeeded to the Presidency on the death of Roosevelt.

It was her turn to be surprised, and the Senator explained: "If the Republicans control Congress, the Government will be divided, and each will blame the other for failure. We'll be drifting for two years almost without a Government, and the times are too critical for that."

The reporter was a good prophet. She called him after the election and asked, "Do you remember our conversation, and you saying Truman should resign if the party lost control of Congress?"

He remembered, but didn't think his comment was important.

"Can I quote you on that?"

"Sure," he said, but added humorously, "No one is going to pay any attention to that. You probably won't even get it on the wire."

This is typical of Fulbright's innocence about news and the political system. He is constantly being surprised that some statement of his should wind up on page one and become the subject of furious debate.

The Senator's invitation to Harry Truman to resign was, of course, front paged for several days, and brought astonishment, shock and laughter to the political community.

President Truman's reaction was an exclamatory, "That over-educated Oxford SOB!"

IX

IN THE RED-BRICK courthouses of Arkansas, men are always willing to interrupt their leisurely routine to talk about Bill Fulbright. He occupies the place in their imagination of the favored son who went away and made good. Pride is mingled with a curious speculation as to how come. All this in the slow amiable conversation of the courthouse oracles.

One such sage remarked with the air of a man who had spoken this wisdom before and received a good audience, "You know, if Bill Fulbright would wind up in hell, he'd find some way to tidy up the place and make it more comfortable for him. He's not a fellow to accept the intolerable."

This is what the Senator did in the long winter of 1946–1947 that began with the first snows of December and ended when the cherry blossoms bloomed in April. He tidied up hell. The fantasy that the suffering and terror of World War II were so great men would eschew force and violence faded before the hell of reality: the outbreak of the Cold War, the heavy Russian boots trampling about Eastern Europe, the failure to give the United Nations peace-keeping powers, the military messianism in Washington.

Within Washington, the pressure for military action against Russia built up. It came from many sources. The Catholic Church was emotionally aroused by the loss of the faithful in Poland and Hungary, and a fear that the ugly brute would move West. This view was reflected in the hyperbole of Representative John McCormack of Massachusetts and the ecclesiastical warnings of Cardinal Spellman. The Pentagon, particularly the Air Force, was anxious to make the Strategic Air Command (SAC) the atomic guardian of Christendom.

And John Foster Dulles was busying about with his air of the benevolent curate urging the good guys against evil. After the 1946 elections put the GOP into power in Congress, President Truman established Dulles in the State Department as a superadviser.

In mid-January, Dulles publicly urged that the coal and steel of the Rhine basin be the heart of a West European industrial system strong enough to contain Russia. Dulles had long been lobbying against the Roosevelt plan of depriving Germany of its war-making potential by putting a tight rein on heavy industry, which had been one of FDR's schemes to mollify the Russians. The Dulles speech was tagged by the supersuspicious Soviets as a deliberate move to rebuild Germany as a military machine against the U.S.S.R. The next month Dulles attacked "appeasement" of the Russians and urged a "vigorous" containment. In February, too, the new Secretary of State, General George C. Marshall, announced Dulles would go with him to the April meeting of foreign ministers in Moscow as a consultant. This also alarmed the simplistic Russians.

The Cold War gathered momentum in Washington. The wind of disquiet was filled with alarms and suspicions, many of which have proved groundless. The fear was of a frightful conspiracy by Moscow to take over the world by military action, guerrilla movements, strikes and political agitation. Anything which threatened the *status quo* was attributed to Moscow. Actually, as we know now, most of the uprisings and agitation in Western Europe were local heavings rather than part of a master plan of the Kremlin. Stalin was, in fact, uneasy over the eruptions. He was having enough trouble within his own empire, and he feared being thrown into a war with the United States by overzealous comrades along the fringes.

Senator Fulbright, too, was drawn along by the winds of alarm. He had no facts to disprove the rumors, and Russia was behaving so brutally in Eastern Europe and so rudely at international conferences that it became easy to imagine the worst. This experience is basic to the Senator's desire to have all the facts before the United States went too far along the road to war with China in the middle 1960's. The Foreign Relations Committee hearings on both Vietnam and China were an attempt to fill a vacuum with intelligent information.

The extent of the Cold War feeling was indicated on March 6, 1947, when President Truman said "freedom" was more important than peace, and listed as the key freedoms, freedom of worship, speech and (private) enterprise, and said the system "could survive in America only if it became a world system."

A specific crisis forced this rhetoric to a test. Greece was falling apart. Ruined by war and corruption, it struggled between Communism and a limited democracy. A leftist guerrilla force controlled much of the country. The British had been spending three-quarters of a billion dollars a year and garrisoning a large army there to keep Greece from collapsing. This was a major Churchill policy, to keep Communism and Russia from gaining a hold on the Mediterranean. The British voters, though, threw out his party, and the Labor Government on February 24, 1947, advised Washington it would give up the job in Greece as of March 31.

Washington was convinced the Greek revolution was the work of Moscow, and prepared to take over the role of protector. However, an entirely different view is reported by Djilas, the former Yugoslav Communist leader, in his *Conversations with Stalin.*

He tells of a meeting in Moscow in February, 1948, when the Soviet leader turned to Kardelj, the Yugoslav Vice Premier, and said, "The uprising in Greece has to fold up . . . No, they have no prospect of success at all. What do you think, that Great Britain and the United States—the United States the most powerful state in the world—will permit you to break their line of communication in the Mediterranean Sea! Nonsense. And we have no navy. The uprising in Greece must be stopped, and as quickly as possible."

Djilas speculated that Stalin did not want another unreliable Communist state in the Balkans "not to speak of possible international complications, which were assuming an increasingly threatening shape and could, if not drag him into war, then endanger his already-won positions."

To a grim and tense joint session of Congress on March 12, President Truman outlined his Greek-Turkish aid program. He asked for money and guns to keep Greece from Communist control, and gave a broad policy of American intervention, now known as the Truman Doctrine. We would move to protect any peoples threatened by Communist pressure anywhere, again on the assumption any Communist act outside of the Soviet empire was a hostile act planned in Moscow. Truman said, "It must be the policy of the United States to support free peoples who are resisting attempted subjugation by armed minorities or outside pressure." The President himself wrote the word "must" in pencil in place of "should" and generally toughened up the tone of the original draft from the State Department.

Secretary of State George Marshall made futile efforts to patch up the torn fabric of East-West relations. He had a frustrating meeting with Stalin and Molotov. In Washington, military strategies to meet Russian threats were outlined in secret to Congressional committees.

Senator Fulbright is somewhat persuaded today that the Cold War, in part, was the result of a breakdown in communications and political intelligence on both sides of the Iron Curtain. Neither Washington nor Moscow made any great attempt to understand the society and mores of the other, but created fantasies. The Russian one was standard Marx with a strong dose of Dostoevski. The confusion and lack of any rational understanding of Russia in the United States were underlined by Senator Fulbright in a talk to Arkansans. He said, "I talked to Secretary Marshall, and he is confused about the Russians. None of us understands what is going on there. But we all agree, we must prevent the Russians from taking over Western Europe." He was also disturbed by those in Washington who seemed happy to contemplate a holy war with Russia. He remarked, "They seem to get a sensuous pleasure out of talking about war. I can see the need to fight the Russians, if they move westward, but I don't get any pleasure out of contemplating it."

To Fulbright there was some comfort in the Washington scene in the presence of Secretary Marshall and his calm and humane view of America's role in the world. His philosophy was pointed up that June under the huge elms in the Harvard Yard, as the Secretary said, "Our policy is not directed against any country, or doctrine, but against hunger, poverty, desperation and chaos. Its purpose should be the revival of a working economy in the world so as to permit the emergence of political and social conditions in which free institutions can exist." This was the logic of the Marshall Plan, in which the United States sought to build up the shaky economies of Western Europe.

Senator Fulbright has refined this thesis in a number of speeches on the social and political upheavals in Latin America, Asia and Africa. A man will not work to overthrow his government, he argues, if he has a decent job, food and a home, as well as basic liberties. A prosperous and fair economy is the best guarantee against revolution. In some places, this cannot be accomplished without revolution. The

United States should be prepared to accept and even encourage some revolutionary movements as essential to progress and to prevent Communists from gaining control. This view was implicit in his critique of the Johnson Administration's handling of the Dominican Republic crisis.

But his main concern during this period of the late 1940's was Europe. It was a Europe he knew and valued, as one does an old friend. The long-range salvation for Europe, he thought, was a united Europe. United it could stand off any threat from the East, military or political.

The thought came to him from a reading of Benjamin Franklin's letters. To a friend in France, Franklin wrote on October 22, 1787: "I send you enclos'd the propos'd new federal constitution for these States. I was engaged 4 months of the last summer in the Convention that form'd it. It is now sent by Congress to the several states for their confirmation. If it succeeds I do not see why you might not in Europe carry the Project of good Henry the 4th in execution by forming a Federal Union and one Grand Republick of all different states and kingdoms, by means of a like convention. For we had many Interests to reconcile."

One Grand Republick of Europe would relieve individual states of heavy military burdens; they would contribute to a common defense. A common market without tariffs or duties, as within the United States, would stabilize the economy. There would be no need, for example, for small countries to develop their own expensive steel industries.

On March 21, 1947, Fulbright and Senator Elbert Thomas of Utah introduced a resolution "providing that this Congress favors the creation of a United States of Europe within the framework of the United Nations."

He plugged for it during the debate on the Greek-Turkish aid: "This isn't a new idea. For centuries the leading thinkers and statesmen of the world have urged the creation of a federated Europe as the best method of bringing peace and prosperity to that unhappy region, as one of the essential conditions for a peaceful world. We know that so long as this senseless conglomeration of separate political and economic entities exists there is little hope for the peace and prosperity of the world. We also know that the most propitious time to move forward is just after society has been disturbed by some great upheaval, leaving it in an unstable and fluid state."

The Senator observed the press generally thought the idea was swell, but the timing bad. He disagreed. "I think the only opportunity to bring the nations of Europe together is now." They were asking for assistance, and we could indicate the aid might depend on how they got together to solve their own problems.

He admitted critics thought the plan Utopian. But, he recalled, "the United States of America was, in the beginning, branded Utopian and its failure predicted by those who, if they were here today, would look with derision on this proposal." He pointed out that Europe was united for several centuries under the Roman Empire. Later, in the ninth century, Charles the Great united Europe from Spain to the Elbe River. There were no major cultural differences within Western Europe; the political systems were much alike. This land mass of two billion square miles and three hundred million people and a going industrial society, if united, could raise living standards and be strong enough to hold off any enemy.

Otherwise, he pointed out, the American commitment to Europe might go on indefinitely. "How do we finally work out from under these obligations?" he asked.

This question is typical of Fulbright. He is a conservative fiscally, and he believes the underprivileged and the poor should help themselves. He thinks, for example, that India has not worked diligently enough in social, agricultural and economic reforms, and he rather admires the up-from-the-bootstraps efforts by China with little or no outside aid.

Senator Fulbright thought the United States of Europe should not be a closed club, but keep the door open to any Eastern European nation that could become free enough of Russia to join.

Official reaction was hostile. As the Senator has mentioned, a nation screwing itself into a war psychology is not the best place to plant new ideas. It spews them out like a slot machine rejecting slugs.

The Russians were also outraged. They saw this resolution as an imperialist scheme of the United States to put Germany back in the saddle and in control of European industry. The Moscow Radio carried the usual (for that period) unimaginative diatribes against Fulbright. The State Department had enough trouble without trying to get the sensitive and squabbling European family together. The kindest remarks were, "Oh, my God!" The chairman of the Senate Foreign Relations Committee thought it was a lot of damn nonsense.

The resolution died, with only slight mourning.

Two years later, as a member of the Foreign Relations Committee, the Senator from Arkansas retained his enthusiasm for federation, and he had another clash with his old antagonist, the condescending Dean Acheson. Acheson was by then Secretary of State and the West's chief diplomatic Cold War warrior, and as such, the Senator thought, should be anxious to strengthen Western Europe.

It is not altogether clear why, but these two men of superior intellect did not get along well. Fulbright regarded Acheson as somewhat stuffy, but sympathized in a very real way with his problems and was outraged by the Republican and McCarthy attacks upon him. Acheson seemed to feel required to throw cold water on the Senator's ideas.

The Secretary had a habit of playing very close to the power structure. He enjoyed his respectability. Fulbright was a maverick.

At a hearing on American policy in Europe on a Friday morning in early February, 1949, Fulbright was questioning Acheson about the proposed Council of Europe. Was there within it "any real delegation of power"?

Secretary Acheson said not.

In other words, Fulbright countered, it is just another meeting place?

A little haughtily the Secretary said, "When you say it is just another meeting place, the important thing is that it is the meeting place. It furnishes an opportunity for discussions, consultation and recommendations."

But this isn't enough, Fulbright argued. The nations of Europe have been talking and consulting for centuries, and nothing has happened. Didn't the Secretary agree that European nations needed economic integration to be fiscally sound?

Yes, he agreed.

"Do you think we can have lasting economic integration without political unity?"

The Secretary said, "Political integration would be almost impossible on account of the great disparity between the countries."

"You feel then," Fulbright asked, "that they cannot be unified politically until they reach a parity on such things as per capita income and their cultural levels?"

This is what might be called one of Fulbright's "needling" questions. When he gets what he thinks is a runaround, he tries to force the other to reveal what he is hiding by a series of sharp stabs.

"No, I did not say that," Acheson snapped. "But I think they have to make greater progress."

"Do you think there is much more disparity among any of these countries than between Arkansas and Connecticut?"

"Of course there are greater differences."

"In per capita income? I doubt it."

"I am not talking about per capita income."

"That is one of the basic criteria," Fulbright said.

"I am talking about reaching an equilibrium. I think you have to do that before you can get closer political connection between the areas." This view of the Secretary obviously slammed the door against any American encouragement for European union. It also would have prevented or considerably delayed the American union.

The persistent heretic from Arkansas became blunter. He said our foreign aid program—based on the Marshall Plan concept, now an accepted part of American policy—was hindering, not helping the integration of Europe. The fault lay, he believed, in the management of the Marshall Plan, rather than the philosophy. The Senator thought an economic union was essential, and this would lead to political unity. The American aid program, he now concluded, was slowing down the movement toward economic union. This was by "paying the deficits" of individual countries, and by giving specific countries money to build facilities available elsewhere in Europe. He cited funds for steel plants in Norway.

"There is really a growth of nationalism in these states, because they are getting their funds from us," he said. "If they weren't able to get them, I think they would try to make a more efficient economy within the European area."

"I suppose one could draw that conclusion."

"It seems to me," the Senator said, still pursuing the thought, "that in the past people have taken these important steps forward because they had to. Not because in some conference room they sat around and decided it was a reasonable thing to do. In our own country, we did it because of great difficulties among the states and the outbreak of practically warfare. Something had to be done, not because it was wise, but because of serious disintegration. After you achieve peace and prosperity, there's no need for doing anything."

The Secretary replied very icily, "I find it difficult to carry on this discussion, because I do not know what you are asking me. Your view, it seems to me, is that the best thing to do is do nothing, to let the situation get as bad as it possibly can, and out of that in some undisclosed way, we are going to move toward higher economic and political unity. If that is your thesis . . ."

Senator Fulbright interrupted him: "My thesis is this: since we are undertaking this obligation and paying so much money, one of the aims should be to unify these countries. But we don't say a word to them about integrating."

Acheson replied, "Nobody has suggested that anyone take the attitude that you have just described."

"I thought it was the attitude."

"You are quite wrong about it."

Chairman Connally pushed into the discussion. He grumbled, "I would feel disposed to take disciplinary action against anybody in the ECA [foreign aid agency] who exceeded his authority, and began to meddle with the political situation in Europe. It is not the purpose of this bill to deal with the politics of Europe, either for a union or halfway between them."

This is typical of the response of The Establishment, with a few exceptions, to the Senator's modest proposals for change. He is not a revolutionary, his schemes are never radical; he probably will be classed by future historians as a farseeing conservative.

His own explanation is that the bureaucracy has become rigid, and actually is far more opposed to change than the public. "Opening those doors and letting a little fresh wind in has become a Herculean task," he has remarked.

At this hearing, Fulbright criticized the plans for the Council of Europe. "There's no delegation of power. It's simply a forum. It doesn't look like much of a step," he said.

"I think if you feel that way about it, you are entitled to that view," Acheson answered. "It is not the view I hold."

Senator Fulbright struck at what he considered the crucial weakness of the aid program. In the exchange, Secretary Acheson very nearly lost his temper.

The Senator said, "It's very difficult to justify continuing a program that has no end, and does nothing to give any assurance it can support itself in the future."

Acheson retorted, "I do not want to leave it at that."

"That is apparently the attitude of the Department."

Connally broke in again, "The Secretary has a right to answer that."

"I think it is quite unfair and wrong of you," Acheson stated, "to say that this is the attitude of the Department. Our aim, first, is to get economic independence by 1952. I do not think your statement gave a fair picture."

Fulbright once again was prophetic. At this writing, the United States is still spending considerable sums for the defense and economic stability of Western Europe. As one associate of Fulbright said, "We sure missed the boat. We had a chance then, but today Europe is drifting apart, and De Gaulle has turned NATO into a joke." The time has passed, barring a fresh cycle of war, depression and revolution, for federation.

By one of those ironies that seem to dog Fulbright's career, two months after his exchange with Acheson, a special United Nations Commission on Europe agreed entirely with him. An Associated Press report from Geneva which an assistant put on his desk said: "The Commission said European nations, striving for an economic come-back, are tripping over their own isolationism, and the European Recovery Program is aggravating the situation. The Marshall Plan, through European Recovery Program, pours in money with the avowed intention of helping to integrate European economy; European nations themselves adopt plans to integrate it, but the observable trends are away from integration, the Commission reported. For lack of such integration, it continued, national economy is disintegrating all over the continent . . . In spite of this recovery, it held the general outlook is poor because of a persistent dollar shortage and the almost total absence of integration of the economic plans of the various European nations."

The Senator said gloomily during the next foreign aid debate, "Our aid is building up and reinforcing the traditional nationalism in each country. They will indefinitely be dependent upon our supplying them with dollars either as gifts or loans."

The hostility and indifference of official Washington put off for a generation or more the reality of "one Grand Republick." This marked the end, too, of Senator Fulbright's more idealistic period, when he thought governments would react quickly and reasonably to constructive ideas. He believes that man carries within himself the seeds of his own salvation from war and hunger. He, that is man, is frustrated by the bureaucracies and pressure groups.

The Senator from Arkansas turned more and more into a critic chipping away at these granite structures and trying to reach and reason with the people. He is not a gentle critic; this is part of the paradox of J. William Fulbright.

X ❋

In APRIL, 1951, Senator Fulbright was asking America if it wanted "a moment of imperial glory" or "to preserve the peace by the difficult, democratic process of persuasion and compromise."

This was during his first hand-to-hand fight, so to speak, with the military mind and its swelling influence on the political scene. His antagonist was the colorful hero, General Douglas MacArthur.

MacArthur was by then an almost legendary figure, and a controversial one. President Roosevelt, according to his secretary, Grace Tully, regarded MacArthur as one of the two men most dangerous to our democracy. The other was Huey Long. But to millions he was an idol.

MacArthur wanted to turn the Korean War into an attack upon China. Specifically, he wanted to bomb Manchurian bases, blockade the Chinese mainland, and "unleash" Nationalist China to invade the Communist coast. This would have required American ships and air cover. Fifteen years later, Fulbright found traces of this thinking in the Johnson Administration's Vietnam policy.

Long before the dispute reached the public or Congress, MacArthur had been wrangling with Washington. He held the Prussian view that once a debate had reached the shooting stage, all major decisions should be made by the field commander. Also, MacArthur had an old grievance against Washington, claiming it shortchanged him during World War II by giving first priorities of men and matériel to Europe, whereas, to him, Asia was the more important battleground. This was the "Asia First" view that still pervades much of the Navy, and parts of the State Department, CIA and other services. Dean Rusk was an "Asia First" man.

From the beginning of the Korean War, the Joint Chiefs of Staff feared it might be a Sino-Soviet trap to lure us into battle in Asia, where we would be at a disadvantage, and bleed us. The Joint Chiefs continually worried about MacArthur going too far, and committing us to a land war on the mainland.

So on September 25, 1950, the Joint Chiefs sent him a directive ordering the general to make "special efforts" to find out if Russia or China would intervene if our forces went beyond the 38th parallel, as MacArthur intended. MacArthur replied he did not want any conditions placed on his movement northward. Washington retreated.

Within the next few days, China warned it would not permit actions beyond the 38th parallel, and there were reports of heavy Chinese troop movements to the border of North Korea. MacArthur informed Washington this was sheer bluff and nonsense, that China and Russia "have decided against further investment in a lost cause." Within the Washington councils, Rusk, then Assistant Secretary of State for Far Eastern Affairs, agreed with the general.

In mid-October, President Truman was so concerned he went to Wake Island to talk personally with MacArthur. He asked, "What are the chances of Chinese or Soviet interference?"

The general replied, "Very little . . . We are no longer fearful of their intervention . . ." As he spoke 120,000 Chinese were already across the Yalu River.

On October 24, MacArthur ordered his toops onward to the Yalu. The Joint Chiefs urgently cabled him this was not in accord with the September 27 directive. He replied he had sufficient latitude in the directive. According to the official Army history, the Joint Chiefs considered he had disobeyed the directive. However, they did not countermand his order to the troops. On November 3, the Joint Chiefs cabled their anxiety about "overt intervention," and he answered there were "many fundamental logical reasons against it [Chinese intervention]."

A few days later, two Chinese divisions, equipped with the latest Russian rockets fired from trucks, struck at Unsan. They cut off a large United Nations force with huge losses. The Chinese had employed an ancient tactic, one noted by Marco Polo; the enemy is drawn on and on until he is overextended and caught in a trap, then the noose is pulled.

MacArthur's reaction was to bomb bridges halfway across the

Yalu River, over the objections of the Joint Chiefs. The war escalated to a new turn, without seriously halting Chinese reinforcements. Chinese MIG planes attacked U.S. bombers. MacArthur then wanted to chase the MIG's back to their bases in Manchuria.

In late March, 1951, General MacArthur openly defied the Joint Chiefs and the President by taking the issue of his plan—to bomb the bases, blockade China and invade the mainland—into the political arena in an exchange of letters with Representative Joe Martin, the No. 1 Republican leader. On April 5, Martin made a speech in the House and gave the press copies of MacArthur's letter to him.

The MacArthur thesis was almost exactly that of President Johnson and Secretary Rusk fifteen years later. MacArthur said in his letter: "It seems strangely difficult for some to realize that here in Asia is where the Communist conspirators have elected to make their play for global conquest, and that we have joined the issue thus raised on the battlefield; that here we fight Europe's war with arms while the diplomats there still fight it with words; that if we lose the war to Communism in Asia the fall of Europe is inevitable, win it and Europe most probably would avoid war and yet preserve freedom. As you point out, we must win. There is no substitute for victory."

Truman removed MacArthur. The general shot back that this was "a new and heretofore unknown and dangerous concept that the members of our Armed Forces owe primary allegiance or loyalty to those who temporarily exercise the authority of the Executive Branch of the Government, rather than to the country and to the Constitution which they are sworn to defend."

Fulbright, the constitutionalist, was now thoroughly alarmed. He told the Senate:

"It is rare in history that a major question of Government policy is presented so forcibly, so dramatically to a nation. General MacArthur has drawn the issue. Our Founding Fathers decided that the President is the front rider as commander in chief of our Armed Forces. If the nation is not now content with this solution, it may amend the Constitution." "MacArthur," he said in his soft, almost inaudible voice, "reminds me a little of the great crusader of the twelfth century who is riding out in a four-engined bomber to eradicate the evils of Communism from the world . . . One cannot fail to recall that Napoleon on every occasion expressed the most profound sympathy and concern for his troops, yet Napoleon brought about the greatest slaughter of troops the world has ever known."

But MacArthur, and his revolt and proposals to expand the war, were popular with a number of Americans. He was enthusiastically invited to address a joint session of Congress, and Representative Martin predicted to reporters the general would be his party's nominee for President. A stampede seemed under way.

Fulbright stood up, and asked, "Are we to proceed as a great power in the grand imperial manner of the past, or as a member of the United Nations, one among sixty trying to preserve peace by the difficult, democratic process of persuasion and compromise." The MacArthur path, he thought, was the lure of empire that overcomes every strong power, even so wise a one as Athens, and in the case of Athens, Napoleon and Kaiser Wilhelm, led to suffering and ruin.

The general's plans to bomb China "are opposed not only by his own government, but also by the governments of the free world, on military and political grounds . . . Boldness and bravery are one thing; recklessness and headlong dispatch are another. In war, as in life generally, prudent men want to pay a price commensurate with the gain, to weigh the benefits against the risks."

He asked how much the conquest of China would cost in men and material and whether Russia would not intervene. "And if Russia intervened, would we not then, while precipitating the third world war, doom our Far Eastern forces to destruction, lose Japan, and lay all of Southeast Asia open to easy invasion? . . . Shall we make over-all strategy, involving the life or death of millions of peoples, without consulting our allies? Shall we commit them to a world war without their consent? Do we prefer to face Russia alone? Shall we gain Chiang Kai-shek and lose Britain, France, Italy, the Low Countries, Scandinavia, Greece and Turkey?"

The great problem, as Fulbright now saw it, was not so much how to contain Russia or even China, for we had the immense military power. It was rather how to contain the rashness of a country with a strength unknown to history and, it seemed at times, spoiling for a fight. He tried, in his own thinking and study, to isolate this rashness, find out where it lay. The military was divided, with the Asia First school for MacArthur, and such men as George Marshall and Omar Bradley opposed. MacArthur picked up strong support among the old isolationists and new radical right. Hamilton Fish later helped organize a group to work for MacArthur's election as President. Barry Goldwater mourned "the waste of this magnificent talent." And there was the usual ragtag of hotheads and oppositionists.

Senator Russell, chairman of the Armed Services Committee, and Fulbright thought an examination of the facts before a Senate panel might clear the air. The Armed Services and Foreign Relations Committees came together under the gavel of Russell, a former judge. MacArthur was invited to testify, and at first declined. When he appeared in early May in the packed Senate caucus room, he announced, "I appear today not as a voluntary witness."

Never before had so much been at stake in a Congressional investigation. When the general sat down, photographers surrounded him, for he was the public idol. His views seemed to have caught the public fancy.

MacArthur was read an Administration statement, "What we are trying to do is to maintain peace and security without a general war . . ."

The general replied, "That policy seems to me to introduce a new concept into military operations—the concept of appeasement, the concept that when you use force, you can limit the force."

Fifteen years later, at the closed door Foreign Relations Committee hearings on Vietnam, Fulbright accused Defense Secretary Robert McNamara of failing to place a limit on the use of American force.

General MacArthur was asked if his recommendations would not mean that the United States would have to stand alone.

He replied frankly, "If the other nations of the world haven't got sense enough to see where appeasement leads, why then we had best protect ourselves and go it alone." This view came up again in the Vietnam war.

MacArthur's most challenging questioners were three—Fulbright, Wayne Morse, and Brien McMahon. Fulbright's technique is that of a great trial lawyer; by a combination of disarming charm and artful questions, he lets the witness entangle himself.

Fulbright addressed MacArthur most amiably. He began with pleasantries about the general's Arkansas birth. He asked gently, what did he think would most influence the Russians to intervene?

MacArthur said the size of the opposing force.

"Would it make them more aggressive if they had a relative increase over our forces? Is that a fair thing to say?" Fulbright asked. He spoke with an almost eager goodwill.

General MacArthur felt himself at ease before this friendly Arkansan. He answered, "The greater relative strength they possess would probably be an inducement, if they decided to go to force, instead of the present political force."

"Then it is fair to say that you feel that an expansion of our forces should take place, rather than a reduction?"

"I most assuredly do."

Other Senators looked at one another in surprise. What was Fulbright up to? But at his next statement, there were smiles at the press tables. He had very gently led the great general into a trap.

Fulbright read a statement, not giving the source, saying that the cost of maintaining 3,500,000 men in the Armed Forces indefinitely would wreck the economy. The author called for a cut of half a million in the Armed Forces, and a $20 billion reduction in the budget.

"Do you think that that is a safe doctrine?" the Senator asked mildly.

MacArthur knew what was up. He said he could not discuss details of military planning.

"I think it is important to have your judgment now. I don't see this as inconsistent," the pleasant drawl went on.

"I am not able to pass judgment."

"Is a substantial reduction warranted in view of the world situation?"

Plainly unhappy, the general said, "I can only believe in a state of adequate preparedness. I haven't the information to give you a concrete answer."

By this stratagem, Fulbright had made MacArthur show his other hat, that of the aspiring politician, and in so doing dimmed some of his luster as a decisive military authority. The MacArthur backers, and Joe Martin was among the most prominent, had hoped to persuade the source of this quotation, Senator Robert Taft, to surrender his GOP delegates to MacArthur.

Still in a gentle tone, slightly humorous, Fulbright went on: "Senator Taft said he should use the Chinese Nationalists, bomb Chinese bases, and cut the defense budget. Don't these seem contradictory?"

MacArthur was irritated. He said, "I said when I addressed this august body I was not going to be drawn into politics, and I am not." (He later was not only a candidate for President, but keynote speaker at the GOP National Convention.) "I believe that is as much of a political question as anything else."

The Senator from Arkansas lectured him mildly, "It seems to me, General, this is a little different from an ordinary political controversy. Here is a question that Congress has to decide, the defense of this country. I don't know anyone better qualified to give us advice on that very important question . . . To undertake a greater obligation with fewer forces simply confuses a nonmilitary man, as myself."

Senator Russell also urged MacArthur to express himself on this subject. He would not.

The Senator from Arkansas next challenged the general's military judgment. He began: "One of the things that seems very important and has not been developed is: why, in view of the difficulties the Japanese had over thirteen years in subduing the Chinese, do you feel that with a few additional troops and air power, we could subdue them? I believe the Japanese had a much greater military establishment than we have now."

MacArthur's manner was condescending. He said, "The objective of Japan in China was to seize and exploit the whole country, a very large order. Our objective is a limited one—to put sufficient pressure on the Chinese that they would withdraw their troops and cease their depredations in the area of North Korea."

The Senator persisted: "I assume if you undertake a project you are going to do whatever it takes to accomplish it. You are not going to undertake, and then not go through with it. As long as China is not subdued, as long as there is a Communist group anywhere in China, they may be able to oppose you . . . The Japanese airplanes dominated the air, and yet in thirteen to fifteen years they could not subdue the Chinese. I wonder if the very primitive nature of the Chinese isn't a great defense. You cannot get at them and destroy them, as you would a highly industrialized nation."

The big room was quiet during the questioning. The spectators sensed this was not the polite give-and-take that had been murmured all day. These men were deadly antagonists.

MacArthur replied, "You have only to destroy their political ability to maintain an army on foreign soil. When you destroy their power to build guns, the munitions to supply the food for an aggressive army, they will have to cease being an aggressive army."

This argument was repeated fifteen years later as the Johnson Administration's rationale for bombing North Vietnam.

Yes, Fulbright told the general, but the Chinese received their munitions from the Russians. All they made themselves were pistols. There was a buzz in the caucus room. General MacArthur had been caught wide open. He tried to recover, saying, "The whole process of modern war depends upon the logistical potential of supplying your troops, feeding them and giving them the necessary munitions, all of the intricate paraphernalia of modern armies. The Chinese capacity is very limited. They live only a few jumps ahead of starvation. They are vulnerable to blockade. A very modest military effort on our part, I believe, will have an excellent chance of bringing an end to the Korean slaughter."

He suggested a severe blockade would create famine and fifteen million deaths from hunger.

Fulbright came quickly back, the hound on the chase: "China was not appreciably better off twenty years ago than now. Japan did bomb her communications. I don't recall that resulted in fifteen or even ten million dead. There were no more than the usual number of starving."

"Not all of the Japanese forces were concentrated in China."

"During the eight years before Pearl Harbor, they concentrated solely on China, didn't they?"

There was an uneasy silence.

The drawling voice, unemotional, almost pedantic took up again. "General, if we accept your basic philosophy of war, and that is to proceed to victory without any dillydallying, without any of what you call appeasement, without anything short of decisive victory, then there is no stopping point once we are committed. Then what happens to us?"

MacArthur looked at him stonily.

"If we become committed in China," the Senator said, "Russia is really given a free hand in Europe and the rest of the world. What happens in the Middle East and Europe, if we are committed to very large ground and air forces in China? I think this is a central question, and I was hoping you would develop it."

General MacArthur did not choose. Instead, he spoke with the words of the political demagogue, "The alternative, Senator, is to sacrifice thousands and thousands and thousands of American boys month after month. Not only that, but you will have sacrificed the entire Korean nation and its people. If you do not save her, you are going to destroy her . . . I have been here two days now, and I have heard no proposition yet, outside the one made by the Joint Chiefs of Staff and myself, which would offer a successful conclusion of the Korean War. I believe it would mean that, if you don't attempt to bring this to a short and honorable conclusion [by his formula], it means not only the indefinite sacrifice of life, but, equally important, degradation and sacrifice of our moral tone."

Senator Fulbright, sitting behind the committee table with his slight fixed smile, wondered about the "moral tone" of a proposal which would admittedly starve fifteen million people to death and spread a modern war to the land mass of Asia for an indefinite period. Morality, it seemed, was determined by where you sat.

The Senator elected to answer MacArthur. It was, to him, a challenge he could not avoid. He replied, "Our objective is to minimize the loss of American lives and the expenditure of treasure. The loss of life going on today is so sad and terrible, it is proper to consider that a mistake might result in ten times greater loss in the near future. This is what we are trying to balance off. The issue is whether there is a reasonable opportunity to stop our losses, rather than vastly increase them."

There was a final and revealing clash of ideas. The Senator said, "There is just one other idea, General, that I think many of us are confused about. That is the idea that anything short of complete victory in an all-out effort to end it by force of arms in the Orient would be called 'appeasement.' It does not necessarily seem to me that a negotiated peace, for example, is necessarily appeasement. Do you think so?"

A bit wearily, for this had been a long and exhausting day, the general told him, "Senator, I have my own definition of appeasement that might disagree with yours. I believe that when you enter into war, you should use sufficient force to impose your will upon the enemy."

Late that afternoon when the television floodlights were turned off, and the general arose from the witness chair and walked stiffly out of the chamber, a few hands clapping at him, he was obviously tired. The tide had turned against him. He was quite possibly baffled. Where were the cheers that rang through the hall in his appearance before the joint session of Congress? In this new forum, the same man, the same persuasions had fallen. The general must have known then he was not going to be the next President.

Senator Fulbright gathered up the notes he had made. He thought of De Tocqueville's horror as, more than a century before, this curious traveler in America heard a priest pray to a large hall, "God, all-powerful! God of War!" There was something in the American frontier character to which war and the success of violence appealed. The thought troubled the scholar from Arkansas.

XI

In the hot July of 1952, the two political parties each camped in Chicago for a week or more. The only cool was a light breeze that came off the lake at nightfall. The political nominating conventions were hot and angry and full of tumult.

The Republicans came first, on July 7. The highly efficient machine put together by Governor Thomas Dewey of New York crushed the Old Guard and nominated General Dwight D. Eisenhower. John Foster Dulles was much in evidence in the resolutions on foreign policy, one of which, designed to draw Polish-American voters away from the Democrats, called for the "liberation" of Eastern Europe.

The Democrats came to town two weeks later, torn and disheveled. The Republicans had named a national hero, and President Truman's popularity was at a disastrous low. The reform Governor of Illinois, Adlai E. Stevenson, a most reluctant candidate, was drafted as the sacrificial lamb.

His suite would hardly seem the best place for urbane conversation between two gentlemen and old friends, but it was. Governor Stevenson and Senator Fulbright talked about the troubled world, as if it were a million miles away and they were studying it by telescope. A secretary who chanced upon this dialogue said, "I'd give anything for a record of those two talking. It was very wonderful and elegant."

They had met as young Government attorneys, Stevenson in the Agricultural Adjustment Administration and Fulbright in the Justice Department; both were a little old-fashioned in their manner and expression, their classical viewpoint, their interest in world affairs. Through the years, they had remained friends, meeting occasionally and corresponding.

Adlai Stevenson's nomination for President was a miracle to Fulbright. He had not hoped that the political system was ready to name a Civilized Man. He dropped everything to devote himself to Stevenson's campaign. He and his assistant, John Erickson, came to Springfield, Illinois, the headquarters, and Fulbright became a policy adviser and, when Stevenson was tied up with state business, the substitute speaker.

His intense feeling about this campaign was revealed as the campaign train moved into Texas. Senator Lyndon Johnson came aboard very quietly before the train reached Dallas, hunted up Fulbright, and told him, "Bill, I'm sorry, but I can't campaign for Adlai in Texas. It would hurt my reelection chances."

Fulbright, usually gentle and understanding, was outraged, and swore at Johnson like a trooper and called him a renegade. So startled was Johnson that he did make a talk on his wife's radio station for Stevenson. Then he lit out for Missouri for the rest of the Stevenson tour of Texas, to speak for Stuart Symington.

In late October, at Richmond, Virginia, Fulbright said, "The issue which overshadows all others is the fitness of the candidate for the Presidency, his ability and competency to understand, to form sound judgments about the most complex and difficult problems any man has ever faced. The candidates' own personal intellect, experience and character are of the utmost importance. Governor Stevenson knows what he is talking about. He has had vast experience in many years in government, and executed delicate matters for the Defense and State Departments in many parts of the world. The mark of greatness is upon him. Above all, he is a reasonable man in a time when so many zealots are on the political scene."

By the time of the Richmond speech, the campaign took a highly ironic turn. The Republican Party, many of whose leaders had been calling stridently for a tougher Asian policy, backing General MacArthur's demands, offered, in effect, to end the Korean War. General Eisenhower would go to Korea personally to see about ending the war, and the slogan, "Bring the Boys Home," played across the land. The "Democratic war" theme was played so heavily that one veteran columnist, Tom Stokes, wrote it was "enough to turn a stomach hardened to political extravagance."

The election was a disaster for Stevenson and Fulbright. They were overwhelmed by the unpopularity of the war and the great hero. The Governor carried only the seven states of the Deep South and the border states of Kentucky and West Virginia. Studies afterward showed that in heavily Democratic urban areas, women and young people switched to Eisenhower in hope of ending the war.

Some of the seeds of the celebrated Dulles-Fulbright feud undoubtedly were sown in that campaign—the Senator's distress at the defeat of his friend, his belief that the Republicans very cynically exploited the Korean War which, in Congress, they had tried to heat up.

His feelings were not improved by Dulles' first speech as Secretary of State. This was his "massive retaliation" address of January 12, 1953. Dulles saw Communism as a monolithic force whose tactic was to overextend the enemy and thus destroy him. This menace would be met by the United States—a strategic reserve of military power, chiefly nuclear bombs and their delivery systems; we would "retaliate instantly, by means and at places of our own choosing." Hanson Baldwin, *The New York Times* military writer, said that massive retaliation in return for any Communist aggressive moves implied "unlimited atomic warfare."

Dulles' acceptance of this so calmly was unquestionably part of his Calvinism. Also, this was a fairly cheap way to run the world, since it did not require a large army or navy.

From Russia, Malenkov said an attack on Russia would start a world war which "means the death of world civilization." The British and our European Allies were shaken. Protests and calls for clarification came to the State Department. This was because if we were to bomb the U.S.S.R., the immediate reaction target of the Russians would be Western Europe. (This was before the intercontinental rockets.)

Dulles had to back down. He said he did not mean "turning every local war into world war. It does not mean that if there is a Communist attack somewhere in Asia, atom or hydrogen bombs will necessarily be dropped on the great industries of China or Russia."

This came at a time of an odd feeling of horror, like the deathly silence in the eye of the hurricane. The monstrous megaton arms race was on. This meant the United States homeland was no longer invulnerable. The Pentagon was busy with its plans. Admiral Arthur W. Radford, the chairman of the Joint Chiefs of Staff, proposed dropping Hiroshima-strength bombs in Indochina. Others drew up plans for using tactical nuclear weapons on China to stop the shelling of the offshore island of Quemoy. Americans planned bomb shelters and bought property in the country. Mournful folk songs of nuclear death were sung in coffeehouses and on campuses. The thought of living on the rim of terror corroded the moral structure a little more. Senator Fulbright's mood was indicated by a talk with a correspondent, who saw him sitting alone in the Senate restaurant. "What did you think of Dulles' speech?" the reporter asked. Fulbright groaned. "My God," he said, "the people elect Eisenhower, and he treats Dulles as if he were St. Peter. So Dulles plays Russian roulette with us. There isn't anything you can do about it. I say a few words to the contrary, and am called a damn fool. I tell you the Emperor has no clothes, and whether the world is blown to hallelujah before we find out is anyone's guess."

By 1955, he began to speak out. To students at Hofstra College on Long Island he said warmongering and war-making were "a relatively simple, uncomplicated, orthodox procedure for solving internal problems that appeals to unthinking people. The basic trouble is that war is no solution. Victory is no solution." The world's problems were illiteracy, undernourishment and sickness. He scored "unthinking people" who wanted a "showdown" with the Communists, and said there was no "inherent reason" why free and Communist nations could not live on the same planet without fighting.

Of China, then in the news because Senate GOP leader William Knowland wanted to "unleash" Chiang to invade the mainland, the Senator remarked later in Arkansas, "If the leaders of Red China seem willing to abide by minimum standards of civilized conduct, we ought to find a basis for negotiations." He added with a trace of sarcasm, "I do not belong to the Knowland war party."

Fulbright challenged Secretary Dulles directly on Friday afternoon, February 24, 1956. Dulles came to the Foreign Relations Committee to talk about the Middle East. This was at a time when the Soviets had turned into smiling supersalesmen in the Middle East and Africa. Millions had cheered Russian leaders in India and Burma. The Baghdad Pact, a U.S.-supported alliance against Communism in the Middle East, was coming apart at the seams.

The Secretary announced that Russian foreign policy had proved a dismal flop. "The fact is," he said brightly, "the Russians have failed, and they have got to devise new policies."

Fulbright asked him, "You think that the speeches of Khrushchev and other leaders in the Russian Government would indicate a failure in foreign policy?"

"Absolutely, sir."

"I would be most interested to hear why you think that."

The Secretary gave one of his homilies of how "the unity and firmness and resolution of the free nations" had brought down the Soviets.

The Senator told him, "Your testimony is in direct contradiction to many observers."

Under his questioning, Dulles admitted the Soviets had markedly increased production in heavy industry, steel and oil, and "they have somewhat surprised the estimates which have been made."

"Is the situation in France reassuring to you?" Fulbright insisted. France was in the throes of a government crisis, one Cabinet after another falling.

"Well, the French Government is an interesting phenomenon."

The Senator asked about riots in Jordan against the Baghdad Pact, and the Secretary answered, "The riots in Jordan were an unfortunate development."

Three days later in the Senate, the gentleman from Arkansas let Dulles have it.

"Will Secretary of State Dulles tell America the truth about our present peril, or will he say one thing publicly and the opposite privately?" he asked. "Will he give us a fair chance to decide for ourselves, with full knowledge of the facts, what efforts should be made for our salvation, or will he lull us to sleep in an hour when the Soviet Union has launched a powerful diplomatic offensive against us? Will he by his candor rally the free world to trust in American leadership: or, from an apparent craving for popular approval, will he endanger the mutual trust which supports the association of free peoples?

"What we want and what we will support is a Secretary of State who will not treat us as children ready to clap in delight at every fairy story, however fanciful. What we want and will support is a Secretary of State who will come to us, not with packaged solutions to every ill that plagues the world; but who will come to us, instead, with a statement of fact about the nature of those ills. Such a Secretary of State would win our respect for his courage, and for the respect he himself showed the truth. It is my unpleasant duty to say that on Friday of last week, we did not have such a Secretary of State."

Behind these words were the utter frustration with an electorate which made possible the diplomatic fundamentalism of Dulles, which permitted an arms race whose only end was wholesale death, and at the acquiescence of his own colleagues in Congress. He had discovered that among the so-called "liberals," those who voted consistently for labor and civil-rights legislation, there was a strange silence and conformity on foreign policy. They were what David Riesman called "bomber liberals." Much of this conformity was a protective coloring to escape the shrill political accusation of "fellow traveler" in an atmosphere of postwar hysteria much like that following World War I.

His speech broke an uneasy truce over foreign policy and showed Fulbright's independence once again. The truce was Lyndon Johnson's idea. He was the Senate Democratic leader, and argued in the caucus that the Democrats needed a "consensus," which could be woven together by supporting the Eisenhower Administration in foreign policy, while dissenting mildly on labor legislation and civil rights.

The Senator from Arkansas went on: "Is the Government well served when a Secretary of State misleads public opinion, confuses it, feeds it pap, tells it that if it will suppress the proof of its own senses, it will see that Soviet triumphs are really defeats, and Western defeats are really triumphs?"

A Republican came to Dulles' defense. Senator Leverett Saltonstall of Massachusetts said mildly in his charming old New England accent he didn't think the Secretary had made "intentional misrepresentation of facts." Saltonstall added, "I would say that I would take his statement on Friday and again yesterday as being perhaps optimistic —perhaps too optimistic—but certainly we cannot proceed on a basis of gross pessimism."

A year later, Fulbright led a Congressional revolt against Dulles' handling of Middle East affairs. He would have succeeded had not Senator Johnson opposed him.

The background for this rebellion began when Secretary Dulles, in a move to counter Soviet aid to Arab states, offered American economic help for a major Egyptian project, the high dam at Aswan, a $1.2 billion program for drainage, irrigation and hydroelectric power. The United States offered $54.6 million for the first stage, and sympathetic consideration of later requests.

On July 19, 1956, the Egyptian Ambassador called on Secretary Dulles to accept the offer, and was told in language described in the press as "brusque" and "brutal" that we had changed our minds, and were withdrawing our proposed aid.

The reason for this switch has never been made completely clear. Senator Fulbright after his investigation said it had been done in the heat of emotion. He also said cotton-growing states had put pressure on the Administration against the loan, which would increase Egypt's cotton yield. The State Department claimed Dulles became convinced Colonel Nasser, the Egyptian President, was a Soviet tool. The U.S. Ambassador in Cairo opposed withdrawing the offer. Another possibility was intense Jewish feeling against the loan, and the heavy Jewish vote particularly in New York. It was an election year.

At any rate, six days after Dulles withdrew the offer for the Aswan Dam, Colonel Nasser nationalized the Suez Canal. Late in October, the British, French and Israeli armies attacked Egypt, seeking, in part, to regain control of the canal and overthrow Nasser. (At almost the same time, another Dulles' project, "liberation," came to its full circle. The Hungarians revolted against the Soviet-puppet government, and called on the United States for help. *The Washington Post* reported a freedom fighter who had fled to Austria saying, "For eight years the United States has been telling us through Radio Free Europe and the Voice of America to resist Communism but when resistance finally leads to revolution, you stand by and watch Soviet tanks without lifting a finger to help.")

In the Middle East, Russia threatened to use force "to crush the aggressors and restore peace." Washington put pressure both directly on Britain and France and through the United Nations and achieved a cease fire. President Eisenhower won reelection against Governor Stevenson by an even bigger margin, as a peace President who prevented war in the Middle East.

Secretary Dulles moved to put the United States into the power vacuum in the Middle East, an area of 4½ million square miles. This was the Eisenhower Doctrine, which the President presented to Congress on January 5, claiming Russia "long sought to dominate the Middle East." He asked Congress for a free hand on economic and military aid and for armed intervention "against overt armed aggression from any nation controlled by international Communism." The Cold War was pushed in the President's second Inaugural Address, and he stated: "Rarely has the earth known such peril as today." Dulles had taken brinkmanship to the Middle East with its 70 percent of the world's oil reserves.

Hearings on the Eisenhower Doctrine were held before the joint Senate Armed Services and Foreign Relations Committees. Fulbright led the attack on Dulles' credibility, and, according to the press, the Secretary was variously stiff with anger, red-faced and almost shouting before the hearings ended. This was on January 24.

The Senator from Arkansas began by questioning Dulles' statements that $200 million was needed, because the Middle East states were "near bankruptcy."

The Senator said all but Egypt and Jordan had oil revenues and good credit ratings. "Didn't Jordan indicate it would not take money from us?" he asked.

"No."

Fulbright quoted a Reuters dispatch saying the Jordan Foreign Minister rejected a "subsidy" by the United States. "Do you think this is erroneous?" he insisted.

"Yes, sir."

"What evidence do you have?"

"Discussions by the U.S. Ambassador lead us to believe in a favorable decision by the government of Jordan."

Fulbright read the words of the Foreign Minister against accepting American aid. Dulles stared at him with his large blinking eyes.

Fulbright asked, "Is there any significant evidence that some state or states in the Middle East are about to fall under the domination of international Communism, and are planning aggression against other states in the region?"

"That is a possibility."

"Do you wish to give the committee any evidence justifying that?"

Dulles said not in public session; privately. This was a favorite device of the Secretary, and never failed to annoy Fulbright. He remarked later that, of course, a certain amount of diplomatic information must be secret; you cannot conduct world affairs in a fishbowl. "But," he concluded, "to ask the American people to take great risks on faith is not democracy. Nor is it good sense. The information on which the risk is taken may be false, as in the Bay of Pigs. Too often, the information is not factual at all, but bias. Congress, it seems to me, has a responsibility to find out whether we are being guided by hard facts or poppycock."

As the Secretary sat before him, angry and uncomfortable, Fulbright said, "He [Dulles] told this committee that the Russian or Communist menace in the Middle East has created for the United States the most dangerous situation since the end of World War II. At one point in his testimony, he went so far as to say that unless we approve the proposal, he believes it is a very great likelihood that American boys will be required to fight in the Middle East. He emphasized the economic distress in the whole area of the oil-rich states . . . Less than a year ago, the Secretary told us the Russians had made very little progress in the Middle East and the military danger was less than the danger from competitive coexistence."

Some members of the joint committee shifted uneasily at this heresy. Some smiled slightly.

"This resolution is a broad unrestricted grant of power over the Armed Forces and our enormous economic resources. It is a blank check for the Administration to do as it pleases with our soldiers and our money. To justify voting for it, one must indeed have a full and deep confidence in those who are to administer such far-reaching powers.

"Speaking for myself, I need more convincing evidence. I regard the course of action which he has been following as harmful to our interests, as being calculated to weaken the influence of the free world in the Middle East, as disastrous to NATO, and to our friendship with Great Britain and France.

"I suggest we ask the Secretary to review his conduct of foreign relations in the Middle East, at least since the time he visited General Naguib in Cairo and gave him a silver plated pistol. I think the committee should be fully informed of our relations with Colonel Nasser, and why we became involved in the Aswan Dam project and what led to the Secretary's abrupt dismissal of the offer."

He concluded with even blunter words: "I regard it as improvident and unwise to make a grant of authority to disburse large sums of public money, without restrictions of any kind, for objectives which are vague and unspecified, and by people who have disproved their foresight, wisdom and effectiveness in the field of foreign affairs."

Later, at this same hearing, Fulbright questioned sending arms to Pakistan. He said, "By pouring in great quantities of arms we create local problems that may cause an immediate outbreak of hostilities."

Dulles replied stiffly, "We couple any such arms with very specific stipulations against their aggressive use."

"Do you think anyone has any confidence in such a stipulation? Weren't arms given France for NATO used in Africa?"

Senator Fulbright's boldness brought out latent fears, and gave heart to the timid. Others spoke up, and by the first of February, mail to Congressmen was running very heavily against the Eisenhower

Doctine. The Senator on February 17 moved in the joint committee to tame the resolution, and give the President less direct authority. This came after considerable behind-the-scenes skirmishing. Fulbright had gone to Lyndon Johnson and asked him to oppose, individually and as the Democratic leader, "this gargantuan grant of power" which he also said was a "cover-up" for past failures of American policy in the Middle East.

Johnson in his flat Texas drawl said no; in times of crisis we had to support the President, and give him all the tools he needed.

It did not occur to Fulbright then, only much later, that Johnson might have the same simplistic, Old Testament view of the world as Dulles; that in the poor, overfarmed land of southeast Texas in small frame churches, Baptist preachers pounded out a simple good-versus-evil theory of life, and that this was translated into politics by speakers on courthouse lawns.

The Fulbright motion lost in the committee 17 to 10. Another motion by Senator Harry Byrd, the Virginia Democrat, to curtail the spending authority in the resolution was beaten down 17 to 11. Senator Johnson controlled enough votes to save Dulles.

By the summer of the following year, 1958, another crisis sprang in the Middle East, and Senator Fulbright said wryly we were "one foot over the brink." A revolt overthrew the pro-Western regime of Iraq and President Eisenhower sent Marines to Lebanon. The Senator commented: "I do not know where we are heading under the present leadership of this country, which, when it is not weak and desultory, tends to be impetuous and arbitrary. The Administration might well review the validity of the concept of the Baghdad Pact and the Eisenhower Doctrine. If these are as worthless as I believe them to be, it is high time they be reconsidered and abandoned . . . Where will the shock come next time? If we go on as we are—in the fashion of the cat on a hot tin roof—we shall be skipping from one crisis to another all over the globe, unable to get our footing anywhere."

He spoke with shame and disgust of what he thought was the weakness of the Dulles policies; it seemed to him such idiocy for a great and educated people to follow. "Let something go wrong—whether in China or Nigeria—and we have a ready answer: the Soviet Union is behind it. What a perfect formula for the evasion of reality. I suggest that some of the blame belongs closer to home. In the fear of the deviltry of Communism, we have cast ourselves indiscriminately in the role of the defender of the *status quo* throughout the world."

He scornfully listed the products of this policy: lavish economic aid to venal governments parroting an anti-Communist line, help held back from those who did not wish to give this obeisance not out of any affection for Communism, but simply to stay out of the East-West quarrel; "tens of millions of dollars" for "anti-Communist propaganda through the blatant information program," but on cultural and student exchanges "there has been much rending of hair over economy and parsimonious doling out of the shekels"; a "pinch-penny approach" to economic aid, but for military aid "the hand has gone deep and unhesitatingly into the pocket of the American people. We have on a grandiose scale provided peoples of the underdeveloped nations with the weapons of destructive warfare, and have been miserly in providing them with weapons to wage war on their own poverty, economic ills and internal weaknesses."

This was not simply an afternoon's outrage. It was the accumulation of years: the primitive anti-devil worship that so fascinated the American politician from Harry Truman to John Foster Dulles, and let them escape the heartless reality of their own limitations; the trust in bombs and tanks to exorcise the devil, and the arms race; the neglect of all a wise society assures, schools, food, housing, medical care, an atmosphere in which great ideas are born. All mixed up in this was the fact that twice the American people turned away decisively from his man of reason and moderation, Adlai Stevenson. And this was what they bought!

"I do not pretend that there are answers to all our problems," Fulbright said in his dry, inflexionless voice to the Senate. "Some difficulties in human affairs are insoluble. At least, let us try to develop a set of coherent, realistic, well-thought-out objectives and feasible policies to attain them."

XII

IN EARLY 1950, America was struck by what Senator Fulbright called "this swinish blight," more widely known as "McCarthyism." The gentleman from Arkansas is too careful a historian to believe this sprang whole from the earth. It was a virus common to all men, a dread of new ideas exploited by politicians and demagogues into a panic against the "enemy from within."

The first sign of it in America was in 1798 when standpatters among the New England clergy saw in the Jeffersonian liberals, and particularly liberal refugees from Ireland and England, a "Jacobinical plot" and an "international conspiracy" by the "illuminati" against church and state. Leading followers of Jefferson were arrested and, according to *The American Past,* "railroaded through the courts by Federalist judges like the coarse and vindictive Samuel Chase. One ailing Republican editor died from the mistreatment he received in the Boston jail. A Republican official of Otsego County, New York, was forced to travel 200 miles in manacles to the prison in New York City." A Vermont Congressman, who was both Irish and a fiery advocate of Jeffersonian democracy, was arrested for criticizing President Adams in a letter.

In the mid-1800's, violence against Catholic and Irish immigrants was so strong that the "Native Americans," as they called themselves, burned two Catholic churches in Philadelphia and started riots in which twenty-four persons were killed. A larger antiforeign movement, the Know-Nothings, elected governors to seven states and, among other things, stole a stone given for the Washington Monument by the Vatican. After World War I, this same history points out, "An antiforeign and anti-Red hysteria swept the country along with the strikes. Congress investigated Communist propaganda; the FBI seized hundreds of 'radicals' in coast-to-coast raids; and the Justice Department deported 249 'undesirables' to Russia. War veterans smashed up a Socialist newspaper office in New York, and lynched (with gruesome pocketknife emasculation), an I.W.W. member in Centralia, Washington, after a free-for-all gun battle in which four ex-soldiers were killed. Legally elected Socialist legislators were barred from Congress and the New York state legislature."

Fulbright saw the signs again after World War II—a general fear of Communists in the Government, and particularly within the State Department and such weird symbols as the "pumpkin papers." But until February 9, 1950, no demagogue appeared to build these elements into a fire. On that night, Joe McCarthy, at a Republican women's meeting in Wheeling, West Virginia, said, "I have here in my hand a list of 205 . . . a list of names that were made known to the Secretary of State as being members of the Communist Party and who nevertheless are still working and shaping policy in the State Department." (He had no such list, as subsequent investigations revealed.)

The toll of this dreadful disease, Senator Fulbright wrote much later, was, "The free discussion of ideas, the basis for our strength since the days of the Revolutionary War, was stifled. Security was substituted for scientific research. Discoveries which were made were locked in safes instead of becoming available as stimuli for new discoveries. Some of the best minds in the land were expelled from Government service, and a suspicion of educated people was spread throughout the land as if they were enemy aliens. The big doubt came to full flower in an orgy of flamboyant newspaper and television spectacles."

The full force of the McCarthy attack, as the Senator pointed out, was not upon Communists, but on liberals, conservative constitutionalists as Senator Millard Tydings of Maryland, and critics of Generalissimo Chiang Kai-shek in the State Department. Many rushed for cover. Senator Hubert Humphrey introduced an anti-Communist control bill, and told Senator Margaret Smith of Maine he did not dare criticize McCarthy openly for fear of Catholic voters in Minnesota.

Fulbright's reaction to McCarthy was one of both mental and physical revulsion. Once he was on the floor as McCarthy, William Jenner and Herman Welker were speaking. The Senator from Arkansas came out into the lobby and said to a friend in great dismay, "Who are these creatures? Ugh!"

He thought of them in terms of Hitler and his henchmen.

Joe McCarthy was an unlikely demagogue—a bearlike shape, thinning hair, a nervous giggling laugh, and a hoarse voice. He and Fulbright served together on the Banking Committee. There had been questions about McCarthy's receiving $10,000 from a housing company under scrutiny by his subcommittee, supposedly for writing a book on housing. Fulbright said at the time this was "a very questionable practice."

McCarthy began his "fifth column" and "numbers game" of Communists as a device to get attention for his reelection campaign. He immediately got his headlines, and Senator Fulbright noted, "The very fact that the press and public respond so rapidly to the extravagant and ridiculous in their public figures is in itself a strong temptation to a man with a forum like the Senate floor."

McCarthy had a gift for the grandstand play, as referring to "Case Number Eighty-one . . . an extremely dangerous and active Communist, completely disloyal to the United States and loyal to Soviet Russia." Another "case" was the "boss of Alger Hiss . . . in the espionage ring in the State Department." After the GOP sweep of 1952, McCarthy gained his own Senate "investigating" subcommittee which, according to Fulbright, was used to terrorize and blackmail Government agencies. The Senator from Arkansas criticized the FBI for turning over files to McCarthy, and he was the only Senator to refuse to vote funds for these witch hunts. He explained to Robert Sherwood, the playwright, "I don't see why I should buy a gun for the man to shoot decent citizens with."

The first direct conflict between Fulbright and McCarthy was on September 27, 1951 over the nomination of Philip C. Jessup, a Columbia University expert on international law. He was U.S. delegate to the United Nations General Assembly and spent much of his time debating Russia's ferocious purge trial prosecutor, Andrei Vishinsky. As such, he was a leading Cold War orator, a matter which disturbed Fulbright, who did not think the United States should turn the United Nations into a Cold War forum for insults simply because the Russians did.

Jessup was renominated for his post by President Truman, and McCarthy unexpectedly contested the nomination.

It was a part of McCarthy's wild bull attack on critics of Nationalist China. A lobbyist for the Nationalists boasted he "helped materially" in this campaign. The most famous target was General George C. Marshall, because of his "plague on both your houses" critique of Nationalists and Communists. Another target was the Institute for Pacific Relations, whose magazine, *Pacific Affairs,* was unfriendly to Chiang. The institute itself is a respectable organization of scholars and "China hands" in the Government, all the way from Henry Luce to Owen Lattimore, a onetime personal adviser to Chiang who became one of his sharpest critics. Jessup was an active member of the institute.

On the Senate floor, where he was immune from libel, McCarthy accused Jessup of having joined "five organizations which had been officially declared as fronts for and doing the work of the Communist Party."

Then he came before the Foreign Relations Committee, and claimed Jessup was "associated with an organization that has been officially named as a secret front for the Communist Party."

Fulbright challenged him. He asked, "When was this [the institute] cited as a Communist front? What was the 'vicious work' they did?"

McCarthy raised his voice, a familiar technique whenever he was asked an embarrassing question. "I don't propose to go into that. If you want that, you'll have to get the House [Un-American Activities Committee] report."

The contrast in the manner and voice of the two men was striking. McCarthy's voice had an odd quality, a heavy contempt with really terrifying tones of accusation. It admitted no possibility of innocence. The longer he spoke, the more exicted he became and he perspired profusely. He was awkward physically. He insulted anyone who questioned him, as part of his tactic to silence opposition. He later called Fulbright "Halfbright" and referred to the leader of the censure movement as a "senile old man."

Fulbright is finicky about facts. His voice is soft, his manner polite.

Now he asked McCarthy again, "You made a statement about the 'vicious work' they did. What did you have in mind?"

"I have in mind the committee report," he said sulkily. Then he took off on another tack: "When the President says, 'I intend to keep Acheson as long as I am President,' that makes it a political issue. I intend to bring this story to the Americans from the Atlantic to the Pacific." (This was the familiar "guilt" chain. Hiss had worked for

Acheson, so, *ergo,* Acheson too was a part of the "Communist" conspiracy, and Truman in standing by Acheson proved he was a member, too. On another occasion, Fulbright remarked, "To continue to attribute everything to some defect in Secretary Acheson seems to me going a little far afield. If you want to go on back, I suppose you could say all this trouble comes from Eve's action in the Garden of Eden.")

McCarthy again assailed Jessup for his membership in the institute. "What was the extent of his membership?" Fulbright asked.

"I don't know. Philip Jessup and I are not on a dear-Phil, dear-Joe basis."

This was the way it went. Each time Fulbright asked a question, McCarthy slid away from a direct reply. To one question, he answered, "I gave you the evidence. You can evaluate it."

This was too much for the former law professor. He said, "I haven't seen any evidence yet."

"Just a minute, just a minute," shouted McCarthy.

"Are you going to answer my question? Is he a Communist?" No answer. "Is he a Communist?"

"Oh, I don't know if he pays his dues. I haven't been attending their meetings."

"Mr. Chairman," Fulbright said in exasperation, "he is not answering the question. I submit the answers are not responsive."

McCarthy retorted, "Were you through with your speech, Senator?"

"The Senator [McCarthy] leaves out so many significant parts of his testimony that someone else has to supply the information."

McCarthy insisted that the Committee pursue a certain line, and Fulbright said, "The Senator from Wisconsin does not happen to be on this Committee, and it is none of his business what the Committee does along this line."

"Oh, yes it is," McCarthy cried; "the Senator from Wisconsin is representing a lot of people and it is his business."

"This is perfectly ridiculous," the Senator from Arkansas stated. "Are all his cases just as ridiculous?"

McCarthy was sweating, beads of perspiration on his forehead. He replied hoarsely, "I can't keep all the details in my head. I'm dealing with too many of these slimy creatures to do that."

There was a shocked silence. Jessup was a gentleman and a noted scholar. One of the Senators on the panel, R. Alexander Smith, Republican, New Jersey, a former Princeton lecturer, had said, "I

have known you [Jessup] too long to have any doubts about your
loyalty or integrity."

During the hearing, McCarthy threatened the Committee members
with political defeat if they voted for Jessup. Fulbright said, "I want
to say for the record that in all my experience in the Senate never
have I seen a more arrogant or rude witness before a committee."

Three of the five Senators on the panel voted against Jessup. One
was Senator Alexander Smith. So great was the fear of McCarthyism
that many decent men chose to hide until the storm was over.
Fulbright remarked, "When public men indulge themselves in abuse,
when they deny others a fair trial, when they resort to innuendo and
insinuation, to libel, scandal and suspicion, then our democratic
society is outraged and democracy is baffled. It has no apparatus to
deal with the boor, the liar, the lout."

McCarthy, when he could not quench Fulbright's questions and
protests, became more and more frustrated and abusive. He couldn't
understand this man whose knees did not buckle. He shouted once to
reporters that the Senator from Arkansas was "a Goddamned Communist stooge." He boasted everywhere he would defeat him in his
home state.

Once, on the Senate floor, McCarthy became so enraged at Fulbright he lost control of himself completely. The Wisconsin Senator
tried to tie President Eisenhower's hands at the Geneva summit
conference with Khrushchev and Bulganin by a rider calling for the
"liberation" of Eastern Europe. Fulbright forced a voice vote which
meant a repudiation of McCarthy. McCarthy literally screamed, "He
sits there and laughs. It is no laughing matter. He can grin and smirk,
but the enslaved peoples will not grin and smirk when they see what
the Senator has done. I repeat, he has done a great service to the
Communist cause."

Fulbright simply remarked, "It is one of the outstanding characteristics of the junior Senator from Wisconsin that he has a capacity to
disrupt the orderly procedure of whatever body or whatever committee on which he happens to be involved."

There was more to it than that, and Fulbright mentioned once in a
mood of outrage and bitterness, "It may be that Hitler was right. It
may be that the human race is incapable of self-government and that
Fascism is the wave of the future. Some of the developments of recent
months cause one to wonder. The American people are humiliated
before the world. The traditions of Jefferson, Jackson, Lincoln and

Wilson presently are smothered by a pervasive miasma of suspicion and doubt."

He didn't understand why President Eisenhower would not fight "the swinish blight." McCarthy bullied and abused his Secretary of the Army, and called on Government employees to send him privately suspicious information about their colleagues and superiors. Fulbright did not understand Lyndon Johnson's lack of concern, nor Alexander Smith turning his back on his friend, nor the great silence from the Senate liberals.

There was another direct encounter. Fulbright came before the Appropriations Committee asking for funds for the student exchange program. McCarthy had been given a seat on this august body. He asked Fulbright a "clever" question, grinning at his own cleverness: "If a Communist had written a book on fly-fishing, would you be willing to put that into a library abroad?"

Fulbright answered he did not know how far one could "reasonably apply that test" of banning everything created by a Communist. "I wonder whether or not this would apply to the government purchasing a generator from General Electric, whose employees belong to a union infested with Communists. I cannot see the fly-fishing case is relevant."

"It so happens," McCarthy said in his heavy voice, "that I think it is relevant. You are appearing here as a witness before the Committee, and I would like to get the benefit of your study of this problem." He poked a finger in the direction of Fulbright. "Would you purchase the book on fly-fishing?"

Fulbright replied, "I think I have answered the question. I do not think the Senator is the least interested in my views so far as the merits of the matter. If a book is a sufficient contribution to the Communist cause, I would not buy it. The question is how far would you go? Do you think we should refuse to buy a generator when a Communist may have worked on it?"

"I've spent six months on this and I know a bit about the program," McCarthy blustered, "and when a Senator comes before a committee and says he wants to advise us on what we should do, I would like to get his ideas."

"If a lecturer gives the Fourth Amendment to a committee, do you think he should be sent over?" McCarthy demanded.

"That is debatable. I can imagine intelligent persons refusing to answer the question as submitting them to indignity."

McCarthy put into the record statements of students who had been given Fulbright scholarships and who, he said "condemn the American way of life."

Fulbright asked that statements by other scholars praising America be shown, too.

Continually through the hearing, McCarthy interrupted Fulbright's testimony. At one point, he demanded that Fulbright be put under oath. Again, he shouted, "I don't want the witness to disappear."

Finally Fulbright told the chairman, "I would be perfectly willing to answer the questions of all members except the Senator from Wisconsin who, I am clear, is determined to destroy my testimony."

In the Senate and in his mail, Fulbright was regularly attacked for opposing McCarthy. He told the Senate, "I should like to say that I am tired of name-calling directed at anyone who does not agree with the other fellow. I am prepared to debate the principles in which I believe. I am not, however, prepared to indulge in any contest of name-calling, for not only is this repulsive but it is also, as I see it, an offense to manners that govern the conduct of decent men and it is anti-democratic in the operation of a democratic society."

His mail was filled with such nonsensical hatred as: "You dirty, low down, evil minded traitor and filthy minded rat . . . You have been a party to the Roosevelt-Truman-Acheson-Hiss gang of traitors and the henchman for the Jew Deal . . . I would spit on you but you would not be worthy of my saliva . . . You will end up in the lake of fire . . . You are a phony pinko punk."

Senator Fulbright was at a loss to understand what McCarthy's purpose was. He said, "McCarthyism seized upon the legitimate fear Americans have about real or potential Communist subversion, then he turned it into a battering ram, threatening every conservative institution that makes for constitutional morality. All were brought under attack. All were charged directly or indirectly with service in the case of treason."

General Marshall was associated by McCarthy with "a conspiracy so immense and an infamy so black as to dwarf any previous venture in the history of man." He impugned the patriotism of the president of Harvard, one of the nation's leading bankers, distinguished diplomats, held up Senate work by intimidating accusations at any who showed any skepticism about his charges, browbeat The Voice of America, and conducted "investigations" which the conservative

Senator John McClellan of Arkansas characterized as "one of the most disgraceful episodes in the history of our government." Why?

Fulbright reached an explanation of sorts. "There was a certain method to this madness, for if every corner of our society could be made to appear a nest of treason, then the way would be open for McCarthyism to make its supreme bid for naked power—all in the name of purifying the social order. Every falsehood, so long as it served the power bid, became a higher truth, every deception became a higher faithfulness."

Fulbright is not an activator, nor does he enjoy group activity. But his fear of McCarthyism and where it was leading was so strong he left his isolation. He worked with a small group of Senators on the techniques of censure. When the chief spokesman, Senator Ralph Flanders of Vermont, a conservative businessman, grew tired and disheartened, Fulbright talked to him. He consulted with Senator Margaret Chase Smith, author of the "Declaration of Conscience," on whether to seek impeachment or censure. He thought censure was the more practical. He gave tips on how to get the votes of key Senators he knew. One, a leading Protestant layman, was aroused by reports that a McCarthy investigator had written an article attacking the Protestant clergy.

In the debate over censure, Fulbright said, "I sincerely hope that in voting for censure, we may put a stop to the reckless incitement of the hatreds and fears of people who are suffering from a lack of information or a lack of understanding. . . . I think he [McCarthy] has inspired and aroused fears for which there is no justification. In his charges of infiltration of this Government by disloyal people, he has gone so far that he has made many lose confidence in their own Government, and in a self-governing democracy, I think that is one of the worst things a man can do."

Throughout the debate, Fulbright was dogged by the most faithful of the McCarthy lieutenants, Sentator Herman Welker of Idaho, who threatened to introduce a censure resolution against Fulbright. In one of these exchanges, the Senator from Arkansas revealed the great tension he was under. He said, "I think I have been temperate. I have had great difficulty in restraining my temper. On the other hand the Senator from Idaho will remember an incident last August when the Senator from Wisconsin challenged five or six Senators on the floor. He stated that he was going to prove us to be perjurers or liars. He made a very violent attack upon us. I do not know of any of us who responded in like manner. . . . I must say that the junior Senator from Wisconsin strikes me as having the greatest contempt for the human personality of anyone I have ever seen."

Anyone watching Fulbright in a conflict will recognize that, along with the tension, he is having a devil of a good time. This is the supreme paradox of the man. He is like the actor who is terribly shy and reticent offstage, but becomes a confident and vibrant personality once he steps before the lights. An old Fulbright friend in Arkansas said, "Don't let Bill fool you. He likes a fight, and he fights to win. Miss Roberta was the same way, and he showed that spirit on the football field."

The Senate voted to censure McCarthy 67 to 22, he ceased to be a political force and died a victim of his own violent nature and alcohol in 1957. But Fulbright recognized that individual men are but agents of stronger social forces. The chilling threat to democratic processes had not passed.

He remembered some words of De Tocqueville: "I know of no country in which there is so little independence of mind and real freedom of discussion as in America . . . The will of man is not shattered, but softened, bent and guided; men are seldom forced by it [majority opinion] to act, but they are constantly restrained from acting. Such a power does not destroy, but it compresses, enervates, extinguishes and stupefies a people."

As the Senator thought of this, he decided the ability of the people to get independent thought narrows all the time—fewer newspapers every year, three radio-TV networks. "The general effect," he told an authors' luncheon, "is that people see, watch, read, and listen to only one side of public questions. And this in turn can adversely affect the public man to whom the guidance of public affairs is entrusted. The public man, to achieve anything at all, will not use the open road, but will crowd himself into the path of low intrigue. He will not boldly scout what lies ahead for the nation. He will bend the weight of his energies to having everything stand still. He will voice no prophecies of what ought to be. He will speak only the sterile dogma of the street."

In this society there is only the silence of the tomb, broken by the strident cries of a McCarthy who frightens back into line any who dare to think independently. What can be the end result of all this?

He replied, "It can be a society shaped in the imitation of an

Egyptian mummy; a society where the embalmer holds the highest place of honor; a society of fixed, painted, and hard shells; a society feeding on its dry rot, until the fateful hour when a probing finger, striking the shell from without, makes it collapse on the empty center."

XIII

An excited voice speaking over the telephone from the Senate cloakroom said, "All hell's broken loose. Get the Senator up and over here. We need him."

It was an incredible hour, two-thirty on a bleak winter morning, March 5, 1960. A Senate benumbed by 108 continuous droning hours of Southern filibuster had suddenly come alive—angrily, belligerently, like a sleeper slapped hard on the face. Lyndon Johnson strode up and down the center aisle crying, "It's later than we think," in his penetrating flat drawl.

The galleries had mysteriously filled. Where do people come from at 2:30 in the morning? Reporters stumbled off the leather couches in the pressroom. Senators, rubbing their eyes, flung into the chamber through the swinging doors. On the Republican side of the aisle, Everett Dirksen was in alarmed consultation with his fellows.

The cause of it all, the junior Senator from Arkansas, sat at his desk in the front row with a slight, amused smile. This was Fulbright in a different role. As a critic, yes; but as a partisan and loyal friend, too.

For all intents and purposes, the 1960 political campaign had begun. Fulbright was getting the accumulated complaints of seven years off his chest. He wanted, too, to help his friend, Lyndon, become President. The Senator from Texas, through leaks from the Air Force and information to the Senate Preparedness Subcommittee, had decided the key issue was the Eisenhower Administration in its budget-cutting economies was neglecting defense and research on new weapons, and the Russians had leaped ahead. It was the genesis of the so-called "missile gap" which later proved a myth.

Fulbright had begun to speak before a handful; then Johnson decided it was the time and place for a full-fledged debate. He excitedly told an aide, "Bill Fulbright's spilling out a ton of ammunition. Get the boys over here."

From the beginning, the Senator from Arkansas looked upon the Eisenhower Administration with a melancholy scorn as one that was shipping its oars; he accused it of providing a "bland diet of sugar-coated half truths . . . a devil-may-care attitude" which would "leave the country flat and immobile." He regarded President Eisenhower as a hoax upon the American people; a placebo for their fears and confusion propped up on the throne by cynical politicians. The *Baltimore Sun* said in an editorial that Eisenhower was "personally obnoxious" to the Senator.

In this early-morning setting, with five Senators in attendance, Fulbright let fly with all his irritation and scorn. Whether the Administration was as remiss as the Senator charged will long be argued, but Fulbright, as usual, managed to find the hole in his antagonist's armor: the bland and simple optimism brought to bear on a terrifying world.

He began, "The Congress has been in session for two months. During that period we have heard the President in his State of the Union address assure the American people that all is right with the world, and that our freedom and our place in the world are secure. We have received the Budget Message and been assured again that all is well—indeed, very good, because we look forward to a budget surplus, albeit we must do without new schools and better missiles."

The reference to missiles was included despite the Senator's dislike of the arms race, and showed the influence of Johnson. Fulbright said it was currently being argued whether the Soviet missile superiority would be "three to one or maybe only two to one." He pointed out we had stood still on defense research, or nearly so, while "the Soviet Union swiftly leaped from the oxcart to the moon," having bound up the injuries of war, developed an industrial plant, manufactured the hydrogen bomb, created the intercontinental rocket and improved mass education. "But how shall we excel in these fields if we are more concerned with keeping up with the Joneses than surpassing the challenges of Khrushchev?" He questioned Eisenhower's budget balancing at the expense of military research and hardware, and accused the Administration of "assumptions of omniscience."

Five years later, in his continual review of his own convictions,

Senator Fulbright changed the priorities, and questioned the value of spending billions on trying to reach the moon first, while poverty and illiteracy haunted the land.

In this early-morning address, Fulbright questioned the peace of Eisenhower. He asked, "What is our so-called peace? Is it not a monstrous make-believe to which men lend credence so that thereby they may have the prospect of another day under the sun?

"Men have anciently yearned for a universal commonwealth. Now we have it. But it is a commonwealth of fear kept going by a precarious balance of terror, a chilling oscillation between negotiations and incineration. All the world's parts, for the first time, are simultaneously out of joint. And while horrors stalk the earth, weapons of potential universal destruction are hurled to the stars . . . Our communication instruments are superb, yet we cannot communicate with the Russian people who occupy one-sixth of the earth's surface or the Red Chinese who compose about one-fifth of the world's population. Perhaps half of humanity lies beyond our hailing."

He concluded: "This is the melancholy pass to which we have come. It is like the common story of the rich, miserly recluse found starving. There has never been a time when we did not have the resources of men, money and access to knowledge that might have given us a wide lead over any aggressor and made attack upon us suicidal. Yet we have apparently believed we could not afford to spend enough to secure our liberties.

"We stand as a nation, a twentieth-century Babylon, headless and heartless, a big, fat target for the ably led Communist world and the clamoring, poverty-ridden new states . . . Everywhere the implacable cage stalks the unwary bird."

Johnson took up the cry from there. He said defense funds voted by Congress had been "impounded, sunk and hidden" by the Administration, and he kept assistants busy bringing him documents.

Senator Dirksen fired back that Fulbright's views were only "the lay opinion of a man from Arkansas." The *Baltimore Sun* called the speech a "tirade" and asked that Fulbright resign as chairman of the Foreign Relations Committee. Maybe it was, but it accurately reflected the mood of much of the nation, a feeling that the nation was "bloviating" while Ike played golf. It was the constant theme of John Kennedy that autumn, that we must get moving again.

Senator Fulbright is certainly not immune to the undercurrents of public feeling. Indeed, he seems to reflect them most sensitively and long before other politicans catch the trend. While World War II was in progress, he reflected the deep-seated, but rarely spoken, horror of the slaughter and waste. When the Russians began trampling into Eastern Europe, he was appalled at the Soviet "opportunism and fanaticism," the subject of his speech of May 17, 1946. He was frightened by the Dulles brinkmanship and the McCarthy terror, and worried by the Eisenhower do-nothing, and it now appears that millions of silent Americans agreed with him. Finally, his active concern over a spreading war in Southeast Asia touched a chord of American sentiment most politicians had overlooked.

In that same year, 1960, Senator Fulbright seized upon the U-2 incident to demonstrate what he considered the ineptness of the Eisenhower regime.

Eisenhower and Khrushchev had agreed upon a summit meeting in Paris in the late spring. Eisenhower wanted to leave office with the mantle of peace upon him. His chosen successor, Vice-President Nixon, was looking forward to running as the nominee of the "peace party," although he was one of the most militant hawks in Washington, even dismaying a convention of newspaper editors with his proposal for intervention in Southeast Asia.

On May 1, or two weeks before the summit, a U-2 or high-flying American spy plane was shot down well inside Russia. When, some days later, Moscow announced an American plane had been downed, a cover story was invented in Washington. NASA, the space agency, identified this as a weather plane that had strayed off course. The Soviets, obviously delighted at catching us in a lie, produced the pilot and his secret gear. President Eisenhower admitted the truth and took personal responsibility. The Administration adopted a Dullesian view: we did what we did because we were the good guys, and they were the bad.

Khrushchev exploited the Washington statements to break up the Paris conference. On May 24, the Foreign Relations Committee, at Fulbright's suggestion, voted a full inquiry into the U-2 incident and its effect upon foreign policy. Charles E. Bohlen, former U.S. Ambassador to Russia, who accompanied Eisenhower to Paris as an adviser, testified, "Had there been no plane incident, I believe the conference would have run its full course. The plane incident, the whole development connected with this, moved things into a totally new dimension."

Senator Fulbright commented, "Suppose a Russian counterpart of the U-2 had come down over Kansas City on May 1. This event in itself would have brought speeches in the Senate powerful enough to rock the Capitol dome with denunciations of the perfidy of the Soviets on the eve of the summit conference and with demands that the President not go to Paris. But then reflect how much more violent the reaction here would have been if Mr. Khrushchev had said he was personally responsible for the flight and at the same time left the impression that he had every intention of trying it again."

On June 28, Fulbright presented the Committee's report to the Senate and said, "It is never pleasant to admit error in our private lives. It is far more painful for a great nation to admit that its policies have been lacking in wisdom and foresight, and one may be sure that whoever calls attention to the errors will not be thanked for his effort."

He listed what he thought to be the errors: the overflights should have been stopped well before the Paris conference. "Little or no consideration was given to the international consequences of a failure on May 1." The cover story was too specific, "and made us look ridiculous when the full extent of Soviet knowledge was revealed. . . . The gravest mistake was made when the President assumed responsibility for the flight." This declaration was without precedent, and put Eisenhower on the spot; the blame rightly should have been borne by the intelligence agency. "The chief of state embodies in his person the sovereignty and dignity of his country. It is totally unacceptable for one chief of state to impinge upon the sovereignty of another, and much less for him to assert the right to do so."

Finally, Fulbright said, "the self-righteous attitude" of the Government complicated the delicate international situation. This "must have been unbearably provocative to the Soviet Government and contributed substantially to the violence and intemperate bad manners of Mr. Khrushchev at Paris."

The Senator asked that closer control be maintained over intelligence operations, so that incidents like this did not recur. He has consistently criticized the CIA for making foreign policy, and in 1966 tried to have members of the Foreign Relations Committee added to the so-called "watchdog committee" composed exclusively of Armed Services Committee Senators.

The Administration sent chubby, white-haired Alexander Wiley, the ranking Republican on the Committee, to do battle with Fulbright. He was known for his jokes and flowery speeches about cheese. Wiley complained, "The biggest noise and greatest effort to pin blame on U.S. policy seems to be coming—second only to Moscow—from the chairman of the Foreign Relations Committee." He thanked God for Eisenhower and his "honesty and integrity," and said, "by his noble, statesmanlike actions he has made us all proud of him."

Senator Fulbright replied that Wiley's arguments "consist of self-righteous statements. He blames everything on the Communists, and that makes the whole matter very simple. Our Government does not make mistakes, in his opinion, and it interprets every setback as a victory, whether it be the failure of the Paris summit conference or the withdrawal by the Japanese Government of its invitation to the President to visit the country."

Senator Kennedy joined in the criticism, saying America should have expressed regret over the U-2 flight. We had violated international law, and if there were any value to a summit meeting, this slight effort should have been made to keep it going.

These two, Fulbright and Kennedy, were much alike, well educated in American and British schools, somewhat aloof from "the Club" of the Senate, and contemptuous of political clichés. They differed in two important ways. Kennedy was terribly ambitious; Fulbright was content to stay where he was. Kennedy was a part of the Eastern Establishment and Fulbright came from a far different milieu, the Southwest. He was drawn to Johnson, rather than Kennedy, and was disappointed that the convention chose the latter. Later, he came to admire Kennedy whose American University speech was very near the basic Fulbright philosophy. In 1966, in the great parting of the ways between Fulbright and Johnson, the assassinated President's brother, Robert, took up many of the Senator's views.

In the 1960 campaign, Senator Fulbright provided ammunition for Senator Kennedy by needling the State Department, and demanding that the Administration make public a study of worldwide opinion which showed America's prestige at a low ebb. Vice-President Nixon unhappily replied, "I think it's time for my opponent and those who support him to quit downgrading the United States of America."

The election of John Kennedy altered the role of Senator Fulbright considerably. Kennedy wanted him as his Secretary of State, but the Senator knew his free spirit could never fit into this confining role as manager of a vast enterprise, protocol shuffler, Presidential hand holder, and inter-governmental intriguer. He became, instead, a friendly critic, but one not beholden to the Administration, expressing his strong and often prophetic views privately to the President and members of his Cabinet. His first critique was made in late March, 1961.

The coming invasion of Cuba by a refugee army was the worst-kept secret in the world. Newspapers in both the Americas and Europe published accounts of the training camp in Guatemala, and speculated on the strategy. Émigré leaders quarreled in public. The Havana Radio broacast detailed propaganda stories of the leaders, equipment, training and tactics. There was a good deal of word-of-mouth reportage in the diplomatic community.

At a casual meeting with President Kennedy in March, Fulbright briefly raised questions about the plan, which he knew about only from the press. Kennedy invited Fulbright to travel with him on his plane to Florida on March 29. Before the trip, Fulbright talked to Pat Holt, the Committee staff expert on Latin America, and they worked on a memorandum, which the Senator presented to the President on the flight.

He discovered to his surprise this was the eleventh hour. Kennedy aides on the planes were talking excitedly about the invasion, as if it were a ski outing or a Fourth of July picnic. "They didn't seem to have any idea of what they were getting into," he remarked later. "It was just a lark to them."

The memorandum which President Kennedy studied over the Easter holiday made several prophetic points.

Castro, the Senator said, was strengthening his hold, and we could not count on his regime's collapse, or its overthrow from within. The exiles were likely to run up against so much resistance on their landings, they would have to call upon the United States for help. "The question would then arise of whether the United States would be willing to let the enterprise fail (in the probably futile hope of concealing the U.S. role) or whether the United States would respond with progressive assistance. This would include ultimately the use of armed force; and if we came to that, even under the paper cover of legitimacy, we would have undone the work of thirty years of trying to live down earlier interventions. We would also have assumed the responsibility for public order in Cuba, and in the circumstance this would unquestionably be an endless can of worms."

Too, "the United States problem in Latin America is not with governments; it is with people, particularly with workers, peasants and students," and their demands for radical social reform. Our attempt to overthrow Castro "would be denounced from the Rio Grande to Patagonia as an example of imperialism and as the conclusive answer to those who felt the 1960 election presaged a change in U.S. policy."

The Democratic Revolutionary Front of refugees did not have the strong and dynamic leadership to appeal to the masses.

The operation violated the spirit, if not the letter, of the charter of the Organization of American States, treaties and American laws. Laws prohibited enlisting, recruiting, training, arming "foreign military expeditions" unless it was otherwise permitted, as in lend-lease. The Senator noted, "To give this activity even covert support is a piece with the hypocrisy and cynicism for which the United States is constantly denouncing the Soviet Union. This point will not be lost on the rest of the world—nor on our own consciences for that matter."

A few days later in Washington, the President talked over the memorandum with Fulbright. Kennedy was plainly tense and disturbed. It is not clear that, at this moment, he appreciated the memorandum. Emotionally and politically, Kennedy had painted himself into a corner. As a major campaign issue, he cried that the Eisenhower–Nixon Administration had allowed Communism to "come within ninety miles of our shores." He added, "What can a new administration do to end this drift? . . . We must let Mr. Castro know that we do not intend to be pushed around any longer."

But after his election, the CIA handed him, almost as a *fait accompli,* an expedition against Castro. The plan arose in the Eisenhower days, and Guatemala, the host for the émigrés, was anxious to get rid of them. Kennedy had three choices: to toss out the scheme, modify it, or go ahead. There was considerable pressure to enlarge the American role, specifically to provide a standby Air Force group to bomb and strafe if the initial landings failed. Vice-President Johnson strongly backed this view.

If Kennedy accepted Fulbright's advice, he would face the stinging comments of Nixon and GOP leaders that he had "chickened out" after such bold talk on the hustings. This argument was extremely important to him them.

A final review took place April 4 in the State Department. Fulbright was the devil's advocate.

The chief architect of the Bay of Pigs plan, Allen Dulles, the urbane CIA director, did most of the talking. He explained that 1,400 *émigrés,* armed and trained, would land at the Bay of Pigs. They would be given air cover by a squadron of B-26's flown by Cuban crews. CIA would transmit news of the landings to Cuba by special transmitters. The people would rise against Castro. If they were slow to respond, the invaders would go to the mountains and carry on guerrilla warfare from there.

The President called on the chairman of the Joint Chiefs of Staff, General Lyman Lemnitzer. He asked if the plan were "militarily feasible."

General Lemnitzer replied, "If the assumptions of Mr. Dulles are correct, the plan is militarily feasible."

At Fulbright's turn, he said, "Cuba is a thorn in our flesh, but not a dagger in our heart. Our pride rather than our security is at stake here, and we have a great deal to lose. This action would be a violation of our treaties. It would damage us politically in many areas, particularly in Latin America, Asia and Africa, where Communist propaganda has been trying without much success to brand us 'imperialists' and 'warmongers.' "

Also, "I have no evidence that the Cuban people are able and willing at this point to assist any invasion from the outside."

Dulles countered that CIA had highly accurate reports on Cuban sentiment. As it turned out, these reports came from inflamed and imaginative refugees and were without objective corroboration.

Senator Fulbright asked what would happen if the enterprise were called off.

President Kennedy let Dulles answer. He said this would be a disaster. All of Latin America would look upon us as a nation that betrayed its friends. Opposition to Communism would wither away in the southern continent.

"A man's opposition to tyranny doesn't depend on an outsider giving him a gun," Fulbright responded. He argued that the danger from Cuba to the United States was too slight, and the consequences of this move too great. He added, "This may change, and Cuba bears watching. If they should get atomic weapons or missiles from the Russians, we would be justified then in taking direct action to remove the threat."

Two of those present were sympathetic to Fulbright: Adlai Stevenson and Chester Bowles. Stevenson said such an enterprise would be difficult to justify in the United Nations.

The Senator was surprised by Secretary Rusk's acquiescence. He not only agreed to it, he justified the operation. Later, Fulbright remarked, "The Secretary's job was to give the President an accurate picture of the likely political reaction in Latin America, so the President could at least weigh it in the balance."

Fulbright, of course, was overruled. His prophecy was correct. The Cubans did not rise up. The escort planes were shot down. Vice-President Johnson wanted American Air Force planes to enter the battle, saying that we must "will the means" for victory. In the agony of reappraisal, President Kennedy said wistfully, "I should have listened to Senator Fulbright. He was the only one who was right." He wondered whether, if Fulbright had been President and had been under as much pressure as he, he would have gone ahead with the invasion.

One can only guess, but there is an innate stubbornness in Fulbright that stiffens his back in times of great pressure. Indeed, as pressure on him mounts, his assistants can almost see the stiffening process.

A year and a half later, Senator Fulbright was called in again for advice. There was a new Cuban crisis. A Presidential jet picked him up in Arkansas where he was campaigning for reelection. The plane went on to Georgia for Senator Russell, chairman of the Armed Services Committee. They speculated on the emergency, supposing it was the threat of Soviet missiles. This, too, Fulbright had seen as a possibility four years before. He said then, "We have treated constant Soviet preoccupation with our overseas bases as sort of an unreasonable Soviet preoccupation. Speaking for myself, I am frank to admit that I might find myself plagued by an obsession against Soviet bases, if their ballistic launching facilities were in the Caribbean or Mexico."

The two Senators agreed that if missiles were in Cuba, the United States had no alternative. We must get them out, presumably by force.

What happened was this: Khrushchev in an attempt to restore the balance of terror had placed intermediate range missiles in Cuba. It was the first proof that the U.S.S.R. had only a limited supply of long-range ICBM's which could reach America. It was the gamble of a man reaching the end of his political tether. (In 1966, as President Johnson's star went down, Fulbright in private was frankly worried lest he too attempt some rash act.)

Of this White House meeting, the Senator has recalled: "We

convened at the White House at 5 P.M., and were briefed by the President and his advisers on the crisis and on the decisions which had already been taken on how to deal with it. When the President asked for comments, Senator Russell and I advocated the invasion of Cuba by American forces. I, as explained in a memorandum I had hastily prepared, on the ground that a blockade involving as it might a direct, forcible confrontation with Russian ships, would be more likely to provoke a nuclear war, than an invasion which would pit American soldiers against Cuban soldiers and allow the Russians to stand aside.

"Had I been able to formulate my views on the basis of facts rather than a guess as to the nature of the situation, I might have made a different recommendation. In any case, the recommendation I made represented my best judgment at that time, and I thought it my duty to offer it."

Later Senator Fulbright expressed his praise of Kennedy's handling of the episode. He said, "In the Cuban missile crisis, the United States proved to the Soviet Union that a policy of aggression and adventure involved unacceptable risks. . . . It seems reasonable to suggest that the character of the Cold War has, for the present at least, been profoundly altered: by the drawing back of the Soviet Union from extremely aggressive policies; by the explicit repudiation, by both sides, of a policy of 'total victory'; and by the establishment of an American strategic superiority which the Soviet Union appears to have tacitly accepted because it will be exercised by the United States with responsibility and restraint."

In the brief noon, from January 1961 to John Kennedy's assassination, Senator Fulbright worked closely with the Administration. One of his happiest tasks was to help put across President Kennedy's great and lasting triumph, the Nuclear Test Ban Treaty. With Fulbright leading the campaign, the Senate ratified the treaty 80 to 19 on September 24, 1963. This was particularly satisfying to the Senator, because in 1956 he had urged Adlai Stevenson to call for a test ban in the Presidential campaign.

Yet, the Senator from Arkansas remained not a member of the Inner Establishment, but a friendly critic.

XIV

IN THE EARLY spring of 1961, not long after the Bay of Pigs, an assistant handed Senator Fulbright a letter from an Arkansas constituent. He read it with a puzzled frown, looked up and asked, "What kind of madness is this?"

The letter told of a "strategy for survival" conference at Fort Smith, Arkansas, sponsored by the U.S. Army. One of the speakers was Dr. Clifton L. Ganus, Jr., vice president of Harding College at Searcy, Arkansas, sometimes called "the West Point of the ultra-right," and he had said, "Your Representative in this area has voted 89 percent of the time to aid and abet the Communist Party."

The Congressman, of Fulbright's old district in the northwest hill country, was James W. Trimble, a gentle and conservative former judge, an Army reserve major, Legionnaire, Methodist and Mason. That anyone should accuse him of being Communist-inspired or -directed was to the Senator "absolutely unbelievable." That the Army should sponsor such nonsense was equally astounding. These things did not happen in a decent, well-organized society.

Months later, after the hue and cry from the Senator's denouncement of military political propaganda on the home front died down, he said mildly, "I couldn't sit still and let them say dirty stuff about Jim Trimble." More important, Fulbright saw "this swinish blight" rising again.

On this April day, Senator Fulbright told his assistant, Jack Yingling, to bring him all the information he could gather on the Fort Smith conference, checking both in Arkansas and with the Pentagon. He has the scholar's respect for known facts, and rarely makes a speech without either cramming on the subject or conducting a Committee investigation.

A few days later, the Senator had more information. On April 14 and 15, "strategy for survival conferences" were held in Fort Smith and Fayetteville and Little Rock. The conferences seemed, by accident or design, to be zeroing in on Fulbright territory. He was up for reelection the next year. The printed program said the purpose was to "provide an open forum for a frank analysis and discussion . . . of the threats the free world faces from world Communism and the strategy that must be used successfully against it."

The views expressed were, to put it mildly, outrageously opposed to Fullbright's. The speakers were identified with that school that believed the United States had been sold out from within. A speaker at all three meetings was Robert Morris, former counsel of the Senate's version of the House Un-American Activities Committee, the Internal Security Subcommittee. Morris had run with rightist backing for the Senate seat of Clifford Case, the New Jersey Republican moderate, and was badly defeated. Morris spoke on, "No Wonder We Are Losing" and "We Are Losing from Within."

Harding College was involved in the meetings. Its then president had been active in "For America," a curious coalition of rightists, MacArthur generals and isolationists. The college produced the film, *Communism on the Map,* popular in the right-wing circuit.

The tenor of the conferences was that agents of Communism were busily at work within the United States, and planning to take it over. Subversion operated in the seats of the mighty. However, this view of subversion was somewhat different from that of the FBI. A Congressman who voted for mild social reform, as Trimble, was denounced as doing the work of Communism. Tracts from the lunatic fringe were openly passed out.

Fulbright certainly did not deny the right of these people to be heard, but he was startled that an agency of the Federal Government, the Army, was sponsoring the meeting and had collected a captive audience of reservists, businessmen and schoolchildren.

Letters of outrage came to the Senator from Arkansas. A lawyer wrote, "The thing that concerns me most was the prominent part of the Army in planning and promoting these meetings. General Bullock, the area commander, went all out and personally persuaded the Armed Services Committee of the Little Rock Chamber of Commerce to sponsor the meeting in Little Rock. One reserve officer was placed on active duty to promote the meeting. (The program showed this individual in uniform with his brigadier general's star and the title 'State Coordinator.') Attendance was pushed through the Arkansas National Guard and reserve units. Through this activity the meetings and information disseminated had in the public eye the stamp of approval of the Army and National Government."

The first diagnosis of the Senator's staff was that this was a warm-up of a well-advertised and -financed campaign by rightists to defeat Fulbright in the Democratic primary. Rightists had been boasting of getting money from Texas oil millionaires to trounce Fulbright, and Governor Orval Faubus at that point was behaving remarkably like an accomplice.

"But why," asked the Senator, really puzzled, "is the Army mixed up in it?"

The Senator then discovered this was not purely an Arkansas operation. Senator Joseph S. Clark, the Pennsylvania Democrat, told him of a similar rightist-military conference in Pittsburgh. This was a "Fourth-Dimensional Warfare Seminar" sponsored by the Greater Pittsburgh Chamber of Commerce with the aid of the commanding generals of the Army's Second Army and XXI Corps. A civilian aide to the Secretary of the Army was cochairman, and a letter from him appeared on the program on stationery with the seal of the "United States of America War Office."

A retired admiral, Chester Ward, avowed that some of President Kennedy's advisers had philosophies "regarding foreign affairs that would chill the typical American," and named Adlai Stevenson, and George Kennan, the distinguished Kremlinologist and Ambassador to Yugoslavia. The admiral, according to a clipping Senator Clark showed Fulbright, said he "fears a national sellout of freedom in order to buy peace."

Here the centurion's deep craving for the denied total victory, his angry scorn of the calm of peace. The old warriors suffered from the frustrations of modern strategy. They had been trained in their academies and war colleges to believe in nothing but victory. Admiral Ward was simply more articulate. (On his retirement, Ward had been awarded the Legion of Merit for his "realistically expressed convictions concerning the Cold War and the Communist consipiracy," which to Fulbright was evidence of how the official machinery of the military promoted and honored the Cold War mythology.)

At the Pittsburgh meeting, Admiral Ward told his audience—

businessmen, reservists and schoolchildren bussed in—that any negotiations with Russia on disarmament were "appeasement" and that
American foreign policy was playing into Soviet hands. He blamed a
host of events—the U.S.S.R. biting into Eastern Europe, the Communist victory on the Chinese mainland, the French defeat in Indochina,
American foreign policy reactions, and particular individuals. He said
Stevenson "accelerated" the "surrender" to Communism.

Another speaker, Colonel William H. Kintner, chief of long-range
planning for the Army, advocated "an integrated national strategy
based on military power to turn back Communism and extend the
frontiers of freedom." The United States, then, should heavily arm
itself and use military force to drive the Communists out of strategic
areas of Europe and Asia. The participants were told "What You
Can Do in the Fight Against Communism," including:

"Be on the alert for Communist sympathizers in your community,
especially those who can mold public opinion."

"Identify public officials and policies displaying softness toward
Communism. Demand a more patriotic attitude."

"Be wary of films which stress social and moral depravity. Moral
and social subversion are recognized operational methods of the
Communist Party to weaken the moral fiber of this nation."

The seminar was asking for vigilante activities on a wide scale
undreamed of even by McCarthy. A Communist "sympathizer" was
anyone to the left of J. Edgar Hoover; the rightist demonology even
included General Eisenhower.

Senator Fulbright was horrified.

More and more pieces of information came in from across the
nation, in newspaper clippings, magazine articles and letters. The
Senator talked to several correspondents who had written of the
"seminars." Generals and admirals sat on the stages at military-
sponsored seminars while the chief circuit riders of the far right
hectored audiences with their odd ideas. A letter to the editor of *The
Seattle Times* said, "My concern is with the concept which suggests
that any branch of the Armed Forces is the appropriate vehicle for
the dissemination to the civilian population, and particularly to our
youth, of proper attitudes for patriotism and concern for our democratic ideals. This is the nut of the issue."

A number of Senators became interested in Fulbright's information-
gathering, and supplied data. He received reports of out-and-out
partisan harangues, attacks upon Congressmen and Governors, the

passing out of John Birch Society and anti-Semitic tracts at the seminars or "alerts," as they were sometimes called.

He heard, too, of disconcerting troop indoctrination programs, as those of Major General Edwin Walker's in Germany. (The Inspector General's report of this said: "General Walker did personally execute a broad troop information and indoctrination effort within his command to include dependents, that did not completely comply with Army regulations . . . by making speeches, inflammatory and derogatory to past public officials, arranging for speakers who gave inflammatory speeches, quoting and recommending material which was in varying degrees nonfactual, biased and inflammatory . . . Major General Walker, acting in an official capacity, did attempt to influence the members of the 24th Infantry Division and their dependents in the selection of Senatorial and Congressional candidates by recommending the use of voting materials not obtained through military sources . . .") Another high-ranking officer, Vice Admiral Robert Goldthwaite, in a letter to men under his command, recommended they write the Birch Society for information "to identify public officials and policies displaying softness toward communism" and "demand a more patriotic attitude . . . join a citizens group dedicated to upholding American principles and resisting socialism-communism . . . demand that the nation take the offensive in the cold war with the objective of victory over communism."

Senator Fulbright's studies showed a curious pattern among those who undertook these activities. They were chiefly old Asian hands, officers who had served under General MacArthur in World War II or in Korea. General Walker, as a case, was a field commander in Korea.

In June, 1948, MacArthur, in an interview with a writer for the *China Monthly,* a magazine closely identified with the Chinese Nationalists, had been described as "the greatest living American" and quoted as saying that America's problems in Asia—the Nationalists had recently surrendered in Yennan Province—came from "stupidity at the top—treason just below."

A new level of activity by retired officers closely allied with MacArthur began after the Republican Party convention of 1952. When some of MacArthur's backers formed the For America group to gain political control of the Republican Party. Its sponsors included: Hamilton Fish, the onetime isolationist Congressman who in 1943 attacked the Fulbright resolution; "Colonel" Robert McCormick, isolationist publisher of *The Chicago Tribune,* a paper that unfailingly regarded Fulbright suspiciously because of his Oxford degrees, and several of MacArthur's former assistants, all retired. They were Brigadier General Bonner Fellers, his press chief; Lieutenant General George E. Stratemayer, his air commander in Korea, and General James A. Van Fleet, commander of the Eighth Army in Korea.

For America favored withdrawal from the United Nations, repeal of the Federal income tax, and opposition to NATO and civil-rights legislation.

In 1956 this organization hoped to so splinter the vote for President that the election could be thrown into the House of Representatives, and elect General MacArthur. At a "Ten Million Americans for MacArthur" rally in New York sponsored by For America, Senator McCarthy called the general "the contemporary George Washington," and added, "neither Douglas MacArthur nor Washington, if the decision had been his, would have extended the hand of friendship to the Soviet Union as was done last summer in Geneva [by President Eisenhower] . . . General MacArthur's present exile is eloquent testimony to the fact that the reigning liberal bipartisan machine has also cast into exile the principles of national honor, national wisdom, and national freedom . . . General MacArthur's most valuable service has been to put our fight against world Communism in its proper perspective."

A report of the Anti-Defamation League, brought to Senator Fulbright's attention, told of the recruitment of generals and admirals by rightist groups. It said, "Many of the extreme right-wing groups ally themselves to or make use of military figures. The Christian Anti-Communist Crusade uses retired General Wedemeyer (ex-chief of staff to Chiang Kai-shek) at its forums. Billy Hargis' Anti-Christian Crusade employs General Willoughby (MacArthur's intelligence chief in Korea) as its 'intelligence aide.' The John Birch Society's national advisors include a score of retired generals and admirals and one former sergeant, Matthew McKeon, who was court-martialed for leading marine trainees in a death march."

At this point in his investigation, Fulbright began to suspect, but said nothing publicly of it, a secret liaison between a sector of the military and the far right to seize political power, perhaps even install General MacArthur a la De Gaulle.

The Senator saw Secretary of Defense Robert McNamara at a

social function, and asked him in that calm, amiable, rather amused tone he uses for social conversation, "What in the hell are your generals up to?"

The Secretary, of course, wanted to know more, and Fulbright told him. McNamara was so new on the job he did not know of the seminars, and was genuinely shocked.

"I wish you'd write a memorandum and send it to the President, and he'll pass it on to me. This will give me something to work from," the Secretary said. "The sooner the better."

Senator Fulbright and Yingling went over all their materials. A new piece of evidence told of the origin. In May, 1958, Admiral Arthur W. Radford, an old Asian hand, then chairman of the Joint Chiefs of Staff, presented a directive to President Eisenhower that would authorize the military to conduct seminars for civilians. It was signed by President Eisenhower. (Later, General Eisenhower told Senate investigators he did not recall a directive "specifically directing military involvement in the internal problem.") At any rate, the directive existed.

Ringing through all the seminars was the call for "total victory." At a seminar in Chicago in September, 1960, Admiral Radford called for "total victory over the Communist system—not stalemate." He added, "We are confused by fears, the fear of gaining some advantage, the fear of seeming imperialistic, the fear of being unpopular. The massive power providentially given us is frustrated by an abstract idealism that is apart from reality and does not recognize the basic conditions for the effective use of power."

In his military memorandum to President Kennedy, Fulbright stated that the harsh reality behind the concept of "total victory" was "protracted conflict" with Communist nations. This would require, he said: huge secret operations for armed uprisings, a Cold War orientation in American schools and colleges, curtailment of civil liberties as the nation riveted its effort on this mighty undertaking, and "setting up a savage dichotomy between the Communist and Western world, and of making almost every issue a matter of irreconcilable competition."

The seeds of the ultra philosophy were evident to him. He wrote, "Pride in victory and frustration in restraint during the Korean War led to MacArthur's revolt and McCarthyism. . . . If the military is infected with the virus of rightwing radicalism, the danger is worthy of attention. If the military believes the public is, the danger is enhanced. If, by the process of the military 'educating' the public, the fever of both groups is raised, the danger is great indeed. Perhaps it is farfetched to call forth the revolt of the French generals [in 1958] as an example of the ultimate danger. Nevertheless, military officers, French or American, have some common characteristics arising from the profession and there are numerous 'fingers on the trigger' throughout the world."

He recommended a set of reforms: the directive should be reconsidered, military propaganda and troop indoctrination programs should be brought under civilian control, the role of the National War College should be reviewed and limited (the War College is the graduate school for combat officers and strategic concepts), and a long-range program dominated by a board of civilian educators undertaken to expose officers to history, government and foreign policy.

When the memorandum was circulated in the Pentagon, the effect, as one observer noted, "was like dropping a bomb in a cocktail party." The party, that is the military "alerts," was over.

One incident is worth relating. It gives an idea of the fury created by the memorandum. One morning while Fulbright was at a meeting of the Foreign Relations Committee, Strom Thurmond, the South Carolina Senator, a reserve major general, and a speaker at rightist meetings, burst in. He demanded to see the Senator. A flustered secretary directed him to Lee Williams, the administrative assistant.

"I demand a copy of that memorandum," he cried.

Williams was not exactly sure what memorandum Senator Thurmond wanted, and tried tactfully to find out. Thurmond appeared to think the assistant was trying to put him off, and became a bit irate. The conversation was somewhat confused. Thurmond is not the easiest person to understand because of his thick accent. Finally, Williams perceived it was the military memorandum.

He said apologetically, "I would be very glad to give you a copy of the memorandum, Senator, but we don't have a copy here. We really don't."

Thurmond shouted, "I must have a copy of that memorandum within an hour."

"I don't know how that can be done, sir."

"I want that on my desk in an hour." He turned and strode out.

Williams sought out Senator Fulbright at the Committee and recounted the incident.

Fulbright said, "Don't worry about Strom. Who does he think you are, one of his corporals?"

Senator Thurmond did not get the memorandum.

A few days later Fulbright put in *The Congressional Record*. He told the Senate, "I have been surprised by a display of intense interest in a memorandum on propaganda activities of military personnel which I have submitted to the Secretary of Defense. Perhaps I am naïve. I must confess that I was unaware that the subject was one which would arouse great controversy. It was based on my strong belief in the principle of military subordination to civilian control. There has been a strong tradition in this country that it is not the function of the military to educate the public on political issues. Military officers are not elected by the people, and they have no responsibility for the formulation of policies other than military policies. I did not think this constitutional tradition was controversial.

"I must confess to another misapprehension. I was unaware that it was the custom, the practice, or the right of Senators to demand access to the private correspondence of their colleagues. Although I should not have thought it was my duty to open my private files, I would have been quite willing to show the memorandum in question to any Senator who courteously requested to see it. I am not willing, however, to comply with an ultimatum such as I received from the junior Senator from South Carolina on July 21 demanding that he be provided with a copy of the memorandum 'within the next hour.' "

A parody on the Lewis Carroll classic featuring Senator Fulbright and the military was circulated in the Pentagon and Capitol Hill:

> You are old, J. William, the young man said,
> And your hair has become a bit white
> And yet you stand Pentagon brass on their heads;
> Do you think at your age it is right?
>
> In my youth, J. William replied with a drawl
> I feared it might injure the brain.
> But now that I'm perfectly sure they have none,
> Why I do it again and again!

President Kennedy at his news conference on August 10 supported Fulbright, and said nothing could cause more grave damage to the prestige and integrity of the Armed Forces than being mixed up in partisan arguments.

Eleven days later, Senator Fulbright braved the most critical audience of his career. He spoke at the opening session of the National War College and the Industrial College of the Armed Forces at the invitation of the Secretary of Defense. Those below him on the floor were officers and military contractors. His title was "Public Policy and Military Responsibility." He was speaking as an individual Senator.

He began by saying, "It is the constitutional right of all Americans, civilians and military, to hold whatever political views they are led to by conviction and conscience, be they moderate or extreme. Military men in their official status, however, are committing not only themselves but the prestige of the armed services when they promote or appear to sponsor partisan political meetings. They are therefore doing a disservice both to the American people and to the armed services when they lend their support to any groups or organizations which espouse policies that run counter to those of the Commander in Chief and which have the effect of generating distrust and suspicion among the people.

"The appeal of certain ideas espoused by radicals of the right is not difficult to understand. To a nation beset by onerous challenges and responsibilities, they offer deceptively quick and simple solutions. It seems to me that it is these extremists who are advocating a soft approach. Their oversimplifications and their baseless generalities reflect the softness of those who cannot bear to face the burdens of a continuing struggle against a powerful and resourceful enemy. Those who seek to meet the challenge—or, in reality, to evade it—by bold adventures abroad and witch hunts at home are the real devotees of softness—the softness of seeking escape from painful realities by resort to illusory panaceas."

In his soft voice without the overtones of strong persuasion, he stated that radical extremism, either right or left, is the true enemy of democratic society. They may form an unholy combine of "disloyal opposition" which destroyed the Weimar Republic of Germany and plagued postwar Italy and France.

Senator Fulbright looked at the revolutionary world in which Americans must live and operate: "The realities of American foreign policy lie in the fact that the world has undergone revolutionary changes since World War II and that the end of this historic upheaval is not yet in sight. To live in a world of revolution, and to attempt to shape the forces of change toward constructive purposes requires

A future statesman is a
year old.

Senator Fulbright, as a boy, is at left, above his mother, in this snapshot of
the Fulbright family of Fayetteville, Arkansas.

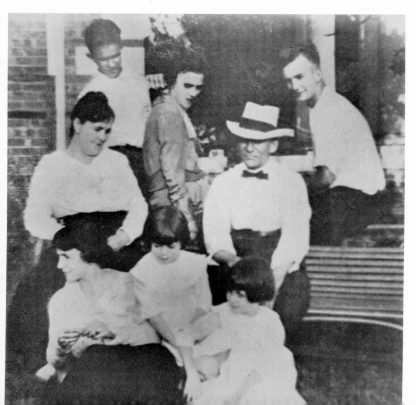

Fulbright was a star halfback at the University of Arkansas, and his exploits are still recalled in the football folklore of the Southwest.

An account of the Rhodes scholarship award in *The Beaumont (Texas) Daily Journal.*

THE BEAUMONT DAILY JOURNAL

kholders to V

Star Athlete, Student

Crack Football And Tennis Player - at University (
Arkansas Wins Rhodes Scholarship

FAYETTEVILLE, Ark., Feb. 16.—
J. W. Fulbright, 19-year-old University of Arkansas senior, winner of the Rhodes scholarship for Arkansas, is one of the most versatile students that ever attended the state university.

He has played halfback on the Arkansas University team for the last three years, receiving his third varsity football letter at the close of the football season just past. He also holds two varsity letters in tennis and was captain of the tennis team last spring.

Fulbright is the youngest student ever to have received the Rhodes scholarship in Arkansas. The scholarship is good for a three-year's tenure at the University of Oxford, England. It carries with it an annual stipend of 350 pounds.

Fulbright will be graduated from the University of Arkansas College of Arts and Sciences at the end of this term in February, but will continue his studies in law at the university for the remainder of the school year.

He will take up his residence in Oxford in October, 1925, where he will specialize in history and economics.

Young Fullbright is from Boonville, Ark., and is a cousin of John W Fullbright of Beaumont.

J. W. FULBRIGHT.

RIGHT: A pensive young man at Oxford.

BELOW: As a member of the Oxford tennis team (1928) Fulbright is at the left in the front row.

The old lodge outside Fayetteville where Fulbright spent his happiest hours as a university professor and president. He is in the foreground by a tree.

Fulbright at the farm with his dog and cattle, 1940.

LEFT: Senator and Mrs. Fulbright on a fishing trip to Colorado, where they vacation every year. The picture is 1956 or 1958.

BELOW: "Miss Roberta," the Senator's mother, in her Fayetteville home, 1950.

ABOVE: As a freshman Congressman who put through a resolution calling for a world organization, he is congratulated by, left, Sol Bloom, chairman of the House Foreign Affairs Committee, and a senior Republican on the committee, Rep. Charles Eaton of New Jersey. BELOW: Representative Fulbright in 1944 when he attended a conference on postwar education in London. At right is Richard A. Butler, then British Minister of Education.

ABOVE: Senator and Mrs. Fulbright greet Fulbright exchange scholars in Japan.

RIGHT: Senator Fulbright with a Japanese expert on "fish farming," a process developed by the Chinese thousands of years ago. Arkansas farmers rotate "fish farming" with rice by flooding the fields. The Senator helped introduce this technique, and obtained funds for a research station at Stuttgart, Arkansas.

OPPOSITE PAGE: The disappointments of the 1952 Presidential election are momentarily forgotten by Senator Fulbright and his good friend, Adlai Stevenson, on an Arkansas hunting trip. From left to right, Senator Russell Long of Louisiana, Fulbright, Senator John Sparkman (Stevenson's running mate), Governor Orval Faubus of Arkansas, said to be the LBJ candidate to run against Fulbright in 1968, and Stevenson. *(Courtesy Sports Illustrated)*

The Senator receives an honorary degree from President Clark Kerr of the University of California at Berkeley in 1960. He has more honorary degrees than any ot'er man in the Senate. *(Courtesy ASUC Photography)*

A Senate Foreign Relations Committee luncheon in March, 1960, in honor of British Prime Minister Harold Macmillan. Left to right, Macmillan, Fulbright, the host; Sir Harold Caccia, British Ambassador to Washington, Senators Alexander Wiley of Wisconsin, John J. Sparkman of Alabama, Wayne Morse of Oregon and Russell B. Long of Louisiana.

ABOVE: Fulbright receiving a pen from President Kennedy at a bill-signing ceremony, possibly the act setting up the Arms Control and Disarmament Agency. Left to right: Fulbright, Senator Hubert Humphrey, chairman of the Disarmament Subcommittee, Rep. Ross Adair of Indiana, Rep. Clement J. Zablocki of Wisconsin, Mrs. Frances P. Bolton of Ohio, all members of the House Foreign Affairs Committee, and President Kennedy. BELOW: Three antagonists in a happier mood, Senator Wayne Morse, Fulbright and Secretary of State Dean Rusk. This apparently was taken following a discussion before the Committee of Latin American Affairs. Morse is chairman of the Latin American subcommittee.

ABOVE: This photograph is in the Senator's private office. It was taken on board the President's private plane, and Johnson has written on it, "To J. William Fulbright. Than whom there is no better. Lyndon B. Johnson. Dec. 13, 1963." BELOW: The Senator is surrounded by reporters and microphones for an impromptu press conference after a session of the Foreign Relations Committee on Vietnam.

The Senator listens skeptically while the President talks, March 20, 1966. Johnson wrote on the photograph, "To Bill, I can see I haven't been very persuasive, Lyndon B. Johnson." *(Courtesy Wide World Photos)*

patience, discipline and sustained effort. Only by the cultivation of these qualities can the American living in the 1960's hope to escape the defeatism and despair that arise when initial efforts fail to produce total victory."

He described the fifteen weeks in the spring of 1947 when American policy was radically overhauled by the Truman Doctrine and the Marshall Plan as "days of imagination and innovation." (He has since become less enthusiastic about the Truman Doctrine, believing it has overcommitted the United States, and transformed its duties into that of guardian of the world.) He added, "The crisis in the 1960's derives from our failure to adopt the now classic policy forms of 1947 to new conditions and challenges."

Senator Fulbright listed the great changes that had taken place since.

The onetime monopoly of nuclear power was gone, and the system of alliances, as NATO, no longer offered substantial protection against Communist imperialism. Instead there was "a highly unstable nuclear stalemate which Winston Churchill has called the 'balance of terror.' "

Western Europe had become politically and economically stable, although still militarily dependent on the United States. (This dependence on the American nuclear deterrent became unacceptable to France.)

Soviet foreign policy had altered from the heavy-handed tactics of Stalin to a more sophisticated, varied and challenging approach.

The former colonial and semicolonial nations of Africa, Asia and Latin America were "caught up in the emotional fervor of nationalism" and "are now the great prize in the struggle between East and West."

To meet the changing world, the Senator believed, "We must now go on to perfect new and varied instruments of foreign policy that go far beyond containment and military alliances. . . . The purpose of our foreign policy is the very gradual improvement of human life on earth. Our success is not guaranteed, and if our efforts are to be coherent and sustained we must accept this fact with sobriety and serenity. Besides patient and continuous effort, we must bring to the task a little of a sense of mission—and I emphasize little. A consuming messianism will surely lead us to false hopes and frustration, while action without purpose is action without meaning or hope."

In the beginning of his lecture, his audience looked at this neat and sober figure in the platform curiously or with hostility. Now there was animation and interest.

He ended, "If we are to meet the challenges of our times, we must reject the false and simple solutions of irresponsible extremists who cannot, or will not, accept the world as it is. We must instead dedicate ourselves to the national purpose with fortitude and discipline. These are the imperatives of military responsibility, as indeed they are the imperatives for all Americans."

His words hung a moment in silence. Then came applause from all over the hall. This applause marked the end of an ugly and perhaps threatening crisis. The American military by this signal accepted his thesis that political education was best left to the civilians. President Kennedy and Secretary McNamara were able to carry out quietly his proposals for reform without revolt or protest from the military.

XV

In the bright October day in 1961 a dusty Ford station wagon hustled along Route 40 on a ridge of the Ozark Mountains. The scent of autumn was in the air, the lingering wood smoke curling lazily in thin white streams from cabins mingling in the crisp air. Ahead, to the right, was a small country store with its faded Coca-Cola sign and a gas pump.

"Let's stop there," the man beside the driver said.

The station wagon slowed, and turned off the pavement into the gravel, the tires crunching the stones. A man, a very tall one, in blue denim overalls emerged from the store, stooping slightly to get through the door, and the driver told him, "Fill her up, please."

His companion got out, looked curiously around him. Here was the old soldier returning home after the war, the look of pleased remembrance. He was plainly not of this place now, a trim, well-dressed, waistcoated man in a city hat.

He went into the store. It was redolent with the smells of cheese and fruit and kerosene and bacon frying in a back room. He spoke to the stout, pink-cheeked woman behind the counter in a soft and pleasant drawl, "How do you do, ma'am," running the words together. "What kind of apples do you have?"

"The best." She recognized him. "Why it's Bill Fulbright! How are you, Senator?"

"I'm fine." He smiled, showing how pleased he was to be remembered. Here a Senator is like a piece of prize personal property, and addressed familiarly.

He explained, "But I'm hungry for a good eating apple. A couple of years ago, I stopped here and got some very good ones."

"Why sure, I remember that, Senator. You were on your way to Fort Smith, and it was a Saturday about this time of the year. We have those apples. Get them off of Ed Green. You remember him, he has the little orchard about five miles off the road at the next fork. It's the soil that makes them so sweet."

Senator Fulbright picked an apple from the wooden crate, shined it on the sleeve of his coat and took a bite.

"That's just the way I remembered it," he said in satisfaction. "Let me take a sack along."

The storekeeper came in. He wiped a big hand on his overalls, and the two shook hands solemnly. Ten minutes later when Fulbright's assistant came in looking for him, the three were discussing apples with great animation.

A secret of the Senator's political success is that he knows a great deal about the life of Arkansas. He has a natural curiosity and a thirst for new knowledge, and can talk about the cash crops of rural Arkansas, cotton, soy beans, rice and chicken, or even apples, with enthusiasm.

This wayside conversation was part of a test of democracy whose results were waited anxiously in much of the civilized world. Would the voters of Arkansas return their statesman to the United States Senate? Journalists from New York, Washington, St. Louis, London and other way parts were traveling the state, as if it were a tiny Balkan nation, to find the answer. They interviewed taxi drivers in Little Rock, courthouse sages, supermarket checkers and farmers. Walter Lippmann expressed his concern: "Senator Fulbright has now begun to run for reelection, and all the signs indicate that over and above the local issues in Arkansas, the campaign will be of great importance to the Nation as a whole. For an important part of the opposition to the Senator . . . comes from radical right extremists like Senator Goldwater among the Republicans and Senator Thurmond among the Democrats. It is highly significant that they have chosen to do battle not with a man of the left, but with as genuine a conservative in the great tradition of conservatism as exists in our public life today. Thus the Arkansas Senatorial campaign will bring a confrontation between traditional American conservatism and a wholly new phenomenon, a radical reaction sailing under the flag of conservatism."

The signs were ominous. A lot of the old fellows who make up the web of local politics—judges, country editors, sheriffs—were saying

Fulbright was through. He might as well face it, and not make the try. People didn't know what in the hell he was talking about, and it didn't have anything to do with the price of chickens. Governor Orval Faubus was going to take him to the cleaners.

The whole of the radical right was directing a great deal of propaganda against Fulbright into Arkansas. This drive had exploded after his military memorandum, which had been the final outrage to the ultras. He had cut off their direct pipeline to the American public with the shutdown of the military "seminars." Also, there was the accumulated bitterness of Fulbright's conflicts with General Mac-Arthur, Joe McCarthy, the "brinkmanship" of Dulles, the military, and over Cuba. The radicals on the right had marked Fulbright as a fallen angel, and thus more dangerous than an ordinary imp of Satan. American politics, at times, becomes peculiarly mixed up with fundamentalist religion.

The *Arkansas Statesman* spoke of a "conservative grassroots rebellion spreading from shore to shore. The people of Arkansas can help save the United States by defeating a man who is a symbol of anti-anti-communism." Radio stations in Texas and Louisiana were pouring out bile against the Senator into Arkansas. Fierce little tracts appeared by the thousands. A small segregationist sheet in the state cried, "Fulbright should be fired." George Benson, president of Arkansas' right-wing Harding College, said, "Fulbright has given comfort to the reds. Attempts to defend the Fulbright memorandum as an effort to keep civilian control over the military are just a lie." The *Shreveport* (Louisiana) *Journal* thundered, "Senator Fulbright's record of appeasement on Cuba and Berlin, as well as his authorship of the memorandum make him a disgrace in the Senate." A New Hampshire paper in an editorial circulated widely in Arkansas referred to him as "the despicable Fulbright." Letters full of bitter charges against the Senator, from out of state, flooded local newspapers.

The elite of the radical right, Senators Goldwater, Thurmond and Tower, and Billy James Hargis came to Arkansas. Texas oil money was slipped in via intermediaries. An Oriental voice called the Senator's office, identified itself as an employee of the Chinese Nationalist Embassy, and confided the Nationalists were contributing cash to his defeat.

The strategy was to persuade Governor Faubus to run against him. Faubus was a onetime radical of the old Populist strain and a rabble-rouser of talent. He had moved agilely to the far right, and became the hero of the hard-line segregationists, because of his defiance of Federal authority to integrate the Little Rock schools. If Faubus didn't run, then his handpicked Congressman, Dr. Dale Alford (elected by a segregationist write-in vote), would.

Fulbright was not without friends, of course. The executive secretary of the Arkansas Education Association charged that opposition to the Senator came from the far-right wing, and named Fulton Lewis, Jr., Dan Smoot, Gearald L. K. Smith, Governor Faubus, Representative Alford, and Dr. Benson. The *Little Rock Gazette* remarked, "The Fulbright opponents simply hope that enough of the John Birch type nonsense has worn through the basic horse sense of the people of Arkansas that Dr. Alford or Mr. Faubus can convince them they have been wrong about Bill Fulbright for twenty years."

Senator Fulbright listened to all the predictions of doom, usually relayed to him by Lee Williams, and said in a slow, patient, good-humored drawl, "Well, before we buy anything, we'd better go back and take a look around ourselves."

To an outsider this casual attitude might seem the height of foolish optimism. Arkansas has just the soil, many feared, where the simplistic arguments of the right could take root. In per capita income, Arkansas is the second poorest state in the union, with $3,184 as the median family income in 1960. It ranked eleventh from the bottom in literacy. Much of the land is submarginal and easily eroded. One British journalist, Kingsley Martin of *The New Statesman,* wrote in some alarm, " 'I don't know much about the John Birch Society, but it's against Communism, isn't it? I am against Communism, so maybe I ought to join it.' The speaker was a farmer in the village of Augusta, about 70 miles from Little Rock; I had fallen into a talk with him just before a meeting to hear Senator Fulbright."

On paper, the Senator had definite weaknesses. A reporter for the *Memphis Commercial Appeal* listed three after a swing about the state: he was an internationalist and cared little for Arkansas' problems, he favored Federal aid to education, and this had become a symbol of integration, and his military memorandum had been so distorted to make it appear he opposed any teaching of the ills of Communism. A fourth and little-mentioned objection was that he never showed any enthusiasm for segregation; he paid a modest lip service to it, ducked comment on the Little Rock incident and did not support the local segregationists and Governor.

If Senator Fulbright should lose the July primary, the whole nervous jelly of American politics would shift to the right, as it did when conservative Senator Millard Tydings of Maryland was defeated, in part by the McCarthy gang. Liberals on foreign policy would be silent or flee to the old clichés. Congress would adjust, regretfully but with the pragmatism of a professional, and the hard line would be back with its tensions and arms race. Southerners would have to pick up the frayed banner of "massive resistance" and give a tired rebel whoop. The Foreign Relations Committee would become again a propaganda sounding board for the Administration.

Amid this speculation, Senator Fulbright was calm and unflustered. He came back to Arkansas in the autumn of 1961, a full year ahead of the election, for a pilgrimage to the crossroads. With an innate shrewdness, he turned this monstrous attack on him to his own advantage. He spoke of the out-of-state letters to Arkansas newspapers, and said, "They are unpleasant to be sure, but I'm confident the people of this state will not be influenced by these 'foreigners.' These groups are well organized and well financed. I assume they tell their members to write these letters, just like labor unions or other organizations have their members write letters to me and other Congressmen. Their views are ultraradical."

The Senator gave fifty talks in school gymnasiums, hotel banquet rooms and church basements in every part of the state. He spoke to service clubs, PTA's and women's groups. He said modestly, "I want to find out what is on the people's minds."

This was perhaps an overinnocent remark. Certainly he wanted to find out what was on the restless public mind—how much the concerted attack of the rightists had cost him and his aloofness from the civil-rights struggle damaged him, what hopes and fears tossed in the minds of his people? But there is more to him than a calculated shrewdness. He has a faith in people that is Rousseauan. He refreshes his spirit in talking to a farmer about his electric co-op or a shopkeeper, his apples. (Once telling of a meeting with members of a rural electric co-op, he remarked, "It's a great experience. They have so much faith in the future. The last twenty years have brought them so much through electricity, they are sure the future will be as rewarding.")

Fulbright also wanted to talk to his voters, calmly and reasonably, before the heat of the campaign. He knew there is a sensitive period, long before the candidates' banners flap on Main Street and buttons are passed out, when voters generally make up their minds. Then is the time to talk and reason with them, and circulate quietly among them without loudspeakers.

He would be up early in the day in the sweet autumn landscape, he and Mrs. Fulbright and his young assistant, Norvill Jones, taking turns driving the station wagon. If there was time, he liked to stop at wayside stores. When he came into a town, he looked up the editor, often going back into the print shop among the presses and linotype to find him, and there in that pleasant clatter, talking of community affairs. There was never any pomp or ceremony about these visits.

He would climb up the wooden stairs of old buildings to see political friends and helpers, and go over local problems with them. These were leisurely affairs, in the slow, friendly manner of the South, interspersed with gossip and yarns and laughter. For a man so urbane, he adjusts easily to these meetings, and his Washington complaint about having to see people who bore him does not exist. The fact is he is not bored, but relaxed by these contacts in Arkansas.

The meeting in the evening would not be large, a few hundred people sitting quietly on folding chairs while he spoke for about ten minutes in what a British reporter referred to as "a soft, lilting accent." The Senator tends to speak less dryly, more warmly before those he thinks of as friends. His accent slips back into the local mood after a few days on the road in Arkansas. A Fort Smith woman wrote the local newspaper, "I had an idea he was an aloof sort of person. I was never more mistaken in my life. If the speech he made and his manner that night are any indication, the Senator is a completely down to earth person, and a very unassuming one. What impressed me the most was his utter sincerity. Has anyone in the history of Arkansas brought more honor to the state?"

What he said was pretty much the same throughout the ten-week grass-roots tour. He spoke of American foreign policy, and how it affected the people of Arkansas. He began October 9 before the Altrusa Club, a women's society in Little Rock, and said, "You can't know how good it is to get back to where life is normal instead of a constant succession of almost insoluble crises and incessant controversy—back to where ninety percent of all conversation is not about the last atomic test, or Syria or the Congo or Laos or Cuba. It is good to hear again of crops and business and football, and to know that at home life goes on."

The Senator continued: "Women by instinct as well as reason have a more lively interest in the concern for the survival of their sons and daughters than most men. Men become so engrossed in making a living, in meeting the challenge of competitors that they sometimes forget that all of this is ultimately futile and senseless should we have another nuclear war . . . If war comes, Arkansas will not be the remote, safe place it has been in previous wars. It will be ground zero, for the Little Rock SAC base and the missile bases in our hills make us a prime target—and instead of husbands and sons being casualties on foreign soil, it will be those at home who will be destroyed in a single blast, or left to shrivel from fallout and contamination. All we have labored for and built in the past one hundred and twenty-five years could be destroyed in a single hour, our families, our farms.

"I know I am sometimes criticized for giving too much attention to foreign affairs. I can only say these so-called foreign affairs are not very foreign when you consider that a nuclear war with Russia, beginning over Berlin or Laos or Cuba or the Congo would certainly be brought home to us here in Arkansas in a most deadly fashion, and I have always assumed that if in any way I can help avoid a war, it is my duty to do so.

"As in any other activity, long study and understanding are necessary if one is to make a contribution. I make no apologies for being interested in foreign affairs, for trying to strengthen our alliances with other free peoples to resist the spread of the Communist empire through foreign aid, by exchange programs with friendly people so that all of us may eventually understand each other, and maybe in time find a way to resolve our differences by reason, rather than by nuclear bombs."

From there, on the road again. The pattern was the same. The schoolhouse, usually; a crowd of from 50 to 250, Fulbright fidgeting while a series of local nabobs praised him (overmuch, he thought), the brief remarks, and then answering questions. This was the shining hour, for the Senator and his audience. He relishes intellectual give-and-take, the challenge to him, the personality of the questioner. To get the debate moving, an assistant plants a few stock questions in the crowd.

There is a hand up. The Senator nods pleasantly.

A voice full of the flavor of the rural small town of the South says, in some embarrassment, "Senator, what do you have to say about this: we're told over the radio that we're in danger of, you know, collapsing from Communists in the Government and the schools and the church?"

Fulbright smiles a little, and replies, "Now, you know that's nonsense. How many Communists do you know at the courthouse?" A ripple of laughter at the idea. "Or among your teachers? Or preachers? Those who are saying these things are guilty of dangerous propaganda. Suppose you were Khrushchev, and you kept hearing all the time of how the United States has been taken over by Communists in the Government and local life? You would be inclined to be bolder and more reckless in dealing with us, wouldn't you? And that could lead to a serious miscalculation and the war none of us want. No, I think internal Communism is a very minor problem with us, and one the FBI can handle quite well. The real danger is from without. I don't think the Russians or the Chinese want to fight us, and will not unless they are overly provoked or they get the wrong idea that we are weak from internal subversion."

He speaks with such a mood of earnestness, without being oratorical, that there is a brief clatter of applause.

Another hand and nod. "They tell us, Senator, that in your memorandum, you wanted to muzzle the generals and keep them from telling us how bad Communism is. What do you say to that?"

He is pleased with the question, and looks very much like a small boy who has a legitimate answer to a complaint from his mother. "All I said was that I didn't think it was the job of the military to educate the public," he replies. "Their job is to defend us militarily, not to tell us what to think. They are not trained to teach; they have little contact with our civilian ways. There is a difference between seeing a danger, as Communism, and in knowing what it is, and how it works, and how to deal with it. Certainly the American people know from their own observation there is a Communist empire. We don't need a general to point that out to us. What we do need is a good deal more intelligent discussion of how to deal with it, and this I favor wholeheartedly."

Sometimes answering a question, he became so enthusiastic he spoke too long. Mrs. Fulbright would tug at his coat, and he would say a little sheepishly, "Well, I've talked long enough, and Mrs. Fulbright thinks I'd better stop before I tire you all out." This would be followed by a boyish smile, and people often remembered this more than anything, and would remark on it. It created a human bond and refuted the talk that he was high and mighty.

Inevitably there would be a question about foreign aid. Full of facts and figures, brimming with them, he pointed out that the major crops of Arkansas are rice, cotton and soy beans. Fifty-six percent of all U.S. grown rice is sold to the export market, 50 percent of the cotton, 30 percent of the beans. Foreign aid builds a market for American goods. He used to have a well on his place outside of Fayetteville, and they always had to prime that pump to get the water flowing. That's the way with foreign aid. The lesson is caught, and heads shake in agreement.

This little exercise in democracy night after night, even with an occasional flash of ugly heckling, is basic to Senator Fulbright's philosophy. He believes with a passion that if the people are told the facts, they will react wisely. He has this Jeffersonian faith, which so many of his colleagues have abandoned and turned cynically to proven clichés. One night in the troubled spring of 1966, Senator Fulbright had dinner with several Senators younger than he, and surprised them by his warm defense of the people. Go to them, and talk to them, he said. Don't sit here and complain and wail. The people are troubled, and they want to understand.

A political compaign is like a love affair. There are moments of the unexpected, and times when it may seem all is lost. Senator Fulbright takes a long-term view, and is not perturbed by episodes that ruin the digestion of his aides. Early in October, 1961, just as he was setting out, the gods seemed to be conspiring against him.

The Senator was asked to comment on the flare-up of the continuing Berlin crisis, and he answered with his customary candor. The crisis, he said, was partly of our own making, we should explore what the Russians meant by "free access," and there were points for negotiation. Then, on October 15, a flap developed over the news that Yugoslav pilots were training at a Texas air base. Congressmen cried out in horror. An outfit calling itself the National Indignation Congress resolved against this aiding of Communism. Fulbright said he thought American training of Yugoslav pilots was sensible; it helped to increase the independence of Belgrade from Moscow.

The Senator's foes seized upon these comments with gleeful enthusiasm. Governor Faubus sounded very much as if he was going to challenge Fulbright for his seat. He said, "I cannot understand why the United States continues to support Communist countries, such as Yugoslavia and Poland, when the aid will be used against us. The free world has lost North Vietnam, lost Laos, and we've just lost Berlin.

The only question is whether we will go to war over it or not. We're going to get some of our American steel back in bombs, just as we got our scrap iron back from Japan at Pearl Harbor."

A few days later, barking at the Senator's heels, the Governor said of Fulbright, "Some Senator said the other day that the reason we've had so much trouble with Cuba is that we didn't treat them well enough, and if we had we wouldn't be having any trouble with them." There were snickers from his audience. This was not entirely a true interpretation of what Fulbright had said in Little Rock; instead, he argued that if we had paid more attention to the economic imbalance in Cuba during the period of our maximum influence, Castro would not have risen and embraced Marxism. Faubus went on; "For years we paid a premium for Cuban sugar at the expense of Louisiana cane growers. Now the addlebrained visionaries come and say, well, we didn't treat them right, and that's why they're such bad boys."

When reporters questioned Faubus, according to *The Gazette,* "The Governor grinned and dodged comment when he was asked whether he felt he could beat Fulbright the next year."

Congressman Alford, speaking before an American Legion group in Hot Springs, said, "Servicemen are being asked to defend the United States, but they are not allowed to speak out. International Communism is running rampant . . . The political sophisticated progressive liberal would rather be Red than dead."

By mid-October, when Senator Fulbright came to the little town of Ozark, where the mountains fall down to hills, the attack of his foes had become more like a farm wife shooing a chicken than the bugles of a great army.

He came to the old red-brick high-school gym before nightfall for a dinner in his honor by the PTA. The basketball nets were drawn up, and long rows of tables covered with white paper were at one end of the gymnasium. The parking lot was filled when the Ford station wagon pulled in; people had come from a radius of fifty miles to hear what Bill had to say for himself. The school kitchen was a-clatter with the women cooking turkey. Some three hundred people sat down together, and were served by girls from the home economics class.

To the uninitiated, the preliminary introductions at a political meeting are a meaningless flow of heavy platitudes. But "The Arkansas Traveler," a columnist for *The Gazette,* found fascinating omens. The president of the Arkansas Western Gas Compnay, a behind-the-scenes power in state politics and a close friend of Governor Faubus, said, "Senator Fulbright is looked on by a majority of Arkansas people as a man the state, nation and world cannot do without." The editor of the Fort Smith paper, a consistent supporter of Faubus, said the Senator had done "a stupendous job for Arkansas over the years," and criticized some voters who were against a man for a single action or statement they didn't like. The Democratic state chairman, a close associate of the Governor, praised the Senator, too. This meant that if Governor Faubus chose to fight Fulbright, it would be without the help of the local political Establishment and its connections with industry and the press.

The introductions droned on and on. When the Senator's time came, he was in a mellow mood. The friendliness of the crowd, the return to a familiar and well-loved area, and the good omens were a part of it. His mouth had relaxed into a smile, his voice was easy, and he had lost the pedagogical manner. Instead, his approach was one of boyish earnestness and charm. (A hard-bitten New York editor said once, "I have never known anyone, and this includes Jack Kennedy, who has the charm of Senator Fulbright when the mood is on him.")

He told these people from the poultry farms and tiny towns of the western Ozarks that foreign policy and their own prosperity were all wrapped up together. The big buyers of Arkansas frozen chickens were West Germany, Belgium and Holland, and their economy had been primed by foreign aid. The money the Government spent overseas was an investment in America's future.

He was worried, he said, about the people that go around disagreeing with their neighbors and calling them Communists. "I get out of patience with these people. Their alarm about Communist penetration of the clergy and schools is a lot of nonsense. I don't think there is any disagreement among Americans that we should combat Communism. There are honest differences on how we can best achieve national security—by fighting a nuclear war, or by strengthening our Allies and having patience and waiting for a time when we can sit down and honestly negotiate differences . . ."

If there was a doubt about the way Arkansas felt about J. William Fulbright, it was dispelled a few nights later in Fort Smith. He spoke in the junior high school at a meeting sponsored by the League of Women Voters. When he appeared, there was a standing ovation which he received with a shy grin. He spoke like the good conversationalist he is when in the right mood. He rambled over a wide range: the space race (he thought it was somewhat ridiculous and we could better spend the money on education), the United Nations, Sino-Soviet relations (the Chinese would love to sic the United States and Russia into mutual destruction), the Common Market, nuclear testing, and ended on a note of optimism. The nuclear stalemate meant the big powers would find ways to avoid war with one another.

As he stopped speaking, glancing with some embarrassment at the clock for he had talked longer than he intended, there was long and enthusiastic applause.

Before the 5,000-mile pilgrimage through the winding hills, the cotton and rice country of the west and south ended, Bill Fulbright had frightened out both Governor Faubus and Representative Alford. Private polls showed the most any contender could pull against the Senator was around 34 percent. The actual primary campaign the next spring and summer against a trucking operator was hardly even an exercise. Fulbright gave only ten speeches, and carried every county but his opponent's. He went on to win handily in the fall, winning every county.

Senator Fulbright and democracy survived the test.

XVI

HUMBUG IS A cash crop in Washington. A great deal of money is spent on its cultivation. Broadly speaking, humbug is the manipulation of public opinion or official policy for a specific end, and usually passes under the guise of "public relations." Sometimes there is a rather nauseous odor attached to it, but not always. Twice in his career, Senator Fulbright has uprooted the humbugs. These creatures invariably respond with cries that they were patriots or respectable businessmen.

He listened to them with that faintly skeptical, almost sardonic smile that has become his landmark. He is the ironic moralist.

His first investigation of morality, or lack of it, was in 1950. Then, as chairman of the Banking Committee, he detected that odor at the Reconstruction Finance Committee, the Government's lending agency to private business. His revelation of mink coats, deep freezes and the conflict of interest of a White House assistant won the damnation of Harry Truman, and the respect of the press.

His was not a gaudy sideshow, but a well-organized, tightly written morality play with moments of comedy. He drew a moral: "A democracy can recover quickly from physical or economic disaster, but when its moral convictions weaken it becomes easy prey for the demagogue or charlatan . . . One of the most disturbing aspects of this problem of moral conduct is the revelation that, among so many influential people, morality has become identical with legality. We are certainly in a tragic plight if the accepted standard by which we measure the integrity of a man in public life is that he keeps within the letter of the law . . . What seems to be new about these scandals is the moral blindness which allows those in responsible positions to accept the practices which the facts reveal. It is bad enough for us to have corruption in our midst, but it is worse if it is to be condoned and accepted as inevitable."

In 1963, after his reelection, Senator Fulbright took another look at the sickly moral climate of Washington. This time he investigated the foreign agent, not the James Bond variety, but the American who accepts money for lobbying, doing public relations or legal work for a foreign government. What he showed was a tale so shocking, one wonders how firm is the ground on which we walk.

He conducted no headline-hunting expedition, and most sessions were held behind closed doors. The Senator has strict views about the Congressional investigation, and once told an assistant, "Our purpose is not to entertain, but to educate. If there is a bad situation here, we must expose it to the public, and seek a legislative reform."

The foreign agent business is based on a fact of modern life. The United States has great boodle to give away—guns, foreign aid, technical assistance, surplus food, sugar quotas; it will subsidize, on occasion, anything from a dam to a war. Also its foreign policy may well affect the economic and political life of a lesser nation. So most nations operate in this marketplace. Since a diplomat of a foreign country is not permitted to meddle in American politics (he may be declared *persona non grata* if he does), Americans are hired to suborn public opinion, manipulate Congress, influence elections, make suggestions to high officials, and bring their prestige, if any, to bear on decisions affecting X country. They are paid very well. The agent may vary from a simon-pure tower of The Establishment, such as former high-ranking State Department officials, to a downright shyster. Much of the cost is borne by the American taxpayer. The practice has become so widespread and profitable that it cannot be rooted out.

Senator Fulbright hopes that reforms can keep the foreign agent business within reasonable limits. He makes a distinction between what he regards as "legitimate" services, as the counsel given foreign governments by the law firms of Dean Acheson, George Ball and Thomas E. Dewey, and the "charlatans."

Two incidents reveal the resistance to reform. When Fulbright tried to stop a foreign agent from getting a large cut out of the Philippine war damages act, a bill the agent lobbied through the House, abuse fell on the Senator. At a Committee conference, a member of the House Foreign Affairs Committee, Representative

Wayne Hays of Ohio, blustered, "Let's say a number of things have turned my House colleagues against your position. Most of all we do not like your arrogant attitude as evidenced by some remarks on the integrity of the House." Hays suggested he go back to Arkansas and be a chicken farmer, since he worried so about Arkansas chickens.

The Senator replied he could decide his role without any help from the gentleman from Ohio.

After the Foreign Relations Committee made its recommendations for tighter controls over the agents, the House took its own sweet time to consider the bill, and it was not passed until mid-1966. (Several high-ranking House members had received campaign contributions directly and indirectly from foreign agents.) At the hearings, the State and Justice Departments displayed only languid concern.

Senator Fulbright's outrage sets him apart, the ghost at the banquet, the Puritan at the revel. This thread of moralism runs through his entire career; it is more than a thread, it is a steel wire. It is the moralism of the Greek who says, this is wrong because it undermines our great society and its freedoms.

He became very aware of the foreign agent during the foreign aid battles. "It was like a gold rush," he explained with a smile. The wild scramble for sugar quotas bothered him. The India Sugar Association, to cite one, paid $100,000 for sugar lobbying, to get its share of the American sugar market raised. Fulbright remarked, "We find ourselves in the strange position of paying to India large sums of dollars and having large sums of these same dollars paid to American citizens to influence the action taken by Congress."

The hearings uncovered some weird shenanigans. The West German Government set up a "front" organization that hired a lobbyist to influence the American Government against a summit conference with the Soviets. (An outgrowth of this phase of the hearings was the Senate Ethics Committee investigation of the conduct of a Senator, Thomas J. Dodd of Connecticut; he allegedly tried to intervene with German authorities to protect the job of this agent.) A public relations firm with a $300,000 contract with Nationalist China boasted that it would get for each dollar spent $6 worth of free space in American media. The Portuguese Government, through a series of intermediaries, paid an American citizen of Portuguese birth $400 a week to set up a Portuguese-American committee to put pressure on Congress to change American policy for Africa.

In the case of Portugal, the prize was far richer than a foreign aid handout. It was the colony of Angola in Africa. Portugal's hold was slipping as independence exploded over the continent. A rebellion by African natives began. Portugal's exploitation of the colony was under attack at the United Nations. The State Department was somewhat critical. So important is American policy these days that strong opposition could well doom the colonial control.

Portugal set out to prevent this. A Portuguese "group" of industrialists hired a public relations firm, Selvage & Lee. Senator Fulbright questioned whether the group was not merely a cover for the government. The PR contacts were with Portuguese officials; they received instructions from Lisbon and the Ambassador in Washington. The firm, in turn, hired an obscure New England lawyer who had hustled up Portuguese-American votes for Senator Kennedy in Massachusetts, and paid him $400 a week.

At the instigation of Selvage & Lee, he—Martin T. Comacho—set up the Portuguese-American Committee on Foreign Affairs, and as its spokesman issued statements written by the PR men. He operated for some months without even registering as a foreign agent.

A typical operation were his letters about an NBC documentary on Angola which the Embassy did not like. Comacho wrote Senator John Pastore of Rhode Island, a state with a large Portuguese-American population. His ghost-writers used the never-fail Cold War clichés, so Senator Pastore read, "The NBC commentary helped to foster this Communist conspiracy . . . to destroy NATO and the free world . . . NBC unwittingly is serving the Communist cause." Similar letters were sent the chairman of NBC, editors of newspapers and key Congressmen. They had no way of knowing that the "Committee" was simply a front for Portugal.

Every Washington angle was cynically exploited. A letter was sent Senator Richard Russell of Georgia, leader of the Southern bloc: "Undoubtedly you are aware of the influence American Negro leaders in the United States have exerted and are exerting on the African policy of this country."

Senator Albert Gore of Tennessee, a member of the Foreign Relations Committee, criticized Portugal's handling of Angola. Comacho fired off a letter, written by Selvage & Lee, to some two hundred Tennessee newspapers on the letterhead of his "Committee." He said: "We wish to emphasize that the members of the Portuguese-American Committee on Foreign Affairs are citizens of the United

States and that our first interest is the security and welfare of the United States . . . We are communicating with you because we strongly feel that the Angola situation has been misrepresented by forces which wish to break the Western alliance asunder, and eventually to destroy both Portugal and the United States."

Fulbright asked Comacho, "Don't you think this is a rather serious interference with the democratic processes of this country?"

He didn't think so.

"Did the members of the Portuguese-American Committee pass upon this letter?"

"No, sir."

"They had never seen it, had they?"

"No."

"And it was never sent them, was it?"

"No."

Far from regretting this hoodwinking of the American public and political community, those involved cried out about their right of free speech and petition. Oh, yes, the Senator replied, but the public has a right, too; it has a right to know you are a paid foreign agent and you speak for a foreign principal.

The hearings had their moments of comedy, even farce. One involved a name-dropper. Washington is the ideal habitat for this creature, for here he may live quite handsomely and toil little, thanks to a fat retainer from a naïve client. He is generally a pleasant fellow. He laughs at the jokes of the great, opens doors for them, helps them on with their coats, finds drinks for them, and does odd political jobs. His office is plastered with autographed pictures which in the hyperbole of politics means little, but to the client bespeaks Influence.

Michael Deane in his letters to his Dominican Republican contact was a persistent name-dropper. Arthur Schlesinger was "a personal friend of mine and interested in a favorable manner in the problem of the Dominican [sugar] quota." Hubert Humphrey was "also a friend of mine. He and I have been through many political campaigns together." The Secretary of Agriculture was "a friend of mine of long standing." The Assistant Secretary of State for Latin America was referred to by his nickname.

Senator Fulbright commented to the Committee; "We are concerned with the fact that Mr. Deane appears to have been hired to influence our foreign policy because of his domestic political associations. We are concerned, too, with a foreign principal's effort, by hiring a political lobbyist, to inject partisan politics into what was essentially a bipartisan policy."

In his *curriculum vitae* to the Dominicans, Deane gave sixteen lines to his political connections. While to a Washington cave dweller they might appear trifling, as "member, board of governors, National Capitol Democratic Club," he seemed to have impressed the Dominicans. He was hired to get the Dominican sugar quota restored after a break between Washington and the dictatorial Trujillo regime during the Eisenhower Administration. He was to receive $54,000. Deane was a master of the influence.

He wrote in one memo: "On Tuesday, March 28, the Senate Finance Committee went into executive session, and I waited until they finished and Senator Byrd briefed us. [This was actually a press briefing.] The thing we had to work with was the fact that we had a Democratic Congress and a Republican President. Using that situation we skillfully and discreetly . . ."

Asked about this, Deane said, "I think I am giving myself too much credit. One tends to do that a bit when they have a client who is outside Washington."

Fulbright demanded, "Are you saying you were lying to your clients?"

He said not.

"Well, you were misleading them." Later, accused of another stretching of the truth, Deane said defensively, "You find the best law firms in town doing the same thing." He was probably correct.

In another memo, he said, "I have been fighting to maintain the Dominican Republic's allocation from one end of Washington to another. I have seen and talked to people from the top echelon of Government to the bottom. At this moment, I am leaving shortly for an appointment with Adolf Berle, Jr., in the State Department . . ."

Of this prose, Deane confessed, "It may be what I would consider just taking a bit of liberty with the English language."

Another memo related, "This morning I received an invitation from the President to attend a reception on May 25 at the White House."

Senator Fulbright is a relentless questioner, and, as in this case, forces the quarry to admit his own error.

The Senator asked, "Why did you put this in the letter? What is the significance of this?"

Deane had a lapse of memory. "I don't know, sir."

"Were you invited by the President?"

"I was invited by, for a certain occasion, yes, sir; I can't recall the nature of the occasion."

"The letter says, 'I received an invitation from the President.' Did you in fact receive an invitation from the President?"

"It was an invitation, sir, I think from the National Democratic Committee on behalf of the President to come for a reception at the White House."

"Then did you receive an invitation from the President, yes or no?"

"No."

Later Deane assured his client, "Both Schlesinger and I and other White House persons are actively advocating the allocation of the 209,120 short tons of sugar to the Dominican Republic."

Senator Fulbright demanded, "Was Mr. Schlesinger actively advocating the allocation?"

"No, sir."

This was the way it went. He even sent the transcript of a press conference of Senator Fulbright without labeling it as such. The inference was that it was of a private talk with him. The Senator pointed out Deane had mispelled his name.

There was a moral. Fulbright said, "In effect, you are deceiving your client, and this could well have had an effect upon their policy vis-à-vis the United States. I think this is much more serious than just a little puffing."

Thus the tale of the tinhorn dictator and the name-dropper. Another case with a touch of the grotesque was that of West Germany.

After World War II, the most emotional bar to the growth of Germany as an industrial giant and a military power was the horror of the Jews. This was an important factor in the behind-the-scenes scuffle in the United States over German policy. The Morgenthau plan adopted during the Roosevelt Administration would curtail German heavy industry. Secretary Dulles, whose law firm had once represented German interests, wanted to build Germany as a foil against Russia. A group of German industrialists and bankers hired as their American agent a Jewish public relations man with political connections. He, in turn, wrote speeches for Jewish Congressmen backing a strong West Germany.

The operator was "General" Julius Klein. His title came from the

Illinois National Guard, his political base from the Jewish War Veterans which he headed. He received $125,000 to $150,000 a year for his services to the Germans.

Senator Fulbright was able to expose the intimate connection of the regime of Chancellor Adenauer with the "Forderkreis," as Klein called his group. Klein used the German Embassy's diplomatic pouch for sending materials to Germany. A note from the Frankfurter Bank of July 12, 1962, introduced at the committee hearing, said, "Such payments come in from circles of trade and industry and through the Deustche Bundesbank for account of Government offices." Klein wrote in a memo, "Our organization has been for quite some time the personal public relations consultant to Chancellor Adenauer, Minister Erhard, and Foreign Minister Dr. von Brentano . . ." Again, in a separate note, "You all must realize this is a self-serving instrument of Bonn and nothing else."

Fulbright tried to pin down Klein about his clients, and asked him whom he really represented.

He responded, "All I know is, all I am interested in, is to get paid. Where they got their money and how is their business."

"You are not interested in who pays you?"

"I am not. I don't care where the money comes from as long as it doesn't come from Nazis or Communists."

One aim of the "group" was related in a memo in the Klein files, saying its "purpose is to promote Germany's cause vis-à-vis the summit conference. We have agreed to extend the campaign to the United States, to disseminate information here so that the American people may understand the serious problem facing Germany if there should be a compromise with the Soviet Union."

This purpose was stretched rather thin in one case. The Vice President in a speech in West Berlin had praised Mayor Willy Brandt as a matter of course. This seemed to have alarmed Klein or his principals, because Brandt was the leader of the Social Democratic Party, the political opposition to Adenauer's Christian Democratic Union and its ally, the further-to-the-right Free Democratic Party. "General" Klein sent a telegram to the President, protesting that the Vice President's remarks served Mayor Brandt, and "if Adenauer loses [the election], Khrushchev will hail it as a repudiation of NATO. I hope you will find a way to declare publicly that the U.S. appreciates the loyalty of the Adenauer government to the Western cause. If this is not done," he feared, the Communists would exploit the plug for Brandt. He added apocalyptically, "Put this down as another defeat for America."

There is no record the President ever responded to this farfetched idea.

In a letter to his principals, Klein told of buying tickets to political dinners.

"You are telling your clients," Fulbright remarked, "that you are going to engage in political activities, aren't you, in this letter?"

Not at a loss for words, Klein replied, "From the moment I open my eyes in the morning until I go to sleep as a good American, I am interested and I am doing politics, yes, sir."

Toward the close of the hearing, the Senator remarked, "When you write a telegram to the President or you approach a Senator you apparently take the position that if you do that in your own mind out of patriotism and love of your country that makes it wholly immune from the control or influence of the Foreign Agents Registration Act. I believe your counsel will agree that in many laws that is not quite the answer."

"Have I lost my right as a citizen if I write my President?" complained the foreign agent.

This viewpoint represented, as the Senator pointed out, the curious way in which some individuals manipulate their own morals; they give a high and lofty purpose—patriotism is well thought of—to acts which, if not illegal, are ethically doubtful, but which serve the individual's pocketbook. This is dangerous to a state, because it causes the public to question scornfully any patriotic statement, or put it down automatically as humbug.

Another operation boasted it would arouse American opinion for a major war in Asia. The fee was $300,000. The American press, TV, newsreels and magazines were used, and, indeed, many editors apparently decided as long as the material was technically good and free, why worry. Some editors were rewarded by free vacations in Mexico.

The Hamilton Wright Organization in a letter to the Nationalist Chinese Ambassador to the United Nations stated: "As you well know, every Senator, Representative, politician and even our President—is first, last and always 'the servant of the American people.' It is the votes of the people that put these men in office. It is their job to carry out what the voters want. To inform the voters, to make them 'Free China' conscious, is the first step toward these objectives. The entire effort behind this campaign would be to arouse public opinion in the United States, Canada, South America and Europe, and to create a sympathetic understanding of Free China that would have dramatic impact on members of the UN [against the lifting of trade sanctions on Communist China] . . . Too, this campaign will bring vociferous moral support from the American people when the day comes for a 'return to the mainland.' " This was a reference to Generalissimo Chiang Kai-shek's often promised invasion of China, a military action that would require mammoth American naval and air support.

Further instructions came from the Government Information Office to Hamilton Wright, Sr.: "In our public relations work in the United States, we have met with certain 'sales resistance' on the part of the public. . . . The 'two Chinas' theory has never been totally discredited. There have been talks of admitting the Chinese Communists to the United Nations, of relaxing the embargo of strategic materials to the Chinese mainland and of taking another look at United States policy toward China.

"We want to avoid creating the impression that the building up of Taiwan is an end in itself, that the Government is content in just sitting there, and that we have given up the goal of recovering the mainland. There are other fallacies we wish to correct such as 'Chiang's army is ageing' and 'Taiwanese are not Chinese.' "

Wright assured the Nationalists, "The $300,000 spent on this contract will produce $2,500,000 worth of 'Paid Space' in newspapers, magazines and television. This is based on the regular paid space and advertising rates of the media in which the stories and pictures appear."

The Wrights, in effect, ran a free lunch counter. They cultivated editors, particularly of feature syndicates and newsreels, and subsidized writers. They arranged free trips to Mexico and China for obliging editors. This extra reward was incidental. The Wrights assumed, and the cynicism seemed justified, that editors would use timely and well-written feature stories, film clips or tapes, offered gratis or for a low cost, without questioning whether it was propaganda.

Wright said, "Many of these [syndicate] editors give us direct assignments. In seventy-five percent of the cases, neither the editor of the newspaper—nor the newspaper reader—has any knowledge of where the material originated. In some instances we syndicate our material direct to newspaper editors."

Senator Fulbright asked, "During the period of your representation of Free China did all of the newsreel footage originate with your company?"

"Every foot of it," Wright replied.

During a discussion of the way the Wrights "planted" articles in newspapers, the Senator commented, "The net effect of this was that the *New York Herald Tribune* was accepting pieces prepared by a paid foreign agent, and they were accepting them and giving them to the public as if they were objective news stories."

Wright said, "That is done every day in the week."

"Under the law, the public reading this is entitled to know that this was written by a paid agent, and not just a newsman," Fulbright stated.

This had never been done, Wright protested.

"Do you think if the law required that, it would stop?"

"It would stop us. It would put us out of business in 24 hours . . . It would stop everybody's activity. You would raise havoc in the news field. You would raise havoc with television coverage."

(The *Herald Tribune* said the writers in question were paid by the newspaper and the editors did not know they worked for a China lobby firm. One of the writers wrote the committee, "Only one media, to my knowledge, has admitted to you the truth that it did in fact know of my affiliations, clients served and other relevant facts. It is inexcusable of these news media to comment as evasively as they did, implying covertness on my part to cover up their embarrassment . . .")

Wright complained that the Committee was hurting their "small business."

The question, said Senator Fulbright, was whether the law was being complied with and the public fully aware of the propaganda it was consuming. He read a Supreme Court decision on the act: "The general intention of the act is to prohibit secrecy as to any kind of political activity by foreign agents, resting on the fundamental constitutional principle that our people if adequately informed may be trusted to distinguish between the true and the false, the bill is intended to label information of foreign origins so that hearers and readers may not be deceived by the belief that this information has come from a disinterested source. Such legislation supplements rather than detracts from the prized freedoms guaranteed by the first amendment."

Wright represented what might be called the "public relations morality." He arranged for a syndicate editor to have a grand junket to Mexico, including gay Acapulco. The editor wrote Wright, "You told me the Government would pick up the full tab, so we signed for everything at the Hilton, including the Cook's tour."

Wright was asked, "You do not think this has any bearing upon the objectivity or independence of the news and pictures disseminated by the syndicate?"

Wright replied, "You come to a point now, where do you stop and start in doing business with people? Is there anything wrong in having an editor become better informed on a foreign country, having a firsthand observation?"

The most intricate web of all, and possibly the most effective of all, involved Israel. After the complicated hearings, Senator Fulbright charged that the American Zionist Council was used by an Israeli agency as a channel for propaganda funds "to avoid disclosure of what was being done with the money."

The Senator said the hearings showed that the Zionist Council received $5,100,001.02 from the Jewish Agency for Israel from January 1, 1955 until January 1, 1963, or 80 percent of its funds. The Jewish Agency is sanctioned by the Israeli Government and works in cooperation with it. These funds, according to the Senator, were passed on by the council to public relations outfits and other groups to build public approval of Israeli and Zionist aims.

In every good drama of morals, as Shakespeare so well reckoned, there is always a bit of farce. This came about in a letter a Washington lawyer wrote his credulous client, the Dominican sugar cane interests. The key figure in writing the law on sugar was the chairman of the Senate Finance Committee.

The letter said slyly, "Through channels of personal obligation we have made contact with a powerful law firm in the Senator's home state. The senior member of the firm is the executive officer of the Senator's political machine. The second partner is the son of the Senator's first campaign manager; there are close family connections between this man and the Senator. The third partner is the private confidential attorney for the Senator; he handles important confidential matters for the Senator's machine. All three propose to call upon the Senator on Monday, January 30, to engage his sympathy for the position of the Dominican Republic in respect to sugar legislation. They will represent themselves as being interested purely because of their very close ties of friendship and business with my firm. Each of the three will adopt a different approach to arouse the Senator's sympathy."

The letter, it turned out after much hemming and hawing, was a hoax. The law firm mentioned had no such connections, and had never proposed any such scheme.

The mere fact that such an outlandish plot was even dreamed up to hoodwink a client was a reflection itself upon the moral temper of Washington. And, as if to clinch the sardonic view Senator Fulbright held of this influence peddling, the Senator who objected the loudest to the reforms recommended, and in the holiest of terms, had himself been influenced—at least in the past—by one of the foreign agents under investigation.

The Senator from Arkansas, true to his classical discipline, looks upon these cracks in the wall reasonably. He does not predict the end of the world, although he is concerned by the slow, insidious spread of public fraud. Government, he believes, is based on faith and trust, and when that is eroded by cynical humbuggery, anarchy may follow in its wake.

XVII

IT WAS A LONG and troubled and emotional day. First the shock and daze of horror and unreality. You live and breathe in a world which seems a little mad, out of joint. You are suddenly aware that the hand of fate, accident, is never far away. Then, with that sense of pragmatism all men have, no matter what the disaster, you begin to grope into the future, you begin to reach for saplings to hold on to in the storm. You wonder if there is anything you can do to mend events.

This is how Senator Fulbright saw that Friday in November, 1963. President Kennedy had been assassinated in Dallas. "My God, why did he go there? . . . This is part of the poison that has been spilled all over America since the end of the war by the zealots. Some terrible deed like this was bound to happen. You could sense it coming, as in a Greek tragedy." Fulbright had developed a respect and affection for Jack Kennedy after the Cuban missile crisis. There was a tenuous partnership whose great success was the Senator's steering the Nuclear Test Ban Treaty through the Senate by a vote of 80 to 19. He saw the nation begin to move cautiously and intelligently away from the unspeakable doom of nuclear war, away from the rigid stance of the Cold War. Now what?

Lyndon B. Johnson was sworn in as the thirty-sixth President of the United States. His face looked grim and tight-lipped on television. "Thank God, here is a man of experience and strength." The hand reached out for a sapling, and here, thank God, was a strong tree. This was the way Fulbright, the scholar, world statesman, looked on Lyndon Johnson. Theirs was a friendship out of the ordinary, a psychic attraction of opposites. For a period after the assassination of

John Kennedy, the closest friends of the Johnsons were the Fulbrights. President Johnson, who intuitively draws strength and sustenance from others, gathered a sort of intellectual confidence from this friendship.

Soon after the 1960 election, an Arkansas businessman asked Fulbright what kind of a President Kennedy would be and he replied, "I think he will be a good one, if he makes use of the genius of Lyndon Johnson, and puts him in charge of the legislative program."

This friendship came slowly. When the Texan first moved to the Senate in 1949, Fulbright was a bit repelled by him. He regarded the other as a little vulgar, garrulous and overambitious, trying to move too quickly into the seats of power. Fulbright's aloof disdain was a challenge to Johnson. There is in him an impulse, a demand to win over others. He cannot, it seems, bear indifference; he must be greatly admired or hated. With Fulbright, it is quite the opposite; it is immaterial to him what the emotional response of another is, a display of emotions is bad taste.

Senator Johnson began to give the Arkansan the famous "treatment" and broke through his shell of reserve. Johnson has a gift for finding out the open windows in almost every man, whether he be an old-school politician as Everett Dirksen or an intellectual Fulbright. Senator Fulbright once described "the treatment" to a visitor after reading in the paper how the President persuaded a group of business leaders to do his will. "I can just imagine the operation," Fulbright said in good humor. "He first called up each one individually, and told him how much he relied on his advice, and would he come to the White House. When the businessmen were assembled, Johnson came into the room, addressed each one warmly by his first name and made mention of some small detail that was immensely flattering. He told the group they were the leaders of the country, the ones all others looked to, and the fate of democracy, and, in fact, the whole free world, was in their hands. He needed their help badly. 'I may not be the best President, but I am the only President you have until the people tire of me, and the job is such I can't do it all alone.' A smile, a modest one, at this point. 'Now will you help me.' It's pretty hard to turn him down."

For his part, Johnson seemed to see in Fulbright a shoot of his own life, an intellectual one that never had a chance to grow. Johnson has a haunting sense of inferiority in this area, and sometimes says wryly of himself, "I am your corny President." (He was absolutely furious, though, to learn that members of the Kennedy staff called him "Colonel Cornpone.") Fulbright was the man he imagined he might have been under different circumstances, a tantalizing and, at the same time, cruel image. Johnson was much impressed, too, by Betty Fulbright, the Junior League socialite from Philadelphia. In turn, the warmth of Johnson was able to bring out the sociable Fulbright. The aloof Arkansan, sometimes called "the last Whig" or "The Thinking Man's Senator," became a devoted admirer of this opposite.

There were moments of strain and frustration. Fulbright was not able to persuade Johnson to step down as Secretary Dulles' chief flag-waver on Capitol Hill. The puzzled Fulbright once said, "Damned if I understand what Lyndon sees in him."

Once, Johnson called on Fulbright and the two Oklahoma Senators to help him write and put through natural gas legislation. The Texan was late, and when he came in, a draft was already written. He was inexplicably enraged and shouted, "All right, Goddamn it, do it your own way, then. You don't need me," and stalked out of the room.

There were also moments of revelation. One was in an airplane flying the Atlantic. Vice-President Johnson, Senator Fulbright and their wives attended a NATO meeting, flew to London for an audience with the Queen, and then planed back to Washington. Johnson was exhilarated at the experience, his first participation in international affairs in a commanding role. For several hours on the plane, he tumbled out recollections and comments to his friend. Fulbright compared it to Proust's *Remembrance of Things Past*. "I've never heard anything like it. Details of his life going back to his childhood that were as bright and clear as a garden after the storm. And conversations with people of all kinds. He has a talent for picking out of each contact with another man some significant and revealing detail. He told how he manipulated people, how a little favor would be jotted down in memory as an IOU, and called out later for payment."

On the terrible Friday afternoon of the assassination, Senator Fulbright pondered a good deal about his friend. There would be the shock of the event, like a sudden, thudding blow in the stomach. Lyndon would brace himself grimly and squint into the future, and he would want his friends around to reassure him. He would wake up lonely at night and start telephoning, no matter what the hour.

Mrs. Fulbright had come to the Senator's office, and he told her, "I think we should go to the White House, and be there when he comes in."

So in the gathering dusk of evening, the Fulbrights walked up the driveway of the Executive Mansion. A silent crowd stood in the nightfall coolness, staring at the brightly lit white facade and the autumn flowers in the garden. When Johnson came in at last, he stopped and held Fulbright's hand a long time.

Later in the evening, the Senator was interviewed on television. His tribute to Johnson was, the President said, the "kindliest" he had heard all day. Fulbright said he saw no change in foreign policy. The Senator was asked to reassure the troubled world by speaking over the Voice of America, and he said, "In the Senate, President Johnson was one of the greatest political animals I have ever seen, in the best sense of the word. He had an instinct for politics. He used to call me at seven in the morning or eleven at night, it didn't make any difference when. He was utterly ruthless in his job of making the Senate run. I have the greatest admiration for him in this sense. I think there is a much better than average chance that he will be a great President. I think he knows how to organize, he knows how to get people to work for him. He knows how to arouse their exertions and their own dedication to his purpose."

The depth of their friendship then is shown by a framed photograph propped up on the bookshelf in Fulbright's office. The two men are talking face to face, each smiling and obviously relishing the other. The picture, taken on the Presidential plane, is inscribed, "To J. William Fulbright, Than whom there is no better, Lyndon B. Johnson, December 13, 1963."

Some months later, Lady Byrd Johnson was in the Southwest, and saw an old friend of the Senator's, and was asked if she ever saw the Fulbrights. "Oh, yes," she replied. "They are our best friends. We see them more than anyone else. They come over often for the small parties, and we like to have them on trips down the river on the yacht."

During this time of close friendship, Senator Fulbright's statements on foreign policy were based on what seemed then a correct postulate. This was that the threat to peace came from the radical right and the generals. In 1964, the rightists were taking over control of the Republican Party, and their shrill cries demanding a "tough" policy filled the media. Basically, this was the Korean reflex or MacArthur syndrome that Fulbright had fought for more than a decade. The thesis was: we were not winning in Vietnam, we had lost Cuba because we had failed to use sufficient military strength; and this was due to cowardice and Communist subversion in Washington. Senator Goldwater and his followers called for bombing North Vietnam and heavy defoliation of Vietcong areas in the south. In one speech, Goldwater said one possible weapon applicable to this war would be a low-yield atomic bomb. A vast majority of Americans (if the 1964 election returns were any guide) thought they were about to be engulfed by a strange madness.

President Johnson encouraged the Senator by telling him, "Bill, keep up the good work. You are keeping the generals off my back."

The President became something of a hero to foreign policy liberals on Capitol Hill, not only to Fulbright, because of a lecture he gave them. The gist was, he was under great pressure from violent public opinion and the Pentagon to step up the war in Vietnam, but he held firmly to a moderate course because of his concern for peace. Fulbright was impressed and set out energetically to defeat the counsel of the right and create a more moderate public opinion.

He said then: "American politics in the postwar period has been characterized by a virulent debate between those who counsel patience and reason and those, who in their fear and passion, seem ever ready to plunge the nation into conflict abroad and witch hunts at home . . . The malice and hatred which have become a part of our politics cannot be dismissed as the normal excesses of a basically healthy society. They have become far too common. It was in this prevailing atmosphere of suspicion and hate that the murder of the President was spawned. In an atmosphere in which dissent can be regarded as treason, in which violence is glorified and romanticized, in which direct action is widely preferred to judicial action, assassination is not really a radical departure from acceptable behavior."

He followed this vein in a talk to Government workers, telling them the assassination was a "by-product of our puritanical ways of thinking and the mythology of the frontier. It is to be hoped there will be some redemption for the death of our President. That redemption could issue from a national revulsion against extremism and violence, from a calling forth of the basic decency and humanism of America to heal the wounds of division and hate. We must do more than we are doing now to explore the depths of human motivation. We must learn more than we do now about the pathological roots of violence and unreasoning passion in human behavior. We must recognize that the romanticized cult of the frontier, with its glorification of violence and unrestrained individualism is a childish and dangerous anachronism in a nation which carries the responsibilities for the leadership of the free world in the nuclear age."

At the University of North Carolina on April 7, 1964, he tried to turn that massive and quixotic creature, public opinion, away from the Cold War. If there was a shift, he thought, Johnson would be free to move away from the old myths. The major change in American life wrought by the Cold War, he said, "has been the massive diversion of energy and resources from the creative pursuits of civilized society to the conduct of a constant and interminable struggle for world power . . . It has consumed money and time and talent that could otherwise be used to build schools and homes and hospitals, to remove the blight of ugliness that is spreading over the cities and highways of America, and to overcome the poverty and hopelessness that afflict the lives of one-fifth of the people in an otherwise affluent society. It has put a high premium on avoiding innovation at home because new programs involve controversy as well as expense . . . At least as striking as the inversion of priorities which the Cold War has enforced upon American life is the readiness with which the American people have consented to defer programs for their welfare and happiness in favor of costly military and space programs . . . There is indeed a most striking paradox in the fact that military budgets of over fifty billion dollars are adopted by the Congress after only perfunctory debate, while domestic education and welfare programs involving sums which are mere fractions of the military budget are painstakingly examined and then either considerably reduced or rejected outright. I sometimes suspect that in its zeal for armaments at the expense of education and welfare the Congress tends to overrepresent those of our citizens who are extraordinarily agitated about national security and extraordinarily vigorous about making their agitation known."

This followed by only two weeks Fulbright's major plea for a new foreign policy, one which he felt President Johnson would surely follow if the ground were right. This was "Old Myths and New Realities." It was generally hailed in newspaper editorials and the Senator's mail as a refreshing and sensible look at the world. He merely asked that the United States sheath the sword as the sole weapon of foreign policy, that we examine more closely the background of revolutions and their causes, that we drop our Manifest Destiny stance in negotiations, that we broaden our exchange programs with Communist areas.

Almost hidden in the speech were at least two symptoms of the Senator's disquiet with the President, or at least his advisers. One was, "We Americans would do well to divest ourselves of the silly notion that the issue with Panama is a test of our courage and resolve." The President had shown his famous temper when a mob of Panamanians had torn down an American flag. Although this was a minor problem, Fulbright spent some time spelling out a new policy for the Panama Canal, because he knew of Johnson's emotional feelings about events there. The other was a calm discussion of Cuba, urging his audience to take it easy, that Castro was a nuisance more than a menace, and a threat to little more than our pride. He had heard Johnson express himself explosively about Cuba, and confided to a member of his staff that the President's order cutting the water pipe from the Guantanamo naval base to Cuba was "an act of wanton bravado."

The President's problem, he thought, was that he was egged on by too many hawk-like advisers. One, in particular, was a fellow Texan, Thomas C. Mann, his principal counsel on Latin America. Fulbright said sarcastically of him, "He acts as if he learned about Latin America from dealing with Mexican farmhands in Texas."

Fulbright worked hard to encourage intellectuals to support Johnson in the 1964 election. He made a series of witty attacks upon Senator Goldwater. The best known of these was "The Conservation of a Conservative," in which he said: "A peculiar problem arises from the fact that while Senator Goldwater is himself of a conservative die, his conscience clearly is not. It is in fact an unruly conscience, demanding intermittently that we break off diplomatic relations with the Soviet Union, or that we impose a Western protectorate on the newly independent peoples of Africa, or that we balance the Federal budget while at the same time abolishing the graduated income tax and sawing off the Eastern seaboard—with all its valuable tax money—and letting it float out to sea . . .

"The central proposition of the 'conservative' foreign policy is that peace and freedom can only be secured by a policy of 'total victory' over Communism—preferably, but not necessarily by peaceful means. [The MacArthur syndrome again.] The conflict being one between total virtue—us—and total evil—them—it is not readily susceptible to compromise. It is a struggle, says the Senator, 'between godless people and the people of God,' 'between slavery and freedom.' And he adds, 'I claim that we cannot live with these two philosophies in the world forever. Sometime there'll be only one.'

"What the Republican nominee is getting at, in plain old cowpoke language, is that sooner or later one side or the other is going to have to bite the dust. Why? Anybody who's seen a good old Gary Cooper movie knows why. Whoever heard of cowboys coexisting with Indians? Whoever heard of Wyatt Earp coexisting with Jesse James?"

This was the kind of fun he had with Goldwater, whom he looked upon as a foolish Don Quixote leading on a sinister troop of warmongers and McCarthyites. These extremists, to Fulbright, have for some years been the real enemy to sanity in foreign policy.

At this point, President Johnson's foreign policy seemed reasonable and restrained to Fulbright, by comparison. There was no intimate discussion of foreign policy between the two friends, but this, in itself, was no cause for alarm. Johnson had always played his cards close to the chest, giving out reassuring generalizations but keeping specifics very much to himself. John Kennedy used to say his Vice President was like a Mississippi riverboat gambler.

The atmosphere of 1964 with its great assault by Goldwater upon the Middle Ground Establishment was not fertile soil for skeptical questioning of Johnson. It was like a community divided on many issues suddenly called out to fight a forest fire, and thinking only of putting out the blaze. It was unthinkable to wonder if the fire chief might be pouring a little gasoline on the sly.

This political attack from the right was like a great veil obscuring events in Asia, and President Johnson's course of action in Vietnam. The Foreign Relations Committee, looking back on events later, pointed out that on January 27, 1964, Secretary McNamara told the House Armed Services Committee, "The survival of an independent government in South Vietnam is so important to the security of Southeast Asia and to the free world that I can conceive of no alternative than to take all necessary measure with our capability to prevent a Communist victory." This was an open-end commitment. Secretary Rusk at a press conference February 7 of that year threw cold water on proposals for neutralizing South Vietnam. The leader of the military coup, General Nguyen Khanh, called for attacks on North Vietnam. Peace appeals by President de Gaulle, U Thant and Russia were rejected by the United States that summer. On August 2 and 4,

American destroyers were "attacked" in the Gulf of Tonkin off North Vietnam by PT boats, and on August 4 President Johnson ordered U.S. air attacks on North Vietnam. The following day, he asked Congress for unusual powers for military action in Southeast Asia, and Senator Fulbright led the campaign in the Senate for passage of this resolution.

Not all of Washington believed that President Johnson was completely candid about Vietnam or the peace he so ardently espoused in campaign speeches, or that there was a clear-cut choice between Johnson and Goldwater.

There was some dissent. Washington was startled by a sermon preached on September 13, 1964, by the Very Reverend Francis B. Sayre, Jr., dean of the Washington Cathedral. Dean Sayre was a pillar of the liberal community and a father confessor to many statesmen. He said: "I suspect that thousands, even millions, of our countrymen this summer, viewing the extavaganzas that were produced at the Cow Palace in San Francisco and at Convention Hall at Atlantic City, felt something like the Israelites must have felt when finally they were thrust into exile . . . We beheld a pair of gatherings at the summit of political power, each of which was completely dominated by a single man—the one, a man of dangerous ignorance and devastating uncertainty; the other a man whose public house is splendid in its every appearance, but whose private lack of ethic must inevitably produce termites at the very foundation. The electorate of this mighty nation is left homeless, then, by such a pair of nominees. It knows not where to turn. Our people are in a great dilemma, and there is no corner of the country which you may visit today where you do not feel this profoundly. We stared fascinated at the forces that have produced such a sterile choice for us: frustration and a federation of hostilities in one party; and, in the other, behind a goodly façade, only a cynical manipulation of power . . ."

This was almost a lone voice; some forty-two million voted for Johnson, and twenty-six million for Goldwater. Throughout the campaign, Johnson spoke in a voice of moderation tremendously reassuring to his old friend. Fulbright thought the nation might be moving away from its fascination with Manifest Destiny and military power.

Then in early spring of 1965, another crisis dumped upon Washington, and it created for Senator Fulbright a shadow which lengthened and lengthened and finally obliterated the old friendship. As the

Senator tells the story: "On the afternoon of April 28, the leaders of Congress were called to an emergency meeting at the White House. We were told that the revolution that had broken out four days before in the Dominican Republic had gotten completely out of hand, that Americans and other foreigners on the scene were in great danger, and that American Marines would be landed in Santo Domingo that night for the sole purpose of protecting the lives of Americans and other foreigners. None of the Congressional leaders expressed disapproval of the action planned by the President."

Some 2,500 Americans and very substantial investments, a good deal of it in oil, were in the Dominican Republic which shares with Haiti the island that lies between Cuba and Puerto Rico.

The point the Senator has made since is, Congress cannot take for granted that what an Administration tells it about a foreign crisis is the whole truth. (He does not blame President Johnson, and makes a point of his personal loyalty to the President.) He uses the Dominican crisis as an example of the failure of an Executive to give the facts to Congress candidly, and of Congress for failing to use its own resources to get the facts.

The Dominican Republic had long been a Caribbean trouble spot. This most ancient of Spanish settlements in America, discovered by Columbus in 1492, had been ruled since the 1930's by a flamboyant dictator, Generalissimo Rafael Trujillo. As the foreign agents' investigation showed, he had meddled excessively in American politics, hiring an Assistant Secretary of State (retired) as his sugar lobbyist, along with alleged insiders, lavishly entertained close relatives of key U.S. Government officials, gave a medal to the House Democratic leader, and retained the law firm of a Senator. The United States cancelled the Dominican sugar quota when Trujillo was implicated in a plot to murder the moderate President of Venezuela, Rómulo Betancourt. Trujillo was himself assassinated in May, 1961.

Elections the next year gave the left of center candidate, Juan Bosch, a 2 to 1 majority, and he was hailed by the Kennedy Administration as a sign of better things to come. Bosch talked of renegotiating the contract with Standard Oil of New Jersey, saying the contract was "harmful to national interests." This did not make him any friends in Washington. In 1963 a military coup led by Air Force General Wessin y Wessin ousted Bosch, and President Kennedy broke off diplomatic relations and withdrew economic aid.

One of Johnson's first foreign policy moves was to recognize the three-man ruling junta set up by the military. Fulbright thought this was at the behest of Johnson's old Texas friend, Thomas Mann, elevated to the job of Assistant Secretary of State for Latin America. This change of policy was done in a typical Johnson manner. He called members of the Foreign Relations Committee, plus Democratic and GOP leaders to the White House, and in effect announced the recognition by a briefing. Under Secretary of State George Ball said the junta was about to fall, because it was not recognized, and the State Department recommended this step.

President Johnson turned to Fulbright and asked eagerly, "What do you think, Bill?"

The President obviously wanted the Senator to say yes, go ahead. This was the politician in Johnson, exploiting friendship, using it to manipulate his own programs.

Fulbright thought it was the old game all over again—the Administration cooking up its own plans in closed rooms and then calling in Congress at the last minute to give the plans a stamp of OK. He did not like it, and replied, "In a case like this, when the Congress has no information of its own, and the State Department presumably has the facts, we have no alternative but to support the Department."

The only outright refusal came from Senator Wayne Morse, chairman of the Latin-American subcommittee. He asked the President first to consult with the governments of Venezuela and Chile. Mike Mansfield, like Fulbright, gave his reluctant assent.

Eighteen months later, the Dominican Republic spilled over again. On April 24, 1965, forces friendly to Bosch staged an uprising and civil war broke out. The military side of the revolt was broken by General Wessin's planes, tanks and troops, but sporadic fighting continued and demonstrations for Bosch grew. The military regime was in increasing difficulty. President Johnson sent in the Marines on April 28, a day in which there had been heavy fighting in Santo Domingo. The Voice of America moved two radio stations to Santo Domingo, and they broadcast what *The New York Times* called "a biased selection of news."

On television April 30, President Johnson declared, "We took this step when, and only when, we were officially notified by police and military officials of the Dominican Republic that they were no longer in a position to guarantee the safety of American and foreign nationals and to preserve law and order."

American correspondents came to Santo Domingo, and their dispatches raised questions that sorely disturbed Senator Fulbright. He was uneasy but silent.

The President undertook a barnstorming type of salesmanship to win over influential leaders. He called in Congressmen, businessmen and newspaper editors and said, "I'll tell you why I sent troops in there to protect those people. It reminds me of a story I heard as a youngster when Huey Long was up here and everybody was denouncing him because he had taken a sound truck and went into Arkansas and helped elect the first woman elected to the Senate, Mrs. Caraway. Other Senators denounced him for forgetting States' Rights and going into another state and meddling there. Huey listened all afternoon to those speeches, and then he looked at Joe Robinson, the most powerful man in the Senate; he was a big, robust, rotund fellow with a cigar in the corner of his mouth, and he walked over to Joe and put a hand on his shoulder in a very affectionate, friendly way and said, 'I wasn't in Arkansas to dictate to any human being. All I went to Arkansas for was to pull these big pot-bellied politicians off this poor little woman's neck."

It was hardly the kind of story to overjoy Fulbright. He did not regard Huey Long as a model statesman, and twelve years after this incident he had defeated Mrs. Caraway in the Democratic primary.

Another incident added to the questions Fulbright was asking himself about his old friend. Ever since the Panama crisis, the Senator had a corner of anxiety about Johnson, whether he would follow his volatile anger and moods or a more sober consensus of Administration and Congressional advice. Johnson appeared at an AFL-CIO meeting in Washington and in a rather frenzied appeal for backing of his Dominican action said, "We don't propose to sit here in our rocking chair with our hands folded and let the Communists set up any government in the Western Hemisphere."

This was widely interpreted, correctly or not, as a Freudian slip and related to Johnson's private comments on President Kennedy at the time of the Bay of Pigs. He was reported to have called Kennedy "a rocking chair President who let the Communists stay in charge of Cuba, when we could have thrown them out with a few American planes."

The appeal to the labor heads did not sound to Fulbright like the calm Johnson. He was astounded when on May 2 President Johnson said that in the Dominican Republic "some 1,500 innocent people were murdered and shot and their heads cut off." (A subsequent investigation by the Foreign Relations Committee failed to find any evidence of this.) Johnson also stated, "What began as a popular democratic revolution committed to a democracy and social justice very shortly moved and was taken over and really seized and placed in the hands of a band of Communist conspirators."

There were a series of what seemed, at least to Fulbright, thoughtless statements by Johnson. At a televised press conference, he said, "As we talked to the Ambassador [in Santo Domingo] to confirm the horror and tragedy and the unbelievable fact that they were firing on Americans and the American Embassy, he was talking to us from under a desk while bullets were going through his window." (A little more than a year later, Ambassador Bennett appeared before the Committee and was asked about this statement. He said it was not true, that "some exaggeration" crept into reports.)

Newspapers began to question the authenticity of Administration reports, and a debate began. The State Department reacted by attacking individual newsmen. This debate shook the credibility of the Administration, and added to the alarm and outrage of the gentleman from Arkansas.

This was the beginning of his disenchantment, and its extent was revealed as he said that autumn: "Four months later, after an exhaustive review of the Dominican crisis by the Senate Foreign Relations Committee meeting in closed sessions, it was clear beyond a reasonable doubt that, while saving American lives may have been a factor in the decision to intervene on April 28, the major reason was a determination on the part of the United States Government to defeat the rebel, or constitutionalist forces whose victory at that time was imminent. Had I known in April what I knew in August, I most certainly would have objected to the American intervention in the Dominican Republic."

In such prudent, careful words a friendship was ended, and Senator Fulbright moved out into his most challenging role.

XVIII

SENATOR FULBRIGHT's investigation of the Dominican crisis brought on the rage of the President, and in the interaction the Senator started off on a new and independent path. Highly respectable American newspapers and their correspondents had complained that U.S. officials in Santo Domingo and Washington were peddling wild rumors as facts.

This complaint became a focus for Fulbright's growing worry over what he thought were gyrations of foreign policy in both the Dominican Republic and Vietnam. His old friend was sounding and acting more like Barry Goldwater, because, the Senator thought, of bad advice and poor intelligence. Fulbright could imagine Johnson receiving a stream of exaggerated reports and reacting like a cider jug in the sun. Lyndon Johnson was a doer, and in times of crisis he had to do something. If he had been told by his own officials that Communists were taking over the Dominican Republic, he would pace up and down and then order the ships and Marines to move.

The Senator from Arkansas determined to find out who was feeding false information to the President, and why. He thought of the investigation as protecting Johnson.

He began with a list of fifty-three alleged Communists prepared by the CIA. Correspondents in Santo Domingo were told that the fifty-three were active in the rebel camp, that the rebels were using "Communist" street-fighting methods and "Castro-style" propaganda, and had committed "Castro-style atrocities." One atrocity story, dropped after newsmen asked for proof, was that rebels put twelve policemen before a firing squad, cut off their heads, and paraded them on poles. There seemed to be an attempt to persuade the

American public that Communists were trying to take over the Dominican Republic, and by the vilest means. The stories did not check out.

Reporters were concerned, too, by the Voice of America. The Embassy gave the figure of fifty-three Communists to correspondents. This was duly reported, giving the source. However, the Voice of America broadcast that *The New York Times* reported fifty-three Communists were involved in the rebel camp.

The journalists demanded to see the list of Communists. The numbers had been altered twice. Finally they were given a copy of a CIA document and set out to check it. "The result was a shambles," according to *The Review* of the Columbia University School of Journalism.

The Review listed four other false stories. Officials denied that rebel prisoners were turned over to the military junta by U.S. troops, although reporters had seen this being done. Officials denied they were allowing armed Dominicans, from either side, through American lines. Reporters saw truckloads of armed junta trucks going through, particularly when the junta began a campaign on May 15 to wipe out the rebels north of the corridor. Officials denied there was a joint command with the junta. Reporters saw such commands at San Isidro airport. Officials denied there were jointly manned checkpoints searching for weapons. Reporters saw the checkpoints. *The Review* stated: "Too many times there seemed to be a determined, even aggressive, effort to give reporters incorrect, exaggerated, or half-true information."

When Tad Szulc, *The New York Times* correspondent and a veteran observer of the Latin-American scene, returned to Washington from Santo Domingo, Fulbright talked to him. What the Senator heard disturbed him even more. He related events in the Caribbean to the Vietnam war, and wondered if, perhaps, the Gulf of Tonkin alarm the year before was based, too, on alarming exaggerations which then had been carefully covered up.

For a time in 1965, the Dominican and Vietnam crises weaved together. The Dominican crisis was, historically, less important, but it had the effect of stirring Senator Fulbright into open outrage. It led him to ask searching questions on Vietnam. If he had not been disillusioned by Administration conduct in the Dominican Republic, he probably would not have dug so deeply into Asian moves.

The Senator asked Szulc for a memorandum of the facts as he and his fellow journalists saw them. This became a basic document guiding Fulbright in his investigation, much to the chagrin of the State Department. A spokesman complained that the chairman of the Foreign Relations Committee was taking the word of a mere journalist over that of the Department.

Fulbright told the Committee, "I propose that we look into the facts in the Dominican Republic. There is a dispute, and I think we owe it to ourselves and the people to find out the truth."

He did not take this step casually. He sensed the consequences. The Administration would be furious at being revealed, officially, by a Senate committee as a crew of liars. Later, on a television interview, he said, "I am in a most uncomfortable position. I admire the President. It makes me sad to have to criticize his policies. But I think we have a duty up here in the Senate to find out the truth."

The investigation was discreet. The Secretary of State and his associates were not submitted to the public stare, as in the later Vietnam hearings. They testified behind closed doors, filling 660 pages of testimony. Fulbright also studied State Department cables and intelligence reports in detail. This discretion stemmed not only from a desire not to irritate the President. Fulbright felt at that time the Administration had simply been careless in the Dominican crisis, that uncertain rumors were carried from a low level all the way to the President, and, if this was pointed out, a reform would take place.

If he had been convinced from the beginning that this was a deliberate steer over to a tough line, he would not have been so sparing. When the Senator began his probe, he was concerned and anxious, but not disillusioned.

Much of the time during the investigation he was isolated from the White House. The President groused to visitors about "Bill Fulbright sitting up there on the Hill and running his own Goddamn cute shows, and not caring how he hurts national unity."

(Fulbright was asked later if he worried about damaging unity and encouraging the enemy. He replied, "Certainly I do. It is something to weigh and weigh carefully. But I must also weigh the consequences of a wrong policy and nuclear war.")

While the investigation was in progress, during the summer of 1965, President Johnson abruptly switched tactics and began courting the Senator again.

Fulbright was invited to the White House. Secretary Rusk was called in and told to consult regularly with the Senator. The President said, "Now you two Rhodes scholars ought to be able to get together," as if they were two Rotarians from Mason City, Iowa.

The Senator from Arkansas attempted to "educate" the President. These talks were utterly futile to each man.

Johnson was, in almost an Oriental sense, a schemer. His operations were endless and intricate. He believed almost every man had a price. If a Senator came to him and said, "Lyndon, I can't go along with this bill, it's against my grain," the chances were he wanted his coffee sweetened by a deal. The President had patched together pieces of legislation out of the whims and sectional differences of ninety odd men. In this game, the shine on the surface was as important as the taste of the apple beneath. He used his boundless energies to get a bill through, and did not care how much it was altered, so long as it bore the title. This was the consensus process. Once Senator Fulbright took up an important treaty with Johnson and began to explain it. The Texan said impatiently, "I don't give a damn about that. Just tell me how many votes you need."

William H. White wrote of him, "When he [Johnson] thought of America, he thought of it either in primitive terms of Fourth of July patriotism or else as groups of people, forces, individuals, leaders, lobbies, pressures that he has spent his life in intermeshing. He was ill at ease with the broad phraseologies, purposes and meanings of civilization." He was a fundamentalist politically and religiously. At a Washington prayer breakfast with Billy Graham, Johnson used as his text, "They that wait upon the Lord shall renew their strength; they shall mount up with wings as eagles; They shall run, and not be weary; and they shall walk, and not be faint."

In the talks with Fulbright that summer, Johnson's aim was simple and practical—to keep Bill Fulbright shut up. He thought he could accomplish this by sweet-talking him, grinning, telling him a funny story, asking about the latest grandchild and Betty. Months later, after Fulbright had sharply criticized the Administration, and the press was saying he was immune to Johnson charm, the President still thought he could bring his friend back into line by sweet talk. He boasted to White House reporters they could soon get a picture of the two in great amity.

That fall, President Johnson telephoned a member of the Foreign Relations Committee and said he couldn't understand why Bill Fulbright was shooting off his mouth, that it must be the fault of Carl Marcy, the chief of staff of the Committee, and wasn't there some way to get rid of him. This was close to idiotic. Marcy was a cautious and conservative career man, and not particularly close to Fulbright. In the early spring of 1966, the White House was circulating reports that Fulbright's revolt was due to Seth Tillman, his speech writer—an equally ridiculous supposition.

Fulbright, for his part, is baffled by the man with no ear for reason. He assumes everyone is susceptible to logic and fact. The one or two members of the Committee impervious to this approach can upset his humor for days. Nor does he have any sympathy with the view that a man's convictions are a subject for haggling and dealing. To him, the only way a conviction can be changed is by new information.

His critics like to argue that Fulbright has been fickle on foreign aid. Instead, his approach is typical of his single-mindedness. In 1943, he believed the United States should help in the reconstruction of the world, but through an international agency. In the crisis of 1945–1946, when it seemed likely that Russia might try to take over a crippled Western Europe by exploiting its economic chaos, he fought for American aid as a temporary measure. In the mid-1950's, he suspected the United States was using aid as a power weapon, was becoming too much involved in the internal affairs of recipient nations, and was doing quite a bit of mischief. He told Secretary Dulles that giving arms to India and Pakistan was breeding war. By 1964, he was so disenchanted, he did not think he should champion the aid bill. By 1966, he thought the Cold War had abated enough that American aid should be channeled through such an agency as the World Bank. He feared our unilateral aid was propping up corrupt and reactionary regimes.

That summer, during these strange conversations, Senator Fulbright became aware the President was not listening to him. At one session, as the Senator was reaching the climax of an argument, Johnson suddenly dropped his glazed look, picked up the telephone on his desk and began crisply speaking to Secretary McNamara about the supersonic bomber.

"He was just enduring me," Fulbright remarked later. "I figure that the whole time I was speaking, he was turning that bomber over in his mind."

The Senator's choice of action was narrowed. He recognized he could not persuade Johnson to change his policy. He was not personally angry with him, and steadfastly refused to join any intrigues against him.

Fulbright would have preferred that the Committee issue a report on its investigation, and offer recommendations. But the Committee was split five ways to breakfast. A consensus, bringing them all together, would be a fraud.

The only choice, as he saw it, was for him to speak plainly in the Senate. So in the evenings, on long ruled paper, he began to write in a firm hand, "United States policy in the Dominican crisis was characterized initially by over-timidity and subsequently by over-reaction. Throughout the whole affair, it has also been characterized by lack of candor."

Even before the speech was given, it caused a stir. The Senator gave a draft to Lee Williams, his administrative assistant, and looked over his glasses with a slight ironic smile and said, "Let me know what you think of it."

Williams read the speech and said in alarm, "My Lord, Senator, you give this and the President will throw the book at you. You practically call him a liar."

Fulbright said politely no, he misunderstood. The point he was trying to make was that the President had been grossly misinformed. That outrageous statement about 1,500 people having their heads cut off; nothing to it. The Senator wanted to call attention to a failure in communications, and the dangers for this in other crises. We could plunge, unthinking into a terrible war.

Williams said that was not the way the President would see it.

The Senator shrugged his shoulders. That would be most unfortunate. He treasured his friend's goodwill. He said mildly, "If I perform any function, it's to get the Senate and the people to think about these matters, and hope that wiser men than I can improve our policies. We can't afford any more Dominican interventions. It would destroy any hope of controlling the direction of revolutions in Latin America."

His assistant said the Administration might withdraw its choice of Arkansas for an atomic reactor. Fulbright thought not. "The President," he said, "understands the logistics of power. The two Senators from Arkansas are chairmen of committees, and I don't think he is going to declare war on them."

On the morning of September 15, Fulbright sent a copy of his speech to President Johnson with a letter: "This speech contains my personal comments and conclusions on the information which was brought forth in the hearings. As you will note,

I believe that important mistakes were made. I further believe that a public discussion of recent events in the Dominican Republic, even though it brings forth viewpoints which are critical of actions taken by your Administration, will be of long term benefit in correcting past errors, helping to prevent their repetition in the future, and thereby advancing the broader purposes of your policy in Latin America. It is in the hope of assisting you toward these ends, and for this reason only, that I have prepared my remarks.

"Another purpose of my statement is to provide a measure of reassurance for those liberals and reformers in Latin America who were distressed by our Dominican actions, just as you did in your outstanding statement to the Latin-American Ambassabors on August 17. I believe that the people of Latin America whose efforts are essential to the success of the Alliance for Progress are in need of reassurance that the United States remains committed to the goals of social reform. I know that you are doing a great deal to provide such reassurance, and one of my purposes in this speech will be to supplement your own efforts in this field."

That afternoon, the Senator spoke dryly and unemotionally, "Very close to the beginning of the revolution, United States policy makers decided that it should not be allowed to succeed. The decision seems to me to have been based on exaggerated estimates of Communist influence and on distaste for the return to power of Juan Bosch or of a government controlled by his party."

This was a direct challenge to a major Administration theme, or, "cover story." The President had declared the reason for the Marine landings was to protect Americans living in the Dominican Republic.

The relentless voice of conscience went on: "The United States on the basis of fragmentary evidence of Communist participation, assumed from the beginning that the revolution was Communist-dominated, or would certainly become so. We misread prevailing tendencies in Latin America by overlooking or ignoring the fact that any reform movement is likely to attract Communist support. We thus failed to perceive that if we are automatically to oppose any reform movement that Communists adhere to, we are likely to end up opposing every reform movement, making ourselves the prisoners of reactionaries who wish to preserve the *status quo*.

"The principal reason for the failure of American policy in Santo Domingo was faulty advice given the President by his representatives in the Dominican Republic at the time of acute crisis . . . inadequate evidence . . . false information . . . misjudgment of the facts."

The development of the crisis, he thought, showed how each hasty decision reduced the range of options "so that errors are compounded and finally, there are few if any options except to follow through on an ill-conceived course of action. Beyond a certain point the Dominican story acquired some of the inevitability of a Greek tragedy."

He asked if this was part of a basic shift in attitude toward Latin America. "We cannot successfully advance the cause of popular democracy and at the same time align ourselves with corrupt and reactionary oligarchies; yet that is what we seem to be trying to do. The movement of the future in Latin America is social revolution. The question is whether it is to be Communist or democratic revolution, and the choice which Latin America makes will depend in part on how the United States uses its influence."

On the facts of the episode, he said the evidence showed the Communists did not take part in planning the revolt, that they never had control of it. They did have influence, "but the degree of that influence remains a matter of speculation."

His final indictment was: "In their panic lest the Dominican Republic become another Cuba, some of our officials seem to have forgotten that virtually all reform movements attract some Communist support, that there is an important difference between Communist support and Communist control, that it is quite possible to compete with the Communists for influence in a reform movement rather than to abandon it to them, and, most important of all, that economic development and social justice are themselves the primary and most reliable security against Communist subversion . . . Intervention . . . was a mistake of panic and timidity . . . a grievous mistake . . .

"One is led to the conclusion that United States policy makers were unduly timid and alarmist in refusing to gamble on the forces of reform and social change. The bitter irony of such timidity is that by casting its lot with the forces of the *status quo,* the United States almost certainly helped the Communists to acquire converts whom they otherwise could not have won . . . United States policy was marred by a lack of candor and by misinformation."

He thought, in conclusion, that the United States should have acted through the Organization of American States. This would have given policy makers a time to pause and think, and bring collective judgment into play.

President Johnson's reaction came from the guts. It was immediate, swift and terrible and gave credence to those who thought the errors in the Dominican Republic crisis did not come from panicky Foreign Service officers, but from Lyndon Johnson's panic that he would preside over another Cuba; that he had intensely personalized the consequences to himself, to his "honor," to his political prestige.

Johnson organized an attack of a sort rarely seen in Washington. Columnist Joseph Kraft said it was "not unlike the stoning reserved by high priests of primitive communities for those who question the efficacy of blood sacrifice." Marquis Childs added, "The full force of Administration spokesmen, big and little, was leveled against Fulbright; the voices turned up high did not so much seek to refute the criticism as to discredit the critic. At the lowest level, as represented by Senator Russell Long of Louisiana, the majority whip, the suggestion was that if you didn't believe Communists were about to take over the Dominican Republic, then you must have more sympathy for Communism than you know. On careful re-reading of the Fulbright speech, it is hard to discover why the reaction was as though it had been an offense against majesty . . . The example of a Senator birched for faulting the Administration raises a troubling question; Is any dialogue at all possible on the great issues of foreign policy?"

Two newspaper columns often used by the White House as a part of its personal artillery opened up. The Evans-Novak column complained: "In critical matters of foreign policy, how candid should a Senator of Fulbright's prestige be in attacking and undermining the Government's policy in such a dangerous confrontation . . . By dramatizing so harshly his own disillusion with the U.S. decision to intervene, the Senator gives the most extreme anti-U.S. political factions in the Dominican Republic a ready made presidential campaign text." William S. White, Johnson's close personal friend and a fellow Texan, railed at "Fulbright's folly," and said he had "created a poignant crisis for the orderly conduct of American foreign policy."

Senator Thomas Dodd of Connecticut, added to the attack in what *The Washington Post* referred to as "this tawdry, if familiar tactic" of his which had the "tacit blessing" of the Administration.

The sugary voice of Everett Dirksen chimed in. Even Senator Russell joined in, a bit sheepishly. He defended the American Ambassador in Santo Domingo, saying he has known him "as a small

boy," had known his "father and mother and both of his grand-
fathers" and only last year ate "with Ambassador Bennett's father
and mother in the rolling red clay hills of northeast Georgia."

Secretary McNamara called a press conference and said there was
"no question in my mind" that American citizens in the Dominican
Republic were endangered by the revolution. Fulbright had stated,
"The danger to American lives was more a pretext than a reason for
the massive United States intervention."

Finally, Johnson stage-managed a House resolution supporting
him. By a vote of 315 to 52 the House endorsed unilateral use of
force by the United States anywhere in the hemisphere to prevent a
Communist take-over. That the resolution defied the charter of the
O.A.S. did not seem to bother the President.

The fury of the assault disturbed some who supported the intervention. Senator Margaret Chase Smith, author of the "Declaration
of Conscience" in the McCarthy era, said: "I not only defend his
[Fulbright's] right to express his deeply felt views and his sharp
dissent; I admire him for speaking his mind and conscience. I admire
him for his courage to run counter to conformity and the overwhelming majority. God forbid that the United States Senate ever becomes
so shackled by conformity or dominated by a tyranny of the majority
that any Senator has to become a mental mute with his voice silenced
for fear of being castigated for expressing convictions that do not
conform with the overwhelming majority."

Senator Fulbright was honestly surprised by the fury of the Administration reaction. He remarked, "I wanted to start a discussion
about Latin-American policy, and, instead, find myself in the center
of a heated argument. It is unpleasant and reminiscent of Mc-
Carthyism."

On October 22, he replied formally in the Senate, and defined his
role as the critic. He said: "I concluded after hearing the testimony of
Administration witnesses that I could do more to encourage carefully
considered policies in the future by initiating a public discussion than
by acquiescing silently to a policy I believed mistaken. It seemed to
me . . . I was performing a service to the Administration by state-
ing my views publicly.

"A Senator has a duty to support his President and his party, but
he also has a duty to express his views on major issues. I believe that
the chairman of the Committee on Foreign Relations has a special
obligation to offer the best advice he can on matters of foreign policy;

it is an obligation which is inherent in the chairmanship which takes precedence over party loyalty, which has nothing to do with whether the chairman's views are solicited or desired by people in the executive branch . . . I am not impressed with suggestions that I had no right to speak."

He had some orderly advice for his old friend: "A consensus is a fine thing insofar as it represents a genuine reconciliation of differences; it is a miscarriage of democratic procedures insofar as it represents the concealment of differences. I think we Americans tend to put too high a value on unanimity, as if there were something dangerous and illegitimate about honest differences of opinion honestly expressed by honest men. Probably because we have been united about so many things for so long, we tend to be mistrustful of intellectual dissent, confusing it with personal hostility and political disloyalty."

The Dominican critique shuffled the cards in Washington. It showed that all the mighty power of the American President, could not silence an outraged conscience. It led others, not quite so bold, to speak their minds. Within the Democratic Party, the doves began to fly away from the hawks. Robert Kennedy, probably thinking ahead to 1972, moved closely toward Fulbright on foreign policy while Vice-President Humphrey flapped like a hawk.

The critique and the reaction Senator Fulbright set on a path of opposition, and from the Dominican crisis he went on to examine Vietnam and foreign aid. Along this path, he lost a friend and this was painful. But he has a classic strength, and with Euripides believes, "Waste not fresh tears over old griefs."

XIX

IN ALMOST EVERY man's life are a few days he would like to burn and forget. For Senator Fulbright these are two days in the fevered summer of 1964, August 6 and 7.

Of his own conduct then, he says now with a bewildered shake of his head, but without the slightest tone of self-pity, "It was an aberration. I can't vouch for what I said then. I don't know whether what I said was true. I just don't understand what happened."

In a formal address almost two years later, the Senator cited this period as an example of the failure by Congress to exercise a proper "deliberative function" and inadequate Presidential consultation with the legislative.

This is a painful honesty few would essay. But to the Senator from Arkansas truth is important. His search for the truth of August 6 and 7 has turned him from the king's advocate to leader of the opposition.

On those two days, he turned over to the President his immense personal prestige and put on the shelf, for the nonce, his sharp blade of skeptical inquiry. It was an act of personal and political loyalty to Johnson.

On the afternoon of August 6, Fulbright rose from his seat in the front row slightly to the right of the Vice President and said, "I recommend the prompt and overwhelming endorsement of the Resolution now before the Senate. The Resolution . . . endorses the wise and necessay action by President Johnson in ordering the Seventh Fleet and its air units to take appropriate measures in response to the unprovoked attacks on American naval vessels by North Vietnamese torpedo boats. The resolution further expresses the approval and support of the Congress for the determination of the President to take such action as may be necessary, now and in the future, to restrain or repel Communist aggression in Southeast Asia."

The resolution, cosponsored by Fulbright, was in the language of the Cold War: "Whereas, naval units of the Communist regime in North Vietnam, in violation of the principles of the Charter of the United Nations and of international law, have deliberately and repeatedly attacked United States naval vessels lawfully present in international waters, and have thereby created a serious threat to international peace.

"Whereas, these attacks are part of a deliberate and systematic campaign of aggression,

"The Congress approves and supports the determination of the President, as Commander in Chief, to take all necessary measures to repel any armed attack against the forces of the United States and to prevent further aggression. The resolution shall expire when the President shall determine that the peace and security of the area is reasonably assured by international conditions created by the action of the United Nations or otherwise, except that it may be terminated earlier by concurrent resolution of the Congress."

The events which brought on the resolution were, according to the Administration version: on August 2, the U.S. destroyer *Maddox* was in the Gulf of Tonkin about thirty miles off the North Vietnam mainland. Three enemy torpedo boats approached "in attack formation." They were some miles apart. The *Maddox* was about 2,500 tons, heavily armored and with great firepower, and, in addition, had air support from the carrier, *Ticonderoga*. "In accordance with naval practice," the *Maddox* fired three warning shots across the bows of the approaching vessels. The PT boats responded by firing torpedoes and machine guns. The *Maddox* and four planes from the *Ticonderoga* opened fire. There was no injury or damage to the destroyer or planes; two PT boats were damaged, a third got a direct hit.

Two days later, the *Maddox* and another destroyer were fired on by PT boats; no damage, two enemy craft sunk.

President Johnson responded swiftly, as he did seven months later after a raid on a U.S. outpost in Vietnam, and again in the Dominican crisis. He ordered naval planes to attack and destroy PT boat bases in North Vietnam and their oil storage depots. He also: moved

new attack planes into South Vietnam and Thailand, sent antisub-
marine units into the South China Sea, and alerted Army and Marine
groups for action in Vietnam.

Crosby Noyes of *The Washington Star* saw this reaction as a
sudden change in Vietnam strategy, the loosening of restraint. He
wrote: "The air strikes . . . mark a sharp departure from established American policy of studious restraint in the face of provocation. There has been no lack of such provocation . . . American
planes on patrol and reconnaissance missions have been shot down
by Russian, Chinese and satellite forces . . . In all these situations,
the policy of restraint prevailed . . . This policy, in South East
Asia, at least, has now given way to one of prompt and vigorous
retaliation . . . The mounting of 64 bombing sorties against bases
in North Vietnam is an entirely unprecedented version of a 'fitting'
response to provocation. It is difficult to explain the departure on the
basis of threats which North Vietnamese PT boats represented . . ."

Some journalists were less surprised. Columnist Ralph de Toledano had written on June 22: "Some journalist friends of the
Administration have been urged to lay the ground work for public
acceptance of what the pundits call an 'escalated' war in Vietnam.
President Johnson has already given tentative approval to a plan
calling for military action by the Navy and Air Force against bases,
staging areas and supply depots in North Vietnam . . . If the
politicians have their way, the assault on North Vietnam will take
place in mid-October, where it will have, they hope, the kind of
impact that President Kennedy's announcement of the Cuban missile
crisis and his 'ultimatum' had on the 1962 election."

This cynical view, that an incident would be provoked and a mighty
response ordered for political gain, had some currency on Capitol
Hill. The cloakroom talk was based on the President's known respect
for air power, and his often expressed belief while a Senator that the
war in Vietnam would never be won in the jungles; it would have to
be won with superior air power.

Senator Fulbright (in his later questions about the incident) tended
to think the war hawks played upon the taut temper of the President.
Once, defending Johnson against charges of manipulating events,
Fulbright said, "He has a deep insecurity in some areas, and this
makes him touchy and his temper fly off. He also has a good deal of
the old frontier mentality, the good guys have to draw fast or the bad

Indians will get them. And he has a very great respect for power as a pacifier, that is if you have it and the other party does not. He is quite cautious in attacking equal power."

A third explanation has been offered by a number of scholars headed by Franz Schurmann, director of the Center for Chinese Studies at the University of California. After studying all the public information, their report stated: "At a time when the political situation in Saigon was again deteriorating, and *thereby threatening the alleged legitimacy of the American 'presence,'* Premier Khanh began to call for aggressive action against North Vietnam to reinforce his shaky personal position. At a time when international pressures for bringing the problems of Indochina to the conference table were intensified, the United States not only openly revealed its disinclination to participate but mounted a large-scale bombardment subsequent to an incident, on August 2, which U.S. officials termed minor and to a second incident, on August 4, which, if it actually occurred, terminated in an American victory. Thus, the bombardment of North Vietnam was not only out of all proportion to the incidents alleged to have caused it; it served to worsen a climate which was becoming increasingly favorable to a negotiated settlement and concomitantly, in behalf of larger American objectives, it served to prop up the tottering regime of Premier Nguyen Khanh."

The night of the second Tonkin incident, the President appeared on television and said: "Aggression by terror against the peaceful villages of South Vietnam has now been joined by open aggression on the high seas against the United States of America . . . This is not a jungle war, but a struggle for freedom on every front of human activity."

Johnson held a well-staged emergency meeting at the White House with leaders from Capitol Hill. Secretaries Rusk and McNamara and the CIA director told a tale of Communist aggression, interspersed by a running commentary from the President. The thesis was, the PT boat attacks were part of a grand conspiracy for power by China, comparable to Hitler's move into Czechoslovakia and Russian missiles in Cuba. It was a test of American courage and will to resist. It was plain from the President's remarks, he saw this as a test of his own grit and of American unity. He asked for a resolution in Congress backing his stand.

Whatever the motives, it was a magnificent political feat, worthy of the wildest legends of Johnsoniana. He had pulled Republicans and Democrats both behind him. To critics among the doves, he presented Senator Fulbright as his chief salesman.

Senator Fulbright was the chief Senate sponsor of the resolution for two reasons. He accepted the Administration theory that this would keep the war from widening, that a prompt showing of unity and determination would inhibit North Vietnam from fresh aggression. Second, and probably most important, was the Senator's strong desire to help Lyndon Johnson counter Senator Goldwater's militancy about Vietnam. He felt that Goldwater was a real and present danger to peace. The fear of Goldwater hung like a cloud over much of Washington that summer and autumn, and it influenced the decisions of many men.

Fulbright's role as chief spokesman for the resolution was highly ironic. He had been an ardent opponent of the Middle East resolution, giving President Eisenhower sweeping powers in the Middle East. And he had severe doubts about the first of such resolutions, the Formosa Resolution of 1955. At that time, Senator Walter George, a Georgia Democrat, was chairman of the Foreign Relations Committee, and Fulbright recalls, "On the first Far East crisis, Senator George called us to his hideaway in the Capitol on a Sunday, and—he had a pontifical air anyway—he lectured us on 'the great crisis' developing in the Far East, and the 'Russian-Chinese conspiracy.' He said we must back the President; if we presented a divided front the enemy would be strengthened. It didn't sound very straight to me, but I didn't know any other facts, and felt like a jackass in being presumptuous to ask questions. This was clearance for Eisenhower and Dulles to do what they wanted in Asia, and I didn't like it. Later when the President asked for similar powers in the Middle East, I was disillusioned with Dulles, and I opposed the resolution."

The Bay of Tonkin resolution was rushed through the Senate in "immoderate haste," as Fulbright now ruefully admits. Two days of debate, and then a vote, 88 to 2. Many uneasy questions were asked. They reflected apprehensions that the whole truth was not being told. But there was a political paralysis. Mike Mansfield, the majority leader, knew more than any man there about Vietnam, and was deeply worried. But he felt he could not question Johnson on the eve of a campaign. Everett Dirksen, the minority leader, was so close to Johnson personally he was virtually a captive. The Republican Party had been taken over by Barry Goldwater, who pulled an even faster gun than Johnson.

The in-between group of moderates was restless, but willing to be reassured by Fulbright. Time and again, he wanted to sit down and turn the floor over to Senator Russell, chairman of the Armed Services Committee. But it was from Fulbright they wanted to hear.

In his opening remarks, he said the first assault by the small PT boats was an attack "without provocation," the second incident was "without doubt a calculated act of military aggression," and the American tactic was "an act of self-defense wholly consistent with Article Fifty-one of the United Nations Charter . . . The most notable fact about the American action was its great restraint."

George S. McGovern of South Dakota, the former Food for Freedom administrator, told him, "All of us have been puzzled if not baffled, as to why a little state, such as North Vietnam, should seek a deliberate naval conflict with the United States with the overwhelming naval and air power we have in that area."

He cited a *Washington Post* story. Hanoi claimed that the United States and South Vietnam sent warships to shell two islands near the area where the destroyer *Maddox* met the PT boats. One of them, Hon Me, was a PT boat base. The writer added: "The U.S. has denied that any of its warships shelled the islands. However . . . the State Department denial did not exculpate South Vietnam. It only denied American participation. There are some indications that the South Vietnamese may have attacked the two islands. American officials have declined to discuss that, although U.S. warships on occasion reportedly have escorted South Vietnam vessels part way to their targets."

Wayne Morse of Oregon said, "On Friday, July 31, South Vietnamese naval vessels . . . bombed two North Vietnamese islands. One island is approximately three miles and one approximately five miles from the main coast of North Vietnam . . . The United States knew that the bombing was going to take place . . . When these islands were bombed, American destroyers were on patrol in Tonkin Bay, and they were not sixty or sixty-five miles away . . . One can deny, but the fact that the ships were that close while the bombing took place is bound to be interpreted as provocation."

Fulbright replied, "The best information I have from high officials is that our boats did not convoy or back up any South Vietnamese naval vessels that were engaged in such attacks."

Allen Ellender of Louisiana asked a series of questions about the role of the American Navy in this area. He explained, "I am trying to discover if our forces could have done anything that might have provoked these attacks . . . Is the Senator satisfied from the evidence presented to the Committee that our naval forces did nothing to invite the attack that was made in the last few days?"

He answered, nothing that they were not entitled to do.

Ellender was not satisfied. He asked, "My question was directed as to whether or not the evidence showed any act on our part which might have provoked this attack."

Fulbright said, "I would say categorically that this was not shown. Whatever provocation there may have been arose, if it did arise, from the activity of the North Vietnamese ships."

Some time later, Senator Fulbright received a letter from an admiral who had spent his entire career on destroyers, fought with them in the Pacific in World War II, and rewrote the destroyer tactical manual, giving a different view. Rear Admiral Arnold E. True, retired, held that the *Maddox,* by opening fire, had created "an act of provocation."

Admiral True wrote: "Under International Law, there is no provision for firing 'warning' shots at another man of war. Under certain conditions, they may be used to stop merchant ships. Any shot at a man of war is considered as a hostile shot and invites retaliation as an act of war. There have been many instances of foreign men of war cruising in the vicinity of our coasts which have had American men of war trailing or shadowing them. If any of them had fired at the American ship, it would have been considered as an act of war and the American vessel would have been required to retaliate if possible."

The Admiral also said it would be extremely difficult for the *Maddox* to determine whether the PT boats were in an "attack formation" at that distance. Others have pointed out a curious omission. The United States failed to present any photographic evidence of the August 4 incident, as is common in American presentations to the United Nations Security Council.

A few days after the resolution was passed, the Pentagon, under questioning by reporters, revealed more facts. The day before the attack on the *Maddox,* South Vietnam naval units raided the Communist island bases, and the next day the destroyer sailed north into the gulf. *The Washington Post* concluded: "Whether the Red PT boats intended to attack or merely to investigate the ship is open to question. So is the question of whether at long range the North Vietnamese may have confused the U.S. destroyer with destroyer escorts supplied to South Vietnam . . ."

Another troubling point arose. American ships had been patrolling within the twelve-mile limit recognized by North Vietnam. Thirty-four nations, including South Korea and four of our allies in Latin America, recognize a twelve-mile area as being within their territorial water. Senator Fulbright explained: "They went in at least eleven miles to show that we do not recognize a twelve-mile limit." The incident took place as the *Maddox* was steaming away after having been within the twelve-mile zone.

Senator Nelson inquired, "Recognizing, as we all do, the great sensitivity of all countries, especially enemies, or those hostile to each other, what purpose is served in having our ships go within eleven miles of the North Vietnam coast?"

Senator Hugh Scott of Pennsylvania pointed out that the incident occurred after "numerous warnings" by the Communists against operating within the twelve-mile area.

Fulbright answered, "Why should the United States be so careful about the sensitivities of North Vietnam? We were there for the purpose of observation of what went on in that area, because our people felt it necessary as part of our activities in protecting and helping to protect South Vietnam . . . It has been asserted on the floor, and elsewhere, that the United States is the provocateur, the aggressor, and that we ought to be ashamed of ourselves. I do not subscribe to that view . . . I have no doubt that the moving party has been North Vietnam supported by Red China. I do not see why we should be so responsive to the sensitivities of the North Vietnamese."

For those with long memories, there was strong irony here. Fulbright might have been "Ole Tawm" Connally or Walter George growling at that damn young nuisance from Arkansas.

Nelson said doggedly, "If patrolling that close has no necessary bearing upon the mission we have insisted we have in South Vietnam, it would seem to me that perhaps it is not the exercise of our best judgment to do it . . . It would be mighty risky if Cuban PT boats were firing on Florida, and Russian destroyers were patrolling between us and Cuba, eleven miles out. It would be a grave risk for her to be testing our viewpoint about her patrolling so close when

Cuban boats were firing on Florida. So the question was whether the patrolling that close was really necessary to accomplish our mission. We are, after all, dealing with incinerating the whole world."

Fulbright replied, "I do not see how the case is analagous."

One of the Administration "myths," as the Senator would call them, was shot down by a reporter for *The Washington Post*—the "myth that the incident was deliberately provoked by North Vietnam and Red China. *The Post* said: "As hours and days pass without any sign of any military buildup to retaliate for the U.S. air pounding of Communist torpedo boat bases in North Vietnam . . . American estimates of the crisis are being reexamined . . . Officials are now giving greater weight to the possibility that the Sunday and Tuesday attacks on the destroyers off North Vietnam may not have been an elaborate plot [but] could have been the result of confusion and miscalculation by North Vietnam instead of a deliberate plot joined in by Red China."

The debate was full of uneasiness, and Senator Fulbright was required to give assurances over and over again. John Sherman Cooper of Kentucky, former Ambassador to India, a close personal friend of President Kennedy, asked, "If the President decided that it was necessary to use such force as could lead into war, will we give that authority by this resolution?"

"That's the way I would interpret it."

"I ask these questions, because it is well for the country and for all of us to know what is being undertaken," Senator Cooper explained gravely. "The power provided the President in section two is great."

Fulbright responded: "This provision is intended to give clearance to the President to use his discretion. We all hope and believe that the President will not use this discretion arbitrarily or irresponsibly. We know that he is accustomed to consulting with the Joint Chiefs of Staff and with Congressional leaders. But he does not have to do it. I have no doubt that the President will consult with Congress in case a major change in present policy becomes necessary."

Cooper expressed a lingering doubt, "I believe we have the obligation of understanding fully that there is a distinction between defending our own forces, and taking offensive measures which could lead progressively to a third world war."

The House in a mood of mass patriotic fervor slammed through the resolution with no dissenting votes and hardly any debate. But the Senators had more questions, and so Fulbright was on his feet.

Senator McGovern quoted the then Premier of South Vietnam as demanding the war be taken to the north. Was the Administration likely to do this?

"I do not think there is any danger of that," Fulbright said.

Daniel Brewster of Maryland, a former Marine, said anxiously, "I had an opportunity to see warfare not so very far from this area, and it was very mean. I would look with great dismay on a situation involving the landing of large land armies on the continent of Asia. Is there anything in the resolution which would authorize or recommend or approve the landing of large American armies in Vietnam or in China?"

There was nothing in the resolution that contemplated this. "This is the last thing we would want to do," Fulbright replied. "However, the language of the resolution would not prevent it."

Jacob Javits of New York wanted to know, had the President acted after consulting our SEATO allies, and were they helping us in Vietnam? "It is one thing," Javits said, "to stand alone. It is another to stand with seven other countries implementing a solemn commitment which is just as binding on them as on us. I am sometimes inclined to agree with those who say we cannot be the policeman or guardian of the whole world."

The answer to both questions was in the negative.

Javits hoped there would be joint action in the future. He wanted the United Nations brought in. Fulbright agreed.

The lack of complete trust in the Administration and the faith in Fulbright was indicated by Javits' next statement. He said, "Can the Senator commit himself, as chairman of the Foreign Relations Committee, to be our 'sentinel' to follow through on these matters after the resolution is passed?"

The Senator from Arkansas pledges, "I shall do everything I can, within the limits of my capacity and my position. I am not looking for an expansion of the war. I am looking for any way I can to bring in with us both our Allies and the United Nations.

Javits then said he would agree to the resolution "providing that we would have some feeling in our heart that there will be a really meaningful follow-through, which we have sometimes lacked before."

Senator Nelson said there were sixteen thousand American troops in Vietnam. Did the resolution authorize the President to land as many divisions as he thought necessary "and engage in a direct military assault on North Vietnam."

"I do not know what the limits are," Fulbright replied. "I personally feel that it would be very unwise under any circumstances to put a large land army on the Asian continent. It has been an article of faith ever since I have been in the Senate that we would never be bogged down in Asia."

"We may not be able to control the discretion vested in the Commander in Chief," Nelson reminded him. "I don't think Congress should leave the impression that it consents to a radical change in our mission in South Vietnam." He proposed to add to the resolution these lines: "Our continuing policy is to limit our role to the provision of aid, training assistance and military advice, and it is the sense of Congress that, except when provoked to a greater response, we should continue to avoid a direct military involvement in the Southeast Asia conflict."

Fulbright said he could not accept the amendment. He had no basic disagreement, but felt it would "delay passage of the resolution and cause confusion." He did not explain why such haste was demanded, but it seems likely the President was on the telephone to the cloakroom wanting to know when in hell the Senate was going to vote, and frantic messages were passed to Fulbright.

In his final words, the Senator said that, although he recognized the apprehensions of many colleagues, the job of defending the national security was, after all, that of the President. He concluded in his soft voice, now tired from the long day, "I believe the resolution is calculated to prevent the spread of the war."

His words have turned to acid. By October of 1964, the martial spirit had so risen within the Administration that James Reston wrote in *The New York Times:* "It is difficult to understand why some prominent officials, a few weeks before a national election, should be talking openly about expanding the war, and not only advocating but almost lobbying for such a course of action. It is even possible now to hear officials of this Government talking casually about how easy it would be to 'provoke an incident' in the Gulf of Tonkin which would justify an attack upon North Vietnam." Walter Lippmann reported the existence of a strong clique of war hawks; they believed war with China was inevitable, and urged "preventive war" to smash her nuclear facilities.

Senator Fulbright has spoken with singular honesty about the resolution and his role in it: "The joint resolution was a blank check signed by Congress in an atmosphere of urgency that seemed at the time to preclude debate. Since its adoption the Administration converted the Vietnamese conflict from a civil war in which some American advisers were involved to a major international war in which the principal fighting unit is an American army of two hundred and fifty thousand men. Each time the Senators have raised questions about successive escalations of the war, we have had the blank check of August 7, 1964, waved in our faces as supposed evidence of the overwhelming support of the Congress for a policy in Southeast Asia which, in fact, has been radically changed since the summer of 1964."

The Senator has also noted that a few weeks after the resolution was signed, the Administration received through U Thant, Secretary-General of the United Nations, a proposal from Hanoi for peace talks in Rangoon, and turned down the bid. Congressmen were not told of it. It came to public attention when in November, 1965, Eric Sevareid recounted a despairing conversation with Adlai Stevenson shortly before his death. A State Department spokesman said we did not believe the North Vietnamese were "prepared for serious talks," but newspapers speculated the President did not wish to clutter up the campaign with such a delicate issue as peace negotiations.

Senator Fulbright explains his role with unusual candor: "I trusted the President. I thought he would use the resolution wisely and with restraint. This was just two weeks after the Republican National Convention, and I was influenced by partisanship. Goldwater was so ridiculous and so extreme, I thought the danger of escalating the war would come from him and his followers. I didn't want to make any difficulties for the President in his campaign against Goldwater, whose election I thought would be a disaster. My role in the adoption of the resolution is a source of neither pleasure nor pride to me today."

The events of the next six months shocked and dismayed Senator Fulbright. The war exploded in size and intensity. The crucial event, in his change from Administration hawk to a strongly dissident dove, was the Dominican landings and his investigation. A patient and thorough study proved the Administration had lied or told half-truths about events in the Caribbean.

Even more important, at least to him personally, was a dreadful possibility. If the Administration had not been entirely honest with the facts on the Gulf of Tonkin, he was guilty as an accomplice. For a man who pays such high court to truth, who views war with such horror, this was monstrous.

His troubled conscience became a dynamo. This was the engine behind the most thorough examination of a war ever made by Congress: the Foreign Relations Committe study of Vietnam. At times the search for truth was so baffling and his hopes of bringing facts to the public so frustrated, the Senator put his hands to his forehead and cried out, "Good God, I am discouraged."

XX 🌿

ON THE FIRST day of 1965, three Communist battalions struck and destroyed a larger South Vietnamese force at Binh-Gia.

This was a most ominous sign. The American program of arming and training South Vietnamese troops, on which both Eisenhower and Kennedy relied, was a failure. If the Vietcong were to be held militarily, new and more violent action was demanded. This is why Senator Fulbright later said we drifted into a war through an aid program. We gave money and advice and then, like a gambler putting down his ante, committed ourselves to the whole game.

Congress was restive. On January 3, Senator Frank Church of Idaho, said, "A full-fledged debate on Vietnam is long overdue. At the very least, such a debate would give the American people a better idea of the alternatives available to us." An Associated Press poll of eighty-three Senators showed only seven favored sending in American combat troops or bombing North Vietnam, three wanted to get out immediately, ten favored negotiations now, and thirty-one when the military balance was improved for us. Majority Leader Mansfield privately asked President Johnson to consider President de Gaulle's proposal that all Southeast Asia be neutralized. Senators John Sherman Cooper and Wayne Morse asked that the Geneva Conference which ended the Indochina war be reconvened.

On January 4, in his State of the Union message, President Johnson (and later Secretary Rusk) made it plain we were in Vietnam for keeps. The President said, "We are there because a friendly nation has asked us for help against Communist aggression. Ten years ago the President pledged our help . . . We will not break it now. Second, our own security is tied to the peace of

Asia . . . What is at stake is the cause of freedom, and in that cause America will never be found wanting."

On January 12, Senator Fulbright publicly disagreed. By placing in *The Congressional Record* a magazine interview with Senator Church, the chairman identified himself with a mild dissent and gave the Administration a sure warning. Church said it was a mistake for the United States to intervene after the French defeat, that the issue was largely internal—that is a civil war, instead of the aggression the Administration claimed—and it would be a serious error to enlarge the American role.

Another Vietnamese Premier was ousted in a coup January 27. Senator Ernest Gruening of Alaska said, "We cannot tell from day to day and from hour to hour who or what is the duly constituted legal Government."

At the same time, Senator Fulbright showed his growing disenchantment in two ways. He talked to columnist Holmes Alexander who wrote, "He wants palpable evidence of a chance for victory before he takes out his papers as a booster. Specifically he tells me he would believe in our Vietnam venture if he beheld the flags of more Southeast Asian countries in the anti Communist ranks, and heard the tread of Filipinos, South Koreans, Thais, Australians and New Zealanders . . . Senator Fulbright is beset by another and larger reservation that blocks full commitment. His doubts extend to the whole question of how much emphasis we should give to waging the cold war." According to the column, the Senator said the Cold War was sapping our vitality and growth, and he wanted a high priority for programs "promoting the welfare and happiness of our people."

Secondly, he said he would not serve as floor manager for the Administration's $3.38 billion foreign aid package. The program of the United States giving directly to a foreign nation had, he said, outlived its usefulness. The funds should be channeled through a regional or world authority, so the donor would not become too closely mixed up in the political life of the recipient. Our involvement in Vietnam, he claimed, started with a foreign aid program and is "a pretty horrible example of how foreign aid can get out of control." He also wanted military funds separated from economic development moneys.

William S. White wrote indignantly, "This was an unexampled abdication of the traditional responsibility of a chairman of the Foreign Relations Committee."

Senator Fulbright moved another step away from the Diplomatic Establishment and its obsession with the Cold War in Asia. He said the United States should take the initiative to improve relations with Soviet Russia, by inviting the U.S.S.R. to join with us in aid to India and in developing a new Central American canal, as part of a consortium. The Republican leaders, Senator Dirksen and Congressman Gerald Ford, said the Russians would have to make concessions first. No concession, no deal. Without mentioning them by name, Fulbright spoke of "flag-waving professional patriots." Dirksen replied silkily, "How splendid it would have been if Senator Fulbright's proposal had been available in 1961. We could have helped the Communists build the Berlin wall. Oh international consortium what promise you hold!"

It may have seemed to the suspicious people at the White House that he was deliberately needling the Administration. Not this time. (Senator Fulbright, at times, does take an impish delight in keeping an opponent off-balance. His enjoyment is quite evident in his great good humor and smiles during a Committee hearing when he is jabbing and stinging.) Actually, Fulbright was thinking of ways to cool down the Vietnam war. One, he believed, was to channel our aid through another agency. The second was to improve our relations with Russia, which might then use its good offices to mediate the dispute without humiliating the United States.

On February 6, Soviet Premier Kosygin arrived in Hanoi for talks. On the next day events moved to a high plane of violence. There was an incident much like that in the Gulf of Tonkin. A small guerrilla force attacked a U.S. outpost at Pleiku; eight Americans were killed and more than a hundred wounded by explosives. It was of no great strategic importance. President Johnson responded with a swift retribution, round-the-clock bombings of North Vietnam. They began while Kosygin was still in Hanoi. Johnson did not consult with Congressional leaders or the SEATO allies.

The next day Premier Kosygin announced the Soviet would help Hanoi if North Vietnam were invaded. The Indian Foreign Minister asked for a new Geneva conference.

On February 11, the Vietcong blew up an American barracks at Qui-Nhon, killing nineteen. On February 12, 160 American and Vietnamese planes attacked the north. James Reston wrote in *The New York Times,* "There is doubt all over Washington tonight about both American policy and purpose." Walter Lippmann said a new argument had been introduced into the policy councils, "that the way to stabilize South Vietnam is to wage war against North Vietnam." Hanson Baldwin, *The Times'* military commentator, saw the possibility of 200,000 to a million Americans fighting in Vietnam. Senator Church told his colleagues, "We lost a hundred and fifty-seven thousand dead and wounded in Korea. The fighting cost us $18 billion. But, in the end, we had to go to the conference table. There was no victory for us in Korea."

The whole world was caught in a fever of alarm. A symptom was Secretary General U Thant trying through the United Nations and his own contacts in Asia to bring the Vietnam war to the conference table. The fear expressed in the world press was that more escalation would inevitably bring on World War III.

Yet the raid on Pleiku, the event that brought on the bombing, turned out in press dispatches to have been far more trivial than the Administration originally believed. The first version was that this was a deliberate attack upon the United States, planned in Hanoi probably with Chinese help.

The Associated Press suggested the Vietcong had only exploited bad security at Pleiku. The camp was on an open plain with a view for several miles, so raiders might be easily seen. Yet the guerrillas came across the plain, cut through two lines of barbed wire and laid explosive charges against a wall. The A.P. said: "Anyone who has ever gone to war and fought on a perimeter defense must be asking: what happened to the night patrols? Where were the listening posts? Has the practice of staking out enemy routes of approach been abandoned? Was there no illumination available, such as parachute flares or artificial moonlight—searchlights aimed at the clouds?" The official reply of the Pentagon, the A.P. said, was, "We don't know."

Other facts came to light. The attack was two hours after the end of the cease-fire for the New Year holiday had expired, and more than half the South Vietnamese troops on guard had not returned to the base. *The New York Times* said: "The official explanation of events surrounding the American air strikes on North Vietnam have left a number of important questions unanswered . . . One question involves the use of weapons used by the attacking Vietcong unit. The heaviest were American made 81-mm mortars . . . The question is, therefore, that if the Vietcong unit at Pleiku was using captured weapons, would this sustain the argument that North Vietnam made possible this particular attack?

"Administration sources also contend that the size and intensity of the attack indicated that it was a major blow carefully timed by Hanoi. Yet reports from the field indicate that a company—or less— of Vietcong troops took part. A Vietcong company is estimated to have 200 to 300 men. This is not a large Vietcong assault. Many are much larger. There were American casualties, but the attack was not especially intense. On a number of occasions whole South Vietnamese infantry units up to company size have been wiped out by the Vietcong in night assaults. Another factor advanced by Government sources is a belief that attacks launched the same night at Tuy Hoa and a group of villages near Nhatrang indicated . . . a pattern of over-all direction, probably from Hanoi . . . Since large numbers of Vietcong attacks have taken place throughout South Vietnam on other nights, it is asked, why should this be?"

The Wall Street Journal reported: "Clamor for a negotiated peace was growing in Congress, among key allies and even within Administration councils. . . . In this atmosphere, the latest, most brazen guerilla blow at a U.S. installation in South Vietnam struck many U.S. policy makers, for many different reasons, as just the sort of provocation they have been looking for."

On February 23, the President struck back at his critics through Senator Dodd, a typical Johnson ploy. Dodd said, "The demand that we negotiate now over Vietnam is akin to asking Churchill to negotiate with the Germans at the time of Dunkirk . . . The great majority of those who advocate that we abandon Vietnam to Communism, either by pulling out or negotiating a settlement, have not taken the time to weigh the consequence of defeat [which] would be so catastrophic we simply cannot permit ourselves to think of it . . . It would result in the early disintegration of all our alliances, and in the total eclipse of America as a great nation . . ."

Five days later the President announced continuous bomber strikes on North Vietnam. The intention—to force the Communists into a negotiated settlement the Administration felt it could live with. Apparently, from word circulated on The Hill, Johnson wanted a flat guarantee from Hanoi it would call off the guerrillas, and give no further aid and comfort to rebellious movements.

The war in Vietnam looked to Fulbright "pretty damn dismal." He began reading extensively about Southeast Asia, and particularly Vietnam, and talking informally to scholars.

He found there were a few facts almost everyone accepted. Vietnam was a composite of many fiercely independent tribes and sects, but the people—divided as they were—united to fight the foreign overlord. At no time had the people of this long, densely wooded tropical land ever allowed an occupier peace. The Senator was impressed by the comments of two Vietnamese to *New York Times* reporter Neil Sheehan. One said, "We Vietnamese are somewhat xenophobe. We don't like foreigners, any kind of foreigners, so that you shouldn't be surprised that we don't like you." The other remarked, "Any time legions of prosperous white men descend on a rudimentary Asian society, you are bound to have trouble." Vietnam was a Chinese colony for a thousand years and finally threw off its conquerors in 940. In the late 1800's, Vietnam came under French control, as part of Indochina, and remained so for sixty years. There were rebellions. An anticolonial revolt led chiefly by Communists was put down in 1933.

The Communist influence in the anticolonial agitations and uprisings was probably, the Senator thought, more accidental than deliberate. Vietnamese intellectuals and nationalists tended to go to France, with its large Socialist and Communist blocs, rather than India, where Gandhi's campaign of passive resistance stirred the masses. Ho Chi Minh, the leader of Communist North Vietnam, as a young man drifted to France and fell in with the Socialists, because they opposed a harsh colonial policy. A Communist fraction split off after World War I, and called for immediate independence of colonial areas. Ho, as an ardent nationalist, joined the Communists for this reason. He went to Russia to be trained as a revolutionary and studied at the University of Toilers of the East in Moscow. From there he went to China, at a time when Chiang Kai-shek was working with the Soviets. Ho selected revolutionaries for work in colonial areas of Asia, and many of his agents were trained at the Chinese military academy at Whampoa.

Ho Chi Minh was sent into Vietnam, by (and here there is disagreement) either the Chinese Nationalists or the American OSS (the predecessor of the CIA) during the Japanese occupation. His Vietminh guerrillas, with a strong Communist base not dominated by them, were armed by both China and the United States. The Vietminh by May, 1945, had seized part of North Vietnam, and on September 2 took over Hanoi and proclaimed the "Democratic Republic of Viet-Nam."

The Japanese, as they pulled out, left a native regime in keeping with their theme "Asia for the Asiatics." The ruler was Emperor Bao Dai, who had ruled Annam in central Vietnam under French aegis.

Fate, accident, the whim of the gods again intervened in Vietnam. President Roosevelt strongly opposed a French return to its colonial holdings, and wanted Indochina set up under a United Nations trusteeship, and free of big power control.

He died, the Cold War broke out, and President Truman supported France's claims to its old colonies. During the bitter eight-year war, the United States largely underwrote the costs, and had spent more than a billion dollars by 1953. Many of the guns used by both sides were made in America. "What a tangled web we weave with our military assistance," Senator Fulbright has commented wryly.

The French colonial army, including the Foreign Legion with a goodly share of Nazi veterans in it (no French conscripts served in this war), was defeated in 1954, and the officer class badly depleted. This was a galling defeat, for which the army blamed the "politicians," just as had the German General Staff following World War I. In 1958, following further reverses in Algiers, the military overthrew the Fourth Republic and placed General de Gaulle in power. To Fulbright, with his experience with General MacArthur and the military seminars, this was an ominous succession of events. He believes events of passion and violence in one part of the world influence events elsewhere. For example, the African freedom movement created a new militancy in the American civil rights struggle. The Senator feared the seizure of political power by the generals in France, traditionally a democratic country, would create a more militant and demanding mood by the Pentagon. A year later, oddly enough, the Defense Department was talking of 500,000 troops in Vietnam and a military presence of from five to twenty years.

After the defeat at Dien Bien Phu, the war went to the conference table at Geneva in 1954. The armistice provided that the Vietminh, then physically in possession of three-fourths of Vietnam outside the cities, withdraw to north of the 17th parallel, and the French and the Bao Dai regime to the south. The Geneva declaration promised elections in two years to unify the nation under a single government. There was every reason to believe Ho and his partisans would win.

The United States was not a signer of the Geneva accord, but declared it would "refrain from any threat or use of force to disturb" the agreement, "would view any renewal of the aggression in violation of the aforesaid agreement with grave concern," and "shall continue to seek to achieve unity through free elections, supervised by the United Nations to insure they are concluded fairly."

President Eisenhower's caution about getting into a war without partners and Congressional approval kept the United States out of Indochina in April, 1954, when the French drive was faltering. Secretary Dulles and Vice-President Nixon favored a plan by Admiral Arthur W. Radford, chairman of the Joint Chiefs of Staff, to attack a major supply area close to the Chinese frontier with atomic weapons. On Saturday morning, April 3, Dulles invited five Senators and three Representatives to his office, and there Radford unfurled his plan. Fulbright was not invited, but was told the details by Johnson and Russell.

Dulles presented his "domino" theory, that if Vietnam fell to the Communists all of Asia would fall to them, and the United States would be forced back to Hawaii. He had in his pocket a joint resolution he wanted Congress to back. Senator Johnson said he didn't think we should be asked to take up the burdens alone, with the collapse of the French, and he asked Dulles to shop around with our Allies. The British objected, saying this was likely to lead to World War III in Asia, and it would be a costly land war. By then, Nixon had spilled some of the plan to newspaper editors; their reaction, so soon after Korea, was bad, and doubts grew on Capitol Hill. President Eisenhower then called off the scheme, which, incidentally, a majority of the Joint Chiefs of Staff also opposed. Secretary of the Treasury George Humphrey was against the plan as well because of its heavy demands upon the budget.

The French, tired of the burdens and costs of Indochina, pulled out, and the United States soon moved in to prevent the domino from falling. (The French, now that they are no longer spending lives and treasure in the jungles, are more detached. Foreign Minister Couve de Murville has said, "In Vietnam what is at stake is the fate of a people to whom we are deeply attached. What is probably at stake, too, for a long time to come, is the future relationship between the white and colored peoples, at any rate in Asia. The peace of the world may also be concerned, for whatever may be said, America and China are at grips there.") The precarious regime of Bao Dai was nominally in control of South Vietnam. The civil service was weak and corrupt. A million refugees, many of them Catholics who had been converted by French priests, were pouring into the preponderantly Buddhist south, creating a new friction. Religious warfare had been a part of the

Vietnamese scene for a hundred years. Food and housing were at a premium. The countryside needed agrarian reform. The American presence, hopefully, would stir reform, set up a strong and popular government, and train a first-rate army.

Another factor influencing American intervention was the concern of the Roman Catholic Church for its faithful. Cardinal Spellman had spoken of this to Secretary Dulles. The Cardinal, together with such leading Catholic laymen as Senator Mansfield and Joseph P. Kennedy, had a candidate for the leadership of a reformist government. He was Ngo Dinh Diem, a Vietnamese nationalist of a high caste Catholic family who had spent considerable time in America since 1950. As a young man he was an honest and promising administrator in Annam, and Ho Chi Minh in 1949 offered him the key post of Minister of the Interior. He turned it down, because the Vietminh had murdered his brother.

On July 7, 1954, Bao Dai named Diem Premier, following the American suggestion, and early the next year the U.S. Military Assistance Advisory Group took over training the army. But there was too much disarray, the reforms were too little and too late. A revolt of minority sects spread into large scale dissidence in the spring of 1955, and had to be put down by the army.

On July 25, 1955, with American backing, Diem denounced the elections scheduled for 1956 as part of the Geneva agreement. Diem said the people in the north could not vote freely, and falsified votes would throw the election to Ho. Three months later, a referendum in South Vietnam gave 98 percent of the votes to Diem. This is one of the ironies Senator Fulbright invariably catches. (It was noted in the Senator's Foreign Relations Committee background report on Vietnam.)

The Senator feels the consequences of this were far-reaching. He said later, "Having been betrayed after previous negotiations—by the French in 1946 and by Ngo Dinh Diem in 1955 when, with American complicity, he refused to allow the elections called for in the Geneva accords to take place—the Hanoi Government may now feel that American offers to negotiate peace, which we believe to be genuine, are in reality plots to trick them into yielding through diplomacy what we have been unable to make them yield by force."

The organized terrorism of the Vietcong began soon after this.

Diem was hugged to the American bosom. Vice-President Nixon went to Saigon in 1956 and hailed him and declared, "The militant march of Communism has been halted." In May, 1957, Diem came to Washington and addressed a joint session of Congress. Yet by mid-April, 1960, his regime was in such disfavor in Vietnam through corruption and terror that eighteen leading citizens, ten of them former Ministers, protested: "Continuous arrests fill the jails and prisons to the rafters, as at this precise moment; public opinion and the press are reduced to silence. The same applies to the popular will as translated in certain open elections, in which it is insulted and trampled. Political parties and religious sects have been eliminated. Groups or movements have replaced them. But this substitution has only brought about new oppression against the population without protecting it for that matter against Communist enterprises . . . The size of the territory has shrunk, but the number of civil servants has increased, and still the work does not get done." The army, they said, was divided.

Diem was overthrown and assassinated on November 1, 1963.

A few days after the coup, President Kennedy was so discouraged by the events he told the most outspoken Congressional critic of American policy, Senator Wayne Morse, "You could be right, Wayne. I just don't know. But I'm going to order a review."

The problem that oppressed Kennedy was later put into words by Senator Fulbright: "We are now engaged in a war to 'defend freedom' in South Vietnam. Unlike the Republic of Korea, South Vietnam has an army which operates without notable success and a weak dictatorial government which does not command the loyalty of the South Vietnamese people. The official war aims of the United States Government, as I understand them, are to defeat what is regarded as North Vietnamese aggression, to demonstrate the futility of what the Communists call 'wars of national liberation' and to create conditions under which the South Vietnamese people will be able freely to determine their own future . . . What I do doubt—and doubt very much—is the ability of the United States to achieve these aims by the means being used. I do not question the power of our weapons and the efficiency of our logic. What I do question is the ability of the United States, or France or any other Western nation, to go into a small, alien, undeveloped Asian nation and create stability where there is chaos, the will to fight where there is defeatism, democracy where there is no tradition of it and honest government where corruption is almost a way of life."

President Johnson's first full year in the White House, 1964, was a bad year in Vietnam—a series of coups, increasing gains by the Vietcong, a high desertion rate by new recruits (30 percent by January, 1965), student demonstrations in Saigon and Hue against the war, and a rise in Buddhist dissidence. As 1965 began, a correspondent of Le Croix, the daily of the Catholic Archepiscopate of Paris, wrote from Vietnam: "The escalation continues, implacably. Hate grows on both sides as the immense means at the disposal of the United States comes into play. Already in use are phosphorous bombs, napalm bombs and 'improved' tear gas, and weapons which, it is said, utilize californium and pulverize everything within a radius of forty meters, while in Saigon and elsewhere, cases of terrorism multiply. The distinct impression which emerges from this alarming situation is that the United States is enraged to find itself facing a small adversary which it is unable to overcome."

Senator Fulbright found contradictions in two areas of his research, the Vietcong and the American commitment to Vietnam.

On February 7, 1965, the State Department issued a white paper, which stated, "The hard core of the Communist forces attacking South Viet-Nam are men trained in North Viet-Nam. They are ordered into the South and remain under military discipline of the Military High Command in Hanoi." The war, it said, is "not a spontaneous and local rebellion against the established government." Instead, "a Communist government has set out deliberately to conquer a sovereign people in a neighboring state," the war was "inspired, directed, supplied and controlled" by Hanoi.

Foreign sources told a different tale. Premier Eisaku Sato of Japan sent a senior statesman, Shunichi Matsumotto, to Vietnam to find out the facts for him. He reported that "even the people of Saigon" estimated that the Communists within the Vietcong were "at the most, 30 percent." The noted French journalists, Philippe Devillers, editor of France-Asie, and Jean Lacouture of Le Monde, reported the Vietcong had been formed by veterans of the Vietminh living in the south, after Diem's refusal to agree to the elections and his arrest of Vietminh veterans; that Diem's excesses and lack of reforms brought it recruits, and that it was more militant than Hanoi. According to this view, the Vietcong received support from the north only after the Vietcong threatened to go to the Chinese in 1960. Hanoi did not wish to become too closely connected with the Vietcong for fear of U.S. reprisals on the north.

On the matter of supplies, Bernard B. Fall, the most widely quoted

Vietnam expert living in America, told *The Washington Post* that documents of the International Control Commission in Saigon "seem to show that less than 7 percent of the captured weapons [from the Vietcong between 1962 and 1964] are of Communist origin," that is, made in a Communist country. Instead, according to Fall, Devillers and Lacouture, most of the guns came from South Vietnam deserters and army stores. Malcolm W. Browne, the Associated Press reporter who won a Pulitzer Prize for his dispatches from Vietnam, stated, "Intelligence experts feel less than 10 percent and probably more like 2 percent of the Viet Cong's stock of modern weapons is Communist made," and "only a small part of Viet Cong increase in strength has resulted from infiltration of North Vietnamese Communist troops into South Vietnam."

Browne described the National Liberation Front, the political arm of the Vietcong, as a Communist-front organization "appealing for the support of every social class," and with "strong, but subtle ties to Hanoi." Nonetheless, he wrote, "Western intelligence experts believe that the proportion of Communists is probably extremely small."

On the American commitment, the Administration pointed to a letter of President Eisenhower to Diem on October 23, 1954, and the Southeast Asia Collective Defense Treaty of 1955. In the first, Eisenhower offered economic aid on the condition that "standards of performance" were maintained. He said, "The purpose of this offer is to assist the Government of Viet-Nam in developing and maintaining a strong, viable state, capable of resisting attempted subversion or aggression through military means." President Kennedy said in September, 1963, "In the final analysis, it's their war. They're the ones who have to win it or lose it. We can help, give them equipment, we can send our men out there as advisers, but they have to win it."

The SEATO treaty looked at two possibilities, armed attack and subversion. If there was an attack, member nations would act "to meet the common danger." This would be almost automatic. The treaty's chief architect, Secretary Dulles, explained to Senators in late January, 1955, how he thought of "attack"; he took the conventional view, as when Hitler's tanks rolled into Poland, or, in this case, North Vietnamese and Chinese battalions pushed south. He thought such attacks could be deterred by massive American air and sea power, operating mainly from aircraft carriers. (President Eisenhower's chief military adviser was an admiral with strong Asia First leanings. The

giant American air base at Cam Ranh in 1966 showed President
Johnson's long flirtation with the Air Force.)

In case of subversion, including guerrilla warfare, SEATO members would consult one another on the action to be taken. This was a
more deliberative step. In 1964 when the Vietnam war was escalated, there was no "armed attack" from the north. Even by stretching a point, the PT boat maneuvers were hardly in this class. To
Fulbright, the legalist, this weakened our case for leaning on the
SEATO treaty. He mused aloud, "Throughout history the world has
suffered from idealists who have fallen victim to the fatuous illusion
that they and they alone are in possession of the key of paradise and
are guilty of an excess of zeal. The true believer makes war in the
name of peace and commits murder in the name of human happiness." Americans had an inheritance of intolerance from the Puritans
which was "harsh and ascetic and intolerant, promising salvation for
the few, but damnation for the many. Moderation prevails [in
America] until a crisis, and then puritanism responds, and people
look at the world through the distorting prism of a harsh and angry
moralism. When our latent puritanism is aroused, we see principles
where there are only interests, conspiracy where there is only misfortune, and when this view of things prevails, conflicts become
crusades, righteousness becomes the justification for unlimited violence, and claims of morality become delusion and hypocrisy . . .
Our failing, I think, is the mischief or the great virtue of idealism in-
sufficiently tempered by the sobering wisdom of experience. It is this
crusading tendency, so noble in intent, so potentially destructive in its
own consequences that we must guard against in our relations with
the Communist world."

This is basic to his thinking about Vietnam, and our policy there
illustrates for him the faults that lie, usually dormant, within the
American ethic. The American action in Vietnam offends his belief in
cooperative action, moderation, quiet diplomacy, firm civilian controls on the military, political and economic reforms in dealing with a
revolutionary movement, the maintenance of civil liberties.

A few days after President Johnson decided on continual bombings, General Maxwell Taylor, then our Ambassador to Saigon,
appeared before the Foreign Relations Committee. Senator Fulbright
sat listening to him, his shoulders hunched over, frowning, the picture
of a troubled man.

After the general finished his statement, Fulbright said slowly, "I am most apprehensive and unhappy about the situation in Vietnam. Whenever fighting is going on, there is the danger it may get out of control. I am not certain we have gone all the way in exploring what kind of a settlement we would accept."

XXI

SENATOR FULBRIGHT began searching for a solution in Vietnam. It was a damnably frustrating task. An answer that might be feasible one day slipped away with the passing of time. The more intense a war between proud peoples grows, the more difficult it is to bring them together. Anger begets its own fire. Also, as he knew, Lyndon Johnson regarded Vietnam as a test of himself. It was the one victory he wanted to win above all others.

Even as the Senator from Arkansas looked for a way out, events were cruel and pressing.

U Thant proposed on March 8, 1965, a preliminary conference on Vietnam. It would include the United States, Russia, Great Britain, France, Communist China and the two Vietnams. The next day, without consulting Congress, the Administration rejected the idea until North Vietnam "ceased its aggression."

Word began circulating through the Capitol Hill grapevine that Johnson had become most interested in the doctrine of "persuasive deterrence." This was the brainchild of the Strategic Air Command, and the President had been particularly close to SAC as a Senator and chairman of the Preparedness Subcommittee. This doctrine was spelled out by the former SAC chief, General Thomas S. Power, in his book, *Design for Survival:* "Let us assume that in the fall of 1964, we would have warned the Communists that unless they ceased supporting the guerillas in South Vietnam, we would destroy a major military depot in North Vietnam [by air attack]. Through radio and leaflets, we would have advised the civilian population living near the depot of our ultimatum and of the exact time of our attack so that the civilians could be evacuated. If the Communists failed to heed our warning and continued to support the rebels, we would have gone through with the threatened attack and destroyed the depot. And if this act of 'persuasive deterrence' had not sufficed, we would have threatened the destruction of another critical target, and, if necessary, would have destroyed it also. We would have continued this strategy until the Communists had found their support of the rebels in South Vietnam too expensive and agreed to stop it."

Senator Fulbright thought this an expansion of the myth of strategic bombing. From his reading, it appeared that heavy bombing did not bring Germany to its knees, nor seriously reduce its production. How could it then be effective against the more primitive and equally nationalistic Asian civilization of North Vietnam?

Events rolled on. On March 22, the Pentagon admitted what the newspapers had been saying for days. "Riot-control" gasses were being used in Vietnam to "save lives." The Federation of American Scientists thought it "morally repugnant that the United States should find itself the party to the use of weapons of indiscriminate effect, with principal effectiveness against civilian populations . . . The characterization of such applications as 'humane' is incomprehensible to say the least. In recent weeks, we have been treated to a succession of stories which have included the employment of napalm against villages, the use of crop-destroying agents, so called defoliating chemicals, and now the use of gas against civilians . . . The use of United States produced chemical and biological weapons in Asia will be interpreted widely as 'field testing.' "

Senator Fulbright saw this as the inevitable "brutalizing" effect of war upon even a civilized and advanced society.

Japan's great mass circulation newspaper, *Asahi,* said Vietnam could sweep all of Asia into war and added, "The war has been continued in complete disregard for the humble hope of happiness and simple wishes for peace and stability of the local inhabitants."

Fulbright saw the possibility that the support of our strongest ally in Asia might be eroded beyond recovery by the Vietnam war, and he asked himself, was it worth it? We must, he thought, consider all the consequences of the war—its effect on the world community, friend and foe alike, on the economy and mood and personal liberties of the United States.

The World Council of Churches asked all involved in Vietnam to take the "necessary risks" to start negotiations and added, "The shift from the battlefield to the conference table will not be facilitated if the United States awaits a clear signal from North Vietnam, or if North Vietnam awaits the withdrawal of U.S. forces." Silence from both sides.

The academic community, and Fullbright felt a close bond with it, was stirring unhappily over the war. Petitions opposing an enlarging of the conflict and asking for negotiations were being circulated on the campuses. A petition at Yale drew more signers than any other faculty petition in a decade. President Johnson was bitterly denounced by a number of leading intellectuals. Lewis Mumford, the writer and critic, holder of the President Medal of Freedom, said in a letter to the President, "You now, casting all caution to the winds, propose to increase the area of senseless destruction . . . without having any other visible means in view than to conceal our political impotence."

The Senator's decision was to appeal once again to his old friend. He would try to present him with a plan for negotiations. His thought about the President was expressed in a private conversation: "He is a very remarkable and complex person. He has an unfortunate sense of inferiority about foreign policy and the old frontier spirit of hitting out against a vexing enemy, and he looks on intellectuals as confused. The hawks around him have, I suspect, been exploiting these traits to get their way."

Fulbright moved cautiously. He talked at length to Senator Russell. The Georgian has a unique position in Washington. A somewhat aloof and lonely man himself, a pillar of The Establishment, he enjoys more than anyone else on The Hill the respect of all. He had helped raise Lyndon Johnson to power in the Senate. He respected Fulbright's intellect. Probably, Fulbright hoped that he and Russell might join in trying to persuade the President to a more moderate course.

The Arkansan told Russell he thought the situation in Vietnam was "pretty damn dismal," and there ought to be an honorable way out before it got beyond control.

Russell said, as he has in public, "I thought we made a mistake when we went in there after the French pulled out, and I tried to tell President Eisenhower. I told him it was a bottomless pit in every way, and we would find ourselves in a few years paying billions and supplying our own men, and involved in a full-scale war at the wrong place. But Dulles had persuaded him we could hold the Chinese by the threat of massive retaliation, and stop the North Vietnamese by building up the southern army. I disagreed. I thought we were in for a great deal of trouble, and would wind up sending our own troops to fight in the jungles, one of the worst possible places in Asia to make a stand."

Senator Russell's objection was a strategic one; this was the wrong place to fight the war for Asia. He thought, though, that the United States had become too deeply involved to pull up stakes now. We would have to press on, using progressively more military strength, and hope to persuade China and North Vietnam to leave Southeast Asia alone, as too costly a morsel.

Fulbright countered that escalation moved the United States and China closer to a war neither wanted. Every time we raised the ante, the enemy would raise its commitment of men and guns to the Vietcong struggle. It was far less costly to them than to us, because of the high ratio, 10 to 1 or 12 to 1, conventional troops needed to fight guerrillas and the long distance from the United States to bring supplies. Finally, he speculated, Chinese "volunteers," the bombing of China, retaliation perhaps in Korea, a Soviet move. Where would it end?

The two Senators looked at one another gloomily.

Fulbright thought a solution was possible. We would have to recast our thinking, move away from our obsession with Communism as the sole enemy. In this case, he felt the enemy was Chinese imperialism. A great empire had been humbled and humiliated by Western power in the nineteenth century, and seemed determined now to push Western influence from Asia and dominate it herself.

Any negotiation with the Chinese or North Vietnamese would be difficult and frustrating, because of this stored-up anger at the Western invader and the doctrines of Communism. But, the Senator said, if we spent as much ingenuity and energy on diplomacy as warmaking, the peace of Southeast Asia could be assured.

An idea had been forming in his mind, and he tried it out on Russell. The strongest barrier to China, he suggested, might be an independent Communist state of Vietnam. The Vietnamese were ardently nationalistic, and unlikely to trade one colonial master, France, for another, China. A Tito-type government of Vietnam could become a stabilizing force.

His thinking was influenced by his interest in Yugoslavia. He spent nine days there in November 1964, and said, "Yugoslavia is more responsible and more reliable in its attitude toward the United States than certain non-Communist governments with whom the United States maintains normal and correct relations. Their policies neither harm their neighbors, nor threaten American interests."

Yugoslavia's independence was possible because the Communists there won their own revolution, they were not put in power by Soviet tanks, they did not allow Russia to install their own puppets, and broke with Moscow in 1948. North Vietnam had some of the same conditions, but the longer the war continued and the more it had to rely upon China, the less independent it could be.

Senator Fullbright admitted the North Vietnamese did not show any great enthusiasm for negotiations at this time. This might be changed by a cessation of the bombings, an agreement to honor the Geneva pledge of elections, and inviting the Vietcong to the conference table.

A few days later, Senator Fulbright sent a memorandum to the President setting forth ideas he had talked over with Russell, and which he has made abundantly clear since. The significance of the memorandum is that the Senator wanted to exhaust all possibilities of "quiet diplomacy" with the Administration before he took his case to the public.

He made several points:

1. It would be a disaster for the United States to try to engage in a massive ground and air war in Southeast Asia. Not only would it be extremely costly, but it would also revive and intensify the Cold War which had begun to cool off following the missile crisis in Cuba, and it would lead to a revival of jingoism in the United States.

2. The threat to Asia was not Communism, as such, but rather Chinese imperialism.

3. The smaller nations of Asia were historically afraid of and independent of China, and a Communist regime in Vietnam independent of China, as Tito was independent of Russia, would be of greater value to world security than weak anti-Communist regimes dependent primarily on U.S. manpower and money.

4. As a way of finding an end to the war, the United States should declare a moratorium in the bombing, make clear our aims, and begin a campaign to persuade the people of Vietnam, north and south, of the economic and political advantages of a free and independent regime.

5. The United States might make its wishes known through Great Britain or Russia that we would accept an independent regime, regardless of its political makeup, and that we would at the same time join in guarantees of the independence of the country and the rights of minorities, and that the regime not be a pawn or satellite of any great power.

6. It would be of advantage to world stability to have a regime in Vietnam oriented to Russia rather than exclusively to China, since at least at this point China was in an agitated and belligerent and resentful mood.

President Johnson was interested enough to invite the Senator to the White House.

Of Johnson's reaction to his arguments, Senator Fulbright merely says, "He was not persuaded."

The President did not believe China would intervene, because of its internal problems and political conflict with Russia. His principal adviser, Secretary Rusk, had predicted that China would not intervene in Korea, either. (He had been Assistant Secretary for Far Eastern Affairs at the time.) Johnson saw North Vietnam, and China behind it, as the enemy, and dismissed the importance of the Vietcong. He believed then that North Vietnam could be so badly damaged by air power it would abandon its "aggression" in the south.

President Johnson's answer to Fulbright, as well as to the seventeen nonaligned nations which on April 1 asked for negotiations, was given April 7 at Johns Hopkins University. The address was a complete disavowal of the subtleties of the Fulbright approach. He said: "The first reality is that North Vietnam has attacked the independent nation of South Vietnam. Its object is total conquest. Of course, some of the people of South Vietnam are participating in an attack on their own government. But trained men and supplies, orders and arms, flow in a constant stream from North to South . . . The rulers of Hanoi are urged on by Peiping . . . The contest in Vietnam is part of a wider pattern of aggressive purpose . . . To dishonor that pledge [to support South Vietnam], to abandon this small and brave nation to its enemies, and to the terror that must follow would be an unforgivable wrong. We are also there to strengthen world order . . . Let no one think for a moment that retreat from Vietnam would bring an end to conflict. The battle would be renewed in one country and then another. The central lesson of our time is that the appetite for aggression is never satisfied . . .

"There are those who wonder why we have a responsibility there. Well, we have it there for the same reason that we have a responsibility for the defense of Europe. World War II was fought in both Europe and Asia, and when it ended, we found ourselves with continued responsibility for the defense of freedom."

There was a sop to Fulbright and the critics in the speech. The President said we were willing to negotiate—on what basis he did not specify—and proposed a billion-dollar economic development plan for Southeast Asia.

Johnson absolutely turned down the idea of calling off the air war. He said, "We know that air attacks will not accomplish all of these purposes. But it is our best and prayerful judgment that they are a necessary part of the surest road to peace."

This was most discouraging to Senator Fulbright. The President's answer to him was no. There followed eleven painful days of irresolution for the Senator. He did not relish the prospect of openly fighting his old friend or the Democratic Administration. He decided on a tactic short of an open break, to see if he could not put pressure on the Administration to alter its course.

Fulbright did this informally. A reporter asked him, "Does the course we are now following in Vietnam offer the best course for an eventual satisfactory settlement, or would you alter the policy?"

He replied carefully, "I have said on numerous occasions that I support the Administration's present policy . . . Within the near future, before the escalation goes too far, a temporary cease-fire might be advisable in order to give the people a little time to contemplate the trouble. The daily bombings are inclined to keep the atmosphere tense, and I think perhaps to make the North Vietnamese dig in, as in Great Britain where the Germans thought the British might sue for peace when they began to bomb them in World War II.

"Well, it didn't work that way. No one knows if a temporary cease-fire, just to give an opportunity for reflection and possibly to go into discussions as proposed by the President, might be feasible. In judging from the press reports, the actions of the Russians and some of the others, that would indicate the prospect for discussions might be enhanced by a temporary cessation of the bombing."

He tossed this out, hoping for Congressional and public reaction. It was hardly a revolutionary statement. An end to the bombings had been proposed by such knowledgeable friends of America as Canadian Prime Minister Lester Pearson and Indian Prime Minister Lal Bahadur Shastri, as well as Pakistani Foreign Minister Ali Bhutto. All had much better information on Saigon and Peking than we did. The position of Fulbright, as chairman of Foreign Relations, gave the proposal a new prestige and urgency.

The Administration responded to this as heresy that must be condemned.

Secretary Rusk said the Administration had considered and rejected the idea, since this "would only encourage the aggressor and dishearten our friends who bear the brunt of the battle."

Secretary McNamara stated, "We have no indication that a cessation of bombings would move the North Vietnamese to discussions leading to termination of their aggression against the South. To end the strikes would discourage and dishearten the people of South Vietnam in their battle against the campaign of terror which is directed against them and which is dependent upon the daily flow of materials from Hanoi."

This flat rejection became embarrassing less than a month later when on May 13 the President halted the bombings for six days, apparently because of public support for the Fulbright idea.

On Capitol Hill, the Administration was hard put to find warriors to throw spears at the Fulbright position. Mansfield, the Majority Leader, personally selected by Johnson as his successor, was as deeply troubled over Vietnam as Fulbright. On May 3, Mansfield urged the Administration to consider the Soviet bid to bring the Geneva powers together. "It is of the utmost importance," he said, "that the question of how to apply the principles of the Geneva agreement be faced as soon as possible. The longer the confrontation is put off, the more the people of North and South Vietnam pay for the delay, and the more likelihood that the present limited conflict will spread into a general war on Asia."

There were actually very few convinced hawks in the Senate. Most of the members sat uneasily in the middle, hoping to stay out of the debate. A group of doves, perhaps ten, followed Fulbright in his suggestion.

Russell Long took the President's side and boasted, "I'm for a strong line. The President is upholding the freedom of a government we are committed to help. If we didn't fight there, we will have to fight somewhere else."

Senator Dirksen added, "If we let up on them now, we will lose face, our prestige will then drop, and that will make it more difficult to end the conflict."

Arthur Krock in *The New York Times* was surprised at what he called "the round of shooting from the hip which the highest officials engaged in, with Fulbright's suggestion as the target. This did not merit the instant hostility it encountered, having been made by the chairman of the Foreign Relations Committee, and offered respectfully as only a tentative proposition. Yet Secretary of State Rusk consigned the idea to the most undesirable category of high policy in times of national emergency . . . President Johnson made his disapproval of a bombing halt very plain . . ."

The Administration then made elaborate statements trying to knock down the points made in the private memorandum. Both Rusk and McNamara at their press conferences sought to prove North Vietnam was the true "enemy," the Vietcong of little or no importance. Rusk said, "There is no evidence that the Vietcong has any significant popular following in South Vietnam." McNamara gave a great many statistics to attempt to prove the Vietcong was the North Vietnamese Army in disguise. He also sought to show the effectiveness of the bombings by maps and more statistics.

Nevertheless, Fulbright's statement had the hoped-for effect. It widened the debate and gave an aura of respectability to dissent. *The Christian Science Monitor* on May 1 said, "The voices of doubt grow," and quoted a number of political leaders. Senator George Aiken of Vermont, the senior Republican, said, "It is plain now that unless reason returns to the world, we will be headed into the most devastating conflict the world has ever known. It is difficult for me to understand what our Defense Department and our executive branch are thinking of when they send two hundred planes to blow up a bridge. It is simply braggadocio. Those people there, I suppose, are not in a mood to negotiate when they see everything they have worked for being blown to pieces by a huge air fleet." Another senior Republican, Frank Carlson of Kansas, said, "A deep concern is growing over the country." Mansfield reported his mail running heavily in favor of negotiations to end the fighting. Church noted his was 20 to 1 for a peaceful settlement. Letters to the Foreign Relations Committee were 90 percent for a lull in the bombings.

Not only events in Vietnam, the Senator's proposal and the Administration reaction, but the landings in the Dominican Republic in April created many "voices of doubt."

Fulbright was by now determined to open up a wide debate. On May 5, while in Strasbourg for the European Consultative Assembly, he asked for a Vietnam settlement on the basis of the Geneva agreement. "There would have to be really free elections," he told journalists. "They would have to be supervised. Probably by the United Nations. And I think the result would probably be an independent nationalist regime, because I don't think the people there would inevitably vote for a sort of Red Chinese regime."

The reaction in Western Europe was favorable, somewhat to the dismay of columnist Joseph Alsop who complained, "Senators like Fulbright, Mansfield, and even Gruening and Morse have been made to sound like the true voice of America, whereas they represent no more than 10 percent. The result is a gravely distorted picture."

William S. White denounced "a small but screechingly articulate Democratic splinter in the Senate" speaking "monstrously dangerous falsehoods . . . modern day appeasers and isolationists . . . noisy and fatally foolish fringe groups" and professors "who believe in dishonoring the honorable commitments of this country." The heat was on the gentleman from Arkansas.

From Saigon, General Taylor was sending reports—which did not prove accurate—of a huge buildup of the Vietcong for a final massed drive as in the last days of the French–Vietminh war.

Thus it was an angry and troubled President who called Congressional leaders to the White House on Sunday, May 2, sat them around the Cabinet table and lectured them on criticism from Congress. The column, "Inside Report," said, "He made it clear he was upset about the Capitol Hill sniping—Democratic sniping against the United States hard line in Vietnam and the Dominican Republic. Through most of the monologue, Mr. Johnson was glaring at Senator J. William Fulbright of Arkansas, his old friend who has called for a pause in the bombing of North Vietnam. Mr. Johnson implied that Congress ought to show the world it really backs up his policies."

The President's humor was indicated by another incident. He went up to Senator Church at a White House gathering and asked bluntly, "Who did you talk to before you made that speech on Vietnam?"

Church said he had talked to Walter Lippmann.

"All right," said Johnson grimly, "next time you want a dam for Idaho, you go talk to Walter Lippmann." And he turned away.

Yet it was plain, despite the bad humor of the White House, the Fulbright "splinter" had brought about the May 13–19 break in the bombings. The Senator thought the lull was too short and not accompanied by the necessary quiet diplomacy. But the lesson was not lost on him. He could accomplish more by speaking up and stirring the dust than by private memoranda and talks in the White House.

XXII

CAPITOL HILL awakens slowly in the morning. With the sunrise, crews of workmen swab the tiled floors in the Capitol, then young men, many of them college students, drag the big canvas mailbags bulging with letters from home down the halls. The silent offices, still smelling of yesterday's cigaret and cigar smoke, are opened up from eight to nine. When Senator Fulbright arrives soon after eight o'clock, driving his old Mercedes through the thickening crawl on Constitution Avenue, the new Senate Office Building has the sleepy, unhurried mood of a small town on Sunday morning.

He picks up the morning newspapers, and retires into the sanctuary of his private office. For thirty minutes or perhaps an hour, the Senator will sit alone with the news and his thoughts. He is a man who needs quiet and solitude as much as a diabetic needs insulin. Unhurried, uninterrupted reflection is a precious part of his day. His mind sparks with ideas, hundreds of them. Listening to him think aloud is a dazzling experience, for the orderly and even cautious Fulbright moves swiftly in the array of thoughts.

In his solitary moments, the Senator sorts out and organizes his thoughts with a Germanic thoroughness and self-discipline. This idea he puts aside as not timely or impractical; another fits in with a bit of history.

One morning of early June, 1965, he came into the office at the usual hour, picked up *The New York Times,* and went into his office to read. He had a sense of foreboding. It was about the "fundamental reality of Vietnam," as Senator Mansfield described it in an impassioned speech in the Senate. This was the "bleeding . . . by Vietnamese and Americans . . . by Communist and anti-Communist

Vietnamese and mostly, in all probability, by simple peasants who cannot distinguish one from the other, and whose greatest wish is to be spared the ravages of war. In all probability these people want peace and a minimum of contact with distant Saigon and distant Hanoi, not to speak of the places which they have scarcely heard about, Peking, Moscow, or Washington."

The Senator read with quickening interest a story by Hanson Baldwin, *The Times'* military writer. He predicted that American troops in Vietnam would be increased to a full battle army of 250,000 to 300,000 men. This meant a drastic change of policy and a new escalation—without consulting Congress or its leaders. Fulbright recalled that a year before, Secretary McNamara said, "I don't believe that anyone in our government believes that the addition of U.S. ground combat troops in South Vietnam or the introduction of such troops would favorably affect the situation there." Ambassador Henry Cabot Lodge had advised that large numbers of ground troops would make us appear "a colonial power, and I think it's been pretty well established that colonialism is over."

A few days before, Fulbright had said, "The Communism of Eastern Europe and the Soviet Union is slowly being humanized. The terror of Stalin's time has largely disappeared. The Hungarian Government now tolerates a degree of individual liberty. Rumania produces a defiantly national Communism. Yugoslavia seems slowly and hesitatingly to be coming to accept the legitimacy of doubt about Communism itself . . . As it becomes clear to each side that it is safe and profitable to do business with each other, ideological barriers can be expected gradually to erode away . . . Communists have unalterable bonds of humanity with all other men and these bonds of humanity can be the instrument of change . . ."

Now, the growing struggle in Asia, with both sides implacable. The Communist Vietnamese insisting that their land be cleared of foreign "imperialists"; Secretary Rusk, just as implacable, an old China hand, insisting that Communism advance not one step; and Lyndon Johnson's brand of patriotism, much like Teddy Roosevelt's, whipped up like the sea in a gale. As the Senator had said that spring, "A good many Americans are disposed to regard the Cold War as a struggle between two ways of life, one true and good the other unalterably evil. It would be ironic indeed were we to fall victim to the contagion of fanaticism that we find repugnant in Communism."

He had hinted in a talk at Johns Hopkins University of his daring idea—an independent Communist state of Vietnam. He said, "We have reached the point at which the fact that a country is Communist does not in itself tell us that the country is hostile to the United States from the point of view of political and strategic interest. I think we have reached the point at which certain Communist countries must be regarded as more friendly to the United States than certain non-Communist countries. As we survey the growing variety of Communist governments, we find that their profession of Marxist-Leninist beliefs tells us very little about how they can be expected to behave . . . I think we ought to ask ourselves hypothetically whether a Communist regime that leans away from China is worse or better from the viewpoint of our political and strategic interests than a non-Communist state, such as Indonesia or Cambodia, that leans toward China." He had presented this idea as a conservative, saying, "The point of view I have been commending is intended literally to conserve the world—a world whose civilization can be destroyed at any time if either of the two great powers should choose or feel driven to do so. It is an approach that accepts the world as it is, with all its existing nations and ideologies, and with all its existing qualities and shortcomings."

Senator Fulbright is one of the last of the great conservatives of Anglo-American tradition. He cherishes American institutions and traditions, and hopes to salvage them from the upheavals of the world by adjusting to change, rather than trying to fight the pull of the tide. He differs utterly from the modern radical who says we must pull down and build anew.

It is typical of him that in this dilemma of concern in the late spring of 1965, he took a course of compromise first. He went to see President Johnson on Monday, June 14.

This was much like every other talk he has had with Johnson on Vietnam, Fulbright sitting quiet and restless while the President lectured him at a machine-gun clip, words tumbling over each other in that peculiarly flat drawl. There was a compulsion in Johnson to prove, perhaps to himself as much as to his visitor, that he was absolutely right on Vietnam, seeing himself as a kind of Archangel Michael protecting the world against Communism. Perhaps, as Alistair Cooke has suggested, this man "with the ego of Goliath" and with obvious shortcomings in experience in foreign affairs was trying "to overcompensate for the general view that he would be inept at foreign policy."

He went flaying away with words at the Senator. All right, Bill, you think we should negotiate. Let me show you how many times we have offered to talk to them. (Scraps of memoranda pulled from the pockets.) They have spit in our eyes. How do you negotiate with folks like that? (An eager, compelling stare with those bright eyes.) And the military pressing every day to take stronger action. The generals and CIA are telling us the Communists will start a full-scale offensive when the heavy monsoon rains sweep in, and the South Vietnamese defense may crack and fall apart.

Two and a half months later, on September 1, an A.P. dispatch from Saigon noted, "Military analysts are asking themselves if the Viet Cong ever planned such an offensive in the first place." Coupling this bad advice with MacArthur's intelligence dictum that the Chinese would not enter the Korean War, Senator Fulbright has wondered how often faulty military intelligence, representing wishes rather than fact, may be a major cause for foreign policy errors.

Still, how does a Senator, even the chairman of the Foreign Relations Committee answer a President who waves intelligence bulletins? For the most part, Fulbright listened.

When he had a chance to speak, the Senator said he was going to oppose, publicly, a further escalation of the war. Johnson said he hoped his friend would point out how patient he had been, how in his April 7 speech he offered unconditional discussions with North Vietnam, and Hanoi and Peking denounced him for his pains. Good God, he didn't want to send American boys out there to die, but our freedom and liberty were in danger. (Again, the sudden brightness in the eyes.)

At that time, Senator Fulbright believed the President was sincere. Since then, perhaps a year later, he has had nagging doubts; did Johnson really want to end the war before he had changed the face of Asia as a monument to himself, as the pharaohs raised their pyramids?

On the afternoon of June 15, the Senate was exasperated over taxes. The cultivated, Down East voice of Paul Douglas and the excited Louisiana drawl of Russell Long were heard in the chamber. Visitors moved like a river through the galleries. They lighted long enough to catch a glimpse of a familiar figure ("Oh, there's Bobby Kennedy"), and moved on. The press gallery was largely vacant, a few earnest wire service fellows copying down pertinent snatches, bored financial writers—that was about it.

Senator Fulbright rose from his desk and said wryly, "I regret to digress a few minutes to speak on another subject, but since we have been preoccupied with taxes, it will not hurt to pay attention to another subject for a moment."

His next words were challenging, "It is clear to all reasonable Americans that a complete military victory in Vietnam, though theoretically attainable, can in fact be attained only at a cost far exceeding the requirements of our interest and our honor. . . . Our policy therefore has been and should remain one of determination to end the war at the earliest possible time by a negotiated settlement involving major concessions by both sides."

He was against a withdrawal, "because such action would betray our obligation to people we have promised to defend, because it would weaken or destroy the credibility of American guarantees to other countries, and because [it] would encourage the view in Peking . . . that guerrilla wars supported from outside are a relatively safe and inexpensive way of expanding Communist power."

He opposed stepping up the war, because: "the bombing thus far of North Vietnam has failed to weaken the military capacity of the Vietcong in any visible way . . . escalation would invite the intervention or infiltration on a large scale of North Vietnamese troops . . . this in turn would probably draw the United States into a bloody and protracted jungle war in which the strategic advantages would be with the other side; and, finally, because the only alternative to such a land war would then be a further expansion of the air war [so] as to invite either massive Chinese military intervention in many vulnerable areas in Southeast Asia or general nuclear war."

He praised the President for his "steadfastness and statesmanship" in resisting pressures for stepping up the war. (The *New York Herald Tribune* at the time reported a decision had already been made to increase American troops in Vietnam.) Fulbright also related Communist rejections of peace talks.

The Senator from Arkansas offered his own program: back up the South Vietnam army so that it would not be crushed in the expected monsoon offensive, "offer the Communist a reasonable and attractive alternative to military victory . . . At such time as it becomes clear to all interested parties that neither side can expect to win a complete military victory, I think it would be appropriate and desirable for the United States to reiterate forcefully and explicitly its willingness to negotiate a compromise peace and thereafter to join with other countries in mounting a large-scale program for the economic and social development of southeast Asia." He thought the Geneva accord of 1954 offered the base for a new settlement.

He concluded with a comment: "It may be that the major lesson of this tragic conflict will be a new appreciation of the power of nationalism in Southeast Asia and indeed in all of the world's emerging nations . . . The tragedy of Vietnam is that for many reasons, including the intransigence of a colonial power and the initial failure of the United States to appreciate the consequences of that intransigence, the nationalist movement became associated with and largely subordinate to the Communist movement. In the postwar era, it has been demonstrated repeatedly that nationalism is a stronger force than Communism, and that the association of the two is neither inevitable nor natural. In the past it has come about when the West has set itself in opposition to the national aspirations of emerging peoples."

In other words, the Vietnamese wanted independence from the foreign overlord, and this was far more important to them than the brand of politics of the guerrillas.

Considering Fulbright's private thoughts, this was a mild speech. He deliberately disciplined himself to keep open the channels of communication with the President, and show him there was another side. In the only note of criticism, he said he thought the May bombing pause was "too short, but it must be noted that the suspension elicited no response whatever from Hanoi and Peking." He approved of the use of American ground troops "to secure what we have possession of."

His frail hope for peace was that both sides, in time, would realize they could not win a great victory, and be willing to make meaningful concessions.

Yet, mild as the statement was, there was worried opposition. Senator Leverett Saltonstall of Massachusetts was afraid that any understandings reached at the conference table would be disregarded by the Communists later. In his patrician Yankee voice he said, "This is the great difficulty which we face, which, perhaps, the Senator did not describe very fully."

Fulbright, wearily, a little discouraged, replied, "I don't minimize the difficulties. I know they are very great. I was trying to make the point, and the major point, that I do not want to expand this conflict into an all-out war, either of worldwide proportions or even as large as the war in Korea. I did not think the Korean war was beneficial to the world or to that country.

"I don't believe that anyone with modern weapons could ever hope to come out of a war with any profit at all. Weapons are too destructive. We know that science has made modern war intolerable. War used to be a lot of fun for a lot of people. However, that is not the point anymore."

Senator Saltonstall said, "We must be optimistic and support the President."

Fulbright left the chamber with the feeling, my God, how do you talk to people, how do you wake them up from their pipe dreams of the good American and the bad Communist, and make them see the reality of modern war. Words, thoughts, seemed unable to penetrate the fantasy.

Two days later, *The New York Times* editorialized, "His views should be read by every American—and we hope they will be read abroad as an authoritative statement." *The Times* thought Fulbright's words would counter the clamor for "total war" coming from the military. The *Baltimore Sun* said, "Mr. Fulbright is in the true sense a thinking man. When he speaks, after carefully marshalling his thoughts, he always contributes to a dialogue or debate." The *Philadelphia Inquirer* believed, "There is much logic to Senator Fulbright's views." *The Christian Science Monitor* spoke of the "healthy debate" which Fulbright set in motion.

Senator Mansfield, who had noted a few days before that this had been "a sad week in Vietnam, another government has fallen, the nineteenth coup," applauded Fulbright. His had been "a most constructive contribution, and in the best traditions of the Senate."

President Johnson might have added to the applause. The Senator had generously gone out of his way to praise his friend. ("President Johnson has resisted these pressures with steadfastness and statesmanship, and remains committed to the goal of ending the war at the earliest possible time by negotiations without preconditions. In so doing, he is providing the leadership appropriate to a great nation.") But there is something primitive about Lyndon Johnson's demands for loyalty. Johnson could not fathom why Fulbright should resist his strategy for winning the war by increasing military power.

The President would tell visitors, why, I made that man chairman! It was not quite that simple, but Johnson tended in his own mind to simplify his relations with others. Fulbright had been the ranking

Democratic member of Foreign Relations when, in February 6, 1959, the chairman, the delightful, aged Rhode Island millionaire, Theodore Green, voluntarily quit the chairmanship. Green was in his eighties, dozed at the hearings, and presented an ineffectual image. The Democrats, getting ready for the 1960 elections with the theme they would get things moving, were unhappy with Green. The newspapers suggested that the elderly Senator step down. Senator Johnson arranged this as a kind of broker. The transfer of power was inevitable, but a broker, and particularly if he is even mildly egotistical, likes to take credit.

A few days after the Fulbright speech, the President called an impromptu press conference. The *Washington News* said of it: "President Johnson has thrown down a challenge to the Congressional critics of his policies in Vietnam. He dares them, in effect, to try to repeal the resolution the House and Senate passed last August after the Tonkin Gulf shooting incident. The resolution gave Congressional blessing in advance to anything President Johnson might do in Vietnam. And the President made it clear yesterday during a long, rambling 'impromptu' press conference that he isn't going to let his former colleagues on Capitol Hill forget that they gave him a green light to do anything he decides to do is necessary in Vietnam."

The usual stable of Johnsonian warriors came trotting out to tilt their lances. Senator Dirksen called Fulbright "naïve," and said, "Any who talk of concessions by the United States have an obligation to specify the kinds of concessions which they are prepared to advocate. They have an obligation, too, to indicate the limits beyond which concessions cannot be made."

Fulbright answered, "My apprehension is that little by little this will escalate into a general war. No man can or should spell out concessions now."

Senator Dodd placed in *The Congressional Record* support for Johnson's policy by George Meany, president of the AFL-CIO, and McGeorge Bundy, the former Harvard dean who had stayed on with Johnson as security coordinator.

In a sense, the President's outrage at the Fulbright speech was justified. The "consensus" was only a thin crust, and Fulbright had broken through the crust. The mere fact that the prestigious chairman of the Foreign Relations Committee had dared raise questions stirred a general debate.

From the younger Republicans, that is in the House, hints of future criticism poured out. Congressman Melvin Laird, the chief GOP ideologist, said in a TV interview that if Johnson abandoned "total victory," the Republicans might walk out on him. Also, paradoxically, Laird pointed out that President Eisenhower opposed escalating the ground war in Vietnam.

Senator Fulbright thought "total victory" was either the cry of the zealot or a cheap political gimmick. He remarked, "I must confess to some difficulty in understanding precisely what 'total victory' means in this age of ideological conflict and nuclear weapons. Certainly the term is a stirring one. It has a romantic ring. It quickens the blood. But it would be beneficial if those who call for total victory would spell out precisely how it might be achieved, and, more important, what we would do with total victory once we won it. Is it to be won by nuclear war—a war at which the very least would cost the lives of tens of millions of people on both sides, devastate most or all of our great cities, and mutilate or utterly destory a civilization which has been built over thousands of years? Or can total victory be won without war—by some brilliant stroke of diplomacy or by arguments of such compelling logic that the Communists will abandon their grand imperialistic design?"

There was open support for Fulbright's caution in the Senate on both sides of the aisle.

Frank Church, a Democrat, said, "Unless we are nothing but a mock parliament, we must honor our constitutional responsibility to advise and consent on the country's foreign policy." Jacob Javits, the New York Republican, answered the President's argument that Congress had given him a blank check in 1964. He said, "The words of that mandate no longer mean what we intended in the light of the situation at that time."

This debate was cabled around the world. The press galleries of Capitol Hill begin to fill up with the unfamiliar faces of foreign correspondents and columnists.

Senator Fulbright moved up his criticism another notch in a June 19 reunion of Rhodes scholars. "Until a short time ago," he said, "it seemed that the world might be [moving toward peace], but in recent months events have taken an ominous turn. For varied and complex reasons the nations are sliding back into the self-righteous and crusading spirit of the Cold War. We are hearing very much these days about honor and principles of peace and freedom and national liberation, and it is all being accompanied by rising tension and violence."

This is a classic Fulbright theme, and one borrowed from the Greek tragedians. The United States, as the most powerful nation, had a duty to exercise restraint and seek ingenious solutions, instead of shouting about its honor.

Thus, raising the level of war in Vietnam, he believed, wakened the devils elsewhere in Asia. He was prophetic. The American escalation in Vietnam was followed by Indonesian attacks upon Malaysia, the Indian-Pakistan clashes, and Chinese raids on the Indian border. Fulbright's overall record of prophecy is pretty good. He warned President Truman that unless atomic energy were put under international control, there would be a monstrous arms race and proliferation. In the critical post-World War II years, he counseled, "We have a choice between two policies, armed might and imperialism on the one hand or rules of law enforcement by the United Nations on the other. We must arm to the teeth and increase our strength by domination of strategic bases in the Atlantic as well as the Pacific if we are to rely solely upon our own might for our security." He told Secretary Dulles that arms shipments to India and Pakistan would lead to war between the two. He argued that the Eisenhower Doctrine was an unwise grant of unlimited power to the President, and would lead future Presidents into war on the basis of patriotic generalities in a Senate resolution. He warned President Kennedy the Bay of Pigs would be a fiasco.

He told the scholars, "As an objective of foreign policy 'peace with freedom' is a dubious concept. The difficulty about peace is that practically everybody wants it but practically everybody wants something else more. The difficulty about freedom is that the form of it most desired in the world is the freedom to work one's will upon others . . .

"I don't suggest that 'peace with freedom' is an unworthy object of our foreign policy, but only that the pursuit of it with too much zeal is the surest way to lose it. Of all the faculties of man none is more perfectly developed than the talent for cutting general principles to the specifications of personal interest and ambition. We Americans sincerely believe that our policies are designed to secure peace and freedom for all men. But the Russians and Chinese may be just as sincere in believing their policies are the way to peace with freedom.

The prospects for peace with freedom would seem to depend on the restraint with which everybody pursues his own particular concept of it."

This view was quite in contrast with what President Johnson was saying in his informal lectures to private groups at the White House. To one such, he said, "If I can leave you with any one thought, it is that you must understand that the integrity of the American commitment is the principal pillar of peace in the world today. If anything happens to the integrity of that commitment, we are lost."

This was a political fundamentalism and a form of moralizing that Fulbright looked upon as nonsense.

President Johnson said further: "I've used the word 'honor' with respect to Vietnam. When I've done so, some have said, Oh, dear me! as if it was an expression out of the eighteenth century—by a king who was upset because his daughter said she wouldn't marry the son of a fellow king. Let me tell you what honor means.

"Toward the end of the Eisenhower Administration, he was presented with an ultimatum by Khrushchev, get out of Berlin in six months. And President Eisenhower said no, you can't do that to the United States. And Khrushchev had to believe that. In the summer of 1961, Khrushchev said to President Kennedy, get out of Berlin or there'll be war, and President Kennedy looked him straight in the eye and said, 'If that is what you want, that's what you'll have. It'll be a cold winter.' And it was utterly important that Mr. Khrushchev believe that. When the Russian missiles entered Cuba, President Kennedy had to say to Khrushchev, those missiles have got to go. Period. Paragraph. They have got to go. And you have a chance to get them out without war. The life of this nation depended on Mr. Khrushchev believing him.

"We are now saying to Hanoi and Peking, 'Gentlemen, you are not going to take over South Vietnam. You are not going to do it.' If you were a Berliner, if you were a Thai, you would be living on the basis of the American commitment. If Moscow or Peking or Hanoi ever thought that commitment was not anything, then no one is more in danger than you or I. We are all of us, the whole nation is in danger.

"That is what honor means in this situation. It takes guts."

This stirring, Texas version of events was not accepted out of hand by our own friends in Europe. The *London Times* in an editorial, "War Without End?" commented: "The limited war is growing into an ever-expanding war. Worse, as the American numbers in the South increase, so it becomes more and more plain, despite the President's denials, that advice and support for the Government of South Vietnam is making warfare defined and conducted predominantly by American power. The more American military power is deployed to the exclusion of political initiatives the more it gives all the political arguments away to its opponents." The Swedish Foreign Minister said the only solution lay in negotiations and stated, "The hard pressed people of Vietnam are paying a high price because their country happens to be in an area where the political and military interests of the big powers clash and the interests of the Vietnamese people are being crushed."

Senator Mansfield proposed that President de Gaulle of France be asked to serve as a peacemaker in Southeast Asia.

Johnson's personal reaction was echoed in William White's column. He cudgeled "a largely Democratic left wing that recoils from any use of force anywhere, for any reason, however honorable."

But the discontent and unease were too great to be stopped by a columnist's spitballs. The greatest blow of all to the President came from his old mentor, Senator Russell. Russell was chairman of the Armed Services Committee, the virtual head of the Appropriations Committee, leader of the Southern bloc, and the man who put Johnson on the ladder to power. He had been seriously ill during the restless summer. On a TV program August 1, the Georgian said bluntly that South Vietnam had "no strategic value for the United States," and we would be justified in pulling out if the South Vietnamese did not want to fight. Russell said the Vietnamese war would cost us $10 to $12 billion a year, and asked if it were worth it. Should there be a plebiscite, the Senator from Georgia reckoned, Ho Chi Minh would win hands down.

The President abruptly changed his tactics. He was again the fox of the Senate, with an instinctive sense of each man's weakness and of the subtle means required to win a vote from the opposition. He called in one highly important Senator facing a difficult race for reelection and, in effect, gave him—for his state—one of the greatest Government contracts ever awarded. Another senior Senator, at heart a country boy, was flattered by being invited to the White House for a very private, informal dinner, and being given as loot: an autographed picture of the President and his family, signed by each Johnson; a pair of silver cuff links with the Presidential seal, an autographed copy of the dinner menu, and a silver tie clasp in the form of an airplane. (This tie clasp was a replica of the reconnaissance plane in which Johnson flew as an observer in World War II, or his version of the Kennedy PT boat tie clasp.) Both Senators ceased their criticism of the Vietnam policy.

Senator Fulbright was asked to the White House and treated as a dear friend. A long arm around the shoulder, the very friendliest remarks. I need your advice, Bill. These military fellows keep shoving escalation at me, and I need ideas from you to fling back at them. The problems I've got, Bill, they are enough to weigh a man down to the ground.

There has been recorded a series of interesting photographs of this brief period of reconciliation. Johnson has a mania for having pictures taken of almost every event in his official life. In one, Fulbright is slouched on the divan, attentive, polite, but not committed. Johnson, his back to the camera, is speaking. McGeorge Bundy is in a chair earnestly following the President and encouraging him with his eyes. Mansfield sits in another corner, quiet and unsmiling. Johnson scrawled on this photograph, "Who listens—maybe—perhaps."

In this thawing atmosphere, there was progress, in Fulbright's view. He was impressed by Justice Arthur Goldberg, the new United Nations Ambassador, and his ability to speak frankly to Johnson. Averell Harriman, the President's roving envoy, found Marshal Tito of Yugoslavia cooperative and willing to explore the possibilities of peace with Ho Chi Minh. (Tito spoke warmly of Senator Fulbright who had been in Yugoslavia the year before.) The President sent a letter to the United Nations offering to collaborate in a formula to end the war. U Thant began working through the labyrinth of nations looking for a solution. There were hints from Washington that the United States would accept Vietcong representatives in a new government of South Vietnam, and let the nation itself decide on unification.

Ho Chi Minh replied in mid-August. Hanoi insisted that the air war be suspended and the Vietcong recognized as the "sole authentic representative of the Vietnamese people." This was an arrogant and disappointing reply, but Senator Fulbright cautioned that it was merely the beginning of an Oriental bargaining.

President Johnson's mood changed abruptly. All right, then, these so-and-sos didn't appreciate a decent appeal, all they understood was power. He would pour it on. The President ordered a step-up of the air strikes on North Vietnam and, for the record, demanded a division of northern troops be withdrawn from the fighting.

The suddenness of this caught many by surprise. According to State Department cables, Marshal Tito and the Soviets were outraged. They had been promised the United States would be moderate and patient during the negotiations, and, now without warning, this new fury. U Thant was dismayed.

Disillusioned, disturbed by a pattern of blind reaction in Vietnam and the Dominican Republic, the Senator from Arkansas spoke out bluntly on September 15. He gave his critique of American actions in Santo Domingo, the story of wild exaggeration, concealment of facts and propping up a military dictatorship with American Armed Forces.

All of the Administraton apparatus, reaching into Congress and the press, turned on Senator Fulbright as if he had been North Vietnam. He sent the President a modest personal letter, assuring him that he meant his friend no harm, that he regarded him as a great man, and his criticism was intended to strengthen rather than weaken the Administration.

On October 4, Pope Paul VI came to New York to address the United Nations and plea for an end to the war in Vietnam. Ten days later, the Defense Department announced the highest draft call since the Korean War. On November 2, Norman R. Morrison, thirty-two, a Quaker, committed suicide by fire in front of the Pentagon "to express his concern over the great loss of life and human suffering caused by the war in Vietnam." On November 11, Secretary McNamara announced the Administration "believes it will be necessary to add further to the strength of U.S. combat forces in Vietnam." On November 15, Correspondent Eric Sevareid reported that the United States had rejected a Hanoi proposal in 1964 that U.S. and North Vietnam representatives meet in Rangoon to discuss a way to end the war. Two days later, the State Department confirmed that another North Vietnamese peace feeler had been made May 20, 1965, during talks in Paris between a Hanoi representative and French officials. On November 18, the Defense Department stated that 108 American soldiers were slain in the week ending November 15.

The depth of Senator Fulbright's discouragement was discovered accidentally. Flying out to New Zealand for a parliamentarians' conference, he stopped at Honolulu and saw there, quite by chance,

Senator Vance Hartke of Indiana, flying home from an Asian trip. They met on Monday, November 21, 1965, and had coffee together. Fulbright said, "My God, I feel so alone. No one seems to give a damn. I feel at times that I am walking among the blind and the deaf."

This was the last wail of what has been described by others as Fulbright's "hand-wringing" period. From that point on he moved to a bolder and more dramatic role, the prosecutor presenting directly to the Amercan people his case against the conduct of foreign policy.

XXIII

WHILE SENATOR FULBRIGHT was in New Zealand, Washington talked of the President's obsession, which was to rawhide his old friend, bring him down in public, make him confess his error. Johnson talked incessantly of it and created a fantasy of himself as a wise and generous patron whose protégé had turned despicably upon him. He appealed to his particular audience, it didn't seem to matter who it was, was any punishment too harsh for a fellow like that? The newspaper column of William S. White was, at times, awkward with rage.

The Washington conversation was more than cocktail gossip. There was a quality deeper, more ominous. Most agreed that Fulbright had said nothing to bring on such a passion for revenge, unless—Unless the Senator in his call for a bombing lull, cease-fire, return to the Geneva agreement, accepting the Vietcong as a bargaining unit, in his belittling of the total evil of Communism and the virtue of total victory had struck at the fires that kept Johnson moving. Was Lyndon Johnson a kind of William Jennings Bryan and Fulbright his Clarence Darrow?

If this were true, the Vietnam war would widen step by terrible step as the President, in an ever more desperate mood, sought the victory over evil that was, in effect, his personal salvation.

Very few in Washington knew what really made Johnson tick. He was an artful dissembler, playing the young liberal for Franklin Roosevelt, the great conservative for the Texas oilmen, the dove of peace for the 1964 electorate. His colleagues had assumed for years he was the essence of The Politician, without basic convictions, but with a miraculous skill at adapting himself to changes in the political temperature, and organizing forces behind him. But his onetime executive assistant, Booth Mooney, in 1956 wrote a book, *The Lyndon Johnson Story,* and described his "strong feelings" on a number of subjects. One was Communism, and Johnson's stated view was the wild and alarmist one which the ultrarightists yawped and stuttered over small radio stations. "International Communism is not merely an object of replusion. It is a deadly threat—a threat to our lives, our liberties and our future. It is a threat because the Communist dictators are not content to practice their tyranny in the nations they control already. They insist that their brand of dictatorship is an export commodity, a form of government that must oppose freedom wherever freedom exists . . . Their objective, which they have never concealed, is a universal dictatorship ruled by themselves . . ."

The sophisticated view of Senator Fulbright, spoken publicly during a war with the Communists, would, therefore, seem the worst kind of heresy to the fundamentalist President.

The chastising of Fulbright became such public knowledge that the cautious Associated Press reported in early December: "It's hardly a secret Fulbright infuriated Johnson when he blasted the use of troops in the Dominican Republic revolt . . . When Fulbright suggested a suspension of the bombings, the President let his press secretary, Bill Moyers, answer for him. Moyers said it would do no good. Some of Fulbright's fellow Senators said he wrote Johnson a get well note when the President was hospitalized last summer, and got in reply a note from a staff member." [In his modest and humble note, the Senator confessed his loyalty and friendship for Johnson, and begged him to understand that this criticism was intended to help, not injure, his Administration.]

"Then early last month Johnson approved a fact finding trip to Europe and Asia, including a Kremlin conference, and five Senators headed by Mike Mansfield. Mansfield said he had discussed it with Johnson for months. Fulbright, as chairman of Foreign Relations, might have seemed logical to head such a delegation. But it is known Fulbright was surprised by the news. And his Committee never authorized the trip. Fulbright meanwhile was going to head a group of Senators going to a parliamentary conference in New Zealand. While Mansfield's team traveled by Air Force jet, Fulbright's was told it would have to get slower planes or commercial transportation. In Australia, Fulbright was asked what he thought of the Australian war effort, and when he was asked how many Australians were serving in

Vietnam and was told it was 1,000, he said it was small compared to the American 165,000. Johnson then sent a message to Australia praising their war effort."

Some newspapers were disturbed by the Johnson attitude. *The New York Times* said, "It may be of little importance if President Johnson chooses not to invite Senator Fulbrght to White House dinners for visiting foreign statesmen. It is a more serious affair if the White House has decided to ignore or bypass the chairman of the Foreign Relations Committee on legislative policy and other matters affecting American foreign policy, as a recent Washington story in *The Times* suggests . . . The Administration will need Senator Fulbright's help on a host of foreign policy problems when Congress returns. It may even find that it needs his wisdom and counsel as well."

The *St. Louis Post-Dispatch* stated, "The national interest would be served by the renewed opportunity for Mr. Fulbright to make his voice heard in White House councils—where he is badly needed."

Max Freedman, whose reportage in *The Manchester Guardian* made him such a favorite with the Kennedy entourage, wrote, "Fulbright has insisted on his right of retaining his independent judgment and of expressing it even when it brought him into disagreement with the Administration. The independence has given him a unique prestige and immense influence. But he has paid a grievous price. Inside the Administration he is often called the Democratic Borah."

The Senator himself was honestly bewildered by the Johnson wrath. But he chose in public to say that talk of the President ostracizing him was nonsense. He told one reporter, "The President wouldn't be human if he didn't dislike some of the things I have said, but beyond that is simply ridiculous. It's silly to say he is punishing me."

This isolation from his old friend and from his councils certainly contributed to Fulbright's loneliness. But he did not allow it to run his life. He set out on a double course, to find out the truth about Vietnam, if possible, and to explain to his fellow Senators the facts as he saw them.

Senator Hartke, who has a talent somewhat akin to Johnson's in organizing, brought together some twenty Senators, including Robert Kennedy, for seminars with Fulbright. "There would have been a lot more," Hartke explained, "if they hadn't been afraid word would get back to Lyndon. His anger is respected on Capitol Hill."

Senator Fulbright acted as the informal chairman of a discussion group. The subject was practical political strategy—what could be done to restrain the Administration, and how to go about it. These seminars were frustrating for Fulbright, because there is no real mechanism in our society for cooling the passions of war.

The Founding Fathers thought they had written in such a mechanism, by giving Congress alone the power to declare war. This has proven, though, a weak brake. Traditionally American public opinion responds ardently to the drums of war, although it may cool off rapidly as in the War of 1812 and Korea. The President is in the best position to beat the drums, if he chooses, and few members of Congress are willing to oppose the public passion. Also, by such devices as the Gulf of Tonkin resolution, Congress has given up this power to declare war (perhaps illegally).

There was talk at these meetings of trying to repeal the resolution or force the President to ask for a declaration of war, but most realized there was no great support in the Senate for such drastic action.

Always the meetings broke up in a feeling of helplessness, and each Senator went his own way to do what he could individually.

Finding out the true state of affairs in Vietnam, South and North, was a problem, even for a man as intellectually ingenious as Fulbright. Knowledge of Vietnam was almost an executive branch monopoly. Here again, the Senator looked to the foreign correspondent for a fresh focus.

In mid-December, the Senator spent several hours talking to one of the very few top authorities on Vietnam, the French journalist Philippe Devillers. Fulbright had been laid up with a cold, and Devillers came to his home and the two sat before a log fire talking.

Devillers had come to Indochina as press aid to General Leclerc after World War II, remained as a correspondent for the Paris newspaper, *Le Monde,* and he was now editor of *France-Asie* and director, Southeast Asia Section, Foundation Nationale des Sciences Politique, University of Paris. His *Histoire de Viet-Nam de 1940 À 1952* and *North Vietnam Today* were classics.

This small, precise-speaking correspondent told a story somewhat at variance from State Department briefings. According to him, armed opposition in South Vietnam did not arise from the north, but because of Diem's attempt to crush all opposition in the south by arrests and terror. His first object was the small private armies of religious sects. When their leaders were killed or arrested, the rank and file took to the bush and became *maquis,* as Devillers put it. The *maquis* was swelled by urban liberals, Trotskyites, Communists, even anti-Diem conservatives. The underground asked Hanoi for help, but was refused. Ho Chi Minh was influenced by the Soviets who did not want to rock the boat in Southeast Asia and start a fight with the United States.

In 1960, under pressure from both the *maquis* and China, Ho allowed the National Liberation Front to organize and gave it help.

The Senator wanted to know how much help.

Devillers said of the 230,000 Viet Cong, only 40,000 were from the north, and half of them were southerners who had fled from Diem and returned to fight. Since 1963, weapons of Russian and Chinese make had been coming to the Vietcong at the rate of 200 tons a month, a very little compared to the 4,000 tons a month the Chinese sent the Vietminh when they were fighting the French during the Indochina war.

Fulbright asked him what he thought the prospects were for a negotiated peace.

Devillers was pessimistic. He talked of his own experience. He had spoken to Ambassador Goldberg at the United Nations, who advised him if Hanoi withdrew a regiment, this would be seen as a signal. This the journalist passed on to a North Vietnamese representative in Paris. According to him the regiment was withdrawn, and the North Vietnamese bitterly stated, "The troops are gone, and the bombing continues."

He had interviewed Ho in August, and was told discussions on "disengagement" could start, if the United States gave tangible evidence it would abide by the Geneva accord and cease aggression.

However, in Washington he was told by Administration officials: if the United States withdrew, or if it allowed the Vietcong a place in a South Vietnamese Government, the Communists would take over with the backing of Hanoi. Walt Rostow, one of the Administration ideologists, compared the situation to Poland and Czechoslovakia prior to the Communist take-over.

The French and Soviet Governments agreed to reconvene the Geneva conference when the time was proper, that is, when there seemed a chance for a settlement. That was not now.

Devillers said he did not think China wanted to go to war over Vietnam. However, he was concerned by a very hard line on China he had heard from Washington officials. It seemed as if the United States was itching to fight the Chinese. Some Pentagon generals wanted to bomb neutral Cambodia, claiming it was a hideout for Vietcong on the run, and that country said if it were attacked, China would be asked for help. In that case, he said with an expressive gesture of his hands, he did not know what China would do.

Fulbright wanted to know if he thought the bombings had affected the war one way or another.

Yes, they had hardened the position of the Vietcong and Hanoi, and created more hatred.

Within a few days, there was considerable private talk in Washington of two separate peace feelers from Hanoi to Washington, one through two Italian travelers and the other via the Hungarian Foreign Minister. One version, reported by *The Manchester Guardian,* said Ho Chi Minh had retreated to three points, a cease-fire, halting of the bombing, and an American willingness to negotiate with the National Liberation Front. Ho, in turn, assured the Italians that Vietnam would be extremely independent and willing to develop close ties with the West. According to *The Guardian,* Pope Paul was most interested and hopeful.

President Johnson was told personally that the door would be automatically closed, if Hanoi or Haiphong were bombed. Within hours, *The Guardian* said, the strike against a power station fifteen miles from Haiphong was ordered.

The study by the several leading scholars at the University of California in 1966 revealed the pattern—whenever it seemed the time might be ripe for a political settlement, the United States escalated the war. Nine "critical periods" were analyzed in the report, which concluded, "The effect of the American actions has been not merely to deepen our military commitment but also to weaken the credibility of the United States government officials who publicly claim that they are searching for a real basis for negotiations."

The Manchester Guardian reiterated what Devillers had told Senator Fulbright, that Washington officials would not accept a neutral coalition government with Communists taking part. The Administration, apparently, wanted to create a West Germany out of South Vietnam, and behind the scenes many of the old architects of the "containment" policy in Europe were working on similar strategy in Asia. Dean Acheson, for one, was being called in for consultation.

The Senator, though, is essentially an optimist. When on December 24, a Christmas truce was proclaimed by the United States, he hoped this might be continued into a cease-fire and general negotiations. On December 26, American forces took the initiative again, because of "heavy Vietcong attacks." Then the bombing war was stilled again, and on December 29, the President sent high-ranking emissaries to world capitals on his "peace offensive."

Fulbright kept a discreet silence, but has since privately referred to this operation as a "charade." He would agree with what his friend, Walter Lippmann, wrote: "The reason why the peace offensive failed is most cogently revealed in the Mansfield report on the state of the war. Mr. Johnson has been trying to obtain by propaganda the victory which he has not been able to obtain on the battlefield—that is to say, the acceptance in the whole of South Vietnam of a government which has lost control of a very large part of South Vietnam . . . The Mansfield report shows that Mr. Rusk's objective—the rule of General Ky or of his successors over the whole of South Vietnam—is unattainable no matter how much the war is escalated." A *New York Times* lead editorial pointed out the chief stumbling block to talks was the program of the (Vietcong) National Liberation Front, and suggested the Administration had taken a doctrinaire attitude. Actually, *The Times* said, all that Hanoi wanted was, "The internal affairs of South Vietnam must be settled by its people without foreign intervention (as stated in the program of the NLF). " The editorial recommended quiet diplomacy to bring about a neutral coalition government to include the South Vietnamese Army, the Vietcong, Buddhists, Catholics, Cao Dai and other political blocs.

Senator Fulbright broke his self-imposed silence on January 21. In West Memphis, Arkansas, he said, "We must decide we want to negotiate. I simply cannot help asking myself if the United States involvement in Vietnam is worth a nuclear war."

The next day, Johnson pointedly praised the Senator's chief home state critic, Governor Orval Faubus.

Two days later, Fulbright was back in Washington, and after the Foreign Relations Committee had spent three hours with Rusk, told reporters, "Despite the fact the peace offensive has been unproductive, it is necessary to keep trying." He thought the Administration should prolong the bombing lull, and negotiate with the NLF. "It is necessary to recognize the Vietcong," he said, "as a legitimate party to a conference. This may determine whether we can hold a conference. The war began as an indigenous rebellion which became dominated by the Communists. The Vietcong have borne the brunt of the fighting since it started. One reason they fight so fanatically with such great losses is their intense feeling that they have been thwarted in their move for national independence. They have been helped from the outside, just as we supported the French beginning in 1950."

He thought it had been a mistake in 1949 not to have recognized the reality of Communist China. The Committee, he said, had asked Rusk to consult with it before bombing raids were started again, but the Secretary replied this was up to the President. Fulbright remarked, "I think a resumption of the bombing would mean we have given up on a settlement."

Senator Fulbright was in a restless frame of mind. He had lost confidence in the Administration, both in the veracity of its statements and its ability to end the war. He wanted to open up a debate on Vietnam. He was ready, even anxious, to drop his customary role of the public philosopher and enter the debate. The debate, he felt, should be open. The Administration policies should be examined publicly and questioned, and alternatives offered. He found good possibility when scanning *The Congressional Record* of January 19. Senator Morse had put in *The Record* the letter of General James M. Gavin to *Harper's Magazine*. The general advocated his "enclave" theory, which to the Senator offered a reasonable, politically acceptable alternative.

On Friday, January 28, the debate began in the crowded Committee hearing room on the fourth floor of the new Senate Office Building. The legal "hook" for the session was a request for an additional $275 million aid for Vietnam. Secretary Rusk, placid, round-faced, sat in the witness chair surrounded by his nervous aides.

Senator Fulbright addressed him in his best Sunday-go-to-meeting manner, a rather courtly and pleasant Southern mien: "These requests for additional aid cannot be considered in a vacuum, but must be related to the overall political and military situation in Vietnam."

Personalities are somewhat unimportant to Senator Fulbright, and he had never inquired into the background of the Georgia tenant farm boy and Rhodes scholar who, Max Frankel, diplomatic correspondent of *The New York Times,* said, was regarded by some as "something of a zealot in his dread of Communist China." He had worn an ROTC uniform from high school on, with "a sense of pride and feeling of privilege," Frankel said, had an "elemental—one Cabinet colleague said 'primitive'—patriotism," served in World War II under General "Vinegar Joe" Stillwell in the Far East, held sub-cabinet assignments in the Defense and State Departments, and was recommended for Secretary by two "activists," Dean Acheson and former Under Secretary of Defense Robert Lovett. Senator Fulbright tended to think of him as a disciple of John Foster Dulles.

What Rusk told the Committee that morning he said again and again, hardly varying a word, in his slow, rather pleasantly prim Georgia voice. It was as if he had obtained some divine wisdom, and felt no need to defend it by logic or exhortation or facts. He never appeared seriously ruffled, although once or twice he flushed under Fulbright's intense questioning.

The Secretary said then, "The heart of the problem in South Vietnam is the effort of North Vietnam to impose its will by force. For that purpose, Hanoi has infiltrated into South Vietnam large quantities of arms and tens of thousands of trained and armed men, including units of the North Vietnamese Regular Army. It is that external aggression, which the north has repeatedly escalated, that is responsible for the presence of U.S. combat forces. [Later, during the questioning, he told Senator Claiborne Pell that North Vietnamese fighting in the south were "about 20 percent" of the Vietcong.]

"While assisting the South Vietnamese to repel this aggression, the United States has made persistent efforts to find a peaceful solution. The initiatives for peace undertaken by us and by many other governments during the last five years are almost innumerable . . . The United States has a clear and direct commitment to the security of South Vietnam against external attack. The integrity of our commitments is absolutely essential to the preservation of peace around the globe . . . The challenge in Vietnam demands the selective application of our U.S. military power in support of the forces of the Government of Vietnam. In the absence of a willingness on the part of the other side to sit down and make peace, there is no alternative—except defeat and surrender—to meeting force with force."

Senator Fulbright's first probes were historical. Why did the United States pour so much money into France's war against the Vietminh, when we had pressed the Dutch into giving up Indonesia? Rusk

thought it was to prevent the Communists from getting "a basic position in Southeast Asia." What was the basis of our commitment? The
SEATO treaty.

"Are we obligated under the treaty?" the Senator asked. The Secretary slid away from a direct answer.

"What is our objective?"

"We believe that the South Vietnamese are entitled to a chance to
make their own decisions about their own affairs; that they are entitled to make them without having them imposed from North
Vietnam or elsewhere from the outside . . ."

Fulbright said with a slight irony, "Do you think they can be a
completely free agent with our occupation of the land with two
hundred thousand or four hundred thousand men?"

This was like the opening passes of a fencing match, all very polite,
even ceremonial. But at the press tables, where these things are
gauged in terms of future coverage, there was no doubt blood would
be drawn. Rusk seemed almost indifferent to the Committee. He was
the martyr who had taken his vows and was waiting, perhaps not
without some happy anticipation, the rack and fire. Fulbright, plainly,
had determined on a basic review of Vietnam policy. Like a prosecutor, he was laying the groundwork with selective questions.

Fulbright came back in the second round to ask, "What is the
explanation of why in 1956, contrary to the terms of the Geneva
accords, elections were not held? You have stated several times that
the aggression started in 1960. But the events between 1954, when
the agreement was signed, and 1960 were not without significance?"

The Secretary replied that neither the South Vietnamese nor the
American Government had signed the agreements.

"Why didn't we sign it?" Fulbright asked quickly.

"My general impression is, the United States was at that time not
persuaded that this was the best way to settle this affair . . ."

Since we didn't sign, why did we encourage Diem not to follow the
agreement?

"Well, the prospect of free elections in North and South Vietnam
was very poor at that time."

The Senator looked at him with a frown. Here was the incident
which started the armed rebellion in the south, and our only excuse
for it was that the prospects for elections "were very poor at that
time." This was hardly the whole answer.

As the morning wore on, Secretary Rusk remained placid under a torrent of questions that were, if not hostile, at least skeptical. Senator Albert Gore wanted to know what the constitutional basis was for our involvement in Vietnam. The Secretary replied the Gulf of Tonkin resolution.

Gore replied sharply, "I certainly want to disassociate myself with any interpretation that this was a declaration of war."

Fulbright spoke of his own doubts: "There is some feeling that, perhaps, we have intervened in a family quarrel here, and that this intervention may not be justified on the grounds here presented . . . I do not see the specific commitment. I do not see the Southeast Asia treaty . . . None of us are very well briefed on this area because, frankly, I did not anticipate years ago that this was a serious situation. I mean anything like this. There is unhappiness at what is going on there, this expansion of the war."

The concerns of thirteen perplexed Senators flashed on millions of television screens caught the public mood of uncertainty and apprehension, and the reaction startled official Washington. While the hearing was still going on upstairs, Western Union messengers began bringing piles of telegrams to Senator Fulbright's first-floor office. Letters, hundreds, then thousands of them, began pouring in.

Secretary Rusk might have stilled the troubled public mind, but he did not. He behaved, instead, as though the involvement in Vietnam was too mystic to be entrusted to mere men. Actually, Rusk was too much in the shadow of Lyndon Johnson to be candid. Candor was never a trait Johnson appreciated.

Senator Fulbright, never one to court public opinion in the arena, was surprised by the magnitude of the response. He had not expected so many Americans were troubled by Vietnam. The mail from his own state showed a depth of feeling he had not anticipated. The *Arkansas Democrat* of Little Rock, reflecting sentiment in the state, said, "Any war is wasteful, destructive and takes an appalling toll of lives. Certainly it is the prime desire of the whole nation to end this dirty business as soon as possible."

The Senator remarked, "I've been in Congress quite a long time, and I don't recall any issue about which there is so much apprehension."

The Committee scheduled new hearings, with Secretary McNamara to appear on the following Friday, and General Gavin shortly after.

President Johnson reacted strongly. On January 30, he summoned Congressional leaders to the White House and announced he was resuming the bombing. He glared at the group and demanded if there were any objections. There were, from Mansfield and Fulbright. Johnson listened to Mansfield with an exasperated frown. When Fulbright began in his soft, polite voice, the President turned abruptly away and began talking to Secretary McNamara.

This curt snub was noted by raised eyebrows and questioning eyes. Many were acutely embarrassed.

This was not all. The President ordered McNamara not to testify before an open session of the Committee and told a "surprise" news conference such testimony could endanger "the lives of a good many of our men." Several committee members, Republicans and Democrats, agreed with Morse when he called this "government by secrecy."

Then the President jetted off to Honolulu for a hastily called conference with General Ky, now South Vietnamese Premier thanks to a military coup. For this affair, Johnson took four Cabinet members, the chairman of the Joint Chiefs of Staff, and his security coordinator.

A reporter asked him, "Have any political or military developments prompted this?"

"No," he replied. "Just as I stated, for some time I have been wanting to see them and talk to them, and this seems to be a good time to do it."

The press suggested he had been outraged by the Committee hearings, and scheduled the conference to take the headlines and TV play away from them. This view obviously irked the President, for later Vice-President Humphrey stated, "This was one of the most important meetings of modern times, a blueprint of hope."

Whatever the intention, the result was unhappy. The President was photographed clasping the diminutive Ky in his typical Texan hug. This caused some stir in the world press, because Ky had recently expressed his admiration for Hitler. And among the fiercely nationalistic Vietnamese, Ky became the puppet of the foreign overlord and his days of unquestioned rule numbered.

Senator Fulbright was, at least on the surface, unruffled by Johnson's attitude toward him and the Committee. He said, "All we seek is some information and enlightenment, so that our country's judgment, the judgment of our people of this committee, may be as wise as possible."

XXIV

WHEN NEXT THE Committee met the script might have been written by a Greek tragedian. For, like *The Trojan Women,* it told of the costs and miseries of war, without an end in sight.

The witness was quiet-spoken, competent, intelligent, neutral. Horror should never be overplayed. He was David E. Bell, the AID administrator, one of the new breed of government managers, who in their efficiency and use of statistics seem far away from mortal sweat and tears.

The picture given by his testimony, the remarks of Senators, and material placed in the record was of a small country dazed by the disarray of war. Its economy was being eaten up by inflation, a huge black market and corruption. War had so interrupted its agricultural production that what was once the rice bowl of Asia required $21 million worth of imported rice a year. Without this American aid, Saigon would starve. It was burdened by refugees, 700,000 in one year alone seeking escape from bombings and enemy terror, and ineffectively housed and fed. The war was causing more casualties among civilians than in the military.

The giant, America, was feeling the war, too. Senator Fulbright submitted a staff study showing the cost to the United States of the war in Vietnam for the current year was $15.8 billion.

"This is a rather substantial operation as of now, is it not?" he asked Bell.

"It certainly is."

"And it's growing?"

"Yes, sir."

"You estimate it is going to be less next year?"

"No, more."

Senator Church listed cuts in American domestic programs, as a result of war costs—the school milk program reduced from $103 million to $21 million, agricultural conservation cut $100 million, the watershed program pared back by 45 new starts, $270 million snipped out of aid to public education, and the entire land-grant college fund wiped out.

Church told Bell the cost of one year of the Vietnam war was half the total for the outlay for all unmet needs in American communities for schools, hospitals, water treatment plants and the like.

Other Senators spoke of a lack of clear objectives in Vietnam, of the need for alternatives, of executive secrecy, and these views came from a broad spectrum of conservative Republicans from the Plains States to the liberal urban Senator, Joseph Clark of Pennsylvania. Clark said the Administration would not tell the public of the areas held by opposing forces, even though a map showing them appeared in the magazine, *U.S. News & World Report*.

Fulbright said sarcastically, "It's all right to give it to *U.S. News*. It depends on who gives it."

He was highly pleased with the Committee. To him, it had reached a new height of public service, and shown itself to be thoughtful and fair and diverse in its interests before the staring eye of the TV camera. There were, of course, exceptions. Frank Lausche of Ohio, a somewhat volatile individual with a wild shock of hair and excited manner, interrupted a number of times. Lausche was one of Fulbright's crosses, wished on him by Lyndon Johnson. Once, after a particularly heavy day at the Committee with Lausche, the Senator from Arkansas gloomily suggested to a reporter he might resign the chairmanship.

Senator Morse exasperates him at times, too. He offends Fulbright's sense of decorum, but this is more than balanced by the Arkansan's respect for Morse's spectacular, if sometimes unruly, mind and his courage. He paid an unusual tribute to Morse in the first of his 1966 Johns Hopkins speeches: "In fact, the protesters against the Vietnamese war are in good historical company. On January 12, 1848, Abraham Lincoln rose in the United States House of Representatives and made a speech about the Mexican War worthy of Senator Morse. Lincoln's speech was an explanation of a vote he had recently cast in support of a resolution declaring that the war had been unnecessarily and unconstitutionally begun by President Polk. 'I admit,' he said, 'that such a vote could not be given, in mere party wantonness, and that the one given, is justly censurable, if it have no other, or better foundation. I am one of those who joined in that vote; and I did so under my best impression of the truth of the case."

Senator Fulbright gets along very well with his Republican opposite on the Committee, conservative Bourke Hickenlooper of Iowa, and speaks of him with respect and friendship. Those on the Committee to whom he feels the closest are probably Frank Church of Idaho and Eugene McCarthy of Minnesota.

The televised hearings were, at first, something of a trial to Fulbright. His sense of decorum, again, was painfully startled by the bright TV lighting and the fuss that attends any great show on Capitol Hill. But he was determined to endure it, because this was the most important way to get the Vietnam debate before the public. So he put on dark glasses, and began the ordeal. Then he began to get the feel of it, as he had of campaigning on street corners in small towns of Arkansas. As the telegrams and letters and telephone calls began pouring in, Fulbright was elated. The people were there, and they were watching, and they were catching the message. This was a great classroom, and there was a kind of affectionate rapport between the teacher and much of his class. Too, reluctant as he is to get into a scrap, mooning about it, doubting, vacillating, once he is in the struggle, his spirits pick up rapidly. He enjoys the contest and wants to win.

His first direct, open challenge to the Administration came on the third day of hearings, Tuesday, February 8. President Johnson had been regularly saying no one ever offered alternatives to his own course, and he was pushed heavily for greater escalation by the generals. Now, Senator Fulbright produced a general who offered a militarily feasible alternative, and was able to show that many in the military regarded a land war in Asia, and specifically Vietnam, as a misadventure. Further, he bluntly attacked the air bombardment as pointless.

Lieutenant General James M. Gavin, U.S. Army, retired, was a competent witness. In the military galaxy, he was one of the brightest stars, an innovator of new techniques, a progressive to whom many majors and colonels looked to lift the Army out of its dull old ways and provincialism. He was a paratroop commander in World War II, Assistant Chief of Staff for Plans and Operations during the Indochina War, and then Chief of Research for the Army. He resigned during the Eisenhower Administration in protest of its cutback on research, and was appointed Ambassador to France by President Kennedy, a great admirer. General Gavin, as he sat quietly waiting for the session to begin, did not look like the movie version of the tough, profane paratroop officer, but was more the Ambassador. Even in retirement, General Gavin had probably a wider following among younger officers, as a strategist of the nuclear age, than any other general.

He recounted that at the time of the French defeat at Dien Bien Phu, he was asked by the Chief of Staff, General Matthew Ridgway, to make a thorough study of Vietnam. The question was whether the United States should send in a large force, eight divisions, thirty-eight engineer battalions and auxiliary units, to hold the Hanoi Delta.

"We spent a lot of time worrying about it," he told the Committee. "I knew that I would be responsible for planning the conduct of operations, and I devoted a good deal of talk about it with colleagues who had considerable experience in Southeast Asia and China.

"We finally decided when we were all through that what we were talking about was going to war with Red China under conditions that were appallingly disadvantageous. We were talking about going to war with her thousands and thousands of miles from the heart of our warmaking capacity, and it frankly made little sense to a man who had to go do the fighting. So I was more than pleased to see General Ridgway take the initiative, and it took more courage to do it as he did and say, 'Let's look at this. It makes little sense to do it.' "

President Eisenhower decided against the action, and in his book, *Mandate for Change,* said that to have gone to war then would have been "like hitting the tail of the snake rather than the head."

Senator Fulbright sat, a little slouched over, following General Gavin with an intellectual intensity that is the mark of the scholar. Very little existed for him outside the spoken thoughts of the general.

Gavin then turned to an experience with President Kennedy over Laos. It ran so directly counter to President Johnson's mood and actions in Vietnam that the comparison was striking.

The general said, "Since then, perhaps one of the most interesting experiences I had was with Mr. Kennedy. About a month after going to my post in Paris, he asked me to return to talk about Laos. He was confronted with a very difficult situation . . . I would suspect that if he had sought the advice of the Pentagon, we no doubt would have committed forces and ultimately more divisions and more divisions.

But to Mr. Kennedy this made little sense, and, indeed, the more we talked about it, the more I agreed with him, a landlocked country, remote from the immediate application of sea power and somewhat less of air power seemed to offer a hopeless situation to us.

"He asked me to go Paris and enter into discussions with Souvanna Phouma to see if we could not convince that gentleman that we were interested in a 'free, neutral, independent Laos.' This I undertook. Admittedly it was with some misgivings, because Souvanna Phouma had a reputation of being then very close to the Communists . . . After about six or eight meetings, and very fruitful and fascinating meetings they were for me, we did arrive indeed at a treaty that, hopefully, guaranteed the freedom, neutrality and independence of Laos.

"I was aware then, as I am now, that what our President sought to achieve was a political settlement to what appeared to be a potentially serious military problem. He was absolutely right. He was absolutely right, and we did arrive at that solution."

If President Johnson had been watching this scene, it would have been gall and wormwood to him. How he hated to be reminded President Kennedy did it differently or better! But that thought probably did not occur to Senator Fulbright. He thought in terms of issues and nations, not of individual reactions.

General Gavin went on: "So I decided in the summer or early fall of last year, we had better look hard at our Vietnam commitment, in view of our total spectrum of global commitments, and the changed nature of global strategy. Vietnam was becoming alarmingly out of balance." He was afraid the United States was drifting into greater escalation, and would be tempted to bomb cities, even Peking, and perhaps use the nuclear weapon.

"As man has sought to impose his will on an opponent from the very beginning of recorded history," the general said, "he has sought to use energy in every form that he could get it, bludgeon, metallic penetrating instruments, metallic pellets fired by chemical charges to the explosion of the fission of the atom and fusion of the atom itself. He has finally succeeded in bringing down to the earth the very explosions that take place on the surface of the sun, fission. He has brought the energy of the cosmos itself to the earth. He can no longer use it because it would destroy a major segment of the human race. He is at the end of the search for energy with which to impose his will on fellowmen. He is at the end. Now he must find more discreet means, more discriminating means. He must find greater mobility, rapid data transmission, he must keep these weapons under control. He must know what is going on everywhere as quickly as he can find out so as to keep under control local conflagrations, and thus avoid the major catastrophe that might occur if, thoughtlessly, nuclear weapons were used."

A little more than twenty years ago, Fulbright, sitting cramped and intent in a small committee room, had heard the generals and scientists speak their fears. September, 1945. The danger had moved closer.

The peril, to General Gavin, was that we had committed too much of our power in Vietnam, that if we were confronted in other danger areas, as Korea, Quemoy and Matsu and Thailand, we might be overwhelmed in one or more arenas. Then the temptation to use the bomb would swell into a monstrous desire.

So he tried to carve out a strategy to contain the enemy in Vietnam without further escalations. "We must do the best we can with what we have in hand, keeping in mind the true meaning of global strategy in world affairs today," he warned.

In answer to a question from Senator Fulbright, he said, "I am quite uneasy about an overresponse in Vietnam. There may be variations of nuance to this but I feel the confrontation with the Red Chinese is a real compelling fact of life today. We could get ourselves so deeply involved in Vietnam as to seriously lack the capability if Korea were to reopen, in Thailand if it became very, very serious. I am concerned because our international strategic position is being eroded badly." He was referring to press reports that the Communists might open up new fronts in both Korea and Thailand to relieve pressure in Vietnam.

The general remarked he had heard talk of a million American men in Vietnam. "Is Vietnam at this point worth this investment in national resources, with all the other commitments we have?" he asked. He concluded, "It isn't vital for the future of the United States that we stay. It isn't absolutely essential to our survival or to our future security that we stay there." He did not think "unconditional surrender" of North Vietnam was a prudent goal, and a blockade was not politically feasible because it would lead to a direct military confrontation with important allies in Europe, as well as Soviet Russia.

There were little dramas within the big drama. Senator Stuart

Symington had been Secretary of the Air Force at the peak of the romance over long-range bombing. The Strategic Air Command was going to save the world from Communism; this became a religion with men like Symington. In the Vietnam war, President Johnson was using bombing as an act of retaliation. Questioned by Symington and others, the general thought air power in support of troops and for military targets was justified. But, he added, "I must say I look upon this as one of the great illusions of all times, that through air power you can really win this way. I think the results of the strategic bombing survey will show that as our bombing increased, German production went up until we overran facilities. I don't think you can hold them by bombing nor really win by bombing. . . . Bombing attacks intended to achieve psychological impact through the killing of noncombatants is unquestionably wrong. Likewise, the attack of targets near areas highly populated by civilians are also militarily wrong. The 'urban bombing' concept developed in the immediate post-World War II period is entirely inappropriate in the Vietnamese-type confrontation."

General Gavin's solution was quite simple. Hang on to what we had, including the big urban complexes, to show the enemy we could not be driven out. Lay off the extravagant bombings. Avoid escalation. Seek a political settlement.

He told in surprise of the attacks upon him for advocating a different tactic than the Administration. He said, "I don't know when in my life I have had such techniques used against me where I am charged with having said things I didn't say, and then I am attacked for having said them. I have been accused of retreating, wanting to withdraw, being a turtle, all these things. This is very troublesome and burdensome to me. In fact I almost look upon it more seriously now that I am personally involved in it than Vietnam itself. If this is the state of affairs in the Government, where in the world are we going?"

Senator Fulbright smiled wryly. He said, "I understand that. We sympathize with you."

One of those who had criticized General Gavin was the columnist, Joseph Alsop, whom Senator Clark referred to satirically as "that great military strategist." Clark added, "I suspect, and I have no reason to say this other than that I know Joe Alsop pretty well, he would be dropping bombs on China pretty soon."

Several times during the long day, the talk slid over into the chance of war with China. Without seriously thinking why, the Senators and General Gavin seemed to assume this was almost inevitable. Senator Fulbright, however, frowned and made some notes with his yellow pencil on a pad before him.

Every night for the past week or so, Fulbright had been reading with a growing fascination the classic works on China, its history and culture in anticipation of the forthcoming Committee hearings on China with the top American scholars. Out of this reading was emerging a view somewhat different from the standard clichés.

So he asked General Gavin, "In what respect are they very aggressive, contrasting what they say with what they do?"

The question itself was revealing. In a casual conversation with a member of his staff, Fulbright had remarked, "Often a nation, just like an individual, talks more belligerently than it acts. This is to keep up its own ego, to assure itself of its greatness. It's also to keep the people united and working hard."

The general answered him, "I have been exposed to the filmed reports coming out of China of their militancy, of their training of their youth and their industrial workers and their people in the use of arms, in the military tactics and so forth."

"Do you consider that aggressive necessarily?" Fulbright insisted.

"Not necessarily . . . I think they are supplying the Vietcong with ammunition and medical aid and other logistical support, and certainly they are not passive in that tactical area. Beyond that I don't know that there is much I can say about them, except their published statements about their lack of apprehension about a nuclear war, because of the vast manpower they have, and their charges against the Soviets tending to go along with us in Vietnam, rather than being more militant in opposing us."

"The training of their troops in China, is that an act of aggression?"

"No, no."

"Is there any evidence that they moved troops into Vietnam?"

"There is not at this time. The Chinese I believe have alleged that volunteers would participate if necessary, and they have also been reported as stating flatly that if we think that we can get away with our efforts in Vietnam without Korea being reopened, we are badly mistaken."

"I understand they have made many threats," Fulbright said, pursuing this. "Normally we used the word 'aggression' very loosely."

"If I understand what you are getting at," the general replied, "they haven't made any forays out of China itself, going after other people. Of course, they were into India at one time."

Senator Fulbright recalled that General Maxwell Taylor, then President Kennedy's chief military adviser, told a House subcommittee in 1963 that the fighting was in a disputed area and, "They [the Indians] were edging forward in the disputed area."

What Fulbright was doing was challenging a major and very current myth, that Communist China was an active threat to American security, and was intent on grabbing Southeast Asia. This was, actually, the rationale for the Vietnamese war, that if we withdrew, Vietnam would come under Chinese domination and the "dominoes" would fall one by one until we were fighting, as some Administration partisan said, in Seattle. The Fulbright technique was to question the myth, rather than flatly deny it.

The Senator spoke of a "very interesting article" by a *New York Times* correspondent from Hong Kong. "The whole purport is that the Chinese are alleging they are being encircled," he remarked. "In answer to Senator Hickenlooper, he [General Taylor] advanced, I believe, the thesis that if we didn't stop the Chinese here, we would be encircled. Now who is encircling whom at the present time?"

General Gavin replied, "I would be inclined to believe that the Chinese think they are being pretty well hemmed in."

They were both referring to American military bases and nuclear submarines girding China in an arc from Thailand through South Vietnam, the Philippines, the China Seas, Taiwan, Okinawa, South Korea and Japan.

"Is it a fact, do you think, that relatively speaking they are more encircled today than we are?" Fulbright pressed.

"There is no question about that."

Following this exchange, the Senator adopted a technique borrowed both from the classroom (the tutor and a star pupil) and the debate platform. He asked the leading question, "You know a great deal about both military and political history. Have the Chinese as a nation over the last one hundred or two hundred years been especially aggressive? I use that word to mean military, overt aggression on their neighbors."

"No. They haven't been to my knowledge."

"Who aggressed whom during the last century? Was it China attacking the Western nations or vice versa?"

"The other way around. The Western nations attacking China."

"Was this to a very great extent?"

"Yes. I remember quite well reading about the moving from Tientsin in the Boxer Rebellion, and reviewing the life of Gordon and the British occupation of major segments of China as well as that of other European nations."

"As a matter of fact, various Western nations practically occupied and humiliated and decimated China throughout almost a century, did they not?"

"That is true absolutely."

"Don't you think that might not be a significant element in our present situation?"

"Indeed, surely."

This was a preliminary to Fulbright's cram course on China for the benefit of the Senators and the American public, the seven-day China hearings in March. These meetings brought to the witness table the finest American scholars on China, and were a conscious effort by the Senator to exchange knowledge for myth. In the McCarthy era, as he has pointed out, all but the adherents of Generalissimo Chiang were driven from the Government, even General George Marshall was blatantly maligned, and the United States, in effect, drew down a curtain on this huge and populous area. The result, he believed, was that for more than fifteen years this powerful nation was cordoned off from the West, and its bitterness allowed to fester rather than be treated and alleviated by normal contacts.

His reading of Chinese history led Senator Fulbright to suspect that China would dominate Asia, whether we liked it or not. This was because of three factors—its great culture which existed long before that of the West, its resilience to change and disaster, and its high degree of self-discipline and personal drive.

He remarked during a conversation, "The Chinese have been a highly civilized and decent people, and once this current phase of violent nationalism—a reaction against humiliations from the West, and the most recent from Russia—passes, her influence in Asia might be a force for stability. The best we can do now is stop and take a second look, a more realistic one, and try to help China get past this trying stage in its history. I think U Thant compared it to a nervous breakdown. We can do this by bringing China, reluctant though she may be, into closer contact with the rest of the world, and trying to understand her."

For his pains, the Senator has been denounced by Peking, Nationalist China, and their partisans. It has not discouraged him. His opening of the door for a more reasonable study of China was gratefully received by the Administration, because the United States policy which sealed off China was reaching the end of its rope, and a new policy was needed.

Later on, during the China hearings, the importance of Vietnam to her huge neighbor was emphasized. Professor Benjamin I. Schwartz of Harvard, one of the most prestigious scholars on Communist China, felt Peking would consider the downfall of North Vietnam as a great peril. "That would put them very much in the state of mind that they had when we were approaching the Yalu, an immediate danger to their borders, so that it would be quite erroneous to rule out the possibility, in that event, of a confrontation with China."

Fulbright had earlier anticipated the apprehensions of the China scholars when he told General Gavin, "I want to raise the question whether a conflict [between the United States and China] would be in the interests of anyone. It strikes me it would be against the interests of anyone."

The general replied that such a war could not be waged in a vacuum, that tremendous manpower and possibly nuclear weapons would be involved, and other nations could easily be sucked into the whirlpool.

For the rest of his time—each Senator was allowed ten minutes each round—Fulbright struck deftly at two Administration positions. He did this by sharply pointed questions to shape the general's responses, and clarify his own beliefs.

One Administration position was only hinted at in public, but expressed behind closed doors to the more sympathetic Armed Services Committee. This was that the United States must remain indefinitely in Southeast Asia as a counter to China, that we must substitute our presence as a civilizing influence for that of the French and English. Fulbright felt this position toward an Asia fevered with a new nationalism was madness. Yet huge air and sea bases were being built in South Vietnam for the United States.

Fulbright asked, "Would it be precise to say that we stay there only until we can reach an honorable peace through negotiation?"

"That is exactly my point of view," the general said.

The second position, again never exactly elaborated upon in

public, Secretary Rusk ducking it, was that the United States could not permit a government in Vietnam in which the Communists had a leading role.

"Would you care to describe," Fulbright asked, "what, in your view, is the legitimate objective of this whole operation of the United States. Is it a negotiable peace?"

The general replied: "The objective is to give the South Vietnam people an opportunity to establish a government of their own choosing, a peaceful, free, independent government of their own choosing."

"Of their own choosing, regardless of the nature of that government?"

"Yes, I would say so. If they are happy with it, we are."

This was a long and weary day. Everyone was under great emotional pressure. The bright lights brought on headaches. But Senator Fulbright had achieved a major end in his "seminar." He had shown the American people there were alternatives, that a highly skilled military strategist disagreed with Administration tactics, and that great and terrible dangers lay close by.

At 4:30, at the windup of the hearing, Senator Frank Carlson, a conservative plainsman, a former Governor of Kansas, the kind of individual we like to refer to as a "solid citizen," told the general, "I think you have helped the country a great deal, and I know you have helped the Committee."

The television lights turned off. Senator Fulbright took off his dark glasses and rubbed his hand across his forehead. He was exhausted but pleased.

XXV

BY THURSDAY the hearings had outgrown the Committee room, and were transferred to the huge Senate caucus chamber. The witness and Washington's interest in this heresy against an angry king moved the show, in effect, from a Greenwich Village loft to Broadway. The caucus room with its large Tiffany chandeliers and wine-red drapes was where the other unrehearsed morality plays of the postwar years had been staged. Here MacArthur, McCarthy and Jimmy Hoffa had come and gone.

Before the doors opened, a long queue waited in the third-floor lobby and curled down a dimly lit hall.

The witness was an honored elder of the Foreign Policy Establishment, George F. Kennan. As chairman of the State Department's Policy Planning Committee in 1946, he authored the "containment" plan to hem in Soviet Russia. In 1952, as Ambassador to the U.S.S.R., he was declared *persona non grata* by Stalin and forced to leave.

In producing General Gavin and Kennan, Senator Fulbright executed a bold move. It was as if a duke in his rebellion against the King of England had been able to muster backing from the Archbishop of Canterbury and the Duke of York.

This was a sample of Fulbright's little appreciated shrewdness in playing the Washington wars, or, as a newspaper of 1924 remarked of his football punting, his "uncanny accuracy." On Tuesday, the eminent military strategist disagreed with Pentagon tactics in Vietnam. (On February 10, former Army Chief of Staff Matthew R. Ridgway told an interviewer, "I agree basically with everything that General Gavin said." The four-star general said Gavin's remarks were "magnificently presented.") Now, a distinguished diplomat was expected to add his dissent. Thus, within two days, the gentleman from Arkansas, in plain public view, would be able to knock down the Administration claim of almost unanimous support from the military and The Establishment, and present alternatives. The President continually complained that his critics didn't offer any ideas on how to end the war.

Senator Fulbright has immense personal respect for Kennan, who had thirty-eight years with the Foreign Service, was brought back out of retirement by President Kennedy to be Ambassador to Yugoslavia, and is currently a permanent professor at the Institute for Advanced Study at Princeton and university fellow at Harvard. He has the manner to go along with these honors, white temples and a gravely dignified mien.

The Senator introduced him: "He is one of the most thoughtful and scholarly men I have known to occupy positions in our Government . . . a record unequaled or equaled by very few men."

Kennan explained: "I have not been anxious to press my views on the public, but gladly give them for what they are worth, claiming no particular merit for them except, perhaps, that they flow from an experience with Communist affairs that runs back now for some 38 years, and also from the deepest and most troubled sort of concern that we should find the right course in this truly crucial moment.

"Vietnam is not a region of major military and industrial importance. It is difficult to believe that any decisive developments of the world situation would be determined in normal circumstances by what happens on that territory. If it were not for the considerations of prestige that arise precisely out of our involvement, even a situation in which South Vietnam was controlled exclusively by the Vietcong, while regrettable, and no doubt morally unwarranted, would not, in my opinion, present dangers great enough to justify our direct military intervention.

"Given the situation that exists today among the leading Communist powers, primarily the Sino-Soviet conflict, there is every likelihood that a Communist regime in South Vietnam would follow a fairly independent course . . . I think it should be our Government's aim to liquidate this involvement just as soon as this can be done without inordinate damage to our own prestige or to the stability of conditions in that area."

He disagreed with the Administration theory that by applying the heat, that is military power, the enemy would capitulate. (After all, this tactic had worked most of the time, in a different way, when Lyndon Johnson was majority leader, and he needed votes on a critical bill. You lined up your pressures and you kept it on until the recalcitrant boys yelled for mercy.) "I think this is a most dangerous assumption," Kennan commented, "in light of the experience we have had with Communist elements in the past.

"The North Vietnamese and the Vietcong have between them a great deal of space and manpower to give up if they have to, and the Chinese can give them more it they need it. Fidelity to the Communist tradition would dictate that if really pressed to extremity on the military level, these people should disappear entirely from the open scene and fall back exclusively on an underground political and military existence rather than to accept terms that would be openly humiliating and would represent in their eyes the betrayal of the future political prospects of the cause to which they are dedicated.

"Any rooting out of the Vietcong from South Vietnam could be achieved, if at all, only at the cost of a degree of damage to civilian life and civilian suffering generally for which I would not like to see this country responsible.

"And to attempt to crush North Vietnamese strength to a point where Hanoi could no longer give any support for Vietcong political activity in the south, would almost certainly bring in Chinese forces at some point, whether formally or as volunteers, thus involving us in a military conflict with Communist China in one of the most unfavorable theaters of hostility that we could possibly choose."

He cited three side effects of the war. "Our relations with the Soviet Union have suffered grievously . . . and this at a time when more important things were involved in those relations than what is ultimately involved in Vietnam." Japanese confidence in American policy had suffered sharply, yet this confidence was "the greatest asset we could have in east Asia. As the only major industrial complex in the entire Far East, and the only place where the sinews of modern war can be produced on a formidable scale, Japan is of vital importance to us and to peace and stability in east Asia." And, throughout the world generally there was presented "the spectacle of Americans inflicting grievous injury on the lives of a poor and helpless people, and particularly a people of different race and color."

Ambassador Kennan said, "This involvement seems to me to represent a grievous misplacement of emphasis in our foreign policies as a whole."

He had obviously studied the debate, for he answered key questions before they were asked.

"I would like to know what the commitment really consists of, and how and when it was incurred," he stated. He agreed with General Gavin the best military plan would be to select limited areas which could be safely policed and defended. He did not believe any loss of face would be suffered. Kennan pointed out that "most of our Western European allies . . . have given up great territories within recent years, and sometimes in a very statesmanlike manner."

And, as a historian, he gave the Senators words of wisdom from the past, spoken by John Quincy Adams in 1821.

" ' Wherever the standard of freedom and independence has been or shall be unfurled, there will be America's heart, her benedictions and her prayers. But she goes not abroad in search of monsters to destroy . . .' "

The camera swung to Senator Fulbright. He sat with a yellow pencil in his mouth, listening intently.

" 'She is the well-wisher to the freedom and independence of all. She is the champion and vindicator only of her own. She will recommend the general cause by the countenance of her voice, and by the benignant sympathy of her own example. She well knows that by once enlisting under other banners than her own, were they even the banners of foreign independence, she would involve herself beyond the powers of extrication, in all the wars of interest and intrigue, of individual avarice, envy and ambition, which assume the colors and usurp the standards of freedom. The fundamental maxims of her policy would insensibly change from liberty to force . . . She might become the dictatress of the world. She would no longer be the ruler of her own spirit.' "

Kennan added, "I think that without knowing it, John Quincy Adams spoke very directly and pertinently to us here today."

Senator Fulbright was pleased. Anyone in active political life, and the Senator is no exception, likes to have the trail for new ideas cleared a little in advance. Here was the distinguished diplomat suggesting a course he had proposed to the President privately—that a Communist government in Vietnam, if it were independent, might be the best bargain we could draw from a sorry mess.

Senator Fulbright quickly picked this up, and asked Kennan, didn't he think it might be possible a kind of Asian Yugoslavia might be established in Vietnam, and this would not be opposed to our interests?

"Yes," he replied. "It is not so that when men call themselves Communists some sort of magic transformation takes place within them which makes them wholly different from other human beings or from what they were before. Feelings of nationalism, ordinary feelings, still affect them to a large extent. I think this reality plays a part in all of Vietnam. I don't think they want domination by the Chinese. The fact that there is an alternative to the Chinese within the Communist world, the Soviet Union, in a better position to give them the economic aid they need, I think this represents a state of affairs which would be very, very carefully and sensitively taken into account by any South Vietnamese Communists.

"And so I merely wished to say that while their domination would not be desirable, it might not be perhaps quite as tragic or fatal as many of us assume."

Senator Fulbright nodded his head and remarked, "If any settlement is reached, it is going to be one that is only tolerable, but not satisfactory. Isn't that true?"

"Absolutely true."

The Senator said he gathered from Kennan's remarks that it just wasn't practical to try to tame areas of the world greatly different in culture and language.

Ambassador Kennan feared we were "affected by some sort of illusion of invincibility, a feeling that there is no problem in the world which we, if we wanted to devote enough of our resources to, could not solve." He said firmly, "I disbelieve in this most profoundly. I don't think we can order the political realities of areas in a great many other parts of the world . . . There are limits to what our duties and our capabilities are."

This was very good. Kennan was striking hard at an old myth that the Senator had been picking away at for ten years, but which, unfortunately, the President, his Secretary of State and most of Congress believed. The people probably believed it, too, until it began to rub too hard, as in Korea. We were in the process of disillusioning ourselves, but it was a damn expensive process.

Fulbright's chance to question Kennan came again in the afternoon, and by then new points had come up.

Facing the Ambassador, speaking amiably, the gentleman from Arkansas remarked, "There has been some criticism of this Committee for holding these hearings, that we are giving aid and comfort to our enemies. You are very familiar with the Communists and the whole scene. Do you feel these hearings are in the public interest, or not?"

Kennan replied, "It is my conviction that the implications of this involvement, the complications to which it may lead, are of such magnitude that we shouldn't wander into them without the widest, most serious, most responsible, and most searching sort of public debate."

Senator Fulbright looked at a copy of *The New York Times* on his place at the long table, and read a report from the United Nations: "The solid support given the leaders of South Vietnam by President Johnson in their Honolulu meeting strikes many officials and diplomats here as a barrier to a negotiated settlement of the war. They reason that . . . the increased involvement of the United States in the country's economic, educational and social program, has removed any prospect of forming a more broadly based government with which North Vietnam might be willing to negotiate. This majority view was that the agreements solidified the United States–South Vietnam alliance and would lengthen and expand the war."

He asked Kennan to comment on it.

He replied, "This checks, I must say, entirely with my own opinion. It does seem to me that if we had wanted to develop the prospects for a peaceful solution, the first thing we should have been concerned to do was to retain the independence of our position, and not get it any more closely associated than had to be with another political authority which shares only in part our interest and our aspirations . . . They [the South Vietnamese authorities] have their own axes to grind . . . And I must say it gives me a very, very uneasy feeling to read the joint declaration to which we subscribed the other day with them in Honolulu."

Fulbright was uneasy, too. He could also understand how it happened. Lyndon, impulsive, wanting every stranger to think he is the greatest on earth, putting his long arm around General Ky, and giving him the sweet talk and signing wordy declarations, not realizing this was not Texas politics or the Senate cloakroom, simply wanting to show the people at home, and throughout the world, he could get things done while the critics just talk, talk, talked.

"Do you have any reason to believe," Fulbright asked the witness, "that General Ky has any deep understanding of this kind of a document?"

Kennan said he was skeptical.

As he had with General Gavin, Senator Fulbright tried to develop the point that we were facing a China which in the past several hundred years had not been aggressive, but which was in a stage of nationalism after being badly mistreated by the West. He mentioned the opium war, and asked, "Do you see any excuse for waging a war to force a country to accept opium for the use of their people? This seems to me about as outrageous as any war I can think of!"

Under later questioning, Kennan said he saw three alternatives: we could mount an all-out military effort; or simmer down the conflict, hold on to the enclaves, and bargain for peace; or we could pull out. He favored the second course, and added, "If these alternatives were to be narrowed down to two, to an unlimited commitment to something called victory which I don't quite understand, or to a withdrawal, then I am not sure that I would not prefer the second."

Late in the afternoon, the bright lights were turned out, and Senator Fulbright said gratefully to Kennan, "I only regret that this Committee and the Government had not consulted you more often in the last year or so. I think we all would have benefited from your advice."

A week later, the mood of the hearing abruptly changed. General Maxwell Taylor came straight-backed and bristling with antagonism to the caucus room.

For five years he had been making both military and political policy in Vietnam, as President Kennedy's top military adviser, Ambassador to South Vietnam under Johnson, and currently his special consultant. The general had been to Honolulu with him, and obviously had heard strange and fearful tales of the Committee and its chairman. He came to Capitol Hill grimly to lay down the official line and protect himself from low blows.

General Taylor began: "We are engaged in a clash of purpose and interest with the militant wing of the Communist movement represented by Hanoi, the Vietcong and Peiping. Opposing these Communist forces, in the front rank, stand the Government and people of South Vietnam supported primarily by the United States, but assisted in varying degree by some thirty other nations. The purpose of the Hanoi camp is perfectly clear and has been since 1954. It is to absorb the fifteen million people of South Vietnam into a single Communist state under the leadership of Ho Chi Minh and his associates in Hanoi. In the course of accomplishing this basic purpose, the Communist leaders expect to undermine the position of the United States, and to demonstrate the efficacy of the so-called war of liberation as cheap, safe and disavowable technique for the future expansion of militant Communism . . . Our prupose is . . . the independence of South Vietnam and its freedom from attack . . . We intend to show, too, that the 'war of liberation,' far from being cheap, safe and disavowable, is costly, dangerous and doomed to failure . . . We cannot leave while force and violence threaten them . . ." This was a point of view that allowed no room for differences of opinion, that recognized only one instrument, force. If it truly represented the Administration, it had committed itself privately to an open-end war.

There was, as Fulbright well knew, an irony in these harsh words. In 1961, angry and disillusioned by the advice of the Joint Chiefs of Staff on the Bay of Pigs, President Kennedy turned to General Taylor, then retired, for military counsel, since he was less simplistic and more sophisticated than the usual military mind. But in Vietnam the general had become trapped within events, quite beyond his control, and turned into a true believer.

General Taylor explained the rapid escalation of American forces in Vietnam by some figures. Forces fighting a guerrilla insurrection must have a 10 to 1 or 12 to 1 edge in strength, and the Vietcong had increased its manpower 60,000 within the past year. General Taylor asked himself, "Is this an endless requirement in an open-ended war? I do not believe that anyone can give a completely satisfactory reply to this question . . ." He thought, though, that logistically the Vietcong could not support much larger forces, and heavy air punishment would undermine the "will of the enemy leadership."

He seemed to see the war, in large part, as a struggle for the minds of the North Vietnamese leaders. The American strategy was to keep on the pressure, increasing it, if necessary, to convince Hanoi "that it must mend its ways." The alternative, the general stated, "would be to accept dishonorable terms or continue to sit out the war indefinitely on a supine defensive."

Thus, the Administraton spokesman ruled out the Gavin plan or diplomatic compromise.

General Taylor also expressed a view Senator Fulbright found puzzling. Up to now only the rightist French generals who overthrew the Fourth Republic and then tried to oust General de Gaulle in a military coup, because of his settlement of the Algerian war, had held such a view. This was that the Indochina War was not lost at Dien Bien Phu, but that the French Army was sold out by French politicians.

Fulbright asked him in mild surprise, "You don't consider Dien Bien Phu as a decisive battle? . . . I had always been under the impression that Dien Bien Phu was a rather decisive battle, and that the Vietminh had won the war at this time?"

General Taylor replied stiffly that France had "strong military forces which were not involved at Dien Bien Phu, and could have continued the conflict."

There was a striking philosophic difference between the two men. Here was a general, and a good one and a distinguished one, who believed victory must be won, no matter the cost, as long as troops are left to fight, who saw wars lost by indecision at home, never by the warriors. Here was a Senator, who saw the military as only one weapon in the national arsenal, and one to be used sparingly, and very rarely to the bitter end.

Fulbright told the general, "What does worry me as a representative of the citizens of Arkansas is whether we are justified in pursuing this to this extent . . . It strikes me that the way you described your objective . . . this is just another way of saying 'unconditional surrender.' "

He pointed out that Premier Ky had said after Honolulu he would never negotiate with the NLF, and that the President's most recent speech seemed to be in agreement.

Max Frankel, *The New York Times* diplomatic correspondent, wrote: "General Maxwell D. Taylor brought out in public today what other high officials here have made increasingly plain privately— namely that the U.S. terms for peace in Vietnam are much stiffer than the offer of unconditional negotiations has implied . . . He said the United States could, should and would achieve military and political successes of sufficient magnitude to force the Communists to accept an independent and non-Communist South Vietnam . . . Compromise has no appeal here because the administration concluded long ago that the non-Communist forces of South Vietnam could not long survive in a Saigon coalition with the Communists. It is for that reason . . . that Washington has steadfastly refused to deal with the Vietcong or to recognize them as an independent political force."

The Senator was expressing a growing, uneasy conviction on Capitol Hill, that the President, despite his flamboyant gestures toward peace, was insisting the enemy crawl to him on their bellies, recanting their sins. Fulbright had had some personal experience with Lyndon Johnson on this score. A number of peace feelers had come to the Senator. The Vice President had said, "He needs you." A member of the White House staff had said the same thing, and urged a reconciliation of the old friends. The only problem was that Fulbright was expected to make the first move, and confess his sins.

The Senator said, "If the President wants to see me, he can always pick up the telephone, and I'll come right down and give him whatever help I can."

His technique with General Taylor was that of the highly skilled debater, picking out awkward points in the other's dialogue and examining them in the light. All very well mannered and in good humor.

This so upset the chief Administration patriot on the Committee, Russell Long, son of the "kingfish" dictator, that at one point he shouted, "Mr. Chairman, might I suggest you let the witness answer your question, because you keep making speeches while the witness is answering."

Fulbright said icily, "I wonder if the Senator—he is not the chairman of this Committee—would please wait his turn . . . Continue, General."

That Long's tactic was possibly a well-planned Administration move to disrupt the hearings was indicated when the Louisianan played the same game with Senator Morse.

Senator Fulbright asked General Taylor, "How do you describe the war of 1776? Was that a war of national liberation, or wasn't it?"

The general did not think so.

There had been a discussion of atrocities, and Fulbright said, "If we are going to talk about such things, we are reminded about air raids on Tokyo, or Hiroshima and Nagasaki. Would you call those atrocities or not?"

"No. I would say that was being used against a ruthless enemy executing our prisoners, who attacked us at Pearl Harbor and various places."

The Senator said gently, "Isn't it true that each country always believes the other one commits the atrocities, and that God is on their side? Isn't this typical in all wars?"

The general thought not.

The Senator stated, "Three of the leading military men in our history, Generals MacArthur, Eisenhower and Bradley, have all stated at one time or another that we should never become involved in a major land war in Asia."

The general replied, "The word 'never' is very dangerous for either a military man or a civilian to use."

He did not think the Vietnamese war was a major land war in Asia, and the Senator told him, "It has been stated here that an involvement of up to six hundred thousand men is contemplated by people in authority. I thought that would be considered quite an involvement."

Fulbright went on very earnestly, no longer parrying with his opponent: "I think, General, in all honesty, behind the concern of many of us, is not just Vietnam. There is the possibility, or even probability, of this situation escalating into a war with China. We always hesitate to talk about these things, but that is one of my concerns. I would regret to see us continue this war to the point where we become engaged in an all-out war with China. Many people who are wiser than I believe that this is a possibility."

General Taylor said brusquely, "As we discussed this morning, obviously one cannot rule it out. But I wonder whether our Government, or whether the Congress, would suggest complete supineness on the part of our foreign policy in the Far East, because of that relatively small possibility."

The past came rolling back out of the woolly mists of recent history. General MacArthur ordering his troops north to the Yalu, then demanding the right to bomb Manchurian bases. Dean Rusk saying the Chinese would not enter the war. MacArthur telling the President at Wake Island confidently, "We are no longer in fear of their intervention." Ten days later Chinese forces were at war in Korea.

There was not much the Senator could say to a true believer. Fulbright said more to the unseen audience than to the general: "It would be a great disaster if we became involved in an all-out war against the Chinese on the Asian continent."

General Taylor stared at him stonily.

XXVI

SENATOR FULBRIGHT seemed to be wrestling with a bucket of eels on the final day of the Vietnam hearings, as he questioned Secretary of State Rusk.

A Secretary of State in modern times has an impossible chore. He must uphold the illusion that the United States is ever wise and noble, and the enemy venal and selfish. The enemy changes, from Soviet Russia to mainland China, from Nazi Germany to De Gaullist France. This requires a quick wit and an open mind. The Secretary must adapt himself, day by day, hour by hour, to the mood of the President and the humors of the Joint Chiefs of Staff and the director of the Central Intelligence Agency. An outbreak of candor would be fatal.

Secretary Rusk in his trips to Capitol Hill met the test. His protective covering was a mild, even apologetic manner, like a banker refusing a loan to the local Methodist Church. He spoke in a soft Georgian drawl. His bald head glistened with a theological sincerity. He repeated clichés without tiring, all with a sad and righteous eye.

There was a good deal about him that recalled John Foster Dulles, whom Rusk venerated. With both Dulles and Rusk, their anti-Communism was as sacred as the tablets of Sinai. Indeed, it has been reported that in the councils of the State Department in 1951, Rusk supported General MacArthur's schemes. This liking for military solutions seems to have been a product of his long military service. He was an operations officer and chief of war plans and operations in the China-Burma-India theater in World War II, later a member of the War Plans Division of the General Staff in the Pentagon. He was brought into the State Department by General Marshall. At the hearing, Senator Stuart Symington made a point to stress Rusk's "great experience . . . on military matters."

Senator Fulbright once remarked of Rusk to a fellow Senator, "Every time I look at his face, I have the depressing feeling that no amount of reason or new information will sway him. He is locked in the religion of anti-Communism and the old Asia First strategy. The Secretary looks on Vietnam as a keyhole to China."

At this meeting of the Committee, Friday, February 18, the Secretary's mien was both grievous and stubborn. He was not going to give an inch. Senator Fulbright was not in a charitable mood, either.

At the Honolulu conference, President Johnson had publicly fulminated against the Senate dissenters. An Administration spokesman, presumably Johnson, referred to them bitterly as "a little band of willful men." The Administration tried to organize a public campaign against the critics. Representatives of five veterans' groups were called to the Pentagon and behind closed doors urged by Assistant Secretary of Defense Arthur Sylvester to put pressure on the Foreign Relations Committee and other dissenters. Someone peached, and the story was published in *The Washington Post*.

The desertion rate among South Vietnamese troops had gone up to 14.2 percent in 1965, and great discontent was building up among the Buddhist majority. General William C. Westmoreland, the U.S. commander in Vietnam, had asked for 400,000 American troops by the end of 1966, and 600,000 before 1968. Senator Fulbright figured out in a newsletter to his constituents that forty-one cents of the tax dollar were going for national defense and Vietnam, and the Senator, a tidy economist, was concerned about inflation. *Newsweek* had reported that it appeared, at least, that the United States was planning permanent bases in South Vietnam, as part of its "containment" of China. Senator Goldwater said, "I would like one provocation [by Communist China], just to knock out their atomic capability." Ho Chi Minh had told Egypt's Nasser that total and unconditional cessation of bombing and negotiations with the Vietcong were the "only method by which a political solution for the Vietnam problems can be hoped for."

Senator Fulbright's apprehensions were precisely reflected in a column by Walter Lippmann who wrote: "The promises he [the President] made in Honolulu and which the Vice President is now broadcasting so lavishly in Saigon and Bangkok are—if they are to be taken seriously—an unlimited commitment of American soldiers and

American money . . . We see that as the numbers of our troops and the range of our bombing are escalated and as the theater of the war becomes widened, it is highly probable, indeed, it is well nigh inevitable that the United States will find itself confronting China in a land war on the mainland of Asia . . . The cardinal difference is that our Chinese containment policy is a unilateral one whereas our Stalinist containment policy was shared with and participated in by all the Western Allies."

The stakes at these hearings were, for the Senator, very high. Everything else diminished in scale. He had asked his assistant, Lee Williams, to read a draft of a speech, and he told the Senator, "It's well written, it's timely, it's clear, but I question its political wisdom."

Fulbright replied, "Damn it, I didn't ask you that. I want to know whether it makes the point. That is all that is important."

This morning, the Senator bluntly asked Secretary Rusk, "We would like to know very much how far our commitment to General Ky in Honolulu went; how firm we are to back him in his determination never to negotiate with the National Liberation Front, how many troops we have promised and how much money?"

He suggested Rusk might like to digest his prepared testimony, and proceed to answer the questions. No, indeed. The Secretary and his assistants, with the urgent blessing of the President, had prepared themselves a speech for the twenty-three million housewives watching.

The Secretary of State appealed in what is known as the "soft sell" to ancient fears and prejudices. "We are in Vietnam because the issues posed there are deeply intertwined with our own security and because the outcome of the struggle can profoundly affect the nature of the world in which we and our children will live . . . What we are doing in South Vietnam is part of a process that has continued for a long time—a process of preventing the expansion and extension of Communist domination by the use of force against the weaker nations on the perimeter of Communist power . . . The war is clearly an armed attack, cynically and systematically mounted by the Hanoi regime against the people of South Vietnam." He referred to "world revolution" sought by the Communists. Rusk intimated that the United States would not deal with the Vietcong or its political arm, the National Liberation Front, because these were "Communist front organizations," and "our acceptance of the front in that capacity [as the sole representative of the South Vietnamese people] would in effect mean . . . delivering South Vietnam into the control of the Communist north."

Not all the scholars and commentators on Vietnam believed that Hanoi was insisting on the NLF as the "sole representative." Such authorities as Jean Lacourture, author of *Vietnam Between Two Truces* and currently at Harvard, thought that Hanoi, instead, was insisting only that the NLF be asked to the bargaining table and into an interim government to set up elections.

Fulbright asked Rusk, "Do I understand that General Ky's attitude that he would under no circumstance negotiate with the National Liberation Front is not accepted by the Government?"

The Secretary wriggled out of that one and said, "Now, the circumstances would be drastically changed if Hanoi indicated an interest in peace. I have no doubt that those circumstances would be reviewed by everyone concerned if they developed in that direction, and we could see where we go on that point."

Senator Fulbright said, a little irritably, how could anyone expect Hanoi to move toward negotiations "when we pursue or appear to have taken such an adamant attitude?"

Rusk again showed himself the master of the irrelevant answer, "Well, Mr. Chairman, an adamant attitude has to do with one particular and specific and limited point. We are not asking anything from Hanoi except to stop shooting their neighbors."

With some exasperation, Fulbright said, "The purpose of some of us is to try to get this to a conference table . . . we certainly haven't made much progress. How do we go about doing it if there is a sticking point about whether or not they [the Vietcong] should be admitted to the conference? Everything we have had in testimony is that the Vietcong constitute the major fighting force in South Vietnam. A force, it is admitted by the Pentagon, of two hundred and thirty-six thousand troops . . ."

Rusk said blandly, "If Hanoi would come to the conference table, that is the kind of thing that could be discussed, among other things."

The Senator shook his head. He was baffled. How do you grab these eels? At the close of his questioning time in the morning, he said, "Mr. Secretary, I wish these things appeared as simple to me as they do to you. I am sure it is due to my own obtuseness."

At the noon recess, Fulbright came back to his office, and gave instructions. He didn't want to see anyone or talk to anyone. In the solitude of his private office, among his books, the Senator sat down with pencil and pad. He was disgusted with Rusk's performance, and wrote out his reply in longhand.

In midafternoon, he picked up his statement and began reading it to the Secretary in a dry, unemotional tone: "This morning Senator Carlson raised the question about the failure of our SEATO allies to support us. I think the failure of the SEATO nations to furnish forces is very significant. There are now about 1,600 men from these countries in Vietnam, consisting primarily of Australians, plus about 150 New Zealanders. The forces of other SEATO members are quite small, as he mentioned.

"As I understand it, there are none, or practically none, from Pakistan, the Philippines, Thailand, the United Kingdom, and France. There are none from India, Indonesia and Japan, which are the nearest major countries.

"It seems to me that this fact is explained by their not sharing your view as to the nature of the war, which, as I understand your position, is that it is a clear case of international Communist aggression. I think they believe rather that it is more in the nature of a civil war in which outside parties have become involved. I can see no other logical reason why these countries which are either members of SEATO, or would be subject to attack much more quickly—and are more exposed than we—would not give support if this were truly an example of international Communist aggression. In short, I do not think that they believe their security is at stake or that the SEATO treaty requires their participation in the war . . ."

A flush appeared on Secretary Rusk's neck and spread to his chin.

"A review of the development of this war shows, in my opinion," the Arkansas drawl went on. It is somewhat less pronounced than the Georgia inflections of the Secretary. ". . . that it clearly began as a war of liberation from French colonial rule. It goes back to the time when indigenous Vietnamese nationalists, most unfortunately from our point of view, were led by Communists, notably Ho Chi Minh. These nationalistic Communists were twice betrayed, once by the French in 1946 after they thought they had made an agreement for independence, and later in 1956 by President Diem who, with the support of the Americans, refused to hold unification elections. After 1956, the struggle became a civil war between the Diem government and the Vietcong, the nationalistic Communists remaining in South Vietnam, who believed they were cheated by the Diem government in 1956 . . ."

Reporters who were far enough forward at the long press tables watched Rusk curiously. He sat stiffly, the true believer being flogged.

"After 1960, the character of the war changed, with increased participation by the North Vietnamese and by the United States, and apparently each time one has increased its support the other has responded by a similar increase, to where both sides are now there in very large numbers. In short, I think it is an oversimplification merely to say that this is a clear-cut case of aggression by North Vietnam Communists against a free, independent nation. If that were so, I believe many of the nations I mentioned would be participating in a more positive way. It is this point that I believe is primarily responsible, if not entirely, for the lack of support from our friends. And also, I may say, for a good deal of concern in this Committee."

There was no sting of personality to his comments; there rarely is with Fulbright. He was trying to straighten out the facts, as he saw them.

"As to our efforts to negotiate, the real trouble, it seems to me, is uncertainty as to our terms for peace, not merely the procedure. We have had a lot of very involved and complicated talk about four points and about fourteen points and about the significance of the third point, and where parties to a conference will meet, and who will be there. But I do not recall that we have ever made it crystal clear that we will support an election supervised by an appropriate international body, and that we will accept the results of that election, regardless of how it turns out.

"It is also not clear that we are willing to allow any participation of the NLF, either in a provisional government or at any time, and, therefore, there is no alternative for them but surrender or annihilation. If this is true, there is nothing to negotiate about . . .

"There is the further point of our intentions regarding leaving Vietnam. You have repeated time and again that we are willing to leave and have no desire for permanent bases. But I think few people in Vietnam and I believe in other places can quite understand why we are building such extensive, costly, and large permanent-type bases—harbors, airfields, military housing and so on—if we have any intention of leaving in the foreseeable future.

"Finally, in spite of statements to the contrary, the policy objectives seem to be unconditional surrender of the National Liberation Front. Or to put it another way, that this is not really a limited war, but that we intend to pursue it to victory even though that may result in bringing in the Chinese, and possibly even the Russians, which would force World War III.

"Frankly, Mr. Secretary, we are very much more deeply involved in Vietnam, far more than I ever imagined possible, and I am very worried about future commitments, as for example to Thailand, made without full discussion and consultation, and, I hope, approval, by Congress. I have already stated that I regret that I did not discharge what, in my opinion, I now believe to have been my duty to have full discussion of the 1964 resolution.

"This apprehension on my part has been greatly increased by our unilateral intervention in the Dominican Republic last year which, in my opinion, was a clear violation of our solemn treaty obligations."

The Senator from Arkansas had reached the final, the complete point of disagreement with the Administration. Secretary Rusk had the good sense to recognize he had no answer. He could search his pockets, he could pick out phrases a little different, but until the President changed directions, nothing would satisfy this slight, but stern man before him.

Rusk said in a low voice, "Mr. Chairman, I think I spent almost an hour this morning answering the observations you have made."

At 5:20, the Committee recessed, and Senator Fulbright went back to his office. The evening gloom had gathered outside, and the streets were full of the sounds of the homeward traffic rush. There was a surrealist quality in the contrast between the careless honks and sudden brakings outdoors and the inward thoughts of the Senator. He was certain that strong forces within the Administration did not want peace in Vietnam, they were willing, even anxious, to expand the war into a military showdown with China. The old MacArthur thesis had never died. The militants, and he classed Rusk among them, lived in a fantasy. Communist China was a combination of Hitler's Germany and Stalin's Russia, and they were saving mankind from the barbarians. They were willing to sacrifice NATO, threatening to curtail military aid severely and pull troops out of Europe unless the Allies sent forces to Vietnam. De Gaulle was saying, America is not a good friend and ally, but a fanatic trying to involve us in her military adventures. Europe is better off without her.

And the militants had worked on the President's impulsive, super-patriotic nature, and had so involved his vanity, he was a prisoner. They had him half thinking he was a latter-day Winston Churchill.

The Senator let himself into his office with a key. Lee Williams heard him and came in, with a question on his face. "How did it go?"

Fulbright said wearily, "My God, I don't think we're doing any good at all."

The next morning was Saturday, and the Senator came to the office early looking for someone to talk to. He went into a room where an assistant was working on a letter, and sat down. Fulbright said, "I have to assume that if the people are exposed to information, they will make the right decisions. If I don't assume that, our whole system is worthless, and I am wasting my time."

This was not spoken in a melancholy vein, but more like a man reaffirming his faith. The Senator could be pleased with his experiment in democracy, the hearings. The Administration had been forced to reveal itself. The charade, as he called it spiritedly, of playing we were in Vietnam simply to help the people, and that we were eager for peace was gone. On the next day, James Reston wrote in *The New York Times,* "The Rusk Doctrine makes the Monroe Doctrine or the Truman Doctrine seem rather cheap . . . Mr. Rusk has asked the Senate to contain the expansion of Communism all along the periphery of the Communist empire, by force of arms and without allies, if necessary."

The public response was phenomenal, and this response was braking the Administration. Fulbright saw a great many Arkansans in the early months of 1966, and remarked, "They all wanted to talk about 'the war.' That was the foremost thing on their minds. They don't understand it, it worries them, they have an instinct that it's wrong, and they ask me. I try to give them the reasons." Senator Bourke C. Hickenlooper, the senior Republican on the Committee, told him, "I ran into a hornet's nest on Vietnam during the Easter recess out in Iowa." A privately financed, independent public opinion study on Vietnam was conducted by seven social scientists at Stanford in cooperation with the National Opinion Research Center of the University of Chicago, and could find only 6 percent hawks in the population. Other findings were: 88 percent favor negotiations with the Vietcong, 70 percent would back a United Nations–negotiated truce, 54 percent were for free elections in South Vietnam, even if the Vietcong might win, 52 percent were willing to see the Vietcong in a coalition government, those polled opposed by 2 to 1 a half-million troop commitment in Vietnam, and were against bombing North Vietnamese cities 3 to 2.

For the first four months of 1966, Fulbright received ten to fifteen

requests a day to speak, or a total of 736 invitations, almost all of
them from colleges. When he addressed the National Conference on
Higher Education in Chicago March 14, he received a standing
ovation.

Even in the most timid sector of the public, politics, men were
speaking up. On the Saturday after the Vietnam hearings, Senator
Robert F. Kennedy—with much to gain or lose—recommended that
the Administration offer the Vietcong a share of power in South
Vietnam. He told a press conference we had to admit there were
discontented elements in South Vietnam, both Communist and non-
Communist. "You can kill them or repress them, turn the country
over to them, or admit them to a share of power and responsibility,"
he argued.

The Administration obviously thought the debate had harmed it.
The President complained to visitors, "They [Fulbright and the
dissenters] are trying to push me out of Southeast Asia." His anger
was reflected in the shrill phrases of columnist William S. White. The
Committee, he wrote, had "allowed itself to become a megaphone for
assaults upon simply not the wisdom, but upon the very integrity of
this Nation's war policy in the middle of that war . . . a forum for
this appalling exercise in extremism . . ."

The President's rage at his onetime friend continued to be one of
the little scandals of Washington. To official visitors and even White
House correspondents, Lyndon Johnson sounded off like a mule
skinner. But there was no way, in all his apparatus, he could get to
Fulbright and stop him. He had no price tag, no secret vices, and so
was untouchable to the greatest wheeler-dealer of them all. This
anger boiled over in public on May 12. The Senator had offered the
hand of friendship that afternoon; he complimented the President
before television cameras, calling his Princeton University speech "a
contribution to the national dialogue." That evening at a Democratic
fund raising dinner before six thousand persons, with Fulbright a few
seats from him, President Johnson cried, "You can say one thing
about those hearings, but I don't think this is the place to say it."

Fulbright sat unhappily, drawing slowly on his cigarette. He had
never personalized their quarrel. A week later in a hoarse diatribe to
Democrats in Chicago, Johnson berated the "nervous Nellies" who
did not like his foreign policy. Newspapers and columnists friendly to
Johnson reviled the Senator from Arkansas, as *The London Observer*
noted, as if he were the red Dean of Canterbury.

In the days and weeks that followed, Fulbright's faith in his old friend rusted away. He no longer referred to him in conversation as "the President," but as "this man, LBJ." What concerned him the most was his inability to break into the other's mind and to receive a rational reply. Soon after his controversial speech on the "arrogance of power," Senator Fulbright attended a diplomatic reception at the White House. The President spotted him in the line and came up grinning and asked how any man could be guilty of "arrogance of power when he gets a letter like this from his cook," and drew out a crumpled note ordering him to eat what was put before him, and not ask for more or complain. To Johnson, this answered the argument. To Fulbright it revealed that nothing he had been saying had been understood or considered.

Later, in June, after the President ordered more troops to Vietnam, Senator Fulbright added a postscript in his own handwriting in a letter to a friend: "I note in the papers that they are sending more men to Vietnam. How can we ever change their minds!!!"

By late March, the great debate, or its first installment, was ending. The Vietnam hearings were in print. The China hearings which the Senator hoped would erase another myth were in progress. He announced the Committee would be called to study new crises, NATO would be examined next and probably Vietnam again. The Administration, at least, was on notice its moves would be scrutinized.

On March 22, Senator Fulbright left the stewing pot of Washington for a symbolic journey. He was going back to a campus, this one the University of Connecticut, to talk once again with the young, and reason with them. He understood and sympathized with the young rebellion, their feeling that they were being done in by their elders. In fact, he said at another campus, "It is one of the injustices of life that young men must fight the wars that older men begin. Surely, considering the consequences, it is not improper to question the wisdom and judgment of the makers of our foreign policy. Surely it is the right of citizens of a democracy—especially citizens of military age—to ascertain that the great decisions of war and peace are made with care and deliberation."

The contrast on this trip between the capital and the campus was striking; it resembled the contrast between the weather when he arrived at Storrs, a thick motionless fog, and his welcome in the auditorium. The student newspaper that day featured excerpts from Fulbright speeches and a full-page ad signed by hundreds of students and faculty members, headed, "We the undersigned firmly endorse the work of Senator J. William Fulbright to enlighten the American people to the realities of our current foreign policy—in particular his efforts to bring the war in Vietnam to an immediate end."

No hero was ever greeted with more enthusiasm. The Senator stood smiling, even radiant, his head down modestly. He was stirred, for after all he was a teacher, and to a teacher the hope and belief of the young are very precious. The fog outside was the Old Establishment drifting blindly in a world of change and revolution. Inside, the young were ready to drop old myths and look at new realities.

Fulbright spoke with spirit and warmth. "There are two Americas," he said. "One is the America of Lincoln and Adlai Stevenson; the other is the America of Teddy Roosevelt and General MacArthur. One is generous and humane, the other narrowly egotistical; one is modest and self-critical, the other arrogant and self-righteous; one is sensible, the other romantic; one is good-humored, the other solemn; one is inquiring, the other pontificating; one is moderate and re-strained, the other filled with passionate intensity."

They caught it, and responded with applause.

"After twenty years of world power, the United States must decide which of the two sides of its national character is to predominate—the humanism of Lincoln or the aggressive moralism of Theodore Roosevelt . . . The tendency of recent months has been toward a more strident and aggressive American foreign policy . . . Instead of emphasizing plans for social change, the policy planners and political scientists are conjuring up 'scenarios' of escalation and nuclear confrontation and 'models' of insurgency and counterinsurgency; in Latin America they seem more interested in testing the 'images' of armies than in the progress of social reform. The foremost need of American foreign policy is a renewal of dedication to an 'idea that mankind can hold to'—not a missionary idea full of pomposities about saving the sinful and civilizing the heathen, but a Lincolnian idea expressing what Aldous Huxley called 'the simple human preference for life and peace.' "

A storm of applause halted the Senator, and he stood smiling, waiting for it to pass.

A year ago, he explained, the nation was showing this "preference" in its own social reform program, but this "inspiration and commitment" had disappeared because of the Asian war. We simply did not have "the mental and spiritual resources for such a double effort." He thought "there is a kind of madness in the facile assumption that we can raise the many billions of dollars necessary to rebuild our schools and cities and public transport and eliminate the pollution of air and water while also spending tens of billions to finance an 'open-ended' war in Asia. Even if the material resources can somehow be drawn from an expanding economy, I do not think that the spiritual resources will long be forthcoming from an angry and disappointed people."

This is what he had tried to tell Lyndon Johnson earnestly, beseechingly in the talks in the summer of 1965. He didn't get it. He had grown up with the legend of America, the invincible. And when this private argument failed and Fulbright had spoken openly of these private concerns, how angry the President and his associates had become. They said the criticism was "nonsense," or having no relation to facts which, being secret, could not be revealed, or was helping the enemy. And sometimes they nobly upheld the right of dissent while deploring use of it. The many deceits of power!

"Wars breed war fever; when a nation is involved in a bitter foreign conflict, hopes give way to fears and generous attitudes give way to a false and strident patriotism. That, I believe, is what is happening in America today, and there can be no cure for it except an end to the war in Asia."

The young people picked up his thoughts, and not waiting for his next line pounded their hands together. Outside the fog hung heavily and there was a small rain.

"The tragedy of Vietnam is that a revolution against social injustice and foreign rule has become a contest between Asian Communism and the United States."

The Senator offered his proposal for peace: "The United States should recognize the Vietcong as a belligerent with whom it is prepared to negotiate peace along with the Government of North Vietnam, and we should use our considerable influence to persuade the South Vietnamese Government to do the same. I have also recommended that we state forthrightly and explicitly in advance of negotiations, that we are prepared to conclude a peace agreement providing for an internationally supervised election to determine the future of South Vietnam, and, further, that we are prepared to accept the outcome of such an election, whatever the outcome might be."

This historian placed Vietnam in its proper place, as part of the overall Southeast Asia dilemma. "The prospect for a lasting peace here," he advised, "depends far more than the resolution of that issue [the power struggle between America and China] than on who is to participate in a South Vietnamese Government. As long as America and China are competitors for predominance in Southeast Asia, there can be no lasting peace or stability in that part of the world."

What then? He proposed, "It would seem to me highly advisable that we indicate to the Chinese that we are prepared to remove American military power, but from all Southeast Asia in return for a commitment on the part of China to abstain from military intervention and respect the political independence of Southeast Asian states."

They burst in with applause to show their approval. Senator Fulbright left them, as every good teacher should, with questions to ponder.

"Are we to be the friend or the enemy of the social revolutions of Asia and Latin America? Are we to regard the Communist countries as more or less normal states with whom we can have more or less normal relations, or are we to regard them indiscriminately as purveyors of an evil ideology with whom we can never reconcile? And, finally, are we to regard ourselves as a friend and counselor and possibly as an example for those around the world who seek freedom and who also want our help, or are we to play the role of God's avenging angel, the appointed missionary of freedom in a wicked and benighted world?"

They rose in a standing ovation. The slight man with the glasses low on his nose, smiling boyishly, looked benevolently on them. This was a rare moment of rapport. To the young, he was a hope that had been stunned by the death of John Kennedy and the swift rise of a war society. His was the soft voice of reason, not the stale rhetoric of politics. He spoke of a hope they cherished, of a world in which men could live together, if they worked at it and tried to understand one another. And to Senator Fulbright, the young, if they had the time, had the sense to rescue man from his fate. What he was trying to do was find the time for them.

Outside, the fog slowly began to lift in the thin spring rain.

Epilogue

THE SUMMER OF 1966 was angry and troubled in Washington, reflecting the mood of the President.

Senator Fulbright had an intimate glimpse of this mood in mid-June. President Johnson called him to his office and talked to him privately for an hour, a highly emotional harangue. We must win a military victory; if the enemy persist in their defiance, we will grind them to ashes. They cannot stand up to our power; they must collapse before the Congressional elections.

The Senator had never seen Johnson so insecure, so frenetic. He seemed to be desperately trying to convince himself, as well as his old friend.

Fulbright went back to Capitol Hill very troubled. He told members of his staff he was afraid the President was beyond a rational discussion of Vietnam. The Senator feared that while Johnson was in this mood, he was capable of almost any recklessness, including the bombing of China.

The next step-up of the war came on June 28, bombing of oil depots near Hanoi and Haiphong. Fulbright said, "I am fearful that this is one more step toward the ultimate war." He pointed out to Under Secretary of State George W. Ball how each time there was a move for negotiations on Vietnam, the United States widened the war. This last time, after a responsible Canadian mission went to Hanoi, stories began streaming out of Washington of new bombings and more troops. "This might lead them to believe we are not interested in a negotiated peace, as distinguished from complete surrender," the Senator said.

An angry Mike Mansfield, the Senate majority leader, said the bombings would "make the road to the negotiating table that much more difficult," a view shared by Robert Kennedy. George Aiken, the dean of Senate Republicans, said in a voice shaking with emotion, "I think some of the people advising the President want to get China into the war one way or another." Sixteen House Democrats said the action "further commits this nation to a profoundly dangerous policy of brinkmanship."

On the following Sunday, the Archbishop of Baltimore in a pastoral letter urged all American Catholics to "exert whatever moral, civic influences" they could to keep the war "within moral bounds." He was concerned by "those harsh voices" that "argue against restraint" and who press for "decisions which the Christian conscience could not endorse."

Elsewhere, our oldest and best friends, England, Canada, France, deplored the new bombings. The Vatican weekly, *L'Osservatore Della Domenica,* said, "American policy is being damaged, and not only in Asia." Japan, key to our Asian strategy, warned that rising opposition in Japan to the war might compromise American bases there. The Chinese Communist Foreign Minister said his country would support North Vietnam "to the very end." Chinese troops were reported on the border in Kwangsi Province ready for action "at any time" against the Americans.

President Johnson heated up his attack on home front critics, "dismissing concerned fellow-citizens who question his actions as puny patriots, who would 'tuck their tails and run' away from South Vietnam," according to Edward P. Morgan. Marquis Childs added, "What we have heard so far is merely a prelude to a drumfire that promises to grow in volume." The Defense Department announced that soldiers who would not fight in Vietnam could be prosecuted and sentenced to death. The FBI accused attachés of Communist nations in Washington of plots to obtain U.S. secrets, and William S. White wrote a column titled, "Red Menace Is Real." There were fresh blows at Senator Fulbright, obviously engineered by the White House to silence the most important critic and shut off Committee hearings. A bit of consolation came to the Senator from a well-wisher. This was a copy of Congressman Abraham Lincoln's critique of President Polk's message on war with Mexico, in which Lincoln said: "The President would have gone farther in his proof if it had not been for the small matter that the truth would not permit him . . . Now I propose to show that the whole of this—issue and evidence—is, from the beginning to end, the sheerest deception . . . As to the mode of terminating the war and securing the peace, the President is equally wandering and indefinite . . . He is a bewildered, confounded and miserably perplexed man."

On July 13, the President spread the American mission to all Asia. *The Washington Post* remarked that this speech and Secretary Rusk's news conference "appeared to imbed the United States more deeply than ever in a commitment to exert its physical might, its political power, and its psychological impact, as a 'shield' for all the non-Communist nations of Asia."

In the middle of July, Senator Fulbright sat on the green leather couch in his quiet, shaded office, and talked of the future. His tone was earnest and troubled, but his voice gentle.

"I am very pessimistic," he said. "A war is like a stream at flood. The higher the level, the more is dragged in. We have been raising the level steadily. The Communist powers probably will feel required to respond by more supplies, perhaps volunteers, and will be trapped in the flood just as we are. I think it likely the war will spread in intensity and area.

"Suppose we can win total victory? Suppose we can change the tides of history for a few years by sheer military power. What do we have? Ruin almost as complete as Troy, and a hatred for the white intruder that will plague our sons and their sons."

The Senator was silent for a moment, and commented, more a question to himself than a statement, "Will man ever escape from this trap of violence?"

He shook his head and went on: "I am very concerned about my country. I have never felt this way before. I wake up at nights, and I think, we are capable of so much progress, so much good, and we toss away men, money, resources, goodwill like pennies into a savage war—for what?

"If the Great Society had stuck to its goals, it could have been the beginning of the golden age of America. With the money we are spending in Vietnam, as well as the creative energy, we could build a magnificent system of education, make a real dent in the illness of poverty and the cities, and cure the pollution of our water and air. Our mental resources, at least in Washington, are tied up in this war. It is like a glittering ball used in hypnosis.

"I am distressed about my country for another reason. I don't like to see us labeled across the world as a brutal aggressor mauling a small nation with our terrible power. We are not that kind of people." The Senator shrugged his shoulders. "Of course, the people can't always foretell what their leaders will do when the mantle of power falls on them."

He was silent again. When he spoke it was with great spirit. "It is an incredible irony—who would have thought that Lyndon Johnson would take this turn? It is a tragedy that might have been written by the ancient Greeks. He is an extraordinary man, of a greater dynamic force, I think, than Franklin Roosevelt, but has turned it to destruction—not intentionally. I think he was sincere in 1964 when he derided Goldwater's proposals for bombing the North and said, 'We don't want to get tied down in a land war in Asia.' But a man's intentions can be twisted by chance and the effect of power and crisis on his personality. The President received a good deal of bad advice, he acted too hastily, and now we are all caught in a holy war from which, apparently, there is no retreat short of total victory.

"The President talks of Asia as if we had a holy mandate to act as suzerain. This is likely to be an expensive and bitter task, and our record in Vietnam is not impressive. There we have propped up tyrants and generals who wage war on moderate dissent and the priests of the ruling religion; we have brought unceasing struggle, death and inflation. This in the face of a tremendous surge of Asian nationalism, 'Asia for the Asiatics,' as the Japanese called it in World War II. It is part of the flamboyant style of the President to believe that being an American, and a Texan, you can do anything. But there are limits even to our great power. I think often of the Peloponnesian War and the debate by which Alcibiades persuaded Athens by a narrow margin to attack Syracuse. Athens was the strongest power of the Western world. In a few years, worn out by the excesses of constant warfare, Athens fell and the greatest culture the world has known gone.

"When a nation goes to war, justly or unjustly, the leaders use this as an excuse to shut off debate and dissent and create the uniformity of the graveyard. Those of us who ask questions are accused of letting down the boys in Vietnam. Well, they didn't ask to go there; they were ordered there. I would think the best we could do for them would be to work very hard for an honorable peace, one all sides can live with."

The Senator was alone with a moment of thought. Then he said, "This is all like a bad dream. The evils of the past have come back to haunt us. McCarthyism, brinkmanship, the old Asia First dogma, total victory. The theories of Chiang Kai-shek are presented as official American doctrine by the Secretary of State. The mass destruction and cruelty we hoped were ended by World War II and the lesson of Hiroshima. Hypocrisy and misrepresentation have become the daily bread.

"Why? We are told we are combating Communism. I don't understand this human obsession with abstractions. Communism is simply another way to organize society, and subject to the same abuses of any concentration of power. Stalin was a terrible ogre, but he would have been no matter what system he espoused. Communist Yugoslavia is a more open society today than the military regime in South Vietnam, or military dictatorships in Latin America we support.

"If we do get through this trial, there is a lesson we can learn. Revolt against colonial rule and feudalism is the mood of much of the world, and Communists will become involved. We can't stop the revolutions by bombs or even by massive economic grants, any more than you can stop a volcano by throwing in a human sacrifice. But the more advanced nations of the world, working together, can help make the transition to self-rule, equality and human dignity easier."

A friend asked if the Senator didn't think the Vietnam hearings had brought the issues and alternatives clearly before the people. More important in the long run, he thought, were the China hearings. "Before the hearings," he explained," thinking on China was frozen in the public and political mind. By bringing together the scholars with their imaginative ideas and research, the Committee has thawed the ice. China is a very ancient and proud civilization, and has survived calamities and misrule in a way no other society has. It has an immense capacity for regeneration, and we have to understand and live with China. This lesson has been accepted even by the Administration, with some reservations."

What of his own future?

"What can you do? You feel such frustration. I sometimes think I should quit and let someone else try."

A better omen is the last paragraph of a letter the Senator wrote to a constituent: "I think that the people of Arkansas elected me to use my best judgment on matters of such vital importance to their welfare as war and peace, and as long as Congress has not formally declared war I intend to continue to try to do everything I can to bring about a change in our policies."

We will hear more from the uncommon gentleman from Arkansas.

Recent Key Speeches
by Senator Fulbright

FOREIGN POLICY—OLD MYTHS AND NEW REALITIES

Mr. FULBRIGHT. Mr. President, there is an inevitable divergence, attributable to the imperfections of the human mind, between the world as it is and the world as men perceive it. As long as our perceptions are reasonably close to objective reality, it is possible for us to act upon our problems in a rational and appropriate manner. But when our perceptions fail to keep pace with events, when we refuse to believe something because it displeases or frightens us, or because it is simply startlingly unfamiliar, then the gap between fact and perception becomes a chasm, and action becomes irrelevant and irrational.

There has always—and inevitably—been some divergence between the realities of foreign policy and our ideas about it. This divergence has in certain respects been growing, rather than narrowing; and we are handicapped, accordingly, by policies based on old myths, rather than current realities. This divergence is, in my opinion, dangerous and unnecessary—dangerous, because it can reduce foreign policy to a fraudulent game of imagery and appearances; unnecessary, because it can be overcome by the determination of men in high office to dispel prevailing misconceptions by the candid dissemination of unpleasant, but inescapable, facts.

Before commenting on some of the specific areas where I believe our policies are at least partially based on cherished myths, rather than objective facts, I should like to suggest two possible reasons for the growing divergence between the realities and our perceptions of current world politics. The first is the radical change in relations between and within the Communist and the free world; and the second is the tendency of too many of us to confuse means with ends and, accordingly, to adhere to prevailing practices with a fervor befitting immutable principles.

Although it is too soon to render a definitive judgment, there is mounting evidence that events of recent years have wrought profound changes in the character of East-West relations. In the Cuban missile crisis of October 1962, the United States proved to the Soviet Union that a policy of aggression and adventure involved unacceptable risks. In the signing of the test ban treaty, each side in effect assured the other that it was prepared to forego, at least for the present, any bid for a decisive military or political breakthrough. These occurrences, it should be added, took place against the background of the clearly understood strategic superiority—but not supremacy—of the United States.

It seems reasonable, therefore, to suggest that the character of the cold war has, for the present, at least, been profoundly altered: by the drawing back of the Soviet Union from extremely aggressive policies; by the implicit repudiation by both sides of a policy of "total victory"; and by the establishment of an American strategic superiority which the Soviet Union appears to have tacitly accepted because it has been accompanied by assurances that it will be exercised by the United States with responsibility and restraint. These enormously important changes may come to be regarded by historians as the foremost achievements of the Kennedy administration in the field of foreign policy. Their effect has been to commit us to a foreign policy which can accurately—though perhaps not prudently—be defined as one of "peaceful coexistence."

Another of the results of the lowering of tensions between East and West is that each is now free to enjoy the luxury of accelerated strife and squabbling within its own domain. The ideological thunderbolts between Washington and Moscow which until a few years ago seemed a permanent part of our daily lives have become a pale shadow of their former selves. Now instead the United States waits in fascinated apprehension for the Olympian pronouncements that issue from Paris at 6-month intervals while the Russians respond to the crude epithets of Peiping with almost plaintive rejoinders about "those who want to start a war against everybody."

These astonishing changes in the configuration of the postwar world have had an unsettling effect on both public and official opinion in the United States. One reason for this, I believe, lies in the fact that we are a people used to looking at the world, and indeed at ourselves, in moralistic rather than empirical terms. We are predisposed to regard any conflict as a clash between good and evil rather than as simply a clash between conflicting interests. We are inclined to confuse freedom and democracy, which we regard as moral principles, with the way in which they are practiced in America—with capitalism, federalism, and the two-party system, which are not moral principles but simply the preferred and accepted practices of the American people. There is much cant in American moralism and not a little inconsistency. It resembles in some ways the religious faith of the many respectable people who, in Samuel Butler's words, "would be equally horrified to hear the Christian religion doubted or to see it practiced."

Our national vocabulary is full of "self-evident truths" not only about "life, liberty, and happiness," but about a vast number of personal and public issues, including the cold war. It has become one of the "self-evident truths" of the postwar era that just as the President resides in Washington and the Pope in Rome, the Devil resides immutably in Moscow. We have come to regard the Kremlin as the permanent seat of his power and we have grown almost comfortable with a menace which, though unspeakably evil, has had the redeeming virtues of constancy, predictability, and familiarity. Now the Devil has betrayed us by traveling abroad and, worse still, by dispersing himself, turning up now here, now there, and in many places at once, with a devilish disregard for the laboriously constructed frontiers of ideology.

We are confronted with a complex and fluid world situation and we are not adapting ourselves to it. We are clinging to old myths in the face of new realities and we are seeking to escape the contradictions by narrowing the permissible bounds of public discussion, by relegating an increasing number of ideas and viewpoints to a growing category of "unthinkable thoughts." I believe that this tendency can and should be reversed, that it is within our ability, and unquestionably in our interests, to cut loose from established myths and to start thinking some "unthinkable thoughts"—about the cold war and East-West relations, about the underdeveloped countries and particularly those in Latin America, about the changing nature of the Chinese Communist threat in Asia and about the festering war in Vietnam.

The master myth of the cold war is that the Communist bloc is a monolith composed of governments which are not really governments at all but organized conspiracies, divided among themselves perhaps in certain matters of tactics, but all equally resolute and implacable in their determination to destroy the free world.

I believe that the Communist world is indeed hostile to the free world in its general and long-term intentions but that the existence of this animosity in principle is far less important for our foreign policy than the great variations in its intensity and character both in time and among the individual members of the Communist bloc. Only if we recognize these variations, ranging from China, which poses immediate threats to the free world, to Poland and Yugoslavia, which pose none, can we hope to act effectively upon the bloc and to turn its internal differences to our own advantage and to the advantage of those bloc countries which wish to maximize their independence. It is the responsibility of our national leaders both in the executive branch and in Congress, to acknowledge and act upon these realities, even at the cost of saying things which will not win immediate widespread enthusiasm.

For a start, we can acknowledge the fact that the Soviet Union, though still a most formidable adversary, has ceased to be totally and implacably hostile to the West. It has shown a new willingness to enter mutually advantageous arrangements with the West and, thus far at least, to honor them. It has therefore become possible to divert some of our energies from the prosecution of the cold war to the relaxation of the cold war and to deal with the Soviet Union, for certain purposes, as a normal state with normal and traditional interests.

If we are to do these things effectively, we must distinguish between communism as an ideology and the power and policy of the Soviet state. It is not communism as a doctrine, or communism as it is practiced within the Soviet Union or within any other country, that threatens us. How the Soviet Union organizes its internal life, the gods and doctrines that it worships, are matters for the Soviet Union to determine. It is not Communist dogma as espoused within Russia but Communist imperialism that threatens us and other peoples of the non-Communist world. Insofar as a great nation mobilizes its power and resources for aggressive purposes, that nation, regardless of ideology, makes itself our enemy. Insofar as a nation is content to practice its doctrines within its own frontiers, that nation, however repugnant its ideology, is one with which we have no proper quarrel. We must deal with the Soviet Union as a great power, quite apart from differences of ideology. To the extent that the Soviet leaders abandon the global ambitions of Marxist ideology, in fact if not in words, it becomes possible for us to engage in normal relations with them, relations which probably cannot be close or trusting for many years to come but which can be gradually freed of the terror and the tensions of the cold war.

In our relations with the Russians, and indeed in our relations with all nations, we would do well to remember, and to act upon, the words of Pope John in the great Encyclical, Pacem in Terris:

It must be borne in mind, [said Pope John] that to proceed gradually is the law of life in all its expressions, therefore, in human institutions, too, it is not possible to renovate for the better except by working from within them, gradually. Violence has always achieved only destruction, not construction, the kindling of passions, not their pacification, the accumulation of hate and ruin, not the reconciliation of the contending parties. And it has reduced men and parties to the difficult task of rebuilding, after sad experience, on the ruins of discord.

Important opportunities have been created for Western policy by the development of "polycentrism" in the Communist bloc. The Communist nations, as George Kennan has pointed out, are, like the Western nations, currently caught up in a crisis of indecision about their relations with countries outside their own ideological bloc. The choices open to the satellite states are limited but by no means insignificant. They can adhere slavishly to Soviet preferences or they can strike out on their own, within limits, to enter into mutually advantageous relations with the West.

Whether they do so, and to what extent, is to some extent at least within thhe power of the West to determine. If we persist in the view that all Communist regimes are equally hostile and equally threatening to the West, and that we can have no policy toward the captive nations except the eventual overthrow of their Communist regimes, then the West may enforce upon the Communist bloc a degree of unity which the Soviet Union has shown itself to be quite incapable of imposing—just as Stalin in the early postwar years frightened the West into a degree of unity that it almost certainly could not have attained by its own unaided efforts. If, on the other hand, we are willing to reexamine the view that all Communist regimes are alike in the threat which they pose for the West—a view which had a certain validity in Stalin's time—then we may be able to exert an important influence on the course of events within a divided Communist world.

We are to a great extent the victims, and the Soviets the beneficiaries, of our own ideological convictions, and of the curious contradictions which they involve. We consider it a form of subversion of the free world, for example, when the Russians enter trade relations or conclude a consular convention or establish airline connections with a free country in Asia, Africa, or Latin America—and to a certain extent we are right. On the other hand, when it is proposed that we adopt the same strategy in reverse—by extending commercial credits to Poland or Yugoslavia, or by exchanging Ambassadors with a Hungarian regime which has changed considerably in character since the revolution of 1956—then the same patriots who are so alarmed by Soviet activities in the free world charge our policymakers with "giving aid and comfort to the enemy" and with innumerable other categories of idiocy and immorality.

It is time that we resolved this contradiction and separated myth from reality. The myth is that every Communist state is an unmitigated evil and a relentless enemy of the free world; the reality is that some Communist regimes pose a threat to the free world while others pose little or none, and that if we will recognize these distinctions, we ourselves will be able to influence events in the Communist bloc in a way favorable to the security of the free world.

It could well be argued . . .

Writes George Kennan—

That if the major Western Powers had full freedom of movement in devising their own policies, it would be within their power to determine whether the Chinese view, or the Soviet view, or perhaps a view more liberal than either would ultimately prevail within the Communist camp—George Kennan, "Polycentrism and Western Policy," *Foreign Affairs,* January 1964, page 178.

There are numerous areas in which we can seek to reduce the tensions of the cold war and to bring a degree of normalcy into our relations with the Soviet Union and other Communist countries—once we have resolved that it is safe and wise to do so. We have already taken important steps in this direction: the Antarctic and Austrian treaties and the nuclear test ban treaty, the broadening of East-West cultural and educational relations, and the expansion of trade.

On the basis of recent experience and present economic needs, there seems little likelihood of a spectacular increase in trade between Communist and Western countries, even if existing restrictions were to be relaxed. Free world trade with Communist countries has been increasing at a steady but unspectacular rate, and it seems unlikely to be greatly accelerated because of the limited ability of the Communist countries to pay for increased imports. A modest increase in East-West trade may nonetheless serve as a modest instrument of East-West detente—provided that we are able to overcome the myth that trade with Communist countries is a compact with the Devil and to recognize that, on the contrary, trade can serve as an effective and honorable means of advancing both peace and human welfare.

Whether we are to make these philosophic adjustments or not, we cannot escape the fact that our efforts to devise a common Western trade policy are a palpable failure and that our allies are going to trade with the Communist bloc whether we like it or not. The world's major exporting nations are slowly but steadily increasing their trade with the Communist bloc and the bloc countries are showing themselves to be reliable customers. Since 1958 Western Europe has been increasing its exports to the East at the rate of about 7 percent a year, which is nearly the same rate at which its overall world sales have been increasing.

West Germany—one of our close friends—is by far the leading Western nation in trade with the Sino-Soviet bloc. West German exports in bloc countries in 1962 were valued at $749.9 million. Britain was in second place—although not a close second—with exports to Communist countries amounting to $393 million in 1962. France followed with exports worth $313.4 million, and the figure for the United States—consisting largely of surplus food sales to Poland under Public Law 480—stood far below at $125.1 million.

Our allies have made it plain that they propose to expand this trade, in nonstrategic goods, wherever possible. West Germany, in the last 16 months, has exchanged or agreed to exchange trade missions with every country in Eastern Europe except Albania. Britain has indicated that she will soon extend long-term credits to Communist countries, breaching the 5-year limit which the Western allies have hitherto observed. In the light of these facts, it is difficult to see what effect the tight American trade restrictions have other than to deny the United States a substantial share of a profitable market.

The inability of the United States to prevent its partners from trading extensively with the Communist bloc is one good reason for relaxing our own restrictions, but there is a better reason: the potential value of trade—a moderate volume of trade in nonstrategic items—as an instrument for reducing world tensions and strengthening the foundations of peace. I do not think that trade or the nuclear test ban, or any other prospective East-West accommodation, will lead to a grand reconciliation that will end the cold war and usher in the brotherhood of man. At the most, the cumulative effect of all the agreements that are likely to be attainable in the foreseeable future will be the alleviation of the extreme tensions and animosities that threaten the world with nuclear devastation and the gradual conversion of the struggle between communism and the free world into a safer and more tolerable international rivalry, one which may be with us for years and decades to come but which need not be so terrifying and so costly as to distract the nations of the world from the creative pursuits of civilized societies.

There is little in history to justify the expectation that we can either win the cold war or end it immediately and completely. These are favored myths, respectively, of the American right and of the American left. They are, I believe, equal in their unreality and in their disregard for the feasibilities of history. We must disabuse ourselves of them and come to terms, at last, with the realities of a world in which neither good nor evil is absolute and in which those who move events and make history are those who have understood not how much but how little it is within our power to change.

Mr. President, in an address on February 18 at Bad Godesburg, the U.S. Ambassador to Germany, Mr. George McGhee, spoke eloquently and wisely about the character and prospects of relations between the Communist and the free worlds. I ask unanimous consent that Ambassador McGhee's address, "East-West Relations Today," be inserted in the RECORD at the end of my remarks.

The PRESIDING OFFICER (Mr. Kennedy in the chair). Without objection, it is so ordered.

(See exhibit 1.)

Mr. FULBRIGHT. Latin America is one of the areas of the world in which American policy is weakened by a growing divergency between old myths and new realities.

The crisis over the Panama Canal has been unnecessarily protracted for reasons of domestic politics and national pride and sensitivity on both sides— for reasons, that is, of only marginal relavance to the merits of the dispute. I think the Panamanians have unquestionably been more emotional about the dispute than has the United States. I also think that there is less reason for emotionalism on the part of the United States than on the part of Panama. It is important for us to remember that the issue over the canal is only one of a great many in which the United States is involved, and by no means the most important. For Panama, on the other hand, a small nation with a weak economy and an unstable government, the canal is the preeminent factor in the nation's economy and in its foreign relations. Surely in a confrontation so unequal, it is not unreasonable to expect the United States to go a little farther than halfway in the search for a fair settlement.

We Americans would do well, for a start, to divest ourselves of the silly notion that the issue with Panama is a test of our courage and resolve. I believe that the Cuban missile crisis of 1962, involving a confrontation with nuclear weapons and intercontinental missiles, was indeed a test of our courage, and we acquitted ourselves extremely well in that instance. I am unable to understand how a controversy with a small and poor country, with virtually no military capacity, can possibly be regarded as a test of our bravery and will to defend our interests. It takes stubbornness but not courage to reject the entreaties of the weak. The real test in Panama is not of our valor but of our wisdom and judgment and commonsense.

We would also do well to disabuse ourselves of the myth that there is something morally sacred about the treaty of 1903. The fact of the matter is that the treaty was concluded under circumstances that reflect little credit on the United States. It was made possible by Panama's separation from Colombia which probably could not have occurred at that time without the dispatch of U.S. warships to prevent the landing of Colombian troops on the isthmus to put down the Panamanian rebellion. The United States not only intervened in Colombia's internal affairs but did so in violation of a treaty concluded in 1846 under which the United States had guaranteed Colombian sovereignty over the isthmus. President Theodore Roosevelt, as he boasted, "took Panama," and proceeded to negotiate the canal treaty with a compliant Panamanian regime. Panamanians contend that they were "shotgunned" into the treaty of 1903 as the price of U.S. protection against a possible effort by Colombia to recover the isthmus. The contention is not without substance.

It is not my purpose here to relate the events of 60 years ago but only to suggest that there is little basis for a posture of injured innocence and self-righteousness by either side and that we would do much better to resolve the issue on the basis of present realities rather than old myths.

The central reality is that the treaty of 1903 is in certain respects obsolete. The treaty has been revised only twice, in 1936 when the annual rental was raised from $250,000 to $430,000 and other modifications were made, and in 1955 when further changes were made, including an increase in the annual rental to $1.9 million, where it now stands. The canal, of course, contributes far more to the Panamanian economy in the form of wages paid to Panamanian workers and purchases made in Panama. The fact remains, nonetheless, that the annual rental of $1.9 million is a modest sum and should probably be increased. There are other issues, relating to hiring policies for Panamanian workers in the zone, the flying of flags, and other symbols of national pride and sovereignty. The basic problem about the treaty, however, is the exercise of American control over a part of the territory of Panama in this age of intense nationalist and anticolonialist feeling. Justly or not, the Panamanians feel that they are being treated as a colony, or a quasi-colony, of the United States, and this feeling is accentuated by the contrast between the standard of living of the Panamanians, with a per capita income of about $429 a year, and that of the Americans living in the Canal Zone—immediately adjacent to Panama, of course, and within it—with a per capita income of $4,228 a year. That is approximately 10 times greater. It is the profound social and economic aliena-tion between Panama and the Canal Zone, and its impact on the national feeling of the Panamanians, that underlies the current crisis.

Under these circumstances, it seems to me entirely proper and necessary for the United States to take the initiative in proposing new arrangements that would redress some of Panama's grievances against the treaty as it now stands. I see no reason—certainly no reason of "weakness" or "dishonor"—why the United States cannot put an end to the semantic debate over whether treaty revisions are to be "negotiated" or "discussed" by stating positively and clearly that it is prepared to negotiate revisions in the canal treaty and to submit such changes as are made to the Senate for its advice and consent.

I think it is necessary for the United States to do this even though a commitment to revise the treaty may be widely criticized at home. It is the responsibility of the President and his advisers, in situations of this sort, to exercise their own best judgment as to where the national interest lies even though this may necessitate unpopular decisions.

An agreement to "negotiate" revisions is not an agreement to negotiate any particular revision. It would leave us completely free to determine what revi-sions, and how many revisions, we would be willing to accept. If there is any doubt about this, one can find ample reassurance in the proceedings at Geneva, where several years of "negotiations" for "general and complete disarmament" still leave us with the greatest arsenal of weapons in the history of the world.

The problem of Cuba is more difficult than that of Panama, and far more heavily burdened with the deadweight of old myths and prohibitions against "unthinkable thoughts." I think the time is overdue for a candid reevaluation of our Cuban policy even though it may also lead to distasteful conclusions.

There are and have been three options open to the United States with respect to Cuba: first, the removal of the Castro regime by invading and occupying the island; second, an effort to weaken and ultimately bring down the regime by a policy of political and economic boycott; and finally, acceptance of the Communist regime as a disagreeable reality and annoyance but one which is not likely to be removed in the near future because of the unavailability of acceptable means of removing it.

The first option, invasion, has been tried in a halfhearted way and found wanting. It is generally acknowledged that the invasion and occupation of Cuba, besides violating our obligations as a member of the United Nations and of the Organization of American States, would have explosive consequences in Latin America and elsewhere and might precipitate a global nuclear war. I know of no responsible statesman who advocates this approach. It has been rejected by our Government and by public opinion and I think that, barring some grave provocation, it can be ruled out as a feasible policy for the United States.

The approach which we have adopted has been the second of those mentioned, an effort to weaken and eventually bring down the Castro regime by a policy of political and economic boycott. This policy has taken the form of extensive restrictions against trade with Cuba by United States citizens, of the exclusion of Cuba from the inter-American system and efforts to secure Latin American support in isolating Cuba politically and economically, and of diplomatic efforts, backed by certain trade and aid sanctions, to persuade other free world countries to maintain economic boycotts against Cuba.

This policy, it now seems clear, has been a failure, and there is no reason to believe that it will succeed in the future. Our efforts to persuade our allies to terminate their trade with Cuba have been generally rebuffed. The prevailing attitude was perhaps best expressed by a British manufacturer who, in response to American criticisms of the sale of British buses to Cuba, said: "If America has a surplus of wheat, we have a surplus of buses."

In cutting off military assistance to Great Britain, France, and Yugoslavia under the provisions of Section 620 of the Foreign Assistance Act of 1963, the United States has wielded a stuffed club. The amounts of aid involved are infinitesimal; the chances of gaining compliance with our boycott policy are nil; and the annoyance of the countries concerned may be considerable. What we terminated with respect to Britain and France, in fact, can hardly be called aid; it was more of a sales promotion program under which British and French military leaders were brought to the United States to see—and to buy—advanced American weapons. Terminating this program was in itself of little importance; Britain and France do not need our assistance. But terminating the program as a sanction against their trade with Cuba can have no real effect other than to create an illusory image of "toughness" for the benefit of our own people.

Free world exports to Cuba have, on the whole, been declining over recent years, but overall imports have been rising since 1961.

Mr. President, I ask unanimous consent that there be inserted in the RECORD at the conclusion of my remarks two tables provided by the Department of State showing the trade of selected free world countries with Cuba from 1958 to 1963.

The PRESIDING OFFICER. Without objection, it is so ordered.

(See exhibit 2).

Mr. FULBRIGHT. Mr. President, the figures shown in these tables provide little basis for expecting the early termination of free world trade with Cuba. The export table shows U.S. exports to Cuba in both 1962 and 1963 exceeding those of any other free world country. These American exports consisted almost entirely of ransom payments for the Bay of Pigs prisoners and should not be confused with normal trade.

There is an interesting feature to this table, which may not be well known. It is that the exports from Cuba to various allies of ours, particularly Japan, the United Kingdom, Morocco, and others have been going up, and have been very substantial. This reflects, I believe, the importation from Cuba of sugar to a great extent, and also accounts for the accumulation by Cuba of substantial foreign aid as a result of the dramatic increase in the price of sugar during the past couple of years.

The exports from the free world to Cuba have been going up in similar instances, in the case of Japan, but generally speaking they have not been increasing. Of course, since 1958, when we accounted for more than half of Cuba's exports, they have gone down rather dramatically. In any case, the tables will speak for themselves.

I should like to make it very clear that I am not arguing against the desirability of an economic boycott against the Castro regime but against its feasibility. The effort has been made and all the fulminations we can utter about sanctions and retaliation against free world countries that trade with Cuba cannot long conceal the fact that the boycott policy is a failure.

The boycott policy has not failed because of any "weakness" or "timidity" on the part of our Government. This charge, so frequently heard, is one of the most pernicious myths to have been inflicted on the American people. The boycott policy has failed because the United States is not omnipotent and cannot be. The basic reality to be faced is that it is simply not within our power to compel our allies to cut off their trade with Cuba, unless we are prepared to take drastic sanctions against them, such as closing our own markets to any foreign company that does business in Cuba, as proposed by Mr. Nixon. We can do this, of coures, but if we do, we ought first to be very sure as apparently Mr. Nixon is, that the Cuban boycott is more important than good relations with our closest allies. In fact, even the most drastic sanctions are as likely to be rewarded with defiance as with compliance. For practical purposes, all we can do is to ask other countries to take the measures with respect to Cuba which we recommend. We have done so and in some areas have been success- ful. In other areas, notably that of the economic boycott, we have asked for the full cooperation of other free world countries and it has been largely denied. It remains for us to decide whether we will respond with a sustained outburst of hollow and ill-tempered threats, all the while comforting ourselves with the myth that we can get anything we want if we only try hard enough—or, in this case, shout loud enough—or we can acknowledge the failure of our efforts and proceed, coolly and rationally, to reexamine the policies which we now pursue in relation to the interests they are intended to serve.

The prospects of bringing down the Castro regime by political and economic boycott have never been very good. Even if a general free world boycott were successfully applied against Cuba, it is unlikely that the Russians would refuse to carry the extra financial burden and thereby permit the only Communist regime in the Western Hemisphere to collapse. We are thus compelled to recognize that there is probably no way of bringing down the Castro regime by means of economic pressures unless we are prepared to impose a blockade against nonmilitary shipments from the Soviet Union. Exactly such a policy has been recommended by some of our more reckless politicians, but the preponderance of informed opinion is that a blockade against Soviet shipments of nonmilitary supplies to Cuba would be extravagantly dangerous, carrying the strong possibility of a confrontation that could explode into nuclear war.

Having ruled out military invasion and blockade, and recognizing the failure of the boycott policy, we are compelled to consider the third of the three options open to us with respect to Cuba: the acceptance of the continued existence of the Castro regime as a distasteful nuisance but not an intolerable danger so long as the nations of the hemisphere are prepared to meet their obligations of collective defense under the Rio Treaty.

In recent years we have become transfixed with Cuba, making it far more important in both our foreign relations and in our domestic life than its size and influence warrant. We have flattered a noisy but minor demagog by treating him as if he were a Napoleonic menace. Communist Cuba has been a disruptive and subversive influence in Venezuela and other countries of the hemisphere, and there is no doubt that both we and our Latin American partners would be better off if the Castro regime did not exist. But it is important to bear in mind that, despite their best efforts, the Cuban Communists have not succeeded in subverting the hemisphere and that in Venezuela, for example, where communism has made a major effort to gain power through terrorism, it has been repudiated by a people who in a free election have committed themselves to the course of liberal democracy. It is necessary to weigh the desirability of an objective against the feasibility of its attainment, and when we do this with respect to Cuba, I think we are bound to conclude that Castro is a nuisance but not a grave threat to the United States and that he cannot be gotten rid of except by means that are wholly disproportionate to the objective. Cuban communism does pose a grave threat to other Latin American countries, but this threat can be dealt with by prompt and vigorous use of the established procedures of the inter-American system against any act of aggression.

I think that we must abandon the myth that Cuban communism is a transitory menace that is going to collapse or disappear in the immediate future and face up to two basic realities about Cuba: first, that the Castro regime is not on the verge of collapse and is not likely to be overthrown by any policies which we are now pursuing or can reasonably undertake; and second, that the continued existence of the Castro regime, though inimical to our interests and policies, is not an insuperable obstacle to the attainment of our objectives, unless we make it so by permitting it to poison our politics at home and to divert us from more important tasks in the hemisphere.

The policy of the United States with respect to Latin America as a whole is predicated on the assumption that social revolution can be accomplished without violent upheaval. This is the guiding principle of the Alliance for Progress and it may in time be vindicated. We are entitled to hope so and it is wise and necessary for us to do all that we can to advance the prospects of peaceful and orderly reform.

At the same time, we must be under no illusions as to the extreme difficulty of uprooting long-established ruling oligarchies without disruptions involving lesser or greater degrees of violence. The historical odds are probably against the prospects of peaceful social revolution. There are places, of course, where it has occurred and others where it seems likely to occur. In Latin America, the chances for such basic change by peaceful means seem bright in Colombia and Venezuela and certain other countries; in Mexico, many basic changes have been made by peaceful means, but these came in the wake of a violent revolution. In other Latin American countries, the power of ruling oligarchies is so solidly established and their ignorance so great that there seems little prospect of accomplishing economic growth or social reform by means short of the forcible overthrow of established authorities.

I am not predicting violent revolutions in Latin America or elsewhere. Still less am I advocating them. I wish only to suggest that violent social revolutions are a possibility in countries where feudal oligarchies resist all meaningful change by peaceful means. We must not, in our preference for the democratic procedures envisioned by the Charter of Punta del Este, close our minds to the possibility that democratic procedures may fail in certain countries and that where democracy does fail violent social convulsions may occur.

We would do well, while continuing our efforts to promote peaceful change through the Alliance for Progress, to consider what our reactions might be in the event of the outbreak of genuine social revolution in one or more Latin American countries. Such a revolution did occur in Bolivia, and we accepted it calmly and sensibly. But if a violent social revolution were to break out in one of the larger Latin American countries? Would we feel certain that it was Cuban or Soviet inspired? Would we wish to intervene on the side of established authority? Or would we be willing to tolerate or even support a revolution if it was seen to be not Communist but similar in nature to the Mexican revolution or the Nasser revolution in Egypt?

These are hypothetical questions and there is no readily available set of answers to them. But they are questions which we should be thinking about because they have to do with problems that could become real and urgent with great suddenness. We should be considering, for example, what groups in particular countries might conceivably lead revolutionary movements, and if we can identify them, we should be considering how we might communicate with them and influence them in such a way that their movements, if successful, will not pursue courses detrimental to our security and our interests.

The Far East is another area of the world in which American policy is handicapped by the divergence of old myths and new realities. Particularly with respect to China, an elaborate vocabulary of make-believe has become compulsory in both official and public discussion. We are committed, with respect to China and other areas in Asia, to inflexible policies of long standing from which we hesitate to depart because of the attribution to these policies of an aura of mystical sanctity. It may be that a thorough reevaluation of our Far Eastern policies would lead us to the conclusion that they are sound and wise, or at least that they represent the best available options. It may be, on the other hand, that a reevaluation would point up the need for greater or lesser changes in our policies. The point is that, whatever the outcome of a rethinking of policy might be, we have been unwilling to undertake it because of the fear of many Government officials, undoubtedly well founded, that even the suggestion of new policies toward China or Vietnam would provoke a vehement public outcry.

I do not think the United States can, or should, recognize Communist China, or acquiesce in its admission to the United Nations under present circumstances. It would be unwise to do so, because there is nothing to be gained by it so long as the Peiping regime maintains its attitude of implacable hostility toward the United States. I do not believe, however, that this state of affairs is necessarily permanent. As we have seen in our relations with Germany and Japan, hostility can give way in an astonishingly short time to close friendship; and, as we have seen in our relations with China, the reverse can occur with equal speed. It is not impossible that in time our relations with China will change again—if not to friendship, then perhaps to "competitive coexistence." It would therefore be extremely useful if we could introduce an element of flexibility, or, more precisely, of the capacity to be flexible, into our relations with Communist China.

We would do well, as former Assistant Secretary Hilsman has recommended, to maintain an "open door" to the possibility of improved relations with Communist China in the future. For a start, we must jar open our minds to certain realities about China, of which the foremost is that there really are not "two Chinas," but only one—mainland China; and that it is ruled by Communists, and is likely to remain so for the indefinite future. Once we accept this fact, it becomes possible to reflect on the conditions under which it might be possible for us to enter into relatively normal relations with mainland China. One condition, of course, must be the abandonment by the Chinese Communists, tacitly, if not explicitly, of their intention to conquer and incorporate Taiwan. This seems unlikely now; but far more surprising changes have occurred in politics, and it is quite possible that a new generation of leaders in Peiping and Taipei may put a quiet end to the Chinese civil war, thus opening the possibility of entirely new patterns of international relations in the Far East.

Should such changes occur, they will open important opportunities for American policy; and it is to be hoped that we shall be able and willing to take advantage of them. It seems possible, for instance, that an atmosphere of reduced tensions in the Far East might make it possible to strengthen world peace by drawing mainland China into existing East-West agreements in such fields as disarmament, trade, and educational exchange.

These are long-range prospects, which may or may not materialize. In the immediate future, we are confronted with possible changes in the Far East resulting from recent French diplomacy.

French recognition of Communist China, although untimely and carried out in a way that can hardly be considered friendly to the United States, may nonetheless serve a constructive long-term purpose, by unfreezing a situation in which many countries, none more than the United States, are committed to inflexible policies by long-established commitments and the pressures of domestic public opinion. One way or another, the French initiative may help generate a new situation in which the United States, as well as other countries, will find it possible to reevaluate its basic policies in the Far East.

The situation in Vietnam poses a far more pressing need for a reevaluation of American policy. Other than withdrawal, which I do not think can be realistically considered under present circumstances, three options are open to us in Vietnam: First, continuation of the antiguerrilla war within South Vietnam, along with renewed American efforts to increase the military effectiveness of the South Vietnamese Army and the political effectiveness of the South Vietnamese Government; second, an attempt to end the war, through negotiations for the neutralization of South Vietnam, or of both North and South Vietnam; and, finally, the expansion of the scale of the war, either by the direct commitment of large numbers of American troops or by equipping the South Vietnamese Army to attack North Vietnamese territory, possibly by means of commando-type operations from the sea or the air.

It is difficult to see how a negotiation, under present military circumstances, could lead to termination of the war under conditions that would preserve the freedom of South Vietnam. It is extremely difficult for a party to a negotiation to achieve by diplomacy objectives which it has conspicuously failed to win by warfare. The hard fact of the matter is that our bargaining position is at present a weak one; and until the equation of advantages between the two sides has been substantially altered in our favor, there can be little prospect of a negotiated settlement which would secure the independence of a non-Communist South Vietnam.

Recent initiatives by France, calling for the neutralization of Vietnam, have tended to confuse the situation, without altering it in any fundamental way. France could, perhaps, play a constructive mediating role if she were willing to consult and cooperate with the United States. For somewhat obscure reasons, however, France has chosen to take an independent initiative. This is puzzling to Americans, who recall that the United States contributed $1.2 billion to France's war in Indochina of a decade ago—which was 70 percent of the total cost of the conflict. Whatever its motivation, the problem posed by French intervention in southeast Asia is that while France may set off an unforeseeable chain of events, she is neither a major military force nor a major economic force in the Far East, and is therefore unlikely to be able to control or greatly influence the events which her initiative may precipitate.

It seems clear that only two realistic options are open to us in Vietnam in the immediate future: the expansion of the conflict in one way or another, or a renewed effort to bolster the capacity of the South Vietnamese to prosecute the war successfully on its present scale. The matter calls for thorough examination by responsible officials in the executive branch; and until they have had an opportunity to evaluate the contingencies and feasibilities of the options open to us, it seems to me that we have no choice but to support the South Vietnamese Government and Army by the most effective means available. Whatever specific policy decisions are made, it should be clear to all concerned that the United States will continue to meet its obligations and fulfill its commitments with respect to Vietnam.

These, I believe, are some, although by no means all, of the issues of foreign policy in which it is essential to reevaluate longstanding ideas and commitments in the light of new and changing realities. In all the issues which I have discussed, American policy has to one degree or another been less effective than it might have been because of our national tendency to equate means with ends and therefore to attach a mythological sanctity to policies and practices which in themselves have no moral content or value except insofar as they contribute to the achievement of some valid national objective. I believe that we must try to overcome this excessive moralism, which binds us to old myths and blinds us to new realities and, worse still, leads us to regard new and unfamiliar ideas with fear and mistrust.

We must dare to think about "unthinkable" things. We must learn to explore all of the options and possibilities that confront us in a complex and rapidly changing world. We must learn to welcome rather than fear the voices of dissent and not to recoil in horror whenever some heretic suggests that Castro may survive or that Khrushchev is not as bad a fellow as Stalin was. We must overcome our susceptibility to "shock"—a word which I wish could be banned from our newspapers and magazines and especially from the CONGRESSIONAL RECORD.

If Congress and public opinion are unduly susceptible to "shock," the executive branch, and particularly the Department of State, is subject to the malady of chronic and excessive caution. An effective foreign policy is one which concerns itself more with innovation abroad than with conciliation at home. A creative foreign policy—as President Truman, for one, knew—is not necessarily one which wins immediate general approval. It is sometimes necessary for leaders to do unpleasant and unpopular things, because, as Burke pointed out, the duty of the democratic politician to his constituents is not to comply with their every wish and preference but to give them the benefit of, and to be held responsible for, the exercise of his own best judgment.

We must dare to think about "unthinkable things," because when things become "unthinkable," thinking stops and action becomes mindless. If we are to disabuse ourselves of old myths and to act wisely and creatively upon the new realities of our time, we must think and talk about our problems with perfect freedom, remembering, as Woodrow Wilson said, that "The greatest freedom of speech is the greatest safety because, if a man is a fool, the best thing to do is to encourage him to advertise the fact by speaking."

OCTOBER 22, 1965

COMMENTS ON THE DOMINICAN REPUBLIC

Mr. FULBRIGHT. Mr. President, I have followed with interest the comments made by my colleagues, by the press, and by private individuals after my speech of September 15 regarding the Dominican Republic. I have also followed with interest events in the other body that may have been related to my speech.

Much of the discussion, I have noted to my surprise, has been about me rather than about the Dominican Republic and Latin America. Some of these personal comments have been complimentary, and to those who made them I express my thanks. Others have been uncomplimentary, and to those who made them I can only say that our country is still strong enough to survive an occasional dissenting view even though the consensus is virtually unanimous.

There has been a good deal of discussion as to whether it is proper for the chairman of the Senate Foreign Relations Committee to make a speech critical of an administration of his own party which he generally supports. There is something to be said on both sides of this question and it is certainly one which I considered with care before deciding to make my speech on the Dominican Republic. I concluded, after hearing the testimony of administration witnesses in the Committee on Foreign Relations, that I could do more to encourage carefully considered policies in the future by initiating a public discussion than by acquiescing silently on a policy I believed to be mistaken. It seemed to me, therefore, that, despite any controversy and annoyance to individuals, I was performing a service to the administration by stating my views publicly.

I do not like taking a public position criticizing a Democratic administration which in most respects I strongly support; I do not like it at all. Neither do I like being told, as I have been told, that my statement was "irresponsible" or that it has given aid and comfort to the enemies of the United States. I am quite prepared to examine evidence suggesting that my statement contained errors of fact or judgment; I am not prepared to accept the charge that a statement following upon many hours of listening to testimony in the Foreign Relations Committee and many more hours of examining and evaluating relevant documents was irresponsible. Nor do I take kindly to the charge that I gave aid and comfort to the enemies of the United States. If that accusation is to be pressed—and I should hope it would not be—an interesting discussion could be developed as to whether it is my criticisms of U.S. policy in the Dominican Republic or the policy itself which has given aid and comfort to our enemies.

A Senator has a duty to support his President and his party, but he also has a duty to express his views on major issues. In the case of the Dominican crisis I felt that, however reluctant I might be to criticize the administration—and I was very reluctant—it was nonetheless my responsibility to do so, for two principal reasons.

First, I believe that the chairman of the Committee on Foreign Relations has a special obligation to offer the best advice he can on matters of foreign policy; it is an obligation, I believe, which is inherent in the chairmanship, which takes precedence over party loyalty, and which has nothing to do with whether the chairman's views are solicited or desired by people in the executive branch.

Second, I thought it my responsibility to comment on U.S. policy in the Dominican Republic because the political opposition, whose function it is to criticize, was simply not doing so. It did not because it obviously approved of U.S. intervention in the Dominican Republic and presumably, had it been in office, would have done the same thing. The result of this peculiar situation was that a highly controversial policy was being carried out without controversy—without debate, without review, without that necessary calling to account which is a vital part of the democratic process. Again and again, in the weeks following the committee hearing I noted the absence of any challenge to statements appearing in the press and elsewhere which clearly contradicted evidence available to the Committee on Foreign Relations.

Under these circumstances I am not impressed with suggestions that I had no right to speak as I did on Santo Domingo. The real question, it seems to me, is whether I had the right not to speak.

Insofar as it represents a genuine reconciliation of differences, a consensus is a fine thing; insofar as it represents the concealment of differences, it is a miscarriage of democratic procedure. I think we Americans tend to put too high a value on unanimity—on bipartisanship in foreign policy, on politics stopping at the water's edge, on turning a single face to the world—as if there were something dangerous and illegitimate about honest differences of opinion honestly expressed by honest men. Probably because we have been united about so many things for so long, including the basic values of our free society, we tend to be mistrustful of intellectual dissent, confusing it with personal hostility and political disloyalty.

As the distinguished commentator, Marquis Childs, recently noted, we tend in America toward a tyranny of the majority. More than a century ago, Alexis de Tocqueville took note of that tendency in these words:

I know of no country in which there is so little independence of mind and real freedom of discussion as in America. Profound changes have occurred since democracy in America first appeared and yet it may be asked whether recognition of the right of dissent has gained substantially in practice as well as in theory.

Tocqueville was a friend and admirer of the United States but he regarded the tyranny of the majority as the greatest of dangers in a democracy.

The smallest reproach—

He wrote—

irritates its sensibility and the slightest joke that has any foundation in truth renders it indignant; from the forms of its language up to the solid virtues of its character, everything must be made the subject of encomium. No writer, whatever be his eminence, can escape paying this tribute of adulation to his fellow citizens.

A recent Harris survey, showing strong public disapproval of nonconformist opinions, tends to sustain Tocqueville's view of tyranny by the majority. In an article in the Washington Post dated September 27, 1965, Mr. Harris writes:

America has long prided itself as a nation of rugged individualists where the pioneer tradition allows a man to hold his own views and go his own way. However, the latest Harris survey reveals widespread misgivings among many Americans over present-day examples of social, political or intellectual nonconformity.

The man who stands apart from the crowd—because he does not believe in God, because he pickets against the war in Vietnam, because he demonstrates for civil rights—is regarded as harmful to the American way of life by two out of three of his fellow citizens, a survey of a carefully drawn cross-section of the adult public shows.

Far from being the danger many of us make it out to be, responsible dissent is one of the great strengths of democracy. France, for example, is unquestionably in a stronger position today in her relations with the emerging nations of Asia and Africa because during the years of her colonial wars in Indochina and Algeria a large and articulate minority refused to acquiesce in what was being done and, by speaking out, pointed the way to the enlightened policies of the Fifth Republic. The British Labor Party, to take another example, not only protested the Suez invasion in 1956 but did so while the invasion was being carried out; by so doing, the opposition performed the patriotic service of helping Britain to recover its good name in the wake of a disastrous adventure, starting to repair the damage while the damage was still being done.

It seems to me a manifestation of the tyranny of the majority that there has been so much talk about when it is proper for a Senator to make a speech and so little about the subject matter involved, which was the Dominican Republic and Latin America. It was my intention on September 15 to start a discussion about these and not about myself. There is a very great deal to be said about U.S. policy in Latin America—about political and economic reform and the Alliance for Progress, about collective security and the Organization of American States, about social revolutions and the interests of the United States. I should like very much to hear the views of my colleagues on these and other matters, including the suggestion tentatively put forth in my statement of September 15 that an inter-American partnership of equals in the long run might be advanced by a loosening of ties in the short run.

I would especially like to hear the views of my colleagues on the proposition put forth by President Johnson in his address of August 17 to the Latin American Ambassadors to the effect that the United States hopes to see Latin Americans achieve the same kinds of reform through the Alliance for Progress that we seek for ourselves through the Great Society. Starting with this premise, there is much to be said about how the United States can aid and support the true friends of social reform in Latin America—men like President Belaunde Terry of Peru and President Frei of Chile, whose programs for social justice are also, and for that reason, antidotes to communism.

A general discussion of the Latin American policies of the United States would be interesting and rewarding, far more so than personal recriminations about tolerance of communism and infatuation with revolutions. I myself am too old to change, but there is still hope for the United States and Latin America.

Mr. President, in the weeks since I made my speech on the Dominican Republic I have received over 1,500 letters commenting on it. Approximately 90 percent of these letters expressed concern about the way in which the United States intervened in Santo Domingo. This public reaction suggests that a large sector of the American public shares my concern about the Latin American policy of the United States. Many of the letters I received expressed concern about the role of the Department of Defense and the role of the Central Intelligence Agency in the conduct of American foreign policy. Many, I am pleased to note, expressed the conviction that the United States should abide by its obligations of multilateralism and nonintervention under the Charter of the Organization of American States, and a great many expressed the view, in one way or another, that the foreign policy they desired for the United States was one which was true to its own democratic values.

There has been a great deal of press and periodical commentary on my speech of September 15, much of it favorable, much of it unfavorable. I have selected comments, pro and con, which I judge to be representative and which I ask unanimous consent to have printed in the RECORD at this point. For the benefit of those who may not have seen the entire text of my speech, and to provide a point of reference, I ask unanimous consent that the text of my speech be inserted just prior to these insertions in the RECORD.

There being no objection, the speech and material was ordered to be printed in the RECORD, as follows:

[From the CONGRESSIONAL RECORD, Senate, Sept. 15, 1965]

THE SITUATION IN THE DOMINICAN REPUBLIC

MR. FULBRIGHT. Mr. President, the formation of a provisional government in Santo Domingo under the leadership of Dr. Hector Garcia-Godoy is good news. It provides reason for cautious optimism as to the future and testifies as well to the arduous and patient efforts of the OAS mediating team. I wish to pay tribute especially to Ambassador Bunker for his wisdom and patience in handling this difficult affair. The formation of a provisional government is not the end of the Dominican crisis, but it does bring to an end a tragic and dangerous phase of the crisis. Many problems remain, particularly the problem of establishing the authority of a democratic government over the Dominican military. Nonetheless, the situation now seems to be moving into a less dangerous and more hopeful phase. At this time of relative calm it is appropriate, desirable and, I think, necessary to review events in the Dominican Republic, and the U.S. role in those events. The purpose of such a review—and its only purpose—is to develop guidelines for wise and effective policies in the future.

I was in doubt about the advisability of making a statement on the Dominican affair until some of my colleagues made public statements on the floor. Their views on the way in which the committee proceedings were conducted and, indeed, on the Dominican crisis as a whole, are so diametrically opposed to my own that I now consider it my duty to express my personal conclusions drawn from the hearings held by the Committee on Foreign Relations.

The suggestions that have been made that the committee was prejudiced in its approach against the administration's policies are, in my opinion, without merit. The committee was impartial and fair in giving a full and detailed hearing to the administration's point of view, so much so, in fact, that it heard only one witness from outside the Government.

U.S. policy in the Dominican crisis was characterized initially by overtimidity and subsequently by overreaction. Throughout the whole affair, it has also been characterized by a lack of candor.

These are general conclusions I have reached from a painstaking review of the salient features of the extremely complex situation. These judgments are made, of course, with the benefit of hindsight and, in fairness, it must be conceded there were no easy choices available to the United States in the Dominican Republic. Nonetheless, it is the task of diplomacy to make wise decisions when they need to be made and U.S. diplomacy failed to do so in the Dominican crisis.

It cannot be said with assurance that the United States could have changed the course of events by acting differently. What can be said with assurance is that the United States did not take advantage of several opportunities in which it might have changed the course of events. The reason appears to be that, very close to the beginning of the revolution, U.S. policymakers decided that it should not be allowed to succeed. This decision seems to me to have been based on exaggerated estimates of Communist influence in the rebel movement in the initial stages and on distaste for the return to power of Juan Bosch or of a government controlled by Bosch's party, the PRD—Dominican Revolutionary Party.

The question of the degree of Communist influence is of critical importance and I shall comment on it later. The essential point, however, is that the United States, on the basis of ambiguous evidence, assumed almost from the beginning that the revolution was Communist dominated, or would certainly become so. It apparently never occurred to anyone that the United States could also attempt to influence the course which the revolution took. We misread prevailing tendencies in Latin America by overlooking or ignoring the fact that any reform movement is likely to attract Communist support. We thus failed to perceive that if we are automatically to oppose any reform movement that Communists adhere to, we are likely to end up opposing every reform movement, making ourselves the prisoners of reactionaries who wish to preserve the status quo—and the status quo in many countries is not good enough.

The principal reason for the failure of American policy in Santo Domingo was faulty advice given to the President by his representatives in the Dominican Republic at the time of acute crisis. Much of this advice was based on misjudgment of the facts of the situation; some of it appears to have been based on inadequate evidence or, in some cases, simply inaccurate information. On the basis of the information and counsel he received, the President could hardly have acted other than he did.

I am hopeful, and reasonably confident, that the mistakes made by the United States in the Dominican Republic can be retrieved and that it will be possible to avoid repeating them in the future. These purposes can be served, however, only if the shortcomings of U.S. policy are thoroughly reviewed and analyzed. I make my remarks today in the hope of contributing to that process.

The development of the Dominican crisis, beginning on April 24, 1965, provides a classic study of policymaking in a fast-changing situation in which each decision reduces the range of options available for future decisions so that errors are compounded and finally, indeed, there are few if any options except to follow through on an ill-conceived course of action. Beyond a certain point the Dominican story acquired some of the inevitability of a Greek tragedy.

Another theme that emerges from the Dominican crisis is the occurrence of a striking change in U.S. policy toward the Dominican Republic and the possibility—not a certainty, because the signs are ambiguous, but only the possibility—of a major change as well in the general Latin American policies of the United States. Obviously, an important change in the official outlook on Dominican affairs occurred between September 1963, when the United States was vigorously opposed to the overthrow of Juan Bosch, and April 1965, when the United States was either unenthusiastic or actually opposed to his return.

What happened in that period to change the assessment of Bosch from favorable to unfavorable? It is quite true that Bosch as President did not distinguish himself as an administrator, but that was well known in 1963. It is also true, however, and much more to the point as far as the legitimate interests of the United States are concerned, that Bosch had received 58 percent of the votes in a free and honest election and that he was presiding over a reform-minded government in tune with the Alliance for Progress. This is a great deal more than can be said for any other President of the Dominican Republic.

The question therefore remains as to how and why the attitude of the U.S. Government changed so strikingly between September 1963 and April 1965. And the question inevitably arises whether this shift in the administration's attitude toward the Dominican Republic is part of a broader shift in its attitude toward other Latin American countries, whether, to be specific, the U.S. Government now views the vigorous reform movements of Latin America— such as Christian Democracy in Chile, Peru, and Venezuela, APRA in Peru and Accion Democratica in Venezuela—as threatening to the interests of the United States. And if this is the case, what kind of Latin American political movements would now be regarded as friendly to the United States and beneficial to its interests?

I should like to make it very clear that I am raising a question not offering an answer. I am frankly puzzled as to the current attitude of the U.S. Government toward reformist movements in Latin America. On the one hand, President Johnson's deep personal commitment to the philosophy and aims of the Alliance for Progress is clear; it was convincingly expressed, for example, in his speech to the Latin American Ambassadors on the fourth anniversary of the Alliance for Progress—a statement in which the President compared the Alliance for Progress with his own enlightened program for a Great Society at home. On the other hand, one notes a general tendency on the part of our policymakers not to look beyond a Latin American politician's anticommunism. One also notes in certain Government agencies, particularly the Department of Defense, a preoccupation with counterinsurgency, which is to say, with the prospect of revolutions and means of suppressing them. This preoccupation is manifested in dubious and costly research projects, such as the recently discredited Camelot; these studies claim to be scientific but beneath their almost unbelievably opaque language lies an unmistakable military and reactionary bias.

It is of great importance that the uncertainty as to U.S. aims in Latin America be resolved. We cannot successfully advance the cause of popular democracy and at the same time align ourselves with corrupt and reactionary oligarchies; yet that is what we seem to be trying to do. The direction of the Alliance for Progress is toward social revolution in Latin America, the direction of our Dominican intervention is toward the suppression of revolutionary movements which are supported by Communists or suspected of being influenced by Communists. The prospect of an election in 9 months which may conceivably produce a strong democratic government is certainly reassuring on this score, but the fact remains that the reaction of the United States at the time of acute crisis was to intervene forcibly and illegally against a revolution which, had we sought to influence it instead of suppressing it, might have produced a strong popular government without foreign military intervention. Since just about every revolutionary movement is likely to attract Communist support, at least in the beginning, the approach followed in the Dominican Republic, if consistently pursued, must inevitably make us the enemy of all revolutions and therefore the ally of all the unpopular and corrupt oligarchies of the hemisphere.

We simply cannot have it both ways; we must choose between the Alliance for Progress and a foredoomed effort to sustain the status quo in Latin America. The choice which we are to make is the principal unanswered question arising out of the unhappy events in the Dominican Republic and, indeed, the principal unanswered question for the future of our relations with Latin America.

It is not surprising that we Americans are not drawn toward the uncouth revolutionaries of the non-Communist left. We are not, as we like to claim in Fourth of July speeches, the most truly revolutionary nation on earth; we are, on the contrary, much closer to being the most unrevolutionary nation on earth. We are sober and satisfied and comfortable and rich; our institutions are stable and old and even venerable, and our Revolution of 1776, for that matter, was not much of an upheaval compared to the French and Russian revolutions and to current and impending revolutions in Latin America, Asia, and Africa.

Our heritage of stability and conservatism is a great blessing, but it also has the effect of limiting our understanding of the character of social revolution and sometimes as well of the injustices which spawn them. Our understanding of revolutions and their causes is imperfect not because of any failures of mind or character but because of our good fortune since the Civil War in never having experienced sustained social injustice without hope of legal or more or less peaceful remedy. We are called upon, therefore, to give our understanding and our sympathy and support to movements which are alien to our experience and jarring to our preferences and prejudices.

We must try to understand social revolution and the injustices that give it rise because they are the heart and core of the experience of the great majority of people now living in the world. In Latin America we may prefer to associate with the well-bred, well-dressed businessmen who often hold positions of power, but Latin American reformers regard such men as aliens in their own countries who neither identify with their own people nor even sympathize with their aspirations. Such leaders are regarded by educated young Latin Americans as a "consular bourgeoisie," by which they mean business-oriented conservatives who more nearly represent the interests of foreign businessmen than the interests of their own people. Men like Donald Reid—who is one of the better of this category of leaders—may have their merits, but they are not the force of the future in Latin America.

It is the revolutionaries of the non-Communist left who have most of the popular support in Latin America. The Radical Party in Chile, for example, is full of 19th century libertarians whom many North Americans would find highly congenial, but it was recently crushed in national elections by a group of rambunctious, leftist Christian Democrats. It may be argued that the Christian

Democrats are anti-United States, and to a considerable extent some of them are—more so now, it may be noted, than prior to the intervention of the United States in the Dominican Republic—but they are not Communists and they have popular support. They have also come to terms with the American copper companies in Chile; that is something which the predecessor conservative government was unable to do and something which a Communist government would have been unwilling to do.

The movement of the future in Latin America is social revolution. The question is whether it is to be Communist or democratic revolution and the choice which the Latin Americans make will depend in part on how the United States uses its great influence. It should be very clear that the choice is not between social revolution and conservative oligarchy but whether, by supporting reform, we bolster the popular non-Communist left or whether, by supporting unpopular oligarchies, we drive the rising generation of educated and patriotic young Latin Americans to an embittered and hostile form of communism like that of Fidel Castro in Chile.

In my Senate speech of March 25, 1964, I commented as follows on the prospect of revolution:

"I am not predicting violent revolutions in Latin America or elsewhere. Still less am I advocating them. I wish only to suggest that violent social revolutions are a possibility in countries where feudal oligarchies resist all meaningful change by peaceful means. We must not, in our preference for the democratic procedures envisioned by the Charter of Punta del Este, close our minds to the possibility that democratic procedures may fail in certain countries and that where democracy does fail violent social convulsions may occur."

I think that in the case of the Dominican Republic we did close our minds to the causes and to the essential legitimacy of revolution in a country in which democratic procedures had failed. That, I think, is the central fact concerning the participation of the United States in the Dominican revolution and, possibly as well, its major lesson for the future. I turn now to comment on some of the events which began last April 24 in Santo Domingo.

When the Dominican revolution began on Saturday, April 24, the United States had three options available. First, it could have supported the Reid Cabral government; second, it could have supported the revolutionary forces; and third, it could do nothing.

The administration chose the last course. When Donald Reid Cabral asked for U.S. intervention on Sunday morning, April 25, he was given no encouragement. He then resigned, and considerable disagreement ensued over the nature of the government to succeed him. The party of Juan Bosch, the PRD, or Dominican Revolutionary Party, asked for a "U.S. presence" at the transfer of government power but was given no encouragement. Thus, there began at that time a chaotic situation which amounted to civil war in a country without an effective government.

What happened in essence was that the Dominican military refused to support Reid and were equally opposed to Bosch or other PRD leaders as his successor. The PRD, which had the support of some military officers, announced that Rafael Molina Urena, who had been president of the senate during the Bosch regime, would govern as provisional president pending Bosch's return. At this point, the military leaders delivered an ultimatum, which the rebels ignored, and at about 4:30 on the afternoon of April 25 the air force and navy began firing at the National Palace. Later in the day, PRD leaders asked the U.S. Embassy to use its influence to persuade the air force to stop the attacks. The Embassy made it clear it would not intervene on behalf of the rebels, although on the following day, Monday, April 26, the Embassy did persuade the military to stop air attacks for a limited time.

This was the first crucial point in the crisis. If the United States thought that Reid was giving the Dominican Republic the best government it had had or was likely to get, why did the United States not react more vigorously to support him? On the other hand, if the Reid government was thought to be beyond salvation, why did not the United States offer positive encouragement to the moderate forces involved in the coup, if not by providing the "U.S. presence" requested by the PRD, then at least by letting it be known that the United States was not opposed to the prospective change of regimes or by encouraging the return of Juan Bosch to the Dominican Republic? In fact, according to available evidence, the U.S. Government made no effort to contact Bosch in the initial days of the crisis.

The United States was thus at the outset unwilling to support Reid and unwilling to support if not positively opposed to Bosch.

Events of the days following April 24 demonstrated that Reid had so little popular support that it can reasonably be argued that there was nothing the United States could have done, short of armed intervention, to save his regime. The more interesting question is why the United States was so reluctant to see Bosch returned to power. This is part of the larger question of why U.S. attitudes had changed so much since 1963 when Bosch, then in power, was warmly and repeatedly embraced and supported as few if any Latin American presidents have ever been supported by the United States.

The next crucial point in the Dominican story came on Tuesday, April 27, when rebel leaders, including Molina Urena and Caamano Deno, called at the U.S. Embassy seeking mediation and negotiations. At that time the military situation looked very bad for the rebel, or constitutionalist, forces. Ambassador Bennett, who had been instructed four times to work for a cease-fire and for the formation of a military junta, felt he did not have authority to mediate; mediation, in his view, would have been "intervention." Mediation at that point might have been accomplished quietly and without massive military intervention. Twenty-four hours later the Ambassador was pleading for the marines, and as we know some 20,000 soldiers were landed—American soldiers.

On the afternoon of April 27 Gen. Wessin y Wessin's tanks seemed about to cross the Duarte bridge into the city of Santo Domingo and the rebel cause appeared hopeless. When the rebels felt themselves rebuffed at the American Embassy, some of their leaders, including Molina Urena, sought asylum in Latin American embassies in Santo Domingo. The administration has interpreted this as evidence that the non-Communist rebels recognized growing Communist influence in their movement and were consequently abandoning the revolution. Molina Urena has said simply that he sought asylum because he thought the revolutionary cause hopeless.

An opportunity was lost on April 27. Ambassador Bennett was in a position to bring possibly decisive mediating power to bear for a democratic solution, but he chose not to do so on the ground that the exercise of his good offices at that point would have constituted intervention. In the words of Washington Post writer Murrey Marder—one of the press people who, to the best of my knowledge, has not been assailed as prejudiced:

"It can be argued with considerable weight that late Tuesday, April 27, the United States threw away a fateful opportunity to try to prevent the sequence that produced the American intervention. It allowed the relatively leaderless revolt to pass into hands which it was to allege were Communist."

The overriding reason for this mistake was the conviction of U.S. officials, on the basis of evidence which was fragmentary at best, that the rebels were dominated by Communists. A related and perhaps equally important reason for the U.S. Embassy's refusal to mediate on April 27 was the desire for and, at that point, expectation of an antirebel victory. They therefore passed up an important opportunity to reduce or even eliminate Communist influence by encouraging the moderate elements among the rebels and mediating for a democratic solution.

Owing to a degree of disorganization and timidity on the part of the antirebel forces which no one, including the U.S. Embassy and the rebels themselves, anticipated, the rebels were still fighting on the morning of Wednesday, April 28. Ambassador Bennett thereupon urgently recommended that the antirebels under Air Force General de los Santos be furnished 50 walkie-talkies from U.S. Defense Department stocks in Puerto Rico. Repeating this recommendation later in the day, Bennett said that the issue was one between Castroism and its opponents. The antirebels themselves asked for armed U.S. intervention on their side; this request was refused at that time.

During the day, however, the situation deteriorated rapidly, from the point of view of public order in general and of the antirebels in particular. In midafternoon of April 28 Col. Pedro Bartolome Benoit, head of a junta which had been hastily assembled, asked again, this time in writing, for U.S. troops on the ground that this was the only way to prevent a Communist takeover; no mention was made of the junta's inability to protect American lives. This request was denied in Washington, and Benoit was thereupon told that the United States would not intervene unless he said he could not protect American citizens present in the Dominican Republic. Benoit was thus told in effect that if he said American lives were in danger the United States would intervene. And that is precisely what happened.

It was at this point, on April 28, that events acquired something of the predestiny of a Greek tragedy. Subsequent events—the failure of the missions of John Bartlow Martin and McGeorge Bundy, the conversion of the U.S. force into an inter-American force, the enforced stalemate between the rebels under Caamano Deno and the Imbert junta, the OAS mediation and the tortuous negotiations for a provisional government—have all been widely reported and were not fully explored in the committee hearings. In any case, the general direction of events was largely determined by the fateful decision of April 28. Once the marines landed on that day, and especially after they were heavily reinforced in the days immediately following, the die was cast and the United States found itself deeply involved in the Dominican civil conflict, with no visible way to extricate itself, and with its hemisphere relations complicated in a way that few could have foreseen and no one could have desired.

The danger to American lives was more a pretext than a reason for the massive U.S. intervention that began on the evening of April 28. In fact, no American lives were lost in Santo Domingo until the marines began exchanging fire with the rebels after April 28; reports of widespread shooting that endangered American lives turned out to be exaggerated.

Nevertheless, there can be no question that Santo Domingo was not a particularly safe place to be in the last days of April 1965. There was fighting in the streets, aircraft were strafing parts of the city, and there was indiscriminate shooting. I think that the United States would have been justified in landing a small force for the express purpose of removing U.S. citizens and other foreigners from the island. Had such a force been landed and then promptly withdrawn when it had completed its mission, I do not think that any fairminded observer at home or abroad would have considered the United States to have exceeded its rights and responsibilities.

The United States intervened in the Dominican Republic for the purpose of preventing the victory of a revolutionary force which was judged to be Communist dominated. On the basis of Ambassador Bennett's messages to Washington, there is no doubt that the threat of communism rather than danger to American lives was his primary reason for recommending military intervention.

The question of the degree of Communist influence is therefore crucial, but it cannot be answered with certainty. The weight of the evidence is that Communists did not participate in planning the revolution—indeed, there is some indication that it took them by surprise—but that they very rapidly began to try to take advantage of it and to seize control of it. The evidence does not establish that the Communists at any time actually had control of the revolution. There is little doubt that they had influence within the revolutionary movement, but the degree of that influence remains a matter of speculation.

The administration, however, assumed almost from the beginning that the revolution was Communist dominated, or would certainly become so, and that nothing short of forcible opposition could prevent a Communist takeover. In their apprehension lest the Dominican Republic become another Cuba, some of our officials seem to have forgotten that virtually all reform movements attract some Communist support, that there is an important difference between Communist support and Communist control of a political movement, that it is quite possible to compete with the Communists for influence in a reform movement rather than abandon it to them and, most important of all, that economic development and social justice are themselves the primary and most reliable security against Communist subversion.

It is, perhaps, understandable that administration officials should have felt some sense of panic; after all, the Foreign Service officer who had the misfortune to be assigned to the Cuban desk at the time of Castro's rise to power has had his career ruined by congressional committees. Furthermore, even without this consideration, the decisions regarding the Dominican Republic had to be made under great pressure and on the basis of inconclusive information. In charity, this can be accepted as a reason why the decisions were mistaken; but it does not change the conclusion that they were mistaken.

The point I am making is not—emphatically not—that there was no Communist participation in the Dominican crisis, but simply that the administration acted on the premise that the revolution was controlled by Communists—a premise which it failed to establish at the time and has not established since. The issue is not whether there was Communist influence in the Dominican revolution but its degree, which is something on which reasonable men can differ. The burden of proof, however, is on those who take action, and the administration has not proven its assertion of Communist control.

Intervention on the basis of Communist participation as distinguished from control of the Dominican revolution was a mistake in my opinion which also reflects a grievous misreading of the temper of contemporary Latin American politics. Communists are present in all Latin American countries, and they are going to inject themselves into almost any Latin American revolution and try to seize control of it. If any group or any movement with which the Communists associate themselves is going to be automatically condemned in the eyes of the United States, then we have indeed given up all hope of guiding or influencing even to a marginal degree the revolutionary movements and the demands for social change which are sweeping Latin America. Worse, if that is our view, then we have made ourselves the prisoners of the Latin American oligarchs who are engaged in a vain attempt to preserve the status quo—reactionaries who habitually use the term "Communist" very loosely, in part out of emotional predilection and in part in a calculated effort to scare the United States into supporting their selfish and discredited aims.

If the United States had really been intervening to save American lives, as it had a moral if not a strictly legal right to do, it could have done so promptly and then withdrawn and the incident would soon have been forgotten. But the United States did not intervene primarily to save American lives; it intervened to prevent what it conceived to be, a Communist takeover. That meant, in the terms in which the United States defined the situation, that it was intervening against the rebels, who, however heavily they might or might not have been infiltrated by Communists, were also the advocates of the restoration of a freely elected constitutional government which had been forcibly overthrown. It also meant that the United States was intervening for the military and the oligarchy—to the detriment of the Dominican people and to the bitter disappointment of those throughout Latin America who had placed their hopes in the United States and the Alliance for Progress.

On the basis of the record, there is ample justification for concluding that, at least from the time Reid resigned, U.S. policy was directed toward construction of a military junta which hopefully would restore peace and conduct free elections. That is to say that U.S. policy was directed against the return of Bosch and against the success of the rebel movement.

In this connection it is interesting to recall U.S. policy toward Bosch when he was in power in the Dominican Republic between February and September of 1963. He had been elected, as I have already mentioned, in the only free and honest election ever held in the Dominican Republic, in December 1962, with 58 percent of the votes cast.

The United States placed such importance on his success that President Kennedy sent the then Vice President Johnson and Senator Humphrey, among others, to attend his inauguration in February 1963. In September 1963, when he was overthrown in a military coup, the United States made strenuous efforts—which stopped just short of sending the marines—to keep him in power, and thereafter the United States waited almost 3 months before recognizing the successor government. Recognition came, by the way, only after the successor government had conducted military operations against a band of alleged Communist guerrillas in the mountains, and there is a suspicion that the extent of the guerrilla activities was exaggerated by the successor government in order to secure U.S. recognition.

It may be granted that Bosch was no great success as President of the Dominican Republic but, when all his faults have been listed, the fact remains that Bosch was the only freely elected President in Dominican history, the only President who had ever tried, however ineptly, to give the country a decent government, and the only President who was unquestionably in tune with the Alliance for Progress.

Despite these considerations, the United States was at the very least unenthusiastic or, more probably, opposed to Bosch's return to power in April 1965. Bosch himself was apparently not eager to return—he vacillated in the very early stages and some well-informed persons contend that he positively refused to return to the Dominican Republic. In any case, he missed a critical opportunity. But the United States was equally adamant against a return to power of Bosch's party, the PRD, which is the nearest thing to a mass-based, well-organized party that has ever existed in the Dominican Republic. The stated reason was that a PRD government would be Communist dominated.

This might conceivably have happened, but the evidence by no means supports the conclusion that it would have happened. We based our policy on a possibility rather than on anything approaching a likelihood. Obviously, if we based all our policies on the mere possibility of communism, then we would have to set ourselves against just about every progressive political movement in the world, because almost all such movements are subject to at least the theoretical danger of Communist takeover. This approach is not in the national interest; foreign policy must be based on prospects that seem probable, hopeful and susceptible to constructive influence rather than on merely possible dangers.

One is led, therefore, to the conclusion that U.S. policymakers were unduly timid and alarmist in refusing to gamble on the forces of reform and social change. The bitter irony of such timidity is that by casting its lot with the forces of the status quo, in the probably vain hope that these forces could be induced to permit at least some reform and social changes, the United States almost certainly helped the Communists to acquire converts whom they otherwise could not have won.

How vain the hopes of U.S. policymakers were is amply demonstrated by events since April 28. The junta led by Gen. Antonio Imbert, which succeeded the junta led by Colonel Benoit, proved quite intractable and indeed filled the airwaves daily with denunciations of the United States and the Organization of American States for preventing it from wiping out the Communist rebels. These are the same military forces which on April 28 were refusing to fight the rebels and begging for U.S. intervention. Our aim apparently was to use Imbert as a counterpoise to Caamano Deno in the ill-founded hope that non-Communist liberals would be drawn away from the rebel side.

In practice, instead of Imbert becoming our tractable instrument, we, to a certain extent, became his: he clung tenaciously to the power we gave him and was at least as intransigent as the rebels in the protracted negotiations for a provisional government.

The resignation of Imbert and his junta provides grounds for hope that a strong popular government may come to power in the Dominican Republic, but that hope must be tempered by the fact that the military continues to wield great power in Dominican politics—power which it probably would not now have if the United States had not intervened to save it from defeat last April 28. Even with a provisional government installed in Santo Domingo, and with the prospect of an election in 9 months, there remains the basic problem of a deep and widespread demand for social change. The prospect for such social change is circumscribed by the fact that the military has not surrendered and cannot be expected voluntarily to surrender its entrenched position of privilege and outrageous corruption.

The United States has grossly underestimated the symbolism of the Bosch constitution of 1963. It can be argued that this contains unrealistic promises, but it has stirred the hopes and idealism of the Dominican people. The real objections to it, the part of conservative Dominicans, seem to be that it provides for separation of church and state and that it provides that Dominican citizens have the right to live in the Dominican Republic if they so desire—that is, that Dominican citizens who happen also to be Communists cannot be deported. In passing, one may note a similarity to the U.S. Constitution on both of these points.

The United States has also misread the dedication of the Dominican military to the status quo and to its own powers and privileges. It may be said that the United States has overestimated its ability to influence the military while failing to use to the fullest the influence it does have.

The act of United States massive military intervention in the Dominican Republic was a grievous mistake, but if one is going to cross the bridge of intervention, with all of the historical ghosts which it calls forth throughout Latin America, then one might as well cross all the way and not stop in the middle. It is too late for the United States to refrain from intervention; it is not too late to try to redeem some permanent benefit from that intervention. Specifically, I think that the influence of the United States and the Organization of American States should be used to help the Dominican people free themselves from the oppressive weight of a corrupt and privileged military establishment. It is entirely possible, if not likely, that if the military is allowed to retain its power it will overthrow any future government that displeases it just as it has done in the past. The OAS mediating team made a contribution by bringing about the installation of a provisional government; the OAS can still make a solid contribution to Dominican democracy by urging or insisting that as part of a permanent solution the Dominican military establishment be substantially reduced in size and some of the more irresponsible generals be pensioned off or sent on lengthy diplomatic holidays abroad. If the United States and the OAS are going to impose a solution in the Dominican Republic, they might as well impose a good solution as a bad one.

Since preparing these remarks, I note in this morning's press that General

Wessin has been induced to leave the Dominican Republic. This, I believe, is a step in the right direction.

The Foreign Relations Committee's study of the Dominican crisis leads me to draw certain specific conclusions regarding American policy in the Dominican Republic and also suggests some broader considerations regarding relations between the United States and Latin America. My specific conclusions regarding the crisis in Santo Dominigo are as follows:

First. The United States intervened forcibly in the Dominican Republic in the last week of April 1965 not primarily to save American lives, as was then contended, but to prevent the victory of a revolutionary movement which was judged to be Communist-dominated. The decision to land thousands of marines on April 28 was based primarily on the fear of "another Cuba" in Santo Domingo.

Second. This fear was based on fragmentary and inadequate evidence. There is no doubt that Communists participated in the Dominican revolution on the rebel side, probably to a greater extent after than before the landing of U.S. marines on April 28, but just as it cannot be proved that the Communists would not have taken over the revolution neither can it be proved that they would have. There is little basis in the evidence offered the committee for the assertion that the rebels were Communist-dominated or certain to become so; on the contrary, the evidence suggests a chaotic situation in which no single faction was dominant at the outset and in which everybody, including the United States, had opportunities to influence the shape and course of the rebellion.

Third. The United States let pass its best opportunities to influence the course of events. The best opportunities were on April 25, when Juan Bosch's party, the PRD, requested a "United States presence," and on April 27, when the rebels, believing themselves defeated, requested United States mediation for a negotiated settlement. Both requests were rejected, in the first instance for reasons that are not entirely clear but probably because of United States hostility to the PRD, in the second instance because the U.S. Government anticipated and desired a victory of the antirebel forces.

Fourth. U.S. policy toward the Dominican Republic shifted markedly to the right between September 1963 and April 1965. In 1963, the United States strongly supported Bosch and the PRD as enlightened reformers; in 1965 the United States opposed their return to power on the unsubstantiated ground that a Bosch or PRD government would certainly, or almost certainly, become Communist dominated. Thus the United States turned its back on social revolution in Santo Domingo and associated itself with a corrupt and reactionary military oligarchy.

Fifth. U.S. policy was marred by a lack of candor and by misinformation. The former is illustrated by official assertions that U.S. military intervention was primiraly for the purpose of saving American lives; the latter is illustrated by exaggerated reports of massacres and atrocities by the rebels—reports which no one has been able to verify. It was officially asserted, for example—by the President in a press conference on June 17 according to an official State Department bulletin—that "some 1,500 innocent people were murdered and shot, and their heads cut off." There is no evidence to support this statement. A sober examination of such evidence as is available indicates that the Imbert junta was guilty of at least as many atrocities as the rebels.

Sixth. Responsibility for the failure of American policy in Santo Domingo lies primarily with those who advised the President. In the critical days between April 25 and April 28, these officials sent the President exaggerated reports of the danger of a Communist takeover in Santo Domingo and, on the basis of these, recommended U.S. massive military intervention. It is not at all difficult to understand why, on the basis of such advice, the President made the decisions that he made.

Seventh. Underlying the bad advice and unwise actions of the United States was the fear of another Cuba. The specter of a second Communist state in the Western Hemisphere—and its probable repercussions within the United States and possible effects on the careers of those who might be held responsible— seems to have been the most important single factor in distorting the judgment of otherwise sensible and competent men.

I turn now to some broader and long-term implications of the Dominican tragedy, first to some considerations relating to the Organization of American States and its charter, then to the problem of reaction and revolution in Latin America, finally to a suggestion for a freer and, I believe, healthier relationship between the United States and Latin America.

Article 15 of the Charter of the Organization of American States says that:

"No state or group of states has the right to intervene, directly or indirectly, for any reason whatever, in the internal or external affairs of any other state."

Article 17 states that:

"The territory of a State is inviolable; it may not be the object, even temporarily, of military occupation or of other measures of force taken by another State, directly or indirectly, on any grounds whatever."

These clauses are not ambiguous. They mean that, with one exception to be noted, all forms of forcible intervention are absolutely prohibited among the American States. It may be that we should never have accepted this commitment at Bogotá in 1948; it is obvious from all the talk one hears these days about the obsoleteness of the principle of nonintervention that some U.S. officials regret our commitment to it. The fact remains that we are committed to it, not partially or temporarily or insofar as we find it compatible with our vital interests but almost absolutely. It represents our word and our bond and our willingness to honor the solemn commitments embodied in a treaty which was ratified by the Senate on August 28, 1950.

There are those who might concede the point of law who would also argue that such considerations have to do with our ideals rather than our interests and are therefore of secondary importance. I do not believe that is true. We are currently fighting a war in Vietnam, largely, we are told, because it would be a disaster if the United States failed to honor its word and its commitment; the matter, we are told, is one of vital national interest. I do not see why it is any less a matter of vital interest to honor a clear and explicit treaty obligation in the Americas than it is to honor the much more ambiguous and less formal promises we have made to the South Vietnamese.

The sole exception to the prohibitions of articles 15 and 17 is spelled out in article 19 of the OAS Charter, which states that "measures adopted for the maintenance of peace and security in accordance with existing treaties do not constitute a violation of the principles set forth in articles 15 and 17." Article 6 of the Rio Treaty states:

"If the inviolability or the integrity of the territory or the sovereignty or political independence of any American State should be affected by an aggression which is not an armed attack or by an extracontinental or intracontinental conflict, or by any other, fact or situation that might endanger the peace of America, the Organ of Consultation shall meet immediately in order to agree on the measures which must be taken in case of aggression to assist the victim of the aggression or, in any case, the measures which should be taken for the common defense and for the maintenance of the peace and security of the continent."

The United States thus had legal recourse when the Dominican crisis broke on April 24, 1965. We could have called an urgent session of the Council of the OAS for the purpose of invoking article 6 of the Rio Treaty. But we did not do so. The administration has argued that there was no time to consult the OAS, although there was time to consult—or inform—the congressional leadership. The United States thus intervened in the Dominican Republic unilaterally—and illegally.

Advising the Latin American countries of our action after the fact did not constitute compliance with the OAS Charter or the Rio Treaty; nor, indeed, would advising them before the fact have constituted compliance. One does not comply with the law by notifying interested parties in advance of one's intent to violate it. Inter-American law requires consultation for the purpose of shaping a collective decision. Only on the basis of advance consultation and agreement could we have undertaken a legal intervention in the Dominican Republic.

It is possible, had we undertaken such consultations, that our Latin American partners would have delayed a decision; it is possible that they would have refused to authorize collective intervention. My own feeling is that the situation in any case did not justify military intervention except for the limited purpose of evacuating U.S. citizens and other foreigners, but even if it seemed to us that it did, we should not have undertaken it without the advance consent of our Latin American allies. We should not have done so because the word and the honor of the United States were at stake just as much—at least as much—in the Dominican crisis as they are in Vietnam and Korea and Berlin and all the places around the globe which we have committed ourselves to defend.

There is another important reason for compliance with the law. The United States is a conservative power in the world in the sense that most of its vital interests are served by stability and order. Law is the essential foundation of stability and order both within societies and in international relations. A great conference is taking place here in Washington this week on the subject, World Peace Through Law. As a conservative power the United States has a vital interest in upholding and expanding the reign of law in international relations. Insofar as international law is observed, it provides us with stability and order and with a means of predicting the behavior of those with whom we have reciprocal legal obligations. When we violate the law ourselves, whatever short-term advantage may be gained, we are obviously encouraging others to violate the law; we thus encourage disorder and instability and thereby do incalculable damage to our own long-term interests.

There are those who defend U.S. unilateral intervention in the Dominican Republic on the ground that the principle of nonintervention as spelled out in the OAS Charter is obsolete. The argument is unfortunate on two grounds. First, the contention of obsoleteness justifies an effort to bring about changes in the OAS Charter by due process of law, but it does not justify violation of the charter. Second, the view that the principle of nonintervention is obsolete is one held by certain U.S. officials; most Latin Americans would argue that, far from being obsolete, the principle of nonintervention was and remains the heart and core of the inter-American system. Insofar as it is honored, it provided them with something that many in the United States find it hard to believe they could suppose they need: protection from the United States.

Many North Americans seem to believe that, while the United States does indeed participate in Latin American affairs from time to time, sometimes by force, it is done, with the best of intentions, usually indeed to protect the Latin Americans from intervention by somebody else, and therefore cannot really be considered intervention. The trouble with this point of view is that it is not shared by our neighbors to the south. Most of them do think they need protection from the United States and the history of the Monroe Doctrine and the "Roosevelt corollary" suggest that their fears are not entirely without foundation. "Good intentions" are not a very sound basis for judging the fulfillment of contractual obligations. Just about everybody, including the Communists, believes in his own "good intentions." It is a highly subjective criterion of national behavior and has no more than a chance relationship to good results. With whatever justice or lack of it, many Latin Americans are afraid of the United States; however much it may hurt our feelings, they prefer to have their security based on some more objective standard than the good intentions of the United States.

The standard on which they rely most heavily is the principle of nonintervention; however obsolete it may seem to certain U.S. officials, it remains vital and pertinent in Latin America. When we violate it, we are not overriding the mere letter of the law; we are violating what to Latin Americans is its vital heart and core.

The inter-American system is rooted in an implicit contract between the Latin American countries and the United States. In return for our promise not to interfere in their internal affairs they have accepted a role as members of our "sphere" and to support, or at least not to obstruct, our global policies. In the Dominican Republic we violated our part of the bargain; it remains to be seen whether Latin Americans will now feel free to violate theirs.

In the eyes of educated, energetic, and patriotic young Latin Americans— which is to say, the generation that will make or break the Alliance for Progress—the United States committed a worse offense in the Dominican Republic than just intervention; it intervened against social revolution and in support, at least temporarily, of a corrupt, reactionary military oligarchy.

It is not possible at present to assess the depth and extent of disillusion with the United States on the part of democrats and reformers in Latin America. I myself think that it is deep and widespread. Nor am I reassured by assertions on the part of administration officials that a number of Latin American governments have secretly expressed sympathy for our actions in the Dominican Republic while explaining that of course they could not be expected to support us openly. Why cannot they support us openly, unless it is because their sympathy does not represent the views of their own people and they do not dare to express it openly? In fact, real enthusiasm for our Dominican venture has been confined largely to military dictators and ruling oligarchies.

The tragedy of Santo Domingo is that a policy that purported to defeat communism in the shortrun is more likely to have the effect of promoting it in the longrun. Intervention in the Dominican Republic has alienated—temporarily or permanently, depending on our future policies—our real friends in Latin America. These, broadly, are the people of the democratic left—the Christian and social democrats in a number of countries, the APRA Party in Peru, the Accion Democratica Party in Venezuela, and their kindred spirits throughout the hemisphere. By our intervention on the side of a corrupt military oligarchy in the Dominican Republic, we have embarrassed before their own people the democratic reformers who have counseled trust and partnership with the United States. We have lent credence to the idea that the United States is the enemy of social revolution in Latin America and that the only choice Latin Americans have is between communism and reaction.

If those are the available alternatives, if there is no democratic left as a third option, then there is no doubt of the choice that honest and patriotic Latin Americans will make: they will choose communism, not because they want it but because U.S. policy will have foreclosed all other avenues of social revolution and, indeed, all other possibilities except the perpetuation of rule by military juntas and economic oligarchies.

The dominant force in Latin America is the aspiration of increasing numbers of people to personal and national dignity. In the minds of the rising generation there are two principle threats to that aspiration—reaction at home and domination from abroad. As a result of its Dominican actions the United States has allowed itself to become associated with both. We have thereby offended the dignity and self-respect of young and idealistic Latin Americans who must now wonder whether the United States will one day intervene against social revolutions in their own countries, whether one day they will find themselves facing U.S. Marines across barricades in their own home towns.

I, myself, am sure, as I know President Johnson and, indeed, most U.S. citizens are sure, that our country is not now and will not become the enemy of social revolution in Latin America. We have made a mistake in the Dominican Republic, as we did at the Bay of Pigs in 1961, but a single misjudgment does not constitute a doctrine for the conduct of future policy and we remain dedicated to the goals of the Alliance for Progress.

We know this ourselves but it remains to convince our true friends in Latin America that their social revolutions will have our sympathy and support. It will not be easy to do so, because our intervention in Santo Domingo shook if it did not shatter a confidence in the United States that had been built up over 30 years since the liquidation of the Caribbean protectorates and the initiation of the "good neighbor policy."

It will be difficult but it can be done. President Johnson took a positive step on the long road back in his statement of rededication to the Alliance for Progress to the Latin American Ambassadors on August 17. It remains for us to eliminate the ambiguity between the antirevolutionary approach symbolized by Project Camelot and the preoccupation with problems of counterinsurgency on the one hand and the creative approach of the Alliance for Progress on the other. If we do this—and I am both sure that we can and reasonably hopeful that we will—then I think that the Dominican affair will be relegated in history to the status of a single unhappy episode on the long road toward the forging of a new and creative and dignified relationship between the United States and Latin America.

In conclusion, I suggest that a new and healthier relationship between the United States and Latin America must be a freer relationship than that of the past.

The United States is a world power with world responsibilities and to it the inter-American system represents a sensible way of maintaining law and order in the region closest to the United States. To the extent that it functions as we want it to function, one of the inter-American system's important advantages is that it stabilizes relations within the Western Hemisphere and thus frees the United States to act on its worldwide responsibilities.

To Latin Americans, on the other hand, the inter-American system is politically and psychologically confining. It has the effect, so to speak, of cooping them up in the Western Hemisphere, giving them the feeling that there is no way to break out of the usually well-intentioned but often stifling embrace of the United States. In their hearts, I have no doubt, most Latin Americans would like to be free of us, just as a son or daughter coming of age wishes to be free of an overprotective parent. A great many of those Latin Americans for whom Castro still has some appeal—and there are now more, I would guess, than before last April 28—are attracted not, I feel, because they are infatuated with communism, but because Cuba, albeit at the price of almost complete dependency on the Soviet Union, has broken out of the orbit of the United States.

It is the nature of things that small nations do not live comfortably in the shadow of large and powerful nations, regardless of whether the latter are benevolent or overbearing. Belgium has always been uncomfortable about Germany and France; Ireland has never been able to work up much affection for Great Britain. And in recent years some of the Eastern European governments have demonstrated that, despite the Communist ideology which they share with the Soviet Union, they still wish to free themselves as much as they can and as much as they dare from the overbearing power of Russia. It is natural and inevitable that Latin American countries should have some of the same feelings toward the United States.

Perhaps, then, the foremost immediate requirement for a new and more friendly relationship between Latin America and the United States in the long run is not closer ties and new institutional bonds but a loosening of existing ties and institutional bonds. It is an established psychological principle—or, for that matter, just common sense—that the strongest and most viable personal bonds are those which are voluntary, a voluntary bond being, by definition, an arrangement which one is free to enter or not to enter. I do not see why the same principle should not operate in relations between nations. If it does, it would follow that the first step toward stronger ties between Latin America and the United States would be the creation of a situation in which Latin American countries would be free, and would feel free, to maintain or sever existing ties as they see fit and, perhaps more important, to establish new arrangements, both among themselves and with nations outside the hemisphere, in which the United States would not participate.

President Frei of Chile has taken an initiative to this end. He has visited European leaders and apparently indicated that his Christian Democratic Government is interested in establishing new political, economic, and cultural links with European countries. For the reasons suggested, I think this is an intelligent and constructive step.

I think further that it would be a fine thing if Latin American countries were to undertake a program of their own for "building bridges" to the world beyond the Western Hemisphere—to Europe and Asia and Africa, and to the Communist countries if they wish. Such relationships, to be sure, would involve a loosening of ties to the United States in the immediate future, but in the long run, I feel sure, they would make for both happier and stronger bonds with the United States—happier because they would be free, stronger because they would be dignified and self-respecting as they never had been before.

APRIL 21, 1966

THE HIGHER PATRIOTISM

To criticize one's country is to do it a service and pay it a compliment. It is a service because it may spur the country to do better than it is doing; it is a compliment because it evidences a belief that the country can do better than it is doing. "This," said Albert Camus in one of his "Letters to a German Friend," is "what separated us from you; we made demands. You were satisfied to serve the power of your nation and we dreamed of giving ours her truth. . . ."[1]

In a democracy dissent is an act of faith. Like medicine, the test of its value is not its taste but its effects, not how it makes people feel at the moment, but how it inspires them to act thereafter. Criticism may embarrass the country's leaders in the short run but strengthen their hand in the long run; it may destroy a consensus on policy while expressing a consensus of values. Woodrow Wilson once said that there was "such a thing as being too proud to fight"; there is also, or ought to be, such a thing as being too confident to conform, too strong to be silent in the face of apparent error. Criticism, in short, is more than a right; it is an act of patriotism, a higher form of patriotism, I believe, than the familiar rituals of national adulation.

In the three lectures which we begin tonight I am going to criticize America,

1 Albert Camus, Second Letter, December, 1943, *Resistance, Rebellion and Death* (New York: Random House, Inc., 1960), p. 10.

I hope not unfairly, and always in the hope of rendering a service and the confidence of paying a compliment. It is not a pejorative but a tribute to say that America is worthy of criticism. If nonetheless one is charged with a lack of patriotism, I would reply with Camus, "No, I didn't love my country, if pointing out what is unjust in what we love amounts to not loving, if insisting that what we love should measure up to the finest image we have of her amounts to not loving."[2]

What is the finest image of America? To me it is the image of a composite, or better still a synthesis, of diverse peoples and cultures, come together in harmony but not identity, in an open, receptive, generous and creative society. Almost two hundred years ago a Frenchman who had come to live in America posed the question, "What Is an American?" His answer, in part, was the following: "Here individuals of all nations are melted into a new race of men, whose labours and posterity will one day cause great change in the world. Americans are the western pilgrims, who are carrying along with them that great mass of arts, sciences, vigour, and industry, which began long since in the east; they will finish the great circle. The Americans were once scattered all over Europe; here they are incorporated into one of the finest systems of population which has ever appeared, and which will hereafter become distinct by the power of the different climates they inhabit. . . . The American is a new man, who acts upon new principles; he must therefore entertain new ideas and form new opinions. From involuntary idleness, servile dependence, penury, and useless labor, he has passed to toils of a very different nature, rewarded by ample subsistence. —This is an American. . . ."[3]

With due allowance for the author's exuberance, I think that his optimism is not far off the mark. We are an extraordinary nation, endowed with a rich and productive land and a talented and energetic population. Surely a nation so favored is capable of extraordinary achievement, not only in the area of producing and enjoying great wealth—where our achievements have indeed been extraordinary—but also in the area of human and international relations —in which area, it seems to me, our achievements have fallen short of our capacity and promise.

The question that I find intriguing—the question which I have chosen as the theme of these lectures although I have no answer to it—is whether a nation so extraordinarily endowed as the United States can overcome that arrogance of power which has afflicted, weakened, and in some cases destroyed great nations in the past.

The causes of the malady are a mystery but its recurrence is one of the uniformities of history: power tends to confuse itself with virtue and a great nation is peculiarly susceptible to the idea that its power is a sign of God's favor, conferring upon it a special responsibility for other nations—to make them richer and happier and wiser, to remake them, that is, in its own shining image. Power confuses itself with virtue and it also tends to take itself for omnipotence. Once imbued with the idea of a mission, a great nation easily assumes that it has the means as well as the duty to do God's work. The Lord,

2 Albert Camus, "Letters to a German Friend," First Letter; *ibid.,* p. 4.

3 Michel-Guillaume Jean de Crevecoeur, "What Is an American," Letter III (1782) of *Letters from an American Farmer.*

after all, surely would not choose you as His agent and then deny you the
sword with which to work His will. German soldiers in the First World War
wore belt buckles imprinted with the words: "Gott mit uns." It was approximately under this kind of infatuation—an exaggerated sense of power and an
imaginary sense of mission—that the Athenians attacked Syracuse and Napoleon and then Hitler invaded Russia. In plain words, they overextended their
commitments and they came to grief.

My question is whether America can overcome the fatal arrogance of power.
My hope and my belief are that it can, that it has the human resources to
accomplish what few if any great nations have ever accomplished before: to be
confident but also tolerant, and rich but also generous, to be willing to teach
but also willing to learn, to be powerful but also wise. I believe that America is
capable of all of these things; I also believe it is falling short of them.
Gradually but unmistakably we are succumbing to the arrogance of power. In
so doing we are not living up to our capacity and promise; the measure of our
falling short is the measure of the patriot's duty of dissent.

The discharge of that most important duty is handicapped in America by an
unworthy tendency to fear serious criticism of our government. In the abstract
we celebrate freedom of opinion as a vital part of our patriotic liturgy. It is
only when some Americans exercise the right that other Americans are
shocked. No one of course ever criticizes the right of dissent; it is always this
particular instance of it or its exercise under these particular circumstances or
at this particular time that throws people into a blue funk. I am reminded of
Samuel Butler's observation that "People in general are equally horrified at
hearing the Christian religion doubted, and at seeing it practiced."[4]

Intolerance of dissent is a well noted feature of the American national
character. Louis Hartz attributes it to the heritage of a society which was "born
free," a society which is unnerved by deep dissent because it has experienced so
little of it.[5] Alexis de Tocqueville took note of this tendency over a hundred
years ago. "I know of no country," he wrote, "in which there is so little
independence of mind and real freedom of discussion as in America. Profound
changes have occurred since democracy in America first appeared and yet it
may be asked whether recognition of the right of dissent has gained substantially in practice as well as in theory." The malady in Tocqueville's view was
one of democracy itself: ". . . The smallest reproach irritates its sensibility and
the slightest joke that has any foundation in truth renders it indignant; from the
forms of its language up to the solid virtues of its character, everything must be
made the subject of encomium. No writer, whatever be his eminence, can
escape paying this tribute of adulation to his fellow citizens."[6]

From small-town gatherings to high-policy councils Americans are distressed
when a writer or a politician interrupts all this self-congratulation and expresses

[4] *Further Extracts from the Notebooks of Samuel Butler*, A. T. Bartholomew, ed.
(London: Jonathan Cape Press, 1934), p. 120.
[5] Louis Hartz, *The Liberal Tradition in America* (New York: Harcourt, Brace &
World, 1955).
[6] Alexis de Tocqueville, *Democracy in America*, Vol. I (New York: Alfred A.
Knopf, 1945), p. 265.

himself with simple, unadorned candor. As prospective diplomats and professionals in various fields of international relations, many of you will be faced sooner or later with the dilemma of how you can retain your capacity for honest individual judgment in a large organization in which the surest route to advancement is conformity with a barren and oppressive orthodoxy. There are many intelligent, courageous and independent-minded individuals in the Foreign Service of the United States, but I have had occasion to notice that there are also sycophants and conformists, individuals in whose minds the distinction between official policy and personal opinion has disappeared.

A few months ago I met an American poet, Mr. Ned O'Gorman, who had just returned from a visit to Latin America sponsored by the State Department. He said, and previously had written, that he was instructed by American embassy officials in the countries he visited that if he were questioned by students and intellectuals with whom he was scheduled to meet on such "difficult" questions as the Dominican Republic and Vietnam he was to reply that he was "unprepared." Poets, as we all know, are ungovernable people and Mr. O'Gorman proved no exception. He finally rebelled at a meeting with some Brazilian students with the following result as he described it: ". . . the questions came, swirling, battering, bellowing from the classroom. Outside the traffic and the oily electric heat. But I loved it. I was hell bent for clarity. I knew they wanted straight answers and I gave them. I had been gorged to sickness with embassy prudence. The applause was long and loud. The embassy man furious. 'You are taking money dishonestly,' he told me. 'If the government pays you to do this tour you must defend it and not damn it.' It did no good when I explained to him that if I didn't do what I was doing, *then* I'd be taking the money dishonestly. . . ."[7]

A high degree of loyalty to the President's policy is a requirement of good order within the Department of State but it escapes me totally why American diplomats should not be proud to have American poets and professors and politicians demonstrate their country's political and intellectual health by expressing themselves with freedom and candor. As O'Gorman put it, ". . . I spoke with equal force of the glory and the tragedy of America. And that is what terrified the Americans."[8]

The universities—and especially institutions like the School of Advanced International Studies—have a special obligation to train potential public servants in rigorously independent thinking and to acquaint them as well with the need for reconciling loyalty to an organization with personal integrity. It is an extremely important service for the universities to perform because the most valuable public servant, like the true patriot, is one who gives a higher loyalty to his country's ideals than to its current policy and who therefore is willing to criticize as well as to comply.

We must learn to treat our freedom as a source of strength, as an asset to be shown to the world with confidence and pride. No one challenges the value and importance of national consensus, but consensus can be understood in two ways.

[7] "Mission Over, A Controversial Visitor Departs," *The National Catholic Reporter,* August 18, 1965, p. 6.
[8] *Ibid.*

If it is interpreted to mean unquestioning support of existing policies, its effects can only be pernicious and undemocratic, serving to suppress differences rather than to reconcile them. If, on the other hand, consensus is understood to mean a general agreement on goals and values but not necessarily on the best means of realizing them, then and only then does it become a lasting basis of national strength. It is consensus in this sense which has made America strong in the past. Indeed, much of our national success in combining change with continuity can be attributed to the vigorous competition of men and ideas within a context of shared values and generally accepted institutions. It is only through this kind of vigorous competition of ideas that a consensus of values can sometimes be translated into a true consensus of policy. Or as Mark Twain plainly put it: "It were not best that we should all think alike; it is difference of opinion that makes horse races."[9]

Freedom of thought and discussion gives a democracy two concrete advantages over a dictatorship in the making of foreign policy: it diminishes the danger of an irretrievable mistake and it introduces ideas and opportunities that otherwise would not come to light.

The correction of errors in a nation's foreign policy is greatly assisted by the timely raising of voices of criticism within the nation. When the British launched their disastrous attack on Egypt, the Labor Party raised a collective voice of indignation while the military operation was still underway; refusing to be deterred by calls for national unity in a crisis, Labor began the long, painful process of recovering Great Britain's good name at the very moment when the damage was still being done. Similarly, the French intellectuals who protested France's colonial wars in Indochina and Algeria not only upheld the values of French democracy but helped pave the way for the enlightened policies of the Fifth Republic which have made France the most respected Western nation in the underdeveloped world. It was in the hope of performing a similar service for America on a very modest scale that I criticized American intervention in the Dominican Republic in a speech in the Senate last year.

The second great advantage of free discussion to democratic policy makers is its bringing to light of new ideas and the supplanting of old myths with new realities. We Americans are much in need of this benefit because we are severely, if not uniquely, afflicted with a habit of policy making by analogy: North Vietnam's involvement in South Vietnam, for example, is equated with Hitler's invasion of Poland and a parley with the Vietcong would represent another Munich. The treatment of slight and superficial resemblances as if they were full-blooded analogies, as instances, as it were, of history "repeating itself," is a substitute for thinking and a misuse of history. The value of history is not what it seems to prohibit or prescribe but its general indications as to the kinds of policies that are likely to succeed and the kinds that are likely to fail, or, as one historian has suggested, its hints as to what is likely not to happen.

Mark Twain offers guidance on the uses of history. "We should be careful," he wrote, "to get out of an experience only the wisdom that is in it—and stop there; lest we be like the cat that sits down on a hot stove-lid. She will never sit

---

[9] *Pudd'nhead Wilson: Pudd'nhead Wilson's Calendar,* chap. 19.

down on a hot stove-lid again—and that is well; but also she will never sit down on a cold one anymore."[10]

There is a kind of voodoo about American foreign policy. Certain drums have to be beaten regularly to ward off evil spirits—for example, the maledictions which are regularly uttered against North Vietnamese aggression, the "wild men" in Peking, communism in general and President de Gaulle. Certain pledges must be repeated every day lest the whole free world go to rack and ruin—for example, we will never go back on a commitment no matter how unwise; we regard this alliance or that as absolutely "vital" to the free world; and of course we will stand stalwart in Berlin from now until Judgment Day. Certain words must never be uttered except in derision—the word "appeasement," for example, comes as near as any word can to summarizing everything that is regarded by American policy makers as stupid, wicked and disastrous.

I do not suggest that we should heap praise on the Chinese communists, dismantle NATO, abandon Berlin, and seize every opportunity that comes along to appease our enemies. I do suggest the desirability of an atmosphere in which unorthodox ideas would arouse interest rather than horror, reflection rather than emotion. As likely as not, new proposals, carefully examined, would be found wanting and old policies judged sound; what is wanted is not change itself but the capacity for change. Consider the idea of "appeasement": in a free and healthy political atmosphere it would elicit neither horror nor enthusiasm but only interest in what precisely its proponent had in mind. As Winston Churchill once said: "Appeasement in itself may be good or bad according to circumstances. . . . Appeasement from strength is magnanimous and noble and might be the surest and perhaps the only path to world peace."

In addition to its usefulness for redeeming error and introducing new ideas, free and open criticism has a third, more abstract but no less important function in a democracy. It is therapy and catharsis for those who are troubled or dismayed by something their country is doing; it helps to reassert traditional values, to clear the air when it is full of tension and mistrust. There are times in public life as in private life when one must protest, not solely or even primarily because one's protest will be politic or materially productive, but because one's sense of decency is offended, because one is fed up with political craft and public images, or simply because something goes against the grain. The catharsis thus provided may indeed be the most valuable of freedom's uses.

While not unprecedented, protests against a war in the middle of the war are a rare experience for Americans. I see it as a mark of strength and maturity that an articulate minority have raised their voices against the Vietnamese war and that the majority of Americans are enduring this dissent, not without anxiety, to be sure, but with better grace and understanding than would have been the case in any other war of the twentieth century.

It is by no means certain that the relatively healthy atmosphere in which the debate is now taking place will not give way to a new era of McCarthyism. The longer the Vietnamese war goes on without prospect of victory or negotiated peace, the war fever will rise; hopes will give way to fears and tolerance and freedom of discussion will give way to a false and strident patriotism. In Mark

10 *Ibid.,* chap. 11.

Twain's novel, *The Mysterious Stranger,* a benevolent and clairvoyant Satan said the following about war and its effects:

There has never been a just one, never an honorable one—on the part of the instigator of the war. I can see a million years ahead, and this rule will never change in so many as half a dozen instances. The loud little handful—as usual—will shout for the war. The pulpit will—warily and cautiously—object—at first; the great, big, dull bulk of the nation will rub its sleepy eyes and try to make out why there should be a war, and will say, earnestly and indignantly, 'It is unjust and dishonorable and there is no necessity for it.' Then the handful will shout louder. A few fair men on the other side will argue and reason against the war with speech and pen, and at first will have a hearing and be applauded; but it will not last long; those others will outshout them, and presently the anti-war audiences will thin out and lose popularity. Before long you will see this curious thing: the speakers stoned from the platform, and free speech strangled by hordes of furious men who in their secret hearts are still at one with those stoned speakers—as earlier—but do not dare to say so. And now the whole nation—pulpit and all—will take up the war-cry, and shout itself hoarse, and mob any honest man who ventures to open his mouth; and presently such mouths will cease to open. Next the statesmen will invent cheap lies, putting the blame upon the nation that is attacked, and every man will be glad of those conscience-soothing falsities, and will diligently study them, and refuse to examine any refutations of them; and thus he will by and by convince himself that the war is just, and will thank God for the better sleep he enjoys after this process of grotesque self-deception.[11]

Past experience provides little basis for confidence that reason can prevail in an atmosphere of mounting war fever. In a contest between a hawk and dove the hawk has a great advantage, not because it is a better bird but because it is a bigger bird with lethal talons and a highly developed will to use them. Without illusions as to the prospect of success we must try nonetheless to bring reason and restraint into the emotionally charged atmosphere in which the Vietnamese war is now being discussed. Instead of trading epithets about the legitimacy of debate and about who is and is not giving "aid and comfort" to the enemy, we would do well to focus calmly and deliberately on the issue itself, recognizing that all of us make mistakes and that mistakes can only be corrected if they are acknowledged and discussed, and recognizing further that war is not its own justification, that it can and must be discussed unless we are prepared to sacrifice our traditional democratic processes to a false image of national unanimity.

In fact the protesters against the Vietnamese war are in good historical company. On January 12, 1848, Abraham Lincoln rose in the United States House of Representatives and made a speech about the Mexican War worthy of Senator Morse. Lincoln's speech was an explanation of a vote he had recently cast in support of a resolution declaring that the war had been unnecessarily and unconstitutionally begun by President Polk. "I admit," he said, "that such a vote should not be given, in mere party wantonness, and that the one given, is justly censurable, if it have no other, or better foundation. I am one of those

11 Mark Twain, *The Mysterious Stranger* (New York: Harper and Brothers, 1922), pp. 119–120.

who joined in that vote; and I did so under my best impression of the *truth* of the case."[12]

That is exactly what the students and professors and politicians who oppose the Vietnamese war have been doing: they have been acting on their "best impression of the truth of the case." Some of our super-patriots assume that any war the United States fights is a just war, if not indeed a holy crusade, but history does not sustain their view. No reputable historian would deny that the United States has fought some wars which were unjust, unnecessary or both—I would suggest the War of 1812, the Civil War and the Spanish-American War as examples. In an historical frame of reference it seems to me logical and proper to question the wisdom of our present military involvement in Asia.

The wisdom and productivity of the protest movement of students, professors, clergy and others may well be questioned, but their courage, decency and patriotism cannot be doubted. At the very least the student protest movement of the sixties is a moral and intellectual improvement on the panty raids of the fifties. In fact it is a great deal more: it is an expression of the national conscience and a manifestation of traditional American idealism. I agree with the editorial comment of last October's very interesting issue of the *Johns Hopkins Magazine,* in which it was suggested that the "new radical" movement "is not shallow and sophomoric, it is not based on the traditional formula of generational defiance, and it is not the result of an infusion of foreign ideologies. It is based instead on personal disenchantment and the feeling of these radicals that they must repudiate a corrupted vision of society and replace it with a purer one."[13]

Protesters against the Vietnamese war have been held up to scorn on the ground that they wish to "select their wars," by which it is apparently meant that it is hypocritical to object to this particular war while not objecting to war in general. I fail to understand what is reprehensible about trying to make moral distinctions between one war and another, between, for example, resistance to Hitler and intervention in Vietnam. From the time of Grotius to the drafting of the United Nations Charter international lawyers have tried to distinguish between "just wars" and "unjust wars." It is a difficult problem of law and an even more difficult problem of morality, but it is certainly a valid problem and, far from warranting contempt, those who try to solve it deserve our sympathy and respect.

There can be no solution to a problem until it is first acknowledged that there is a problem. When Mr. Moyers reported with respect to the Vietnam protests the President's "surprise that any one citizen would feel toward his country in a way that is not consistent with the national interest," he was denying the existence of a problem as to where in fact the national interest lies. The answer, one must concede, is elusive, but there is indeed a question and it is a sign of the good health of this nation that the question is being widely and clearly posed.

With due respect for the honesty and patriotism of the student demonstra-

[12] *The Collected Works of Abraham Lincoln,* Vol. 1, 1824–1848 (New Brunswick: Rutgers University Press, 1953), p. 431.
[13] "The New Radicals," *The Johns Hopkins Magazine,* October, 1965, pp. 10–11.

tions, I would offer a word of caution to the young people who have organized and participated in them. As most politicians discover sooner or later, the most dramatic expression of grievances is not necessarily the most effective. That would seem to be especially true in the United States, a country which, as I have pointed out, is easily and excessively alarmed by expressions of dissent. We are, for better or worse, an essentially conservative society; in such a society soft words are likely to carry more weight than harsh words and the most effective dissent is dissent that is expressed in an orderly, which is to say, a conservative, manner.

For these reasons direct action such as the burning of draft cards probably does more to retard than to advance the views of those who take such action. The burning of a draft card is a symbolic act, really a form of expression rather than of action, and it is stupid and vindictive to punish it as a crime. But it is also a very unwise act, unwise because it is shocking rather than persuasive to most Americans and because it exposes the individual to personal risk without political reward.

The student, like the politician, must consider not only how to say what he means but also how to say it persuasively. The answer, I think, is that to speak persuasively one must speak in the idiom of the society in which one lives. The form of protest that might be rewarding in Paris or Rome, to say nothing of Saigon or Santo Domingo, would be absolutely disastrous in Washington. Frustrating though it may be to some Americans, it is nonetheless a fact that in America the messages that get through are those that are sent through channels, through the slow, cumbersome institutional channels devised by the founding fathers in 1787.

The good order and democracy of our society therefore depend on the keeping open of these channels. As long as every tendency of opinion among our people can get a full and respectful hearing from the elected representatives of the people, the teach-ins and the draft card burnings and the demonstrations are unlikely to become the principal forms of dissent in America. It is only when the Congress fails to challenge the executive, when the opposition fails to oppose, when politicians join in a spurious consensus behind controversial policies, that the campuses and streets and public squares of America are likely to become the forums of a direct and disorderly democracy.

It is the joint responsibility of politicians and opinion leaders in the universities and elsewhere to keep open the channels of communication between the people and their government. Under the American Constitution the proper institutional channel for that communication is the United States Congress, and especially the Senate, to whose special problems and responsibilities I now turn.

In recent years the Congess has not fully discharged its responsibilities in the field of foreign relations. The reduced role of the Congress and the enhanced role of the President in the making of foreign policy are not the result merely of President Johnson's ideas of consensus; they are the culmination of a trend in the constitutional relationship between President and Congress that began in 1940, that is to say, at the beginning of this age of crisis.

The cause of the change is crisis. The President has the authority and resources to make decisions and take actions in an emergency; the Congress does not. Nor, in my opinion, should it; the proper responsibilities of the Congress are to reflect and review, to advise and criticize, to consent and to withhold consent. In the last twenty-five years American foreign policy has encountered a shattering series of crises and inevitably—or almost inevitably—the effort to cope with these has been executive effort, while the Congress, inspired by patriotism, importuned by Presidents, and deterred by lack of information, has tended to fall in line behind the executive. The result has been an unhinging of traditional constitutional relationships; the Senate's constitutional powers of advice and consent have atrophied into what is widely regarded—though never asserted—to be a duty to give prompt consent with a minimum of advice. The problem is to find a way to restore the constitutional balance, to find ways by which the Senate can discharge its *duty* of advice and consent in an era of permanent crisis.

Presidents must act in emergencies, especially when the country is at war, and of the last five Presidents only one has not had to wage a sizable war for at least a part of his period in office. Beset with the anxieties of a foreign crisis, no President can relish the idea of inviting opinionated and tendentious Senators into his high policy councils. His reluctance is human, but it is not in keeping with the intent of the Constitution. I believe that, as representatives of the people, Senators have the duty, not merely the right, to render advice, not on the day-to-day conduct of foreign policy, but on its direction and philosophy as these are shaped by major decisions. I conclude that, when the President, for reasons with which we can all sympathize, does not invite us into his high policy councils, it is our duty to infiltrate our way in as best we can.

I can illustrate by some personal experiences the extent to which the trend toward executive predominance has gone and the extraordinary difficulty which a Senator has in trying to discharge his responsibility to render useful advice and to grant or withhold his consent with adequate knowledge and sound judgment.

Many of us, at the time of the great Cuban missile crisis of 1962, were in our home states campaigning for re-election. When the President called some of us back—the leadership, appropriate committee chairmen and ranking minority members—we were not told the nature of the emergency about which we were to be consulted or informed, but of course we were able to guess the approximate situation. We convened at the White House at 5 P.M. and were briefed by the President and his advisers on the crisis and on the decisions which had already been taken on how to deal with it. When the President asked for comments, Senator Russell and I advocated the invasion of Cuba by American forces, I, as explained in a memorandum which I had hastily prepared, on the ground that a blockade, involving as it might a direct, forcible confrontation with Russian ships, would be more likely to provoke a nuclear war, than an invasion which would pit American soldiers against Cuban soldiers and allow the Russians to stand aside. Had I been able to formulate my views on the basis of facts rather than a guess as to the nature of the situation, I might have made a different recommendation. In any case, the recommendation I made represented my best judgment at the time and I thought it my duty to offer it.

The decision to blockade Cuba had already been made. The meeting at the

White House broke up after 6 P.M. and President Kennedy went on television at 7 P.M. to announce his decision to the American people. In his book on President Kennedy, Theodore Sorensen refers to the temerity of those of us from the Congress who expressed opinions at the White House meeting as "the only sour note" in all of the decision-making related to the crisis.[14]

On the afternoon of April 28, 1965, the leaders of Congress were called once again to an emergency meeting at the White House. We were told that the revolution that had broken out four days before in the Dominican Republic had gotten completely out of hand, that Americans and other foreigners on the scene were in great danger, and that American marines would be landed in Santo Domingo that night for the sole purpose of protecting the lives of Americans and other foreigners. None of the Congressional leaders expressed disapproval of the action planned by the President. Four months later, after an exhaustive review of the Dominican crisis by the Senate Foreign Relations Committee meeting in closed sessions, it was clear beyond reasonable doubt that, while saving American lives may have been a factor in the decision to intervene on April 28, the major reason was a determination on the part of the United States Government to defeat the rebel, or constitutionalist, forces whose victory at that time was imminent. Had I known in April what I knew in August, I most certainly would have objected to the American intervention in the Dominican Republic.

Almost nine months before the Dominican intervention, on August 5, 1964, the Congress received an urgent request from President Johnson for the immediate adoption of a joint resolution regarding southeast Asia. On August 7, after perfunctory Committee hearings and a brief debate, the Congress, with only two Senators dissenting, adopted the resolution authorizing the President "to take all necessary steps, including the use of armed force," against aggression in southeast Asia. Once again Congress had been asked to show its support for the President in a crisis; once again, without questions or hesitation, it had done so.

The joint resolution of August 7 was a blank check signed by the Congress in an atmosphere of urgency that seemed at the time to preclude debate. Since its adoption the Administration has converted the Vietnamese conflict from a civil war in which some American advisers were involved to a major international war in which the principal fighting unit is an American army of 250 thousand men. Each time that Senators have raised questions about successive escalations of the war, we have had the blank check of August 7, 1964 waved in our faces as supposed evidence of the overwhelming support of the Congress for a policy in southeast Asia which in fact has been radically changed since the summer of 1964.

All this is very frustrating to some of us in the Senate, but we have only ourselves to blame. Had we met our responsibility of careful examination of a Presidential request, had the Senate Foreign Relations Committee held hearings on the resolution before recommending its adoption, had the Senate debated the resolution and considered its implications before giving its overwhelming approval, we might have put limits and qualifications on our endorsement of

[14] *Kennedy* (New York: Harper and Row, Publishers, 1965) p. 702.

future uses of force in southeast Asia, if not in the resolution itself then in the legislative history preceding its adoption. As it was, only Senators Morse and Gruening debated the resolution.

I myself, as Chairman of the Foreign Relations Committee, served as floor manager of the southeast Asia resolution and did all I could to bring about its prompt and overwhelming adoption. I did so because I was confident that President Johnson would use our endorsement with wisdom and restraint. I was also influenced by partisanship: an election campaign was in progress and I had no wish to make any difficulties for the President in his race against a Republican candidate whose election I thought would be a disaster for the country. My role in the adoption of the resolution of August 7, 1964 is a source of neither pleasure nor pride to me today—although I do not regret the outcome of the election.

How then can the Senate discharge its constitutional responsibilities of advice and consent in an age when the direction and philosophy of foreign policy are largely shaped by urgent decisions made at moments of crisis? I regret that I have no definitive formula to offer but I do have some ideas as to how both the Senate as an institution and an individual Senator can meet their constitutional responsibilities.

The Senate as a whole, I think, should undertake to revive and strengthen the deliberative function which it has permitted to atrophy in the course of twenty-five years of crisis. Acting on the premise that dissent is not disloyalty, that a true consensus is shaped by airing our differences rather than suppressing them, the Senate should again become, as it used to be, an institution in which the great issues of American politics are contested with thoroughness, energy and candor. Nor should the Senate allow itself to be too easily swayed by executive pleas for urgency and unanimity, or by allegations of aid and comfort to the enemies of the United States made by officials whose concern may be heightened by a distaste for criticism directed at themselves.

In recent months, the Senate Committee on Foreign Relations has engaged in an experiment in public education. The Committee has made itself available as a forum for the meeting of politicians and professors and, more broadly, as a forum through which recognized experts and scholars could help increase Congressional and public understanding of the problems associated with our involvement in Vietnam and our relations with Communist China. It is my hope that this experiment will not only contribute to public education but will help to restore the Senate to its proper role as adviser to the President on the great issues of foreign policy.

I believe that the public hearings on Vietnam, by bringing before the American people a variety of opinions and disagreements pertaining to the war, and perhaps by helping to restore a degree of balance between the executive and the Congress, have done far more to strengthen the country than to weaken it. The hearings have been criticized on the ground that they conveyed an "image" of the United States as divided over the war. Since the country obviously *is* divided, what was conveyed was a fact rather than an image. As I have already indicated, I see no merit in the view that we should maintain an image of unity even though it is a false image, maintained at the cost of suppressing the normal procedures of democracy.

In coming months, and perhaps years, the Foreign Relations Committee contemplates additional proceedings pertaining to major questions of American foreign policy. It is our expectation that these proceedings may generate controversy. If they do, it will not be because we value controversy for its own sake but rather because we accept it as a condition of intelligent decision-making, as, indeed, the crucible in which a national consensus as to objectives may be translated into a consensus of policy as well.

I should like to say a few words about the problems and decisions that an individual Senator faces in the effort to make a useful contribution to the country's foreign relations.

A Senator who wishes to influence foreign policy must consider the probable results of communicating privately with the executive or, alternatively, of speaking out publicly. I do not see any great principle involved here: it is a matter of how one can better achieve what one hopes to achieve. For my own part, I have used both methods, with results varying according to circumstance. Other things being equal—which they seldom are—I find it more agreeable to communicate privately with Democratic presidents and publicly with Republican presidents.

Since 1961, when the Democrats came back to power, I have made recommendations to the President on a number of occasions through confidential memoranda. In March 1961 I gave President Kennedy a memorandum expressing opposition to the projected invasion of Cuba at the Bay of Pigs; although my recommendation was not accepted, it was given a full and fair hearing by the President and his advisers. In June 1961 I sent the President a memorandum protesting public statements on controversail political issues made by members of the armed forces under the sponsorship of right wing organizations; it resulted in the issuance of an order by Secretary of Defense McNamara restricting such activities and it also produced a lively Senate debate in which I was accused of wishing to "muzzle the military."

In April 1965 I sent President Johnson a memorandum containing certain recommendations on the war in Vietnam, recommendations which I reiterated thereafter in private conversations with high Administration officials. When it became very clear that the Administration did not find my ideas persuasive, I began to make my views known publicly in the hope, if not of bringing about a change in Administration policy, then at least of opening up a debate on that policy.

On the afternoon of September 15, 1965, I made a speech in the Senate criticizing the United States intervention in the Dominican Republic. That morning I had sent a copy of the speech to President Johnson, accompanied by a letter which read, in part, as follows:

"Dear Mr. President:

"Enclosed is a copy of a speech that I plan to make in the Senate regarding the crisis in the Dominican Republic. As you know, my Committee has held extensive hearings on the Dominican matter; this speech contains my personal comments and conclusions on the information which was brought forth in the hearings.

"As you will note, I believe that important mistakes were made. I further believe that a public discussion of recent events in the Dominican Republic, even though it brings forth viewpoints which are critical of actions taken by your Administration, will be of long term benefit in correcting past errors, helping to prevent their repetition in the future, and thereby advancing the broader purposes of your policy in Latin America. It is in the hope of assisting you toward these ends, and for this reason only, that I have prepared my remarks.

. . . . . .

"Another purpose of my statement is to provide a measure of reassurance for those liberals and reformers in Latin America who were distressed by our Dominican actions, just as you did in your outstanding statement to the Latin American ambassadors on August 17. I believe that the people in Latin America whose efforts are essential to the success of the Alliance for Progress are in need of reassurance that the United States remains committed to the goals of social reform. I know that you are doing a great deal to provide such reassurance and one of my purposes in this speech will be to supplement your own efforts in this field."

My speech generated a controversy. A number of my colleagues in the Senate expressed support for my position; others disagreed. Much of the criticism, to my surprise and disappointment, was directed not at what I had said about the Dominican Republic and Latin America but at the propriety of my speaking out at all. As Churchill once said, "I do not resent criticism, even when, for the sake of emphasis, it parts for the time with reality."[15]

I was taken aback, however, by the consternation caused by my breach of the prevailing consensus. With these thoughts in mind, I said in the Senate on October 22, 1965:

". . . I believe that the chairman of the Committee on Foreign Relations has a special obligation to offer the best advice he can on matters of foreign policy; it is an obligation, I believe, which is inherent in the chairmanship, which takes precedence over party loyalty, and which has nothing to do with whether the chairman's views are solicited or desired by people in the executive branch.

. . . . . .

". . . I am not impressed with suggestions that I had no right to speak as I did on Santo Domingo. The real question, it seems to me, is whether I had the right not to speak."[16]

It is difficult to measure the effectiveness of a Senator's speech, because its effect may be something *not* done rather than some specific action or change of policy by the executive. Generally speaking, it seems to me that a Senator's criticism is less likely to affect the case in point than it is to affect some similar

---

[15] Speech in the House of Commons, January 22, 1941.
[16] *Congressional Record,* October 22, 1965, p. 27465.

case in the future. I am inclined to believe, for example, that my criticism of the State Department last summer for its failure to give public support to the Firestone Tire and Rubber Company when it was brought under right wing attack for agreeing to engineer a synthetic rubber plant in Rumania, while it did not revive that transaction, may have encouraged the State Department to give vigorous and timely support to a number of tobacco companies who were subsequently criticized by extremist groups for their purchases of tobacco from certain Eastern European communist countries. As to the effect of my Dominican speech, it may have been a factor in the Administration's support for the Garcia Godoy government in its resistance to pressures by the Dominican military. Its more significant results will be shown in the reaction of the United States Government if it is again confronted with a violent revolution in Latin America. As to my criticisms and those of my colleagues regarding the Vietnamese war, their effect remains to be seen.

Before considering how he will try to influence events a politician must decide which events he proposes to influence and which he will leave largely to the determination of others. The Senate consists of a hundred individuals with fifty separate constituencies and widely varying fields of individual knowledge and interest. There is little that a Senator can accomplish by his own efforts; if he is to have an effect on public policy, he must influence his colleagues. Sometimes, but not often, a colleague's support can be won by charm; it can certainly be lost by rudeness. Occasionally it can be won by persuasive rhetoric; more often it is gotten by trading your support on one issue for his on another, or simply by a general practice of limiting your own initiative to matters of unusual interest or importance while otherwise accepting the recommendations of the committees. And, in some instances, a Senator may influence his colleagues by influencing their constituencies.

Some may regard this process of mutual accommodation as unethical. I do not regard it as unethical, because I do not place my own wishes and judgments on a plane above those of my colleagues. There are no areas of public policy in which I am absolutely sure of the correctness of my opinions, but there are some in which I am reasonably confident of my judgment; it is in these areas that I try to make a contribution. There are other areas in which my knowledge is limited, and in these I prefer to let others take the lead. There are still other areas in which I am proscribed from leadership or initiative by the strong preferences of my constituency.

A politician has no right to ask that he be absolved from public judgment; he may hope, however, that he will be judged principally on the basis of his performance in the areas of his principal effort. He may hope that he will be judged not as a saint or a paragon but as a human being entrusted by his constituents with extraordinary responsibilities but endowed by the Lord with the same problems of judgment and temptation that afflict the rest of the human race.

In conclusion, I reiterate the theme on which I opened and the theme that I will develop further in the next two lectures: that, as a nation extraordinarily endowed with human and material resources, as a nation which is a synthesis of many nations, America has the possibility of escaping that fatal arrogance which so often in the past has been the legacy of great power; that it has the possibility, instead of seeking to remake the world in its own image, of helping to bring about some reconciliation, perhaps even some synthesis, of the rival ideologies of our time.

None of us—student, professor, politician or private citizen—can advance this aim by uncritical support of the policies of the moment. All of us have the responsibility to act upon a higher patriotism, which is to love our country less for what it is than for what we would like it to be.

SOURCES

BOOKS

ALSOP, JOSEPH, and ALSOP, STEWART. *We Accuse*. New York: Simon and Schuster, Inc., 1954.

ANDERSON, JACKSON, and MAY, RONALD M. *McCarthy*. Boston: Beacon Press, 1952.

ANOUILH, JEAN. *Becket*. Coward-McCann, Inc. 1960.

BUTLER, JAMES R. M. *Grand Strategy*. London: H. M. Stationery Office.

BUTTERFIELD, ROGER. *The American Past*. New York: Simon and Schuster, Inc., 1957.

DEVILLERS, PHILIPPE. *North Vietnam Today*. New York: Frederick A. Praeger, Inc., 1962.

DJILAS, MILOVAN. *Conversations with Stalin*. New York: Harcourt, Brace & World, Inc., 1962.

FALL, BERNARD B. *The Two Viet-Nams*. New York: Frederick A. Praeger, Inc., 1963.

FLEMING, D. F. *The Cold War and Its Origins*. New York: Doubleday & Company, Inc., 1961.

FLETCHER, JOHN GOULD. *Arkansas*. Chapel Hill, N.C.: University of North Carolina Press, 1947.

FULBRIGHT, J. WILLIAM. *Fulbright of Arkansas,* ed. Karl Meyer. Washington, D.C.: Robert B. Luce, Inc., 1963.

HAMILTON, EDITH. *The Greek Way*. New York: Modern Library, 1961.

JUNGK, ROBERT. *Brighter Than a Thousand Suns*. New York: Harcourt, Brace and Company, 1958.

LACOUTURE, JEAN. *Vietnam Between Two Truces*. New York: Random House, Inc., 1965.

LILIENTHAL, DAVID. *The Journals of David Lilienthal*. New York: Harper & Row, Publishers, 1964.

MOONEY, BOOTH. *The Lyndon Johnson Story*. Farrar, Straus and Cudahy, 1956.

PIERSON, GEORGE WILSON. *Tocqueville in America*. New York: Doubleday & Company, Inc., 1959.

POWER, GENERAL THOMAS S. *Design for Survival*. Coward-McCann, Inc., 1965.

RASKIN, MARCUS G., and FALL, BERNARD B. *The Vietnam Reader*. New York: Random House, Inc., 1966.

WHITE, THEODORE H. *The Making of the President, 1964*. New York: Atheneum Publishers, 1965.

MAGAZINES

Atlantic Monthly, The Flashback (of the Washington County, Arkansas, Historical Society), *Football Digest, Harper's Magazine, Life, Look, The Texas Observer.*

NEWSPAPERS

Arkansas Gazette, Arkansas Statesman, Baltimore Sun, London Observer, Manchester Guardian, Memphis Commercial Appeal, New Statesman, New York Herald Tribune, The New York Times, Northwest Arkansas Times, St. Louis Post-Dispatch, Seattle Times, Shreveport Journal, The Wall Street Journal, Washington News, The Washington Post, Washington Star.

NEWSPAPER COLUMNISTS

Holmes Alexander, Joseph Alsop, Rowland Evans, Roberta Fulbright, Joseph Kraft, Arthur Krock, Scottie Lanahan, Walter Lippmann, Mary McGrory, Robert Novack, Crosby Noyes, James Reston, Thomas Stokes, Ralph de Toledano, William S. White.

OFFICIAL DOCUMENTS

The Congressional Record; hearings of the House Foreign Affairs Committee; hearings of the Senate Appropriations, Armed Services, Banking, Foreign Relations Committees and *ad hoc* committee on atomic energy control, 1945; special joint hearings of Senate Armed Services and Foreign Relations Committees on the Korean War; the Eisenhower Doctrine; History of the Korean War, U.S. Army; Report of the Inspector-General of the U.S. Army in the case of Major General Edwin Walker; Background Information Relating to the Dominion Republic, Senate Foreign Relations Committee; Background Information Relating to Southeast Asia and Vietnam, Senate Foreign Relations Committee.

MISCELLANY

The speech files of Senator J. William Fulbright; a speech by Kenneth Galbraith; "Meet the Press" for May 15, 1965; statement of the Foreign Policy Association; report of the Anti-Defamation League on ultraright activity; sermon by the Very Reverend Francis B. Sayre, Jr., dean of The Washington Cathedral; study paper on "The Politics of Escalation" by Franz Schurmann *et al.,* bulletin of the Federation of American Scientists on the use of gasses.

INDEX